The Year of the Monkey

猴

年

猴年

The Year of the Monkey

Revolt on Campus
1968–69

WILLIAM J. McGILL

McGraw-Hill Book Company
New York   St. Louis   San Francisco
London   Paris   Tokyo   Toronto

Thomas H. Quinn, Michael Hennelly, and Karen
Seriguchi were the editors of this book. Christine
Aulicino was the designer. Sally Fliess supervised the
production. It was set in Janson by Datapage, Inc.

Printed and bound by R. R. Donnelley and Sons, Inc.

Library of Congress Cataloging in Publication Data
McGill, William J.
    The year of the monkey.
    Bibliography: p.
    Includes index.
    1. University of California, San Diego
2. Student strikes—California—San Diego. I. Title.
LD729.6.S3M33   378'.1981'0979498   82-67
AACR2

ISBN 0-07-044797-X

1 2 3 4 5 6 7 8 9 DODO 8 9 8 7 6 5 4 3 2

Dr. David P. C. Hu of the University of California,
San Diego provided the Chinese caligraphy for the cover.

*To the thousands of students
who helped me
when I was in trouble.*

Contents

Preface

In the 1960s college campuses all over the United States erupted in violent protests. The outbreaks had such a stunning public impact that a flood of popular books, serious monographs, and fact-finding studies began to appear, purporting to explain what was happening and why. Now, 20 years later, it is time to look beyond these first-order explanations in an effort to assess the deeper origins and ultimate costs of this unique generational conflict. We have gained enough perspective to understand the complexity of events we once thought susceptible to easy political interpretations.

Popular literature of the Sixties told us that students were protesting because the government and the social system violated their ideals. The greatest student concerns were American racism and the war in Vietnam. It was true, yet now, in retrospect, other causative factors have emerged.

Undergraduates in the Sixties wanted to be free of discipline and authority. They were especially hostile to conformity. This was also true, yet some early writers were determined to create an aura of political purity around the New Left. They were unwilling to acknowledge that the forces impelling students to protest were psychological as well as political.

Middle-class students in the Sixties came of age at a time of great national affluence. Since the necessities of life were amply provided to them, they were permitted the leisure to concentrate on moral abstractions rather than on the requirements of survival. Young people could pretend to drop out of society without worrying about where their next meal would come from.

It was also an era of unprecedented anxiety. The Sixties generation was the first to grow up in the shadow of nuclear catastrophe and the balance of terror. "Going to the brink" became a catch phrase that chilled undergraduates whose lives lay largely before them. Why, they asked, did things have to be this way?

There were major demographic problems, too. The Sixties generation was part of the great baby boom of the post–World War II period. Students arrived on campus in unprecedented numbers that forced unwanted competition in almost every facet of undergraduate life. Although universities knew the enrollment surge was coming and attempted to meet it, bureaucracies constructed to handle student needs were quickly overwhelmed and broke down.

With all these diverse pressures, students of that period became unusually prone to view themselves as victims, and society as inhumane. It is these often-ignored facets of student protest that must be taken into account in creating a lifelike portrait of the radical movements of the Sixties.

Rather than discuss all these convoluted ideas in the abstract, I decided to put them into a realistic and dramatic context. What emerged was a rather personal story of my first year, 1968–69, as chancellor of the University of California, San Diego (UCSD). No fewer than five major disputes erupted on campus that year. It may well have been the peak period of student unrest in the nation. I sought to describe the five crises, retaining the unbelievable and sometimes hilarious confusions of the events themselves while at the same time providing a serious theoretical account of the underlying forces.

Inevitably as the writing progressed, I discovered that powerful transformations had been taking place in me as I faced the pressures of that freshman year in office. I am a far more hard-bitten individual today than the political innocent described in these pages. Part of the price of any protracted struggle is a progressive desensitization engendered by exposure to conflict.

Everyone agrees that student radicalism began to fade nearly a decade ago. The conclusion of the war in Vietnam and diminishing American affluence during the 1970s are generally credited with turning students away from protest. Today one finds a flourishing political literature on the Sixties. The work is scholarly and not as well known to the general public as the earlier, or popular books on the greening of America. Most of the writing is aimed at discovering what went wrong with the New Left. How did this movement, so filled with youthful vitality and the promise of social reform, flame out into Marxist dogma and self-destructive terrorism in less than ten years? The analysts are political scientists, sociologists, and social historians. They are liberal-minded and sympathetic to the New Left, using modern social theory to interpret the meteoric rise and fall of the movement and its youthful leadership.

In the current literature, the role of the ideological Left is faced honestly, not buried in vapid tributes to student idealism. The whole point of the academic Left in its purest form is that it concerns itself with the frontiers of human goodness and utopian reform rather than with the exercise of power. One of the crucial insights about the New Left that emerges from this literature is the discovery that many student radicals became so preoccupied with attacking centers of power they abandoned the utopian faith that gave the movement its soul.

The time appears to be at hand for a study of student unrest from still another perspective. I was one of a generation of American college presidents caught in the savage drama of the Sixties. Obviously my outlook is different from that of theorists discussing the fate of New Left organizations. I am concerned with the pressures on ordinary students. I want to understand what happened to the believers and followers rather than the leaders. All the ugly dynamics of protest demonstrations are familiar to me, and I know that many non-political students were swept up in the heady excitement of making a gesture toward peace or racial justice. Some students, perhaps many, were badly hurt.

The strange thing is that so few college presidents have ventured to write about it. I suspect it is because several of us were experiencing violence for the first time in our lives. We were repelled and frightened by what we saw. The idea that radical students might serve a high idealism by attacking us because we represented the oppressions of a social order they detested is so absurd as to be almost paranoid.

The college administrators who have the most to say are those who were most damaged. But they have heard dozens of times that the disastrous events in which they were involved were mostly of their own making, and that they lacked sensitivity and compassion at a time when human qualities might have made a crucial difference. They do not want to subject themselves to the humiliation of reliving the past only to be criticized by reviewers who never had to face decisions that might cause injury or death.

Most university presidents came into the academic life searching for a better world. If they failed as leaders, one has to ask what went wrong. If they lacked sensitivity and compassion, was it just a personal shortcoming, or can good people become so hardened by conflict as to lose human qualities valued by students? Perhaps a generation of university leaders failed the test of confrontation not because they were uncompassionate but because they were too gentle, unable to match wits with adversaries who meant to do them harm. These are important questions thus far unanswered in the literature.

I find myself in an unusual position. I managed to survive the worst of it more or less intact. There is no particular need at this point to defend the decisions I made. Hence I may be able to offer readers a deeper understanding of the costs of the conflict. Critics tell us the unrest of the Sixties was a good thing because it served a great cause. It sensitized us to the war in Vietnam and helped us to end it.

Frankly, I grow weary of great causes as I grow older. Perhaps the outcome was worth the price in this instance but I want to examine the question because I watched, often helpless, while the price was being paid. I saw myself become calloused and eventually cynical on the subject of great causes. It was part of the price I had to pay.

I am particularly indebted to the Carnegie Corporation of New York for supporting me unfailingly as I struggled to understand what I had lived through. The University of California, San Diego, after the sensitive intervention of Chancellor Richard Atkinson, made its records and papers available to me. The staff of UCSD's Central Library were of particular assistance in dealing with endless calls for library resources. A dozen colleagues read early drafts and helped me to tighten my presentation. They winnowed out many errors. Most of these experts prefer to remain anonymous.

My dear wife, Ann, stood by my side through all the traumas of my administrative service. When she had a right to expect peace, she was forced to put up with the irrational outbursts that accompanied the creative process in her husband. She sustained me.

Thomas Quinn, Michael Hennelly, and Karen Seriguchi, my McGraw-Hill editors, guided the writing with great professional skill. I am indebted to them for many improvements in organization and for several felicities of language.

Finally, special words of thanks are due to Dr. Kathryn Ringrose, my very able research assistant, who read and edited the manuscript and helped me with the preparation of footnotes. Her work was invaluable.

I am also indebted to Donata Bocko for converting my scratchy penmanship into the "information structure" of a word processing unit in UCSD's campus computer.

Remaining errors of fact and interpretation are my sole responsibility. I fear there may still be many in the sensitive material that fills these pages.

WJM

The
Year
of
the
Monkey

猴年

A Monkey in the Garden

In the twelve-year cycle of the ancient Chinese calendar, 1968 was designated the Year of the Monkey. The monkey god of Chinese mythology is sometimes emblematic of ugliness and trickery. He is said to exercise control over hobgoblins, malicious spirits, and evil influences.

No label could be more appropriate for conveying the trauma of that particular period of my life. The 1968–69 academic year was distinctly and uniquely a monkey year by virtue of an almost incredible succession of disastrous events bedeviling the University of California.

Apart from things happening to the university, the Year of the Monkey had an even deeper personal significance for me. To this day I remain haunted by the effects of hardening transformations that changed me fundamentally as I struggled to survive the brutal pressures of my first year as a chief campus administrator. Hence, although 1980 was again the Year of the Monkey in the Chinese calendar, there can never be another monkey year for me. Mine is the one that began in the late spring of 1968 as the University of California searched for a new chancellor to lead its San Diego campus.

A great deal has happened since then. I was selected as chancellor and served for two years. In 1970 I moved to Columbia University to become its sixteenth president, attempting to extract that fine old institution from the chaos in which it found itself after the 1968 riots. Ten years later I retired and returned to La Jolla. By then I longed for the peace of that paradisal environment so that I could distill the meaning of all that I had seen since 1968. After relinquishing my responsibilities at Columbia voluntarily and with dignity, I hoped I might find a peace of mind that somehow vanished during the monkey year of 1968, but there is no peace.

Sometimes late at night, when the house is still and the slightest sound is audible, I am suddenly awake in the darkness because I think I can hear them chanting again. A jumble of familiar emotions comes flooding through my consciousness: fear and anxiety deep inside, angry combativeness up high, and twinges of curiosity somewhere in between.

"Those bastards are at it again," I say to myself. "What can they want now?"

The confused darkness conjures up flashbacks of masses of young people in the streets outside, angry and yet somehow festive. Bearded young men in shoulder-length hair are hammering on my front door with their fists. Out in the street, oblivious of the angry drivers whose way is blocked, a young mother sits cross-legged on the pavement, cradling her baby in her arms. All around the crowd is chanting:

> One, two, three, four, we don't want your fuckin' war
> The people united will never be defeated
> McGill, McGill, you better start shakin!
> Today's pig is tomorrow's bacon

I slip out of bed and tiptoe toward the front of the house to draw aside the curtain and peep out. As I suspected, for this has happened more than once, there is nothing out there but an empty street and the silent bulk of Mt. Soledad looming in the distance. The oleanders in front of my window are whispering softly in the night breeze. Perhaps it was that sound that wakened me.

This is La Jolla. I am returned to paradise more than 2400 airline miles removed from New York City and Morningside Drive. I must have been dreaming again. The images and sounds so sharply etched moments earlier could only have been creatures of my memory. Those emotions, the sudden combative anger and the fear, were only conditioned reflexes summoned up, as Pavlov explained, by the stimuli to which they were joined long ago.

It is all over, all gone. The SDS, the PLP, the RYM and the D4M are no more except as they exist in the ghostly recesses of my unconscious. But at night when they creep out to enliven my dreams, the soothing calm of the last few years is wiped away in an instant. I am transported back to all the ugliness, the excitement, and the fervent idealism of those times.

Intense or frightening experiences leave indelible marks on the psyche, giving each of us a permanent dualistic existence. For the most part we are taken up with the sights, sounds, and ideas of our waking hours together with the conscious memories they evoke. But in the archeology of the mind there is much else—unformed, inchoate—providing unseen dimensions to everything we do.

Unexpected encounters with this hidden content invest the human condition with its deep fascination. Nothing is ever simple. No one who has really lived is ever quite predictable. Duality presents itself not only in terror-filled dreams but also in the changed appearances of things around us. Sometimes, unexpectedly, they seem all wrong and the discrepancies demand explanation.

When I retired as president of Columbia University in 1980, I supposed that my time of struggle was over. The work was done. The battles were long since fought. Now it was time to decompress, to read all the things that had been put aside, and to try to understand what I had lived through since I moved to the East Coast to take up residence in Nicholas Murray Butler's old house on Manhattan's Upper West Side.

But my return to paradise after a decade was not at all what I had expected it to be. Nothing was quite the same. It was not just that San Diego and its spectacular suburb, La Jolla, had changed. The great population shift to the sunbelt has taken its toll, and the city is much bigger and brusquer than when I left in 1970. San Diego appears to me now the way Los Angeles used to look in the years after World War II, before it became afflicted with serious urban social problems. As for La Jolla, it grew richer while downtown San Diego slid downhill during my ten-year sojourn on the East Coast.

But these obvious things are not what I mean. Even the places that have not changed significantly—my home, the buildings around Revelle Plaza in the University of California, San Diego (UCSD), the chancellor's area in Camp Matthews, and University House—are all somehow inexplicably different. They are in fact so altered from the form in which they are carried in my memory that I find myself estranged from things that ought to be familiar and comforting.

At first it was difficult to put my finger on what was wrong, but as I continued to probe at the hieroglyphics of fleeting thoughts, it finally struck me that the familiar landmarks in La Jolla were too peaceful looking.

When I first saw La Jolla in 1964 I was a 42-year-old professor of psychology in the most productive part of my academic career. Life was stable and predictable. The idea of living and working in Southern California suited my youthful agnostic belief that one's goal should be a state of earthly tranquility reserved for "heaven" by earlier and less enlightened minds. You have to make your own heaven, I used to say. This was before the misfortunes of the mid-1960s rekindled my religious faith and raised doubts about the stability of the society we had built. Hardly any American now believes that we are free to choose our own destinies.

In 1968, amid ominous signs of explosive social unrest, I was unexpectedly selected as UCSD's chancellor. Something was about to blow: you could feel it. Governor Ronald W. Reagan, elected in 1966, was a political conservative whose hostility to the University of California could hardly be more evident. At the same time, New Left radicalism was growing rapidly on campus. It was only a question of weeks or months before these two antagonistic forces collided.

My first year as UCSD chancellor forms the focus of this book. It was an extraordinary year by any standard. Even now I still cannot quite accept the fact that all of it actually happened or that in some crazy way I survived. I also understand dimly that Columbia would have been impossible for me had I not gone through that brutal experience in 1968.

The events of my first year in office govern the chronology of the writing, but there was also a psychological transformation on which the book's conceptual framework is built. As stress mounted, I tore up my faculty roots, parted company with old friends, and did what I had to do.

This transformation was crucial because it was the key to survival. It took me safely from the gentle lifestyle of a faculty member to the crushing pressures of a public arena during a time of revolutionary change. To emerge as a leader, I had to learn to steel myself against the debilitating effects of continuous pressure and to fight in ways the faculty rejected. Most of these changes occurred during that first year. It was one of those bedrock ordeals that colors all subsequent experience.

By the end of the 1968–69 academic year I had become so wound up I could think of nothing but the imperatives of surviving and preserving my rationality, caught between an opaque state administration and ruthless campus adversaries. All sense of the beauty of life was lost for a time. Now when I recall the appearance of buildings and walkways on the

UCSD campus in 1968, I see them largely in the context of the fierce struggles that occurred there.

Today's young women strolling to class in form-fitting designer jeans and spike-heeled sandals appear scandalously erotic and completely out of place to me. So do the clean-shaven, short-haired young men in jogging shorts. I keep waiting for lost-looking barefoot girls with Mona Lisa hair and bearded boys in rough peasant clothes. And when I think of the sights and smells of UCSD, my unconscious generates shards of broken glass and the odor of burning rubber rather than memories of carefully manicured green lawns and the perfume of jasmine.

Perhaps, too, the tumultuous years as chancellor at UCSD and the cruel decade at Columbia have altered me in ways less obvious than changed perceptions.

A dozen years ago I was much more the liberal-minded idealist than I seem to be today. There is a harsh combativeness now that I am not especially proud of. The changes are directly traceable to that first year as chancellor in 1968–69. One might think I was "radicalized" in the wrong direction, but that conclusion would be too simplistic. The political beliefs I hold have altered very little; I have always been repelled by both political extremes. What seems to have happened is that I have become harder and less compassionate.

Psychiatrists remind us constantly about the duality of experience, but the arid abstractions of that genre of analytical prose cannot begin to capture the immediacy or power of the real thing. The best I have seen of recent literary evocations of this duality is the ghostly young Marine sergeant in William Manchester's *Goodbye, Darkness.*[1]

The sergeant emerges in Manchester's dreams to remind the author of the young man he once was and of what he endured in the Pacific war against the Japanese. The sergeant demands to be understood, but the process is excruciating because it involves recovery of long-suppressed memories filled with terror.

When recovery is achieved after revisiting the scenes of combat, the sergeant disappears from the author's dreams. He is laid to rest when the older man discovers and relives the young man's suffering.

I have no young sergeant, or in my case no young chancellor, to haunt my dreams. My consciousness is less sharply divided. The person who hears the chanting and confronts ghostly crowds in the depths of night is the same individual who put his head down peacefully to sleep only hours before. In the confused moments when I am half dreaming and half awake, I cannot tell where I am or if by some psychic accident I have been transported to those times again.

Having explained as best I can the peculiar psychological origins of this book, I should also try to give the reader a feeling for the locale of my story.

The San Diego campus of the University of California (UCSD) is located on the Pacific Coast near the exquisite town of La Jolla about 10 miles north of the city. Even Californians speak with awe when they speak of La Jolla. It is one of the rare places on earth where a traveller can actually feel the nearness of the Garden of Eden.

The university campus is set down on a thousand acres along Torrey Pines mesa. A substantial part of the land was given to the Regents by the city of San Diego. The remainder was granted by the federal government when it decided to close Camp Matthews, a former Marine Corps rifle training facility. The old Marine Corps barracks and administration buildings can still be seen on the east side of campus. They have been spruced up, painted a deep rich brown, planted with shade trees, and in some instances transformed with modern redwood facades.

The chancellor's office is located in Camp Matthews adjacent to an elliptical reception area, where a flag pole and stone tablet memorialize the military origins of the facility. This part of the campus also serves as a staging area for new "colleges" before they move to permanent buildings elsewhere on campus.

The original plan was to have twelve undergraduate colleges at UCSD. Today there are four such colleges, each enrolling about 2300 students.[2] In 1968 there were two: Revelle College, with its permanent buildings in a breathtaking setting west of Camp Matthews, and Muir College, located in the staging area. By 1970 Muir College had begun to move into its permanent campus location north of Revelle, and a third college was ready for staging in Camp Matthews.

UCSD is constructed in accord with a highly original plan. Its early designers sought ways to overcome the coldness and anonymity that typically afflict a large state university enrolling 25,000 students or more.

The designers proposed that the campus be organized into separate undergraduate colleges, each large enough to support an educational concentration. There would be a science college, a humanities and fine arts college, a history-centered college, and so on.

At the same time, all colleges would be small enough to define an environment in which student residence halls could be located. Students and faculty would get to know each other. It was felt that such personal interactions might provide a richer and more satisfying undergraduate experience.

Undergraduates would be expected to spend the majority of their time studying in their home college, but they would also be free to enroll in a variety of courses offered by other colleges.

This complex collegiate structure was to be woven together by a faculty and a group of academic departments forming a major graduate school. Every faculty member would be appointed to a graduate department and also to an undergraduate college.

Finally, the university attempted to develop several important research centers and professional schools. The Scripps Institution of Oceanography, organized in La Jolla in 1912, had long antedated the coming of the campus. Scripps became incorporated into the UCSD structure when the Regents decided to proceed with the development of a major campus at La Jolla in 1957.

The designers of UCSD also provided for a branch of the prestigious Institute of Geophysics and Planetary Physics as well as for the construction of a medical school and a hospital. As time went by it was expected that a law school and perhaps a business school might be developed in response to emerging community needs. A thousand acres offered ample room to grow and to experiment.

The plan was majestic in concept and practical to operate, although a bit on the expensive side. But California was in an ebullient mood as the decade of the 1960s opened. Its population and wealth were growing, and the future seemed to depend on an educated citizenry. Most believed that the ingenious UCSD college plan, together with the resources of the richest state in the union and an unmatched setting, would prove appealing to bright students and would attract one of the finest faculties in the world. Such benefits should certainly outweigh any added expense posed by the replication of small colleges that foreclose the economies of scale pleasing to state budget analysts.

These high expectations were substantially realized from the beginning. UCSD's first undergraduate students were admitted in 1964, and they were among the brightest in the state. By 1965 a core of truly excellent departments had been put together and a uniquely gifted faculty was being recruited.

The buildings of the first college were completed by 1967. It was named for Roger Revelle, former director of Scripps and the principal guiding spirit of UCSD's early planning and development. The Revelle College architectural plan centered on a large open square, that was promptly dubbed Revelle Plaza. Encircling the plaza are a number of light, delicately wrought academic buildings, which seem to float on a landscape of semitropical greenery. In the southwest corner is a cluster of modern residence halls with suites that appeared downright luxurious when I first saw and compared them with the austere monks' cells that passed for college rooms when I was an undergraduate.

In the plaza a large fountain splashes year round, and off in the background, beyond stands of pine and eucalyptus, is the blue-green mass of Soledad, rising out of the Pacific to a height of more than 800 feet between San Diego and La Jolla.

The planners responsible for UCSD did not know that the late 1960s would bring a generation of students whose social disaffection and moral outrage could not be diverted by the creature comforts of a paradisal setting or the intellectual attractions of a brilliant academic plan. The war in Vietnam was a continuing horror that lay a short distance down the road for young males, as selective service began to reach into the colleges. On April 4, 1968, Martin Luther King was murdered in Memphis. Suddenly college campuses were aflame with intense racial feeling, not limited to black students. Less than two months later Robert Kennedy, who had captured the hearts of students with his opposition to the war, was shot dead at a political rally in Los Angeles. There were other outrages, some of them chronicled in these pages. None of it was anything we planned.

UCSD found itself swept into the wave of emotion that cascaded across colleges all over the U.S. I was brought into the chancellor's office in the summer of 1968, just as the wave began to build to a climax. I came to my new duties a bookish professor, someone who had not been in a public fight since childhood.

Two years later I departed for Columbia a veteran of academic combat against student radicals—a struggle I hope never to see again, although logic decrees that this kind of history must repeat itself. After all, it is the essence of youth to protest the defects of an imperfect world.

There is nothing unique about student unrest. Undergraduates rioted continuously in the Middle Ages, and there is no basis for expecting special protections in our own time. The truth is that we allowed ourselves to grow soft in the post–World War II era, as the blandishments of an affluent society turned us away from struggle and discipline toward the expectation of unending progress. If I have learned anything from the experience of the last dozen years, it is that we must never allow ourselves to become soft again, just as we must also never fail to listen seriously to students who protest our shortcomings.

What can today's students understand of my thoughts? They were in grammar school when I was fighting my first battles in Revelle Plaza. All of them are complete strangers to it.

But out in the far corner of the plaza near the fountain, I can still see

Angela Davis, then a graduate student in philosophy, addressing a huge crowd. It was during a sun-drenched noon-hour rally protesting the treatment of black and Chicano students in the spring of 1969.

Miss Davis, slim and beautiful, wearing a white T-shirt and blue jeans, seemed for all the world like a black Joan of Arc standing behind a microphone on the base of the fountain, three feet above thousands of worshipping admirers.

Next to her, waiting to speak, stood Herbert Marcuse, a dignified, elderly, neo-Marxist philosopher, his forehead furrowed in a perpetual frown. He was waiting beside his star pupil, wondering, or so it seemed to me, whether perhaps the revolution of the young and the disenfranchised he had forecast long ago had come at last. Perhaps it might even now be taking shape in the hands of this extraordinary young evangelist of black fury.

Marcuse died peacefully in 1979, his revolution gone awry. He was no longer the dynamic force that he had been a decade earlier. The New Left had collapsed, and Marcuse told friends somewhat wistfully that the students had passed him by.

When I first confronted student unrest in the monkey year, 1968–69, I was at first nearly paralyzed with fear, then appalled, then outraged. Toward the end of the year I became an adversary, fighting back and vowing to survive.

Now I want to tell about it, not in the marvelling praise affected by apologists for the New Left, nor in the simplistic interpretations offered by the mass media, but with faithful adherence to the complexity of the events themselves, and with special compassion for the students, many of whom never fully understood the pressures that caused them to rebel.

CHAPTER
2

The Cleaver Crisis

In the beginning, the unprecedented volatility of undergraduates in the 1960s frightened me. During my first weeks as UCSD chancellor in the summer of 1968, I went out of my way to avoid campus radicals and antiwar demonstrators. There was something attractive about their public yearning for a better world, but among those hundreds of self-styled outcasts there was also a fierce, almost wild-eyed, determination and a hostility to authority that made me nervous.

I was 46 years old and looked on myself as a rather engaging fellow, gifted in the persuasive arts, able to handle nearly any academic problem by bringing people together to discuss it calmly. Demonstrations seemed disorderly and irrational, even frightening. It was much, much later that I learned the laws of theater governing protests. Demonstrations are not irrational. They are just different from our normal ways of expressing grievances and for me, at least, ugly.

Why is it that newswriters and creative artists are so much more attracted by group protests than the rest of us? Perhaps it is because of the theater involved. The action is inherently exciting and dramatic, managing in some primitive way to communicate an impression of history in the making.

Far less drama can be gleaned from the gnawing apprehension that grips the human spirit as we try to cope with unexpected threats or unpredictable dangers. Yet these lonelier struggles probably lie closer to the determinative forces of history than do dramatic public protests.

Many demonstrations are media events.[1] They are staged to get attention. The intent is to change history less by force than by public exposure. Anger, the critical ingredient of any protest, is mostly contrived. Of course, sometimes even a media event can blow up if a few demonstrators get out of control. But the overwhelming majority of group protests in which I found myself over the years played themselves out according to a carefully prearranged and agreed-upon scenario. Protestors, administrators, and even the police had well-rehearsed parts to play before the reporters and television cameras. The advantage of a scenario is that protestors are allowed to make their point; everyone goes away feeling he has done well. One of the essential arts in dealing with protest demonstrations lies in making an accurate preliminary assessment as to whether real trouble is impending or simply another staged event aimed at the media.

In real life, as distinct from the plane of existence defined by media events, anxiety must be overcome and a battle for personal survival must be fought before history can be made. Demonstrators who for the first time must try to find the courage to face even a prearranged arrest, in order to make a point of conscience, understand that their personal decision is far more important than the public drama of their protest tactics. Administrators and public officials often remark on the fears evoked by their initial exposure to an angry crowd even when they are assured by demonstration leaders that their people are under control.

This part of my story centers on the first awful moment of realization that charm and persuasion would not suffice if I intended to survive as chancellor. I would be forced either to run away or to fight publicly against determined and unthinking demonstrators led by clever people who meant us genuine harm. What we were facing was no media event. When I suddenly discovered the full impact of this prospect, I was nearly overcome with anxiety. The memory of it even now brings a chill.

The Regents of the University of California convened at UCSD on Friday, November 22, 1968, in accord with their policy of meeting annually at least once on each campus of the university.[2] They departed at 4:30 on Friday afternoon, leaving us in turmoil over a disputed course, Social Analysis 139X. The course was devised at Berkeley during the previous summer by a special planning committee with strong representation from students. The committee had been set up in the aftermath of the Free Speech Movement in 1965 to consider innovative courses reflecting student concerns.[3] Their big problem was that the student planners designated Eldridge Cleaver, Information Minister of the Black Panther party and author of *Soul on Ice*, to present some ten lectures in the 13-week course. It was felt that Cleaver's articulate commentary on urban racism would be important for students to hear. Faculty who sat on the committee thought that such a plan was not likely to cause difficulty.

But the Regents saw Cleaver as a criminal charged with three counts of assault with intent to commit murder, as well as violation of parole. His trial was pending on these various charges.[4] The idea of listing him among the Berkeley faculty and paying him university funds was enough to send most Regents into orbit. At first they sought to ban the course altogether, but they had long ago delegated that authority to the faculty.[5] Any attempt to bar Cleaver from lecturing would have set off another free speech explosion. They finally decided to attack the problem by imposing strict limits on guest lecturers in courses offered for credit. At their meeting in La Jolla on November 22, 1968, the Regents voted to limit guest lecturers to a single appearance in credit courses and to remove credit for Social Analysis 139X because of the way it was structured.[6]

Students had been following the debate over Cleaver's course with mounting excitement throughout the fall quarter of 1968. There was no doubt where their sympathies lay. The Board of Regents considered its action of November 22 a compromise. They would have preferred to bar Cleaver altogether. Everywhere in the university, however, students were outraged by the "compromise." They saw it as a disavowal of earlier agreements permitting students to plan alternative curricula relevant to their concerns about society. They also knew perfectly well that credit was denied Social Analysis 139X because of Cleaver's involvement. In students' eyes, it was a racist act and an illegitimate use of authority. Student observers angrily walked out of the Regents meeting in the UCSD gymnasium after the deciding vote was taken.

Eldridge Cleaver presented a tough problem. During the years following the Berkeley free speech riots in 1964, the University of California and its Regents had come under increasing criticism from the legislature and public. California, perhaps more than any other state, had poured major resources into its state university system ever since its founding in 1868. This faith was handsomely rewarded by the university's leadership in developing California's industry and agriculture, and by Berkeley's postwar reputation for academic excellence. In 1959 the prestige of the University of California was so great that President Clark Kerr could plan a visionary expansion into nine large campuses across the state. Kerr received virtually complete public and political backing for his master plan despite its projected costs. But then Berkeley blew up in 1964, and a widespread suspicion developed that communists were running amuck on a campus that had once been a source of pride among taxpayers and legislators.[7] When the Cleaver case hit the newspapers critics became downright hostile.[8]

A large segment of the public decided, after reading newspaper reports and listening to protests from state legislators, that the Berkeley faculty and student body were out of control. Letters and telegrams poured in demanding that the Regents retrieve their authority over the university before those other people wrecked it. A key member of the board was Governor Ronald Reagan. Reagan attended every Regents meeting, regularly trailed by dozens, sometimes hundreds, of newspaper and TV reporters. He was handed a rare political opportunity with Social Analysis 139X and Eldridge Cleaver. In September the Governor launched a powerful attack[9] on the university and his fellow Regents for considering a convicted felon and a self-declared revolutionary to be qualified to lecture at Berkeley. He kept up the pressure with inflammatory public statements through the fall.

Reagan had been cast in the movies as the gallant, attractive boy who never quite won the girl. He has used this aura of gallantry with great effect in running for office and generating support for his policies. During the 1960s his background as an actor led many people to underestimate him seriously. Close up, Reagan proved to be a hard-bitten, adroit politician. He acquired formidable bargaining skills while serving as president of the Screen Actors Guild, and he knew how to use personal force to get his way. In the inner circles of the Board of Regents during the fall of 1968, Reagan threatened his colleagues with dire consequences[10] if Cleaver were ever allowed to set foot on the Berkeley campus under official auspices. With the Governor running in overdrive on the subject of Cleaver and flailing his fellow Regents daily in the press, they could see not only their budget but all their hopes for restoring the university's prestige going down the drain.

Thus, it was not easy for the Regents to take the position that Cleaver could lecture in Social Analysis 139X, even without course credit. There were many risks in such a compromise, not the least of them the Governor's militant objections. Moreover, Cleaver was having a field day of his own because of the controversy over the course and the role he would play in it. On the night of October 4th, Cleaver had come down to the

UCSD campus from San Francisco in response to an invitation by students. In the same gymnasium where, six weeks later, the Regents would discredit his course, Cleaver led a crowd of 4,000 chanting "Fuck Ronald Reagan!" His lecture that night bore no relation to the sensitive probing of the American black man's dilemma in *Soul on Ice*.[11] Instead it was an appalling analysis of American society from a Black Panther perspective, full of paranoid rhetoric: good guys (students), bad guys (capitalists and politicians), and pigs (police). A friend of mine on the UCSD faculty called me the next day to say that, with ten lectures of that quality, Social Analysis 139X would not be a course but a foretaste of hell. He was relieved that this travesty would occur at Berkeley and not on our campus.

With these inflammatory developments, the Regents saw no option but to act as they did on November 22nd. The hundred or so UCSD students who rose angrily in the balcony of the UCSD gymnasium as the Regents voted on Social Analysis 139X saw things differently. They stormed out of the meeting late on Friday afternoon, totally frustrated, and went over to the Revelle College Plaza to hold a meeting of their own. During the next 48 hours one meeting followed another in an atmosphere of mounting crisis. Faculty radicals became involved and the group began to increase in size.

None of this was known to me. I had gone home Friday evening at dinner time, hours after the last Regent departed. I was thoroughly worn out by the intense activity and tensions of Regents' week at UCSD, determined to sleep until noon on Saturday and to spend the weekend puttering around the house. The staff of the chancellor's office, however, were apprehensive about what was going on at Revelle College. The dean of student affairs, George Murphy, had given strict orders that the chancellor should not be disturbed. McGill had done his job by conducting the most peaceful Regents meeting of the last six months. He should be allowed some time to decompress.

Later Murphy told me he became alarmed when he discovered that Brad Cleaveland was on the UCSD campus, joining the intense meetings of angry students over the weekend. Cleaveland was not a current UCSD student. He was one of the founders and heavy hitters of the Berkeley Free Speech Movement in 1964. He had enrolled as a graduate student in philosophy at UCSD in 1966 but dropped out and disappeared the following year.

Murphy had been a "baby dean" at Berkeley during the Free Speech Movement and he knew Cleaveland. He understood that Cleaveland's emergence in La Jolla at this critical time was very bad news. But neither

Murphy nor anyone else felt comfortable about disturbing me with their alarm over the unusual weekend activity in Revelle Plaza.

Shortly after midnight on Sunday night, just as my wife and I were turning out the lights and preparing for bed, the doorbell rang. We stared at each other in amazement. No one ever came calling at that hour. But there on the doorstep were two prominent members of the UCSD faculty, Walter Munk, chairman of the academic senate, and Sheldon Schultz, a physicist. Both looked extremely upset.

Munk is a famous geophysicist at the Scripps Institution of Oceanography, one of the major units of UCSD. In 1968 he was 51 years old and at the peak of his career, universally admired among the faculty. He is a gentle man, whose perfect manners and trace of an accent almost immediately betray his Viennese origins. Ordinarily, Walter would be the last person to be found ringing doorbells at midnight. He began by apologizing profusely for disturbing us. Shelly interrupted to say that they had just left a long faculty meeting. They were certain we were headed for serious trouble tomorrow. Despite the lateness of the hour they felt I ought to know so that I could decide what to do.

Munk explained. Earlier on Sunday evening he had attended an informal meeting of sixty members of the faculty called by Dr. Joseph Stokes, who had recently stepped down as dean of UCSD's new medical school. The group met in one of the large lecture halls in Revelle College. They were worried about the intense weekend activity in the College, and all of them were annoyed with the Regents because of the ruling on guest lecturers in the Cleaver case. The Regents had no jurisdiction over course content or staffing. They had simply seized it. Munk hoped for a sensible resolution setting forth faculty objections. A meeting of the academic senate was scheduled for the following Tuesday afternoon. He feared that at the senate meeting radical faculty would demand confrontation with the Regents over the racial implications of the attempt to silence Cleaver. Walter sought to head them off by working up a moderate position that would attract support from the wiser heads on the campus. He went to the Sunday night meeting hoping to persuade his colleagues about the wisdom of such a moderate response.[12]

For hours on Sunday night the informal faculty meeting debated the language of several possible resolutions without success. There was considerable sentiment in favor of censuring the Regents for abrogating the faculty's written authority over course credit. Munk and other conservatives did not want a censure. They understood the public pressure on the Regents in the Cleaver case. They preferred an expression of severe displeasure. And so the meeting argued in circles until late in the evening.

Some time after 11 PM there was a sudden commotion at the door. With no preliminaries of any kind, a large group of students pushed into the room and formed a semicircle facing the faculty. Munk said that there were more than a hundred of them. He had no idea how they discovered the meeting place, although it would not have been difficult. Rumors had been flying back and forth in Revelle College all evening about who was meeting with whom, and Stokes had made no particular effort to keep this faculty meeting a secret.

The spokesman was Barry Shapiro, a redheaded, bearded graduate student in philosophy. Walter had never seen him before, but he was a well-known firebrand to the humanists in the room. Mr. Shapiro did not mince words. The students had voted to strike for the next two days, Monday and Tuesday. They were now asking for faculty support. Solidarity must be shown by cancelling classes and releasing students to a two-day convocation in Revelle Plaza. Representatives of black and Chicano students then made angry speeches demanding restructuring of the university as a humane institution.[13] A lined yellow pad was produced and signatures were demanded on a pledge to cancel classes.[14]

Munk said it was a scene out of Kafka: angry students radiating menace from the front of the room, with many of the faculty intimidated. They began to sign up and to make speeches filled with revolutionary fervor. Munk thought they were trying to outdo the students in expressions of piety. As the student group filed out of the room, someone called for a vote to suspend classes on Monday. It passed, with Munk and Schultz alone in opposition.

Faculty members left glumly one by one. Their effort to head off confrontation had ended in disaster under unanticipated student pressure. The best face Munk could put on it was that it was an informal meeting and the vote had no significance. But now people were asking him to call the chancellor at once to urge suspension of classes the following day. The reasons were unimportant. Any pretext would do. Most were fearful of a serious outbreak in Revelle College if these angry students were opposed.

Munk's report, delivered less than an hour later on my doorstep, was stunning news for an engaging fellow easily frightened by demonstrators. I had supposed that all our troubles ended when the Regents departed safely on Friday afternoon, and now this!

Munk asked what I intended to do. I did not have the faintest idea. It would probably be wise to call an emergency meeting of department chairmen first thing in the morning. He said, "Of course, and good luck!" Schultz nodded.

Their unpleasant duty carried out, the two faculty messengers climbed into the front seat of their automobile, backed swiftly out of my driveway, and sped off into the darkness, leaving me wondering what tomorrow would bring and how in the world we would get out of it.

No sleep at all came that night. I lay tossing fitfully through the early morning hours, my head buzzing with anxiety and thoughts racing aimlessly. At 6:30 I gave up and slipped quietly out of bed, where my wife still lay sound asleep—looking, I thought, outrageously at peace. I showered and dressed, tiptoed silently out of the house, and drove along La Jolla Scenic Drive toward the campus. The drive was not especially scenic that morning. A heavy fog had rolled in from the sea. It streamed in irregular patterns past my windshield, blotting out nearly all the local landmarks. Ten minutes later, I steered into my parking place near the chancellor's office in Camp Matthews at the eastern edge of the campus. I remembered that I had not eaten breakfast. No sleep and no appetite! Thinking about what we were in for, I wished wretchedly that I were a thousand miles away from this damned place.

The chancellor's outer office was completely deserted at 7:30 AM. For nearly an hour I forced myself to work through a pile of administrative papers, but I could not read two consecutive sentences without breaking away to stare at the clock. Efforts to concentrate were getting me nowhere, and eventually I yielded to an urge to call George Murphy at home. It troubled me that my hand seemed to tremble as I dialed his number. What if I should pass out in the middle of this, of all days?

Murphy was UCSD's top administrator for student affairs. Although his office was located near mine, I suspected he would spend little time there today. I wanted to catch him before he became entangled with the strike activities in Revelle Plaza.

George S. Murphy was a handsome, tautly disciplined man in his middle thirties. He had the cool reserve and self-command of a military officer. Yet when he spoke to students or about them, there was a warmth and a tolerance that reminded me of priests I had known as a young man. Murphy was a thoroughly experienced professional in student affairs. He had grown up in Wisconsin and, after graduate study in the Midwest, moved to California to join the staff of the dean of students at Berkeley just prior to the Free Speech Movement. He worked outdoors in Sproul Plaza at Berkeley during the worst of the escalating student protests led by the FSM in 1964.[15] My predecessor had heard about Murphy's cool behavior at Berkeley and was so impressed that he looked George up and successfully recruited him to La Jolla in 1966.

Murphy was sitting at the breakfast table drinking his morning coffee when my call came. I reported last night's disastrous faculty meeting in Revelle College and the alarming extent of faculty support for suspending classes. George told me that his staff had given him essentially the same information at about the time Professors Munk and Schultz were reporting to me outside my front door.

"Boss," he said, "I'm concerned. It looks like a big one, and once it starts we can't be sure where it will go. My people and I will try to stay on top of it, but that faculty vote really bothers me."

I mentioned that I had scheduled a meeting with the department chairmen. Perhaps I might be able to turn them around. I would not suspend classes. It would be unfair to the students who wanted to continue. Murphy accepted the decision. He would go directly from home to Revelle Plaza and I could reach him during the morning by leaving a message with the office of the provost of Revelle College. He would call me periodically to report. I asked whether there was anything else I could do.

"No. It's best that you stay over there to coordinate our activities, Bill. I'll call you if I need you."

At 9:00 AM Anita Tinnerstet, my assistant, arrived. She brought in a telegram announcing a convocation in Revelle Plaza. The organizers were asking me to attend. It was signed by the head of the Revelle College student government.

Anita asked whether there was any reply. Two students who said they represented the "Graduate and Undergraduate Liberation Front" were waiting in the outer office to carry back my answer. I had never heard of the organization. It must have come into existence over the weekend.

"Tell them nothing doing."

She looked at me for a moment, expressionless, turned without a word, and left the office, closing the door very softly behind her.

The phone rang. It was Jack Oswald calling from university headquarters in Berkeley. Oswald, now president of Penn State, was serving as executive vice president of the University of California. Cheerful, corny, and clever, Oswald was the president's liaison with the chancellors. Word had reached University Hall about the trouble down in La Jolla. How did it look to me? I gave him the report I had just passed on to my dean of student affairs.

"Would you consider suspending classes?"

"No, Jack. San Francisco State and Chico State have been shut down by students for campuswide convocations.[16] That must be how our people got the idea. If we close now, I am not sure I can stay in control here. We have to remain open, but I am afraid there may be big trouble."

Oswald reassured me cheerfully. "Bill, I have complete confidence in your ability to handle it."

"I hope I can."

The absence of conviction was so evident that Oswald laughed at the other end of the line. He instructed me to keep in touch with him as our situation developed, and I promised to do so.

No sooner had I put down the phone than Anita was back in the office with word that Professor Munk was outside to escort me to the meeting of department chairmen. They were waiting. Walter looked grave as I told him there would be no suspension of classes. He said, "You're right, but I'm afraid there will be trouble."

For the first time since this whole affair began, I felt a sudden and oddly cleansing surge of anger. Dammit, we were all so fearful of students and the possibility they might go on a rampage that they were successfully bullying us. Unless someone put a stop to it, the bullying would go on and on. We just could not permit it.

The anger had not receded as I strode into the senate conference room to be confronted by a dozen gloomy faces. The chairmen were sprawled around the table in a variety of poses depicting their unhappiness. They did not rise as I entered the room. I considered them for a moment and decided not to sit down. One of the chairmen reported that, on his way over, he had seen a large number of students in Revelle Plaza. They seemed very peaceful. When he passed by, some of them were setting up a sound system, but most were listening quietly to a distinguished chemist[17] explaining that the Regents' compromise on guest lecturers was a victory for the students. I knew that George Murphy and Paul Saltman, the provost of Revelle College, must be somewhere on the fringes of that crowd reminding the organizers that their sound system was in violation of campus rules. We prohibited public address systems in Revelle Plaza before noon.

I leaned forward, spreading both hands in front of me on the conference table, and stared at each chairman in turn. Words came tumbling out in an angry flood that surprised me. My listeners appeared shocked.

We were all being paid excellent salaries by the people of California, and it was about time we realized our obligations under that contract.[18] There would be no strike as long as any UCSD student wanted to attend class. There would be no suspension of classes. The chairmen would return to their departments and advise faculty that those cancelling classes today had a professional duty to inform the chairman in writing and to cite their reasons. I would then consider how to respond, but I was not disposed to be either sympathetic or understanding about the pressures they were under. I was damned mad! This was a university, not a political circus.[19] We had always insisted that the Regents treat us as professionals rather than as state employees. Professional status carried responsibilities and I expected our responsibilities to be met.

Most of the chairmen nodded agreement. One of two registered mild protests. The chairman of philosophy suggested hesitantly that my hard line was unnecessarily confrontational. We ought to listen to the students and work with them. My proposed actions would only make matters worse. I replied that we had not started this and did not want any part of it. Our high opinion of UCSD was hardly compatible with militant, day-long political rallies and sound systems operating in violation of campus rules. Someone reminded me of the strong faculty support for the convocation expressed at last night's meeting. I said I did not believe there was any substantial support. People were intimidated. In any case only the chancellor possessed the authority to suspend classes and I refused to do it.

Reluctantly, I thought, but nevertheless unanimously, the chairmen agreed to carry out my instructions. We shook hands near the door and I wished them all luck as they filed out of the conference room. Munk, who had been standing to one side witnessing this scene, joined me near the door, his eyes twinkling with amusement.

"Bill," he remarked gently, "you managed to get it all off your chest, but you didn't give them a chance. They're really trying to help you."

Years later Munk told me that he had been talking with the chairmen for some time before I was summoned, and there was very little disposition to suspend classes. They looked shocked only because I had unloaded on them without giving them an opportunity to reassure me. I was, as it developed, preaching to the already converted.

Alone again in the chancellor's office, I could not account for the sudden eruption that had welled up within me a few moments earlier in the senate conference room. It certainly was not my style. Irritation mounted as I became fired up by the sound of my own words. Migod, I must have sounded like Reagan! Moreover, it was surprising to see how readily the chairmen agreed. Obviously there could be no real militancy there.

Anita came into the office to remind me that I was scheduled to host a luncheon at noon for the women's auxiliary of University Hospital. The affair had been planned for months. Luncheon was to be served in a pleasant room in the chancellor's administrative area, and I was to be the speaker.

I began to fret. Suppose those damned demonstrators were to come marching over to the office to serenade us or perhaps to throw rocks. Wouldn't that be a delightful prospect for the women's auxiliary. They would take flight and we would never see any of them again.

Had the caterer shown up? The answer was no. Was it possible to divert him, say, to University House at the opposite end of the campus, far from the administrative complex? Anita said she would check. Did we have sufficient time to notify the guests of the new location? She would check.

Fifteen minutes later Anita buzzed on the intercom to report that University House was available. There was also time enough to notify the guests by phone.

It seemed possible to get some work done now. I was still tense, but my morbid feeling of dread had markedly diminished after the session with the chairmen. The refusal to suspend classes had been communicated and it was too late to do anything about that now. As I reflected on it, there had been no decision at all. I had been struggling to face up to what had to be done, and then suddenly, without any real deciding, it was over. I simply blurted it out to Murphy on the phone, and again a few moments later when Anita asked for my response to the telegram.

Shortly after 11 AM the phone rang again—Murphy reporting from Revelle College. There were now about 200 people, graduate students, undergraduates, and a sprinkling of familiar outsiders in Revelle Plaza.[20] They had set up an illegal sound amplification system. Murphy asked them to turn it off. They refused.

The convocation began peacefully enough, with speeches from a number of faculty and student leaders trying to turn the discussion of Cleaver's course toward constructive ends. Then the radical leaders took over the microphone and the crowd began debating whether to attempt to enter classes that were continuing to meet despite the boycott. Several people wanted to do it and to impress on those attending class the importance of joining in the protest. The leaders were still uncertain of their ability to influence the crowd, and so the question was put to a vote. It lost. Murphy was relieved. His staff had reported isolated instances in which classes were entered and arguments had ensued, but the incidents were few in number and were not an important problem for us.

I outlined my meeting with the department chairmen, saying that I believed we now had a good understanding with the faculty. Murphy agreed. He was aware of several faculty who had cancelled classes, urging students to go over to Revelle Plaza. Announcements of such cancellations were made at the convocation, but Murphy had the impression that most classes were meeting.

"It's looking good for us, boss."

I asked Murphy who was in charge of the convocation. He mentioned Barry Shapiro, the graduate student who surfaced in Walter Munk's account of last night's faculty meeting. Two black students, both undergraduates, were prominently positioned near the microphone and were involved in the discussion.

What about faculty?[21] Murphy mentioned a professor of German literature recently arrived from the Free University of Berlin, an assistant professor of philosophy familiar to us as an active radical in Revelle Plaza, and a black assistant professor of English literature. The black was a Jamaican citizen who carried a British passport.[22]

Was Herbert Marcuse there? Marcuse was a social philosopher who had recently achieved international celebrity as the guru and father-figure of the New Left. Murphy said that Marcuse was nowhere in evidence. That was typical. As subsequent events proved, Marcuse was usually ready to urge students to strike, but seldom visible in the resulting crowd scenes.

Murphy did not mention Brad Cleaveland. I would not have known who Cleaveland was, but if Murphy had described his credentials to me, the recitation would certainly have plunged me into deep anxiety. George kept the information to himself.

Paul Saltman then came on the phone. Saltman was a biologist, a huge, physical man whose earthy manner made him popular among undergraduate students. He was provost of Revelle College, the chief administrative officer of UCSD's first undergraduate unit. Saltman greeted me in his familiar, profane way. "Hi, Billy. How do you like your shiny new big-ass job now?" I had been chancellor for less than four months.

"I'm O.K. Do you have everything under control over there in Revelle, Paul?"

"You better believe it. Just let one of those two-bit bastards step out of line today, and I'll deliver his head to you on a plate!"

I laughed nervously, and told both of them that I had moved the University Hospital Auxiliary luncheon over to University House. I would be there between twelve and two if they needed me for any reason.

"It doesn't look as though we'll need to bother you, boss." Murphy was signing off in his own gently mocking fashion.

The luncheon at University House was a triumph: stylish and apparently effortless. It was as though we had planned it down to the last detail. The ladies were too polite to question us on the sudden change in location and I did not volunteer anything. The last thing I wanted to discuss with them was the convocation in Revelle Plaza.

Our guests were twenty-five middle-aged women who had organized themselves as volunteers to raise money, supervise the gift shop, and help out on the floors of the newly acquired University Hospital in the Hillcrest district of San Diego. A number of them were faculty wives. Before we sat down to the beautifully set table in the dining room, they fussed over me in the old-fashioned way that men my age find attractive. It was light years removed from the demonstration activity on the other side of the campus.[23]

The faculty wives introduced me to their associates, volunteers from La Jolla and San Diego with no affiliation to the university, only a desire to be helpful in what they considered our important contribution to their community's health care. Animated conversation sprang up around the table. Gradually I began to put aside my anxieties and to enjoy the meal. I was very hungry. When dessert and demitasse were served, Peggy Marston, the chairman of the auxiliary, rose to make a charming introduction. I thanked her, smiled benignly at the serious, attentive faces turned toward me at the head of the table, and then launched into an earnest, almost fervent, recitation of our hopes and plans for UCSD's medical school. I went on extemporaneously for half an hour, oblivious to the cares that had afflicted me since last night's midnight visitation.

I said goodbye to each of the guests at the door, thanked them for their help, and waved to them as they drove off. It was time to go. Before climbing into my car, I stood for a moment in the garden of University House, staring at the expanse of geraniums for which the house was famous all over San Diego. The sun had burned off the morning fog and the flowers were shining in great mounds of scarlet, with the blue sky and the sea sparkling in the background. My anxiety was beginning to rise again as I wondered what in the world I could do to overcome the problem in Revelle Plaza. If only I had the strength or the cleverness to transplant this peace to the other side of campus. But, of course, the problem over there was the perversity of human nature and the only thing to do was to face up to it. It was a depressing thought. Well, at least Murphy had not called. I looked at my watch. It was ten minutes past two.

The phone in the chancellor's office shattered my concentration. I had been working on the morning's mail after returning from University House. George Murphy was on the line, and the sharp edge in his voice told me we were in serious trouble.

The convocation had moved along through the morning with continuing dialogues on the University of California as a racist institution and the need to restructure UCSD to make our curriculum more relevant and more humane. During the noon hour the crowd grew to 300 people and Murphy began to pick up signs of increasing fervor in the references to Cleaver and the fate of Social Analysis 139X. They were debating again whether they should break into classrooms.

At about 2:00 PM a Revelle College junior came to the microphone and made a stirring personal appeal to the crowd. He said that he had never before participated in a protest. He would be the last person anyone might label as a radical. Yet, listening to the discussion during the last few hours, he had come to realize that the Regents had done a monumental injustice to Cleaver just because he was black. Going to class as though none of this ever happened would be obscene. He was prepared to risk everything in a strike on Cleaver's behalf. They simply could not sit there and do nothing. They had to act.

The speech hit the crowd like a bomb. In a few moments they were in motion, banging on trash can covers, ringing cowbells that were produced as if by magic, and marching around Revelle Plaza shouting "Cleaver, Cleaver" and "Join us, join us." The crowd flooded into the Humanities Library and sought to persuade the people studying there to join the march. There were few takers. An argument ensued when several people in the library asked the demonstrators to leave. Some marchers threw themselves on the floor declaring the library "liberated." The bulk of the crowd moved out, heading for classrooms in the Undergraduate Science Building. Someone found a can of red paint and daubed "Cleaver Hall" in crude letters on the side of the library.

The scene on the ground floor of Undergraduate Science rapidly deteriorated into wild, shouting confusion. In the classrooms, arguments erupted between demonstrators and students. Marchers again threw themselves on the floor and refused to leave. There would be no business as usual while Cleaver was barred from teaching his course, they said.

The remainder of the crowd took off again, crisscrossing the plaza to the Humanities Library Auditorium. Here another large class was thrown into chaos as angry demonstrators burst in demanding an end to instruction. More marchers decided to sit in. They argued loudly with the instructor and students who were asking them to leave.

Diminished now by the loss of people sitting in at the library and the three disrupted classes, the leaders of the convocation returned to the center of Revelle Plaza and began to formulate new demands for suspending classes.

Murphy and his staff followed the marchers, trying to stop them. It was no use. He gave up and moved inside the Revelle provost's office to compare notes with his people. The demonstration was now completely out of hand. Something had to be done at once. Murphy pondered the problem and then had a sudden brainstorm. He tried it out on Saltman, who nodded his head vigorously in assent. Saltman handed Murphy the phone and Murphy dialed my number. It was just before three o'clock.

When I answered, Murphy quickly reviewed the sequence of events in and around Revelle Plaza during the past hour. He said the situation was very serious. Then, "Bill, I need you over here in Revelle Plaza."

"When?"

"Immediately."

"I will be right over."

"I'll be waiting for you, sir."

I hung up the phone clumsily because my hands were shaking. Anxiety experienced repeatedly develops a certain familiarity that makes it almost bearable, but I was new to such pressures in those days and I was gripped with fear. It was as though someone had kicked me in the stomach. My head was buzzing and I felt faint. Somehow I managed to rise from the chair. I put on my jacket and tried to appear casual as I told Anita I was on my way to Revelle Plaza. It must have worked. She barely glanced at me, nodded, and went back to her typing.

Murphy and Saltman sent the deans into the library and the "liberated" classrooms, telling the occupiers they could remain if they chose; no one would remove them. But it would be a damn shame because the demonstrators would miss all the action in Revelle Plaza, where the chancellor would be appearing in ten minutes to speak to the convocation.

It was a masterstroke. The people occupying the three large classrooms and the Humanities Library came pouring out into Revelle Plaza. None of the angry demonstrators could resist this opportunity to confront a hated symbol of administrative authority. Many in the crowd were not angry at all but simply consumed with curiosity. Angry or not, they began to move outdoors into the plaza.

With the departure of the demonstrators, classes resumed in the Undergraduate Science Building and the Humanities Library Auditorium. The instructors told me afterwards that they noticed a reduced attendance following the brief occupation of their classrooms. They suspected many nonpolitical students who had refused to join the demonstration could no longer resist the action outdoors, with the chancellor about to make an appearance before an unruly crowd in the plaza.

It was a lesson I never forgot. I used it repeatedly afterwards, especially during the difficult early years at Columbia. Emotionally aroused demonstrators are like excitable, buzzing moths. The president is the flame. Several times I succeeded in drawing people out of an occupied building simply by going up to the door, waiting until I had attracted a crowd, and then slowly walking away arguing all the while in a loud voice with the demonstrators circling around me. Antipathy to authority is so intense in certain protest groups that they simply cannot resist an opportunity to confront the authority figure. But, of course, I did not understand any of these tactical subtleties in November 1968.

The crowd in Revelle Plaza swelled rapidly to more than 350 people as Murphy's staff spread the word that the chancellor was on his way. While the crowd was beginning to buzz with anticipation, I walked down a lonely lane, lined with young eucalyptus trees, leading from the chancellor's office to Revelle College a half mile distant. My body was literally shaking with fear. I had never been in a public fight in my adult life. Murphy had not told me what he wanted me to do, but I had a good idea that I was to be his instrument for controlling the crowd, and I would have to do it alone. Could I face those angry people without showing them I was afraid? What would I say to them?

Just ahead was a graceful arched footbridge over the arroyo separating Revelle College from Camp Matthews and the chancellor's office. On the far side of the redwood footbridge, standing halfway up the path, was George Murphy, calm and smiling. His gray tweed jacket was carefully buttoned. He held a clipboard in his left hand, and not a hair was out of place.

For the briefest of moments we stood motionless next to each other on the path. He looked at me intently and spoke just one sentence, quietly and deliberately:

"It's up to you now, boss."

I moved quickly up the path toward Revelle Plaza, and without another word, Murphy fell in behind me. I did not want him to see how nervous I was. The thing to do was to keep moving.

As the path opened onto Revelle Plaza at the north end of the Undergraduate Science Building, I had my first clear view of the crowd. Later in the evening, I estimated the number at 500 or more. Murphy thought it was 350 or less, and the next day's newspapers proved him right. It has fascinated me ever since that I tend consistently to overestimate the size of a crowd when I believe they are threatening me.

At the moment I saw them, the crowd also saw me coming. Those on the fringe nearest me began to clap and chant. I could see dripping red-painted letters on the side of the Humanities Library, although I could not make the words out. There were several effigies dangling from branches of the plantings surrounding Revelle Plaza. I learned later that these were depictions of the Regents.

The volume of chanting gradually swelled as I approached. There was no sign of a friendly or even a familiar face anywhere on the outer fringe. Well, this was it! I clamped my jaws tightly shut and moved onto the plaza, but my heart was pounding and my throat was dry. The crowd opened up a pathway, clapping and chanting rhythmically as I passed through: "Power to the pee-pul; power to the pee-pul; power to the pee-pul."

In the center, a half dozen people were standing in a cluster, while all around them the inner segment of the crowd had seated itself on the cement pavement in the warm November afternoon sun. They made a rough circle extending some twenty or thirty yards. One fellow was holding a microphone in his right hand. It was attached to a cord that went snaking through the sitters and disappeared among the successive ranks of those standing. Halfway back in the crowd were two large public address speaker units atop metal poles high above their heads.

The person holding the microphone was a redheaded, bearded fellow who tallied perfectly with Murphy's description of Barry Shapiro. Next to him was a trim young black in an Afro hairdo and wearing a dashiki. On the left of these two students stood four men in their thirties. I recognized three of them: the assistant professor of philosophy, a square-jawed, blond Californian in a white shirt open at the collar; the professor of German literature, short, wiry, wearing granny spectacles and blue denims; and the assistant professor of English literature, tiny, black, almost owlish in appearance, and dressed in a long-sleeved turtleneck. In contrast, the fourth man was turned out almost like a Brooks Brothers fashion model. He wore the Ivy League uniform—tweed jacket, slacks, white button-down shirt, and striped tie. I did not know him. Murphy explained later that this was Brad Cleaveland.

The redhead addressed himself to me as spokesman for the crowd. I stood listening with arms tightly folded so that no one could see my hands. I feared they might be trembling. He said:

"Chancellor McGill, this morning we invited you very politely to attend our convocation, but you refused to come. You rejected our invitation in rather crude language. Now we have forced you to come. (Cheers and applause from the crowd.) We are sick of what you and the Regents are doing to the University of California. Cleaver has been silenced, but you can't silence us. We are demanding that this campus be shut down for the next two days and that you stand here and listen to our demands for restructuring this university so that it can become a humane institution. We demand a new curriculum that will address itself to the racism and imperialism in America today. And we want to know what you intend to do to implement our demands." (Loud cheers and applause.)

Mr. Shapiro handed me the microphone. I took it from him, stepped forward, and began to speak to the crowd.

"I understand what you are trying to do and I do not question your good intentions, but I cannot permit you to influence the rest of the campus to this extent. (Boos and catcalls.) There are thousands of other students here who do not feel your depth of commitment and who want to be left alone so that they can go to school. They have rights too and I am obliged to keep the campus open. (Loud boos, cries of "You're a racist" and "Fuck you, McGill.") I am here to listen to your ideas, but in the University of California it is the faculty and the senate, not the chancellor, who decide matters of courses and curriculum." (The last words drowned out in a chorus of boos; from the back of the crowd "Face the problem, McGill, this is a revolution!")

I was surprised that my voice sounded steady and rather strong. Somewhere a competitive debating spark was being kindled. They could not get away with a performance like this. I gave the microphone back to Shapiro, who handed it to the professor of German literature. He startled me by grabbing the microphone and leaping in front of me like a Cossack dancer. His voice was a shrill half-scream in a seriocomic German accent.

"McGill talks about the faculty senate. I'll tell you what the senate will give you. They will give you shit! (Loud cheers and applause.) You will talk nicely to them and they will say come back next week. Let us talk some more about your nice little course on the ideology of revolution. Next week it will be the week after, and then the week after that. They don't take you seriously. They don't give a shit about you. If you want something, you take it and ram it down their throats. McGill is just another racist who will play you along, but he is really out to fuck you." (Thunderous cheers and applause, cries of "Right on.")

He handed the microphone to the redhead, who immediately gave it back to me. I paused to wait for the noise to settle. The last outburst had revived the anger I felt earlier in the day. My fears were beginning to drop away, but I was still nervous. I tried to get an icy sound into my voice, hoping I would not spoil it by stammering.

"The professor may abuse and insult me all he wishes. I am paid to accept insults, although I believe that the display you have just heard is not what we expect as a standard of conduct from professors at UCSD. (Boos and catcalls.) But I do resent most bitterly the unfair and unreasonable charges he has made about the good faith of the senate and the faculty. They care very much about you. Your intellectual growth is the center of their existence. Sometimes you may feel passionately about one particular approach to politics or society, but that does not guarantee its intellectual substance. We are a university. All our courses are subject to careful review by committees of the faculty before they can be offered to you for degree credit. The professor knows that. He is trying to use you to advance his own political agenda. He owes you an apology for exploiting you, and he owes an apology to every member of our faculty for the lies and misrepresentations he has directed against them." (Restless stirring; cries of "Liar.")

The professor shouted, "No apologies."

The microphone was passed on to the square-jawed young assistant professor of philosophy, who stood poised and relaxed, looking more like an actor than a philosopher. But when he addressed the crowd, it was no actor speaking. The words were the classic rhetoric of a Marxist orator.

The chancellor, he said, was an agent of a criminal regime ruled over by boss-Reagan and his stooges, the Regents. UCSD students were now in the midst of seizing power from their corrupt rulers. It was only by bringing the ordinary activities of the campus to a halt that this illegitimate regime could be overthrown and power restored to the hands of the people. Students must be prepared to fight for control of the decisions central to their lives. (Loud applause.) Chancellor McGill was serving his masters faithfully by trying to talk students back into their former submissiveness. He would have to be confronted with resolute student power. (Applause.)

McGill knew very well, the philosopher continued, that if he were to recommend Social Analysis 139X to the UCSD faculty, they would approve it whether the Regents liked it or not. McGill also knew that if he were to order the campus closed for two days, he could make it stick. The truth was that McGill did not give a damn about what students wanted or about justice for Eldridge Cleaver. McGill preferred word games. He blamed the faculty for this and the Regents for that, pretending he was powerless. McGill had the power. Obviously he had the power to oppress students and everyone in the convocation could see that he was using it. (Loud applause, shouts of "Power to the people.")

Barry Shapiro then took back the microphone, clenched his left fist high above his head, and began to shout:

"McGill, the people here are demanding that you close this campus down. What is your answer?"

"I cannot close the campus. I have an obligation to keep it open. Everything seems simple to you and your philosopher friend over there. It is perfectly acceptable in your eyes for the chancellor to trample on the rights of thousands of UCSD students who want to be left alone to continue their work. You believe that you are morally justified and those who disagree with you have no rights. I have heard too much of that bankrupt philosophy here. Don't you know that Joan of Arc was burned at the stake by priests and bishops who understood in their hearts they were really saving her soul?

"I do not possess that kind of self-assurance. It is difficult to tell whether or not I am acting correctly, so I must play by the rules and try to protect the rights of anyone who might be injured by my decisions. If you wish to remain here tomorrow to consider the future of the university, I will see that you are able to do it without suffering any academic penalty. But I cannot permit you to impose your views on the rest of the campus. When I tell you that jurisdiction over courses at UCSD belongs to the faculty and that I cannot take that jurisdiction into my hands even in what you claim to be a good cause, I am speaking the truth."

From the crowd: "What about the Regents? Suppose the faculty votes to take Social Analysis 139X back from the Regents and give the course at UCSD in spite of them, would you do it?"

"I do not know what I would do. If the senate voted to do that, I would have to take their view very seriously. I suppose I would resign."

"Racist!"

"It may give you pleasure to shout epithets at me. It alters nothing and it certainly does not improve this discussion. I have great admiration for the UCSD faculty. Until last summer I was one of them. I am proud to be a member of the academic senate. But I must do what I believe to be right. That is why I cannot give in to your demands that I close down the campus. It would be unfair to other students. If the faculty were to ask me to take an action in opposition to the Regents, and I believed it to be wrong, I would not criticize the faculty, I would resign."

From the crowd: "McGill, you are a gutless wonder! You can't give us the courses we want. You won't cancel classes for our convocation because it might inconvenience a few bookworms. You can't offend the faculty. Can't you do anything but stand up there and whine about the things you cannot do?" (Applause.)

"Listen, goddam it. You don't scare me speaking like that. You and I are complete strangers. We have never seen one another before in our lives, and yet you address me in that contemptuous way. Where do you get the nerve?" (Loud boos and guffaws.) (Careful McGill, you are losing your cool. Do not let them see an inch of your skin.)

The man in the tweed jacket and striped tie spoke next. The chancellor, he said, deserved credit for his willingness to discuss these difficult questions with students, but not for the quality of his answers. The sad fate of Social Analysis 139X illustrated the corrupt nature of UCSD's curriculum. Most of the prescribed science courses were in fact rooted in the Cold War. They were aimed at producing a scientific and technological elite that would guide the country away from humanity and toward war. UCSD was like a factory producing weapons for the Cold War. The devastation of a peasant population in Vietnam was the predictable result of such scientific elitism. Is that what the chancellor wanted as the educational goal of Revelle College? Why didn't he help students when they tried to learn more about racism, imperialism, and repression? Was there something inherently wrong with such inquiry?

The questions were subtle and dangerous.[24] My reply was hesitant and fumbling. Science was not taught in Revelle College as an instrument of politics but as part of man's effort to use logic to reach a more fundamental understanding of nature than he could acquire with his senses. From the crowd came the demand, "Answer the goddam question!" Instead I turned on the well-groomed speaker.

"Sir, I do not know you. Are you a member of this campus community?" I guessed that he was an outsider. Somehow his clothing did not fit the UCSD activist profile. Apparently I was on target because he shook his head and refused to answer. I repeated the question several times, each time more forcefully, and then I spotted Murphy in the crowd. He was wincing. Apparently I was making some kind of tactical error. I felt embarrassed and gave up.

The black student then took the microphone. His remarks were delivered in a quiet voice to a completely silent, almost rapt, audience. He said that blacks had been white men's slaves for four hundred years. His people would be slaves no longer. The University of California was a white racist institution. Black students were demanding a curriculum relevant to their own history and their black experience. Cleaver's course was the beginning of that effort, and now look at what had happened to it.

The chancellor was to blame for the pitifully small numbers of black students and black faculty at UCSD. "Look around you, Chancellor, at all the missing black and Chicano faces." If changes were not made and very soon, black people would take their revenge on the university. They would leave it in ashes, and it would be what we deserved.

The performance was not especially polished but the simple authenticity[25] of this student's remarks after all the ideological posturing of the last hour caught everyone by surprise. I listened with a sinking feeling and replied that we had no excuses. We had simply failed. Courses in black history and culture were beyond the competence of most of us. They required design by experts and there were only a few at UCSD. A way would have to be found to do it and to enroll more black and Chicano students at UCSD. It was a moral obligation for all of us.

From the crowd: "Cut the bullshit, McGill. You're not fooling anyone."

This was not to be the last time I would feel a strange mixture of physical threat and moral anguish from black students. Angela Davis was standing there in the crowd in Revelle Plaza, coolly surveying us. A few months later she would lead UCSD's minority students in their bitter demands for "Lumumba-Zapata College." It was to be a UCSD undergraduate college in which blacks, Chicanos, and "others" would learn the manifold ways in which they had been oppressed and exploited by the majority white society.

Angela Davis made her debut as a radical organizer with the Lumumba-Zapata demands at UCSD in the spring of 1969. As it turned out, the minority students and I eventually took a proposal to the Regents and the Ford Foundation for a more traditional college, Third College, constructed to meet their needs, but without Miss Davis's remarkable revolutionary curriculum. Third College was one of the pioneering minority-oriented academic programs of the Sixties. When Angela Davis saw that the revolutionary fervor of Lumumba-Zapata was beginning to fade, she turned her attention to other things, but that is another story. I have often wondered how much of UCSD's Third College was laid down in embryonic form on that November afternoon in Revelle Plaza.

When the black student finished speaking, the hostility of the crowd rose dangerously and my fears returned.

I sought to keep my voice steady and my remarks unprovocative. The nervous anxiety I experienced when I first faced the crowd was now transformed into a foreboding of failure. I kept probing for some indication of support from this hostile audience. I simply had to find a way to reach them, but it was not happening.

The sight of a single individual struggling to reason with them failed to evoke the students' sympathy. They saw me as so powerful and their own position as so powerless that they could not perceive any lack of fairness in their effort to pressure me. I wondered whether the venting of so much hostility would gradually diminish the emotional high that had made them so explosive earlier. It did not seem to matter. The argument went on desperately for nearly two hours. The responses of the crowd were shot through with ugliness and obscenity, and kept circling back always to the same basic questions: would I close the campus down as a gesture to their desire to restructure UCSD? Would I revive Cleaver's course?

Slowly the long November shadows were disappearing and the evening fog moved in wisps overhead. There was now a damp chill in the air as twilight deepened. I felt myself shivering uncontrollably, listening with evident weariness to each new flood of angry charges, trying to answer them calmly amid boos and catcalls, trying not to raise my voice or lose my temper.

Then, without any perceptible change in the negative tide of the argument, the injustice of the situation finally struck someone. A bearded young fellow with long, dark, stringy hair, gold-rimmed glasses, and a serious expression, said:

"I am feeling uncomfortable about what has happened to our convocation. We came out here this morning because we did not think they were treating Cleaver like a human being. Now, I am afraid we are not treating the chancellor like a human being."

He was a sophomore or a junior, barely twenty years old, standing halfway back in the crowd. As he spoke, the earnestness of the voice caused heads to turn, and when he finished the turned heads looked downward in a long, embarrassed silence. There was a weak smattering of applause. Somewhere near the front of the crowd a girl with blonde hair tied in twin ponytails stood up and said:

"A lot of us admire the way you have talked to us, Chancellor. We want to apologize for some of the things that people here said to you."

I grinned and blew her a kiss.

Barry Shapiro saw his convocation collapsing and his hold on the crowd beginning to slip away. He announced that he would adjourn the meeting for the day if I would agree to meet them again the next morning. We settled on II AM.

The crowd began to break up as I stood there for a few moments speaking to a little cluster of friendly students in the rapidly gathering darkness. Lights were just coming on at the borders of the plaza. A number of faculty who had watched the last stages of the debate from the fringes of the crowd came forward to congratulate me. I thought, *Now they show up!* Paul Saltman clapped me on the back.

"Billy, you done good!"

Then I saw my dean, George Murphy, standing off to one side, waiting patiently for me to finish. We walked together in the darkness across the arched footbridge back toward the lights of the chancellor's area. When we were out of earshot, he looked at me with a big, shy grin and exclaimed:

"Bill, you were wonderful! You faced down the whole crowd and made them apologize to you. When I saw the hard look in your eyes, I knew they didn't have a chance."

I was still shaking from the chill and perhaps also from emotional exhaustion, but I stopped and stared at him in utter disbelief.

"Good God! George, I have never been so scared in my life."

"Boss, believe me, it didn't show."

Murphy steered me to his office. He sat me down in a soft leather chair, and gave me a steaming cup of coffee, while secretaries and staff crowded into the doorway beaming at us. The word had been spreading all over campus from the offices bordering Revelle Plaza. As the chill and the stiffness ebbed out of my bones, Murphy got up, waved the people away, and closed the door. With every detail fresh in our minds, we exchanged minute impressions of the day's events and the cast of characters. Murphy gave me his estimate of the tactical situation.

It was very favorable. Murphy was certain the strike had collapsed. Classes would now continue normally, and almost no one would be out there with Barry Shapiro tomorrow. He was correct. Next morning there were fewer than a dozen militants in Revelle Plaza when I arrived at II AM, this time surrounded by a friendly crowd of more than a hundred supporters. Following Murphy's advice, I refused to debate with Shapiro because he was operating an illegal sound system in the plaza. My side cheered. I walked out, and that ended it.

During the debriefing in his office Murphy told me about Brad Cleaveland. He explained that I had been pushing the "outsider" business too aggressively, which was why he signalled me to stop. George did not want me to goad Cleaveland into becoming my principal antagonist. I was doing too well against Barry Shapiro. Murphy also told me about Angela Davis. He explained that she was Marcuse's graduate student and had recently become politically active among the black students. Miss Davis is a stunning woman, and I remembered exactly where she had stood in the crowd.

"I'm certain she will be making her move soon, boss. She is very capable."

I sat there in Murphy's office basking in a rising glow of satisfaction.

We managed to get through the day successfully. When I had asked myself earlier how in the world we would ever get out of it, I was thinking passively and I was scared. Now I knew the answer. We had done it by taking events into our own hands.

It was my initial discovery of an important principle. No large problem is ever solved by waiting for it to solve itself. You must go out and take hold of events, shaping them to your own purposes. This was a long distance from the civilized and graceful diplomacy I had envisioned as the chancellor's role. Later on in the evening, after I had a chance to think about it, my satisfaction turned to shudders over the risks associated with this dangerous profession. The next day I chastised Murphy for leaving himself no alternative but to be rescued by a nervous chancellor. He looked at me and grinned maliciously. Would I have preferred to call the police? Besides, he felt I was up to it. Over the years he had learned how to measure his chancellors. He was pretty certain the maneuver would succeed.

I wish to God he had told me beforehand!

Reflecting on this extraordinary episode a dozen years later, I am struck by the idea that the events I am describing, however vivid they are in my memory, must have taken place in another world. Could all this have really happened on this benign, almost languid UCSD campus, now, in 1982, peopled by legions of serious, professionally minded students? It did happen, of course. Somehow we managed to squeak through it, surviving our first major encounter with the explosive tensions of the 1960s. But the total contrast between the wild excitement of that November day in 1968 and today's sunny calm is hard to comprehend. It gives those earlier events a dreamlike quality that grows more unreal with the passage of time.

Anita, my assistant, is dead. A few years afterward she had a heart attack on a golf course in San Diego. Paul Saltman rose to become vice chancellor for academic affairs at UCSD before returning to the faculty in 1980. George Murphy has left the academic life altogether. He is director of employee relations in a high-technology industrial firm in San Diego, and doing quite well.

Recently I managed to trace Brad Cleaveland and Barry Shapiro.[26] Both have settled into middle-class, 40-year-old respectability. The handsome, square-jawed assistant professor of philosophy left the university in 1970 to become a practitioner in one of the therapy cults that abound in Southern California.

Angela Davis returned to UCSD in the winter of 1980 to give a traditional invited lecture in a large auditorium filled with polite listeners, many of them middle-aged. She was running at that time as the Communist Party's vice presidential candidate in the national elections.[27] And everyone knows about Ronald Reagan's career during the intervening decade. Somehow nearly all the major figures of this episode managed to survive and to do well for themselves.

Not long after the Regents' decision on Social Analysis 139X, Eldridge Cleaver fled the country to avoid trial on the charges pending against him. He lived for several years as an unhappy expatriate in Cuba and North Africa, and then tried to find asylum in Europe. Eventually Cleaver returned to the United States in 1975 as a well-publicized, born-again Christian. He supported Governor Reagan in the 1980 presidential campaign and was later reported as trying to join the Mormon Church.

I watched Cleaver on TV explaining his new fundamentalist religious fervor. As I studied his performance, I could not get the memory of his lecture on the night of October 4, 1968, and that Reagan chant, out of my mind. Was his Christian rebirth a put-on? Or was that earlier performance in the UCSD gymnasium a put-on? Which one is the real Cleaver, or is it possible that neither are? The transformation in character is too complete, too suggestive of an unremitting hunger for media attention.

One thing you have to concede about Cleaver, though. He is a survivor. If the events I have recounted teach us anything, it is the importance of being a survivor.

And so it was that when I returned to UCSD in February 1980, reflecting on all that had happened to me in the years since 1968, I revisited Revelle Plaza to search for a particular spot that my memory kept returning to in the intervening years.

It had been raining, but the rain let up briefly and the sun shone intermittently from behind dark clouds. I was looking for a precise spot on the drying pavement, a dark carbonized smudge forming a rough circle about three feet in diameter, but it was gone, or at least I could not find it. No trace of anything remained.

The dark smudge had been there a decade earlier. Young women would come each day to lay fresh-cut flowers and light votive candles around it. It marked the place where on May 10, 1970, a senior in Revelle College doused himself with gasoline and set himself afire. He died shortly afterwards.

It happened without warning on a quiet Sunday afternoon. Revelle Plaza, for the first time in many weeks, was completely peaceful. A few students were sunning themselves and talking in low voices on the benches. The young man came out on the plaza carrying a cardboard sign that read, "In the name of God, end the war."

His father said afterwards that the boy had recently received a draft notice and was brooding about it. "He was not a radical student," his mother added. "He was not affiliated with any political groups. He was never in any demonstrations. He was just too sensitive."

A decade later we do homage to the protestors of the Sixties for ending the war, yet no one seems to care about that young man's real-life struggle in Revelle Plaza, or about any of the others lost along the way. It is as though the full reality of those terrifying moments has become too unbearable even to remember, and now it is easier to concentrate on the attractions of a great cause instead of facing the damage suffered by a generation of students.

I feel a special kinship with that boy. Like me, he faced an overwhelming personal crisis in Revelle Plaza. I survived. He did not. But I had everything going for me, whereas he was naked and alone.

In the few moments I spent there ten years later, I knelt briefly where the flowers once lay, and said a prayer for him.

CHAPTER 3

An
Age
of
Antiheroes

Critics with special talent for charting the hidden dimensions of historical trends that the rest of us perceive only dimly say that we live in an age without heroes. Robert Nisbet's *Twilight of Authority*[1] portrays us as a culture lacking both real heroes and real villains because we have lost a central core of deeply held traditional beliefs. In a wonderfully insightful passage, Nisbet observes that only in relation to sacred things can genuine heroism or villainy emerge.

Of course, rock stars, TV celebrities, and professional football greats still evoke worshipful reactions from millions of fans, but Nisbet's criticism is aimed at an unusually cruel and secular era in American public life. We no longer view our elected leaders as heroic figures. Quite the contrary, a significant fraction of the public appears to want to believe the worst about its leaders, and expects almost routinely to see them exposed as corrupt or downright crooked.[2]

When villainy becomes the expected norm, genuine villains become a rare commodity. It is instructive to ask why so many seemed to enjoy Richard Nixon's downfall. Was it because of the juicy revelations about a corrupt President who in some incredible way managed to bug himself?

Or was it because Mr. Nixon proved to be a genuine villain who had defiled the presidency, one of the few sacred things remaining to us?

There is no doubt that many people felt unrestrained joy over the President's comeuppance. But the spectacle of even a wicked man caught in a trap of his own making, brought to bay by implacable prosecutors and unyielding courts, ought not to be a matter of enjoyment. Anyone suffering such a debacle is a tragic figure. The extraordinary dimensions of Richard Nixon's tragedy might have caused us to be more restrained.

Why do we accord our leaders such low esteem, expecting villainy and taking pleasure when they fall into catastrophe? Why do students turn so easily to antiheroes?[2a] Are we growing cynical over virtually all forms of traditional authority, or have we developed different ideas about what is sacred? The answers to these questions are not simple. It certainly appears that there is much more to the low value put on today's authority figures than just their corruptibility. The denigration of authority and the elevation of antiheroes may be two different pieces of the same puzzle.

This chapter is an effort to account for the remarkable forces that created a contemporary antihero in the person of a UCSD professor, Herbert Marcuse. He was neither a vibrant youthful personality, nor a commanding presence. Marcuse was an elderly political philosopher whose writings were abstract and difficult. His most productive years, from 1930 to 1960, had brought him little but frustration. Yet suddenly, at the end of his career, Marcuse was elevated to heroic stature among the student radicals of the Sixties. They saw him as a spokesman for their alienation and their yearning to be liberated from what they considered the repressive power of an authoritarian state.

It is virtually impossible to review the last stages of Herbert Marcuse's career without also discussing student unrest and the phenomenon of antiheroes. The explanations set forth here and in later chapters are unavoidably controversial. It will become evident that I have little sympathy with New Left revolutionaries. Most of the leaders with whom I dealt struck me as less interested in racial justice or helping the poor than in seizing power. Such bias tends to color my judgment and should be acknowledged at the outset. On the other hand, during those struggles I also acquired a wealth of real experience. I worked in the midst of demonstrations and student pressure tactics continuously for nearly a dozen years after 1968. The views presented here are forged out of that experience, and at this juncture I am no longer much concerned with converting others to my point of view. I simply want to explain what I lived through.

If we are to understand the unrest of the 1960s and Herbert Marcuse's role in it, we should avoid simplistic formulas such as the "generation gap" that dominated the popular media a decade ago.3 We should also try to stay away from apologia depicting the riotous events of the Sixties as a form of moral crusade.4 This sympathetic interpretation is offered principally by revisionist social historians. Neither formulation comes close to anything I saw.

Critical readers will note my repeated expressions of irritation over the gullibility of politically uncommitted students regarding the moral arguments of New Left revolutionaries. Skepticism is an essential tool of logical analysis. It forces high standards of proof for emotionally attractive arguments. Untested beliefs ultimately dominate one's capacity to reason. Proof then becomes superfluous and arguments are self-justifying. This diminished level of logical analysis seems to have been one of the most serious problems of that era. I first became aware of it in the 1960s when I saw that students were rarely interested in testing the New Left's rhetoric.

Faith is central to the human spirit. It is our principal resource against cynicism and despair. But faith as that last disciplined step beyond reason, and the naive faith of the unpracticed mind, are two very different things. I never understood how students could be so sophisticated about radical arguments on the moral issues posed by poverty, racism, and the Vietnam war, and yet also so naive about the political designs of their radical leaders.

Universities certainly failed to understand the vital importance of these moral concerns at the time. We were so involved with our own work and our own ambitions that at first we did not hear what students were trying to tell us. University administrators began the 1960s by abandoning the moral high ground to the New Left. And so over and over again, students—and here I mean the mass of sympathetic followers rather than their radical leaders—were content to let themselves be used by the radicals in what most students felt was a just cause. The mass of followers simply did not want to examine their leadership too closely.

It is almost precisely the opposite of the attitude of the general public toward most of our elected political leadership. Apparently students turned to antiheroes because these people were rebels or outcasts whose estrangement from middle-class values touched something sacred in the student outlook. We must try to understand it if we are to be even modestly successful in unraveling the unrest that filled the 1960s.

As I watched student leaders in those days, it seemed to me that they were giving only lip service to the plight of the poor, the oppression of blacks, and the killing of illiterate peasants in Vietnam. There was nothing especially humane or compassionate in their attitudes toward victims of injustice. Seldom were there genuine tears. The primary interest of student radical leaders seemed to be in political power. They operated at two different levels. Talking to fellow students or to reporters, student leaders expressed moral indignation over the evils they deplored. But at the same time they were trying to build a radical movement, and they saw themselves as its leadership cadre.

The question is, which of these motives was predominant? I have no doubt that it was the desire for power.[5] This is a harsh evaluation, but it is born of years of struggle with successive generations of radical leaders. These young people were bright and they knew it. They were contemptuous of opposition. Everything but compassion had always come easily to them, and they were not in the least hesitant about imposing their views on fellow students, despite a veneer of participatory democracy. Perhaps compassion came to them when they acquired maturity, but what I saw was a hard, scornful, competitive edge.[6]

It would be wrong to depict either the entire New Left or even a substantial part of the student body as power hungry. Many people were attracted to the New Left. Their socialist outlook was conditioned by a genuine concern for goodness, as distinct from power. These people, and I include Marcuse among them, were crusaders for social justice, advocates of a more orderly, more equal society than the one that emerges naturally from corporate capitalism. I can sympathize with such radical thought even though I disagree with it as elitist and utopian.

It is difficult to read Mark Rudd's "Columbia: Notes on a Spring Rebellion"[7] without total skepticism for his motives. In the same way, it is difficult to read Peter Clecak's *Radical Paradoxes*[8] without utter admiration for his commitment to human decency. The distinction is a crucial one, and it constitutes a vital point of orientation for this discussion of student unrest and Herbert Marcuse's role as an antiestablishment hero.

Marcuse articulated a utopian faith in a nonrepressive social order. His faith had an undeniable eloquence and esthetic beauty. Some New Left students, while professing to be Marcuse's postulants, committed intolerable acts—seizing buildings or hostages—that had no visible relation to Marcuse's philosophy. It seemed to me that these actions were reflective of unconscious drives for power and were cloaked in philosophical justification so as to make them seem more morally acceptable.

Many students in the Sixties viewed themselves as victims and outcasts from society. Accordingly, we must be prepared for antiheroes when we attempt to probe their ideals. Consider the outpouring of sympathy and admiration evoked among thousands of University of California students by Eldridge Cleaver in 1968. In his book, *Soul on Ice,* Cleaver had written sensitively about the oppressed condition of the black man in America, but his public appearances were characterized more by gross obscenity and the rapture of defiance than by any beauty of thought.

Many young people who were swept up by Cleaver's defiant posturing in 1968 may well have become skeptical later as they witnessed his latter-day conversion to evangelical Christianity and political conservatism. But when Cleaver was Information Minister of the Black Panthers and a writer for *Ramparts* magazine in the mid-Sixties, students were eager to accept him as a heroic figure. They saw Cleaver as defying a deeply evil, racist power structure. They were willing to join him in what they took to be a crusade for racial justice, even though most of them knew little about Cleaver or his motives. The complexity of Cleaver's motivation has become all too painfully evident in recent years.

Now why should this be? Something fundamental happened in the Sixties, causing millions of university students to jettison moral and political values passed on to them by an earlier American tradition. Even more important, it caused them to abandon minimum standards of reticence or skepticism in evaluating radical alternatives.

Some people believe radical teachers were responsible for this extraordinary change, but that view seems to me to be dead wrong. Everything I saw showed that it was the students who were leading and the instructors who followed.

It is the lack of skepticism that I find so fascinating. Students of the 1960s were remarkably knowledgeable about the evils and contradictions of American society, and yet unbelievably trusting about the motives of revolutionaries preaching constructive change.

During the early 1960s, at the zenith of an age of rationalism in Western society, when cultivated intellectuals were proclaiming the end of ideology, students in large numbers found themselves emotionally moved by the speechmaking of charismatic radicals on issues involving racism and war. Most students did not stop to analyze what caused them to abandon rationalism. Suddenly they were aroused. In the undergraduate mind, reasoned hesitation became supplanted by an overpowering feeling of moral outrage and an urgent demand for direct action.

It is difficult not to be sympathetic with their ideals and their impatience toward evil, but the abandonment of skeptical analysis of barely masked revolutionary appeals issued by people with obvious power motives was amazingly immature in bright students of college age. It was an open invitation to exploitation explainable only by the unprecedented emotional stresses afflicting students at that time.9

I remember David Dellinger telling a student audience in 1971 that racism and genocide are built into the American character by our system of government.10 After all, hadn't George Washington been a slave owner? Nothing short of a socialist revolution could purge us of guilt and make us truly free. No one asked him to produce the evidence for this extraordinary claim. Instead, the audience rose to its feet and cheered. Whatever those students were experiencing, it was not critical judgment. They were pushovers.

The stresses of the 1960s in America are not difficult to identify. We need hardly remind ourselves that it was an era of traumatic events and passionate emotional reactions. Even in the best of times teenagers have difficulty coming to terms with the compromises and imperfections of adult society. In this instance we forced them also to adjust to a decade of seething violence and misguided leadership undermining many of the ideals we had urged upon them as part of their patriotic heritage.

The burning cities, the ugly and sometimes lethal struggle to overcome racial segregation, coupled with unmet demands for black political power, left a legacy of bitterness that stirred deep feelings of injustice among undergraduates. So, too, did the murders of the Kennedys and Martin Luther King, as well as the violence accompanying the marches on the Pentagon and the street battles during the Chicago Democratic convention in 1968. What kind of people would we be if we had not recoiled in horror from events such as these? Perhaps a great deal of turmoil might have been avoided if we ourselves had managed to speak out more forcefully against them at the time.

Most people past the age of forty had come easily to accept the patriotic beliefs engendered by our struggle against the Nazis and the Japanese, but for students in their adolescent years, the Sixties were, as they put it, where it was. Time and again in those days demonstrators would shout *"Sieg heil"* at me, saying in simple language who they felt I was.

Granted, no university chancellor can ever expect to achieve heroic status in the eyes of his students; yet it still seems ridiculous to call him a fascist dictator, even when people are driven by primitive instincts causing them to mistrust all authority. Some groups of students went so far in showing their contempt as to spell "America" in the Nazi style: *Amerika.* Undoubtedly, that metaphor was copiously laden with oedipal content, but it has always seemed to me that these remarkable rhetorical excesses must have been fashioned out of more than youthful rebelliousness.

Few of us who lived through that period of student unrest have experienced anything like it before or since. It was as though some medieval communal hysteria had gripped nearly an entire generation of students, causing them to strike at the traditions that had nurtured them and to venerate a succession of extraordinary antiheroes.

The powerful internal strains of the Sixties were heaped on the ugliness of the war in Vietnam. We seemed intent on pulverizing a peasant population to contain the spread of communism in Asia. Such things were bound to produce a corrosive cynicism among young people. It would have been more shocking, I suppose, had such a cruel awakening from the innocence in which we used to live failed to make a decisive imprint on the outlook of students. They began reacting to the gap between what they had been taught of our national ideals, and what they actually saw. Many of them turned to the brands of humanism espoused by writers and orators of the New Left whose activity was focused on campus.[11] Not all students were converted to the New Left, to be sure; but a significant fraction started listening sympathetically and found themselves strangely stirred by the moral preaching in the campus free-speech area.

Moreover, this new and rapidly growing radical movement provided a political focus around which much of the intellectual life on campus revolved during the mid-Sixties.[12] The New Left defined issues addressed by a wide spectrum of political groups, ranging from active sympathizers on campus through a large center group of normally indifferent students to a small core of hostile conservatives. The political activism of the New Left amplified its effectiveness considerably. A majority of nonactivist students were influenced by New Left oratory and became sympathetic to New Left causes. It would take only one administrative error in the form of inept use of force in breaking up a sit-in or a demonstration, and this group of quiet sympathizers would be transformed into militant activists. With the New Left leadership cultivating these stresses and searching for opportunities, I could almost feel the temperature of the campus rising in the mid-Sixties.

Some critics have argued that the origins of campus protests in the Sixties were far less complicated than the causal structure advanced here. Universities were (and are) formidable bureaucracies. Campus life in the early 1960s must have been endlessly frustrating for students. They were unable to influence their curriculum and were completely frozen out of university governance. As these critics see the situation, a generation of activist students, many of them veterans of the civil rights movement, simply became fed up. They rebelled against an authoritarian rule responsible for so much legitimate frustration.

Innumerable problems of that kind did exist, but in twelve years of day-to-day involvement with students and their frustrations, I do not think I ever saw a mass protest break out directly because of dissatisfaction with campus life.[13] Wherever protests occurred, foci of discontent could always be discovered after the fact, and people would then pounce on these discoveries as the real causes of protest despite the announced grievances, which seemed mainly to be political.

One of the major difficulties with this kind of analysis is that it confuses individual reactions to frustration with the phenomena of group protest. The temper of a crowd is not composed of a multitude of identical individual reactions that move unerringly into spontaneous protest. People tend to be diffusely excited or confused, and a persuasive leadership effort is ordinarily required to capture their attention and to stir them. This process of arousal is typically political, in the sense that protest leaders are motivated by objectives that are consciously political. If legitimate grievances exist that raise the level of emotionalism of a crowd, so much the better. It makes arousal easier and more profound. Hence, while individual frustrations raise the temperature of a crowd, they are seldom enough, in and of themselves, to cause a protest. Some concentrating agent is required, and this generally takes the form of politically toned grievances cited by protest leaders as causes for action. Members of a crowd often have incomplete knowledge of the announced grievances, but are extremely sensitive to leadership and to the emotionalism of those immediately around them. They can be led to act on grievances that they will confess later were discovered for the first time in the crowd situation.

The important point to understand is that group protests are rarely spontaneous. They are more often the result of a highly creative and opportunistic process of leadership applied to an excitable and sympathetic crowd.[14]

Those who took students to be legitimately angry over campus conditions were quite right. But they were wrong if they supposed that this anger led spontaneously to campus protests. Viewing unrest in that way is attractively simple, but it fails to conform to the dynamics of any of the hundreds of protests I saw.

Student radical leaders of the 1960s developed a unique and, for me, almost insufferable moral arrogance when they discovered that their ethical criticisms had genuinely shaken the faculty and were having an impact on liberal writers and critics. Demonstrators began to taunt us with denunciations of "business as usual" while people were dying in Vietnam. "What are *you* doing to stop the war?" became a strident cry I can still sometimes hear in my dreams. Demonstration leaders knew that such rhetoric would direct crowd anger at the campus administration. They seldom paused to examine their own motives or to ask whether what they were doing was just. They simply poured it on, and I came to the cynical conclusion that they were actively seeking to radicalize the campus.

As time passed the moral criticisms tended to become more and more uncontrolled and to range away from the basic issues of poverty and racism with which the protests began, into a host of other student grievances. People in authority reacted defensively, as might be expected. Student anger mounted steadily and began to feed upon itself. There was no way in which such intense emotions could be sustained over an extended period of time. They were bound either to blow up or collapse into exhaustion. And so the dynamic processes that had created both the New Left and the Students for a Democratic Society moved with breathtaking speed. In a bit more than a decade, a radical movement was founded, grew into a national phenomenon, reached its peak, and faded away.

Not much remains of the student Left as we enter the Eighties. Its principal residues seem to be a set of important but hardly radical political reforms, and a markedly diminished quality of thought, both spawned in the Sixties. Even today, undergraduates carry around a heavy burden of poorly analyzed, almost paranoid ideas about society and politics. Ask them whether the FBI and the CIA continue to spy on students and a majority will unhesitatingly say yes. Ask whether American oil companies conspired with the South African government to leak oil into Rhodesia, and the faces around you will light up in knowing smiles. No more evidence is needed. This paranoid quality makes today's students somewhat harder to reason with or to argue with than their preradical predecessors two generations ago. Perhaps those earlier students were more naive, or perhaps the sharpness of thought on campus has begun to decline as skepticism toward moralistic arguments has declined. It is difficult to decide, but I lean toward the latter view.

It seems incorrect to suggest that the young people who came of age in the Sixties did not have their heroes. It would be more correct to say that they did not see us as particularly admirable and that for the last 20 years students have gravitated toward some very unconventional heroes. Today's figures are seldom cast from the mold of the establishment types we once admired. Earlier heroic styles in the grand manner of Charles A.

Lindbergh, General Douglas MacArthur, and perhaps even Franklin D. Roosevelt, have little appeal for modern students. Students of the Sixties were enthralled by Ché Guevara, Bernadette Devlin, and Angela Davis, or that most unlikely figure of all, Herbert Marcuse.

Marcuse was a German-born philosopher who had come to the end of his academic career in 1960 amid a succession of frustrating failures and rejections.[15] Then, suddenly, he found himself vaulted into international prominence when he was discovered by European revolutionary students and was also acclaimed as the philosopher of the New Left in the United States. His rise came principally with the publication of his book *One Dimensional Man* in 1964. It was all rather dizzying and, for Marcuse, apparently quite unexpected.

Marcuse became a living saint of the Left, an object of veneration by counterculture students who streamed in from all over the country to sit at his feet. He was embarrassed by such adulation. Blind admiration from people who understood little of his philosophical position did not appeal to Marcuse. In his professional core Marcuse was a hard-headed European Marxist whose mind had been disciplined to penetrate the thickets of successive negations that characterize dialectical thought. He was impatient with adolescent rebels who experienced revolutionary feelings but regarded such impulses as beyond analysis.

Like many American academics of the post–World War II era, Marcuse was driven out of prewar Germany by the Nazis. As a Marxist and a Jew, his departure from Nazi Germany was inevitable. The alternative would have been a concentration camp. But Marcuse was fortunate, because in 1934, Nicolas Murray Butler, president of Columbia University, invited the members of the Frankfurt Institute for Social Research, Marcuse among them, to come to Columbia.[16] In view of their unwelcome status in their own country, the offer was gratefully accepted.

Despite his excellent academic reputation, Marcuse was not offered a faculty position at Columbia in 1934. The omission was probably due to Columbia's financial problems during the Depression rather than to Marcuse's unorthodox political views. Almost no new appointments were made at Columbia during the decade 1930–1940. But it is difficult to imagine N. M. Butler, that rockbound, conservative Republican, as an admirer of Marcuse's remarkable brand of Freudian Marxism.[17]

In any case, Marcuse spent the next six years as a researcher on Morningside Heights. With the outbreak of war in Europe, he became a naturalized citizen in 1940 and was called to Washington by the Office of Strategic Services, forerunner of the CIA. At the end of the war, he moved over to the State Department as acting head of the Eastern European Section.

After the surrender of Germany and Japan, Marcuse continued in the State Department until 1950. He then taught for brief periods at several universities, Harvard and Columbia among them, but was unable to devise a satisfactory permanent arrangement. Undoubtedly his Marxist views played a role in that problem. It was the nadir of the McCarthy era.

In 1954 Marcuse was at last invited to join the faculty of Brandeis University near Boston, Massachusetts. He served there with distinction until his retirement in 1965 at the age of 67. His books—*Reason and Revolution*, written before the war while he was at Columbia, and *Eros and Civilization*, which appeared in 1955—established a secure academic reputation, but he remained largely unknown to the general public.

Just as Marcuse was preparing to retire from Brandeis in 1964, the newly established San Diego campus of the University of California began searching for outstanding faculty in the humanities and social sciences in an effort to match a remarkably talented group of pure scientists whom Roger Revelle had recruited to La Jolla a few years earlier. Marcuse was offered a postretirement appointment as professor of philosophy at UCSD. This meant that he could expect to be appointed from year to year outside the tenure system for as long as his health and intellectual vigor permitted.[18] It was at just this time that *One Dimensional Man* began to be read widely, and Marcuse found himself a media celebrity, the hero and philosopher of the New Left.[19]

Ironically, during his American period, Marcuse's writings were regularly attacked in the Soviet Union because he no longer believed that the economic exploitation of the proletariat was the driving force behind the revolutionary class struggle. Marcuse observed that Western democracies seemed to have created conditions in the work place and levels of subsistence for workers that would effectively prevent the development of a revolutionary working class. To orthodox Soviet minds this assertion from an ostensible Marxist-Leninist was heresy. Moreover, Marcuse had turned to Freud and to the psychoanalytic concept of repression for a better explanation of the origins of modern man's revolutionary impulses, and this was deemed an even more unpardonable heresy.

In the mid-Sixties Marcuse also found himself under attack in the United States by conservative writers, critics, and politicians on the ground that he was a revolutionary Marxist seducing students into radical activity. Before he found his ultimate niche in history as the hero of the student rebels of the Sixties, Marcuse seemed to have been rejected by everyone, his ideas scorned by critics from both East and West, and his eventual stature as a social philosopher questioned because he had no serious following. He was an unlikely and somewhat unusual heroic figure.

Just what were the ideas that led to Marcuse's rejection by establishments on both sides of the Iron Curtain, and to his adoption by a rising generation of student radicals in the New Left during the mid-Sixties?

Marcuse was a utopian theorist who sought to define an ideal state of liberated existence free of externally enforced and unnecessary political, social, and sexual repression. He saw in such surplus repression one of the driving forces of revolution. In *Eros and Civilization* Marcuse wrote, "In a truly free civilization all laws are self-given by the individuals. . . . Order is freedom only if it is founded on and sustained by the free gratification of the individuals."[20] Is it any wonder that students disenchanted with authority and discipline were drawn to him? Freud had argued that repression was essential to the growth of civilization.

In *One Dimensional Man* Marcuse tells us, "Liberty can be made into a powerful instrument of domination. The range of choice open to the individual is not the decisive factor in determining the degree of human freedom, but *what* can be chosen and what *is* chosen by the individual. . . . Free election of masters does not abolish the masters or the slaves."[21] This remarkable precept became part of the dogma of the New Left.

For those whose search for personal liberation during the 1960s was becoming desperate in an environment perceived as increasingly authoritarian, American life promised only a drab and stultifying satisfaction of human needs, rather like that of George Orwell's *1984*.[22] Moreover, the successes of the American economy were so effective in frustrating nearly all proponents of revolutionary change that the political arm experienced no particular need to repress dissent. Marcuse later called it "repressive tolerance."[23] He observed that industrial society would tolerate radical utopian movements only to the extent that they were guaranteed to be ineffectual. The liberty that most Americans took as a source of pride was in Marcuse's eyes one-dimensional and repressive. He rejected it. Like many visionaries feeling themselves possessed of deeply held but untestable truth, Marcuse was not disposed to be tolerant of "error" and "false consciousness" in his utopia.

Who were these alienated people struggling for self-fulfillment outside the operation of what they viewed as a pernicious, militaristic, and repressive political system, a system that bought off the working masses with creature comforts and meaningless pop culture? They were the people without any direct stake in the benefits of the system: students, academics, the poor, and the disenfranchised minorities. Marcuse had said it. The New Left came to view him not only as its major philosopher, but as a hero as well for having had the courage of such convictions when liberals were concluding that ideology was out of date. Marcuse was, of course, not the New Left's only philosopher. C. Wright Mills in the U.S., Sartre in France, Fanon in North Africa, and Mao in China had all left their imprint. But with Marcuse the magic was unique.

As a theoretical description of previously unrecognized revolutionary tensions in Western society, Marcuse's neo-Marxist analysis was sharp and elegant, but it was also unconventional, especially so for those whose lives had been devoted to reverence for the classical American dream. Accordingly, it was not long before the citizens of Marcuse's new home in Southern California began to revile him as something close to the devil incarnate.

At about the same time, Marcuse was beginning to develop an ardent following in the New Left. A success of that kind is what every social philosopher dreams about, and something that he himself had missed during his earlier productive years. But it meant that a variety of strange-looking and strange-sounding people now began to gather under the shadow of the cross on Mt. Soledad in La Jolla, amidst the affluent Californians and the retired admirals. The mixture proved to be volatile.

Up to this point I have been speaking of the New Left as though it were a monolithic and unified radical movement during the 1960s, but actually it was very diverse. The origins of the movement in the United States can probably be traced most readily to the organizing convention of the Students for a Democratic Society at Port Huron, Michigan, in 1962. That first meeting produced a haunting document, the *Port Huron Statement*,[24] which called for a concentration on the plight of the poor and for a democracy of individual participation to break out of the "crust of apathy and . . . inner-alienation that remain the defining characteristics of American college life." This stress on removing alienation via individual participation in the decisions central to one's life became not only a guiding principle of the New Left, but also a point of contention later on when the New Left's free-wheeling individualism clashed with the realities of political organization.

The development of the movement was greatly accelerated by the moral imponderables of the Vietnam war and the popular appeal of civil rights causes among U.S. college students. In the mid-Sixties there was a rapid growth of SDS chapters (as they were called) on college campuses all across the country.[25] The student Left quickly evolved into a measurable political force. But as early as 1968 a series of ideological conflicts began splitting SDS apart. What had been only a few years earlier an idealistic student organization with vague leftist ties, became an arena of bitter struggle among several doctrinaire Marxist factions: Maoist, Castroite, worker-oriented, terrorist. All were contending for control of SDS and ultimately for leadership of the first indigenous radical youth movement in the modern history of the U.S.[26]

The antiwar activity of the 1960s was not strictly part of the New Left, nor was it essentially radical, although it had a radical fringe. It is nevertheless true that in the years prior to 1965 much of the early campus-based agitation against the U.S. commitment in Vietnam originated with SDS and its myriad offshoot committees. The latter were developed for tactical purposes to exploit issues as they arose on different campuses. A largely successful campaign was undertaken by SDS in the early 1960s to arouse students against ROTC and military recruiting on campus. The effort was later extended to include harassment of representatives of the Dow Chemical Company, a manufacturer of napalm. These agencies were identified by SDS, and subsequently by most students, as hostile intruders representing military interests on campus. Their appearance was guaranteed to provoke organized confrontation.

As the level of violence in Vietnam rose with the Tet Offensive early in 1968 and the subsequent bitter fighting that formed the backdrop of the 1968 presidential campaign, moderately liberal students and faculty nearly everywhere in the country began to show increasing signs of agitation. Thousands participated in teach-ins and marches addressed to the moral issues at stake in Vietnam. These protests came to be viewed by nonradical students and faculty almost as an ethical obligation. They argued that Vietnam was a fruitless war with genocidal possibilities and that we had to get out.

In fact, such ideas had been advanced originally by SDS, but by 1968 Marxist revolutionaries were so evidently in control of SDS, and old-fashioned liberalism was being treated with such obvious disdain by the rank and file of SDS, that a fierce struggle for control of the antiwar movement ensued.

Most moderate students found themselves attracted to the peace-oriented idealism of Senators Eugene McCarthy and Robert Kennedy during the 1968 presidential campaign. But SDS was busy organizing its own antiwar activities. In the University of California and on many other campuses, rallies were arranged virtually on a daily basis by SDS as it attempted to capture leadership of the antiwar movement. These rallies, and spectacular mass demonstrations in Washington, showed the sharp differences in outlook between campus liberals and SDS radicals. Liberals were attempting to influence U.S. war policy by dramatizing the moral ambiguities of Vietnam, whereas the SDS deliberately tried to provoke police assaults that would convert antiwar protests into a powerful tool for radicalization and hence for revolutionary change.

Protests and tensions associated with the war became a condition of daily life on campus in the years between 1968 and 1972. These tensions reached a peak in the spring of 1970 following the so-called Cambodian incursion by U.S. forces. All across the country there was an immediate outburst of protests with an emotional intensity bordering on hysteria. It culminated in the killing of four students by the National Guard at Kent State on May 4, 1970.

Nearly all of us were eventually drawn into the antiwar protests. By the spring of 1970 the atmosphere of emotional anguish was so overwhelming that we simply had to reach out to the thousands of our distraught students, to lead them safely through a period of grave anxiety and danger. Others, notably SDS, were also reaching out, urging their fellow students to rise up and do battle against a demonstrably evil society. Their intent seemed perfectly apparent: it was to provoke counterviolence that would deliver all those antiwar students into the hands of the radical leaders, creating the ferment that was central to their strategy of revolution.

At every major antiwar rally and every march on the Pentagon between 1968 and 1972 there was sure to be a fringe of "crazies" who attempted to turn an ostensibly peaceful event into a violent confrontation with the police. Those of us in positions of responsibility on campus spent nearly all our time trying to calm our students. At the same time we used our hard-won knowledge of New Left tactics to isolate the revolutionaries and render them harmless. At times like these I found myself despairing over the naiveté of moderate students who would tell me that they followed radical leadership because they agreed with the objectives, but not the methods, of the radicals.

It was a fierce but subtle contest, which was, and I think still is, largely misunderstood not only by the general public but by scholarly analysts as well. Occasionally things got out of hand despite our best efforts. Politically innocent young people were moved to do foolish things in displaying their antipathy to the war. Getting arrested or fighting with the cops was seen by many of them as a badge of honor reflecting their commitment. Some were badly hurt. Even now, as I recall the wild irrationality of those times, it is incredible to me that any of us managed to get through them safely.

The largest part of the New Left, or so it seemed to me, was neither Marxist nor ideological in orientation. Early in the Sixties there sprang up on several campuses near the Bay Area in California a number of so-called countercultural student groups. These students banded together in romantic rejection of modern society with its demands for a trained elite. The student counterculture seemed to be rooted in dissatisfaction with the competitive rat race for grades in traditional college curricula.[27] Such competition gave students little opportunity to philosophize or to address the crucial human problems of their time. Countercultural students saw themselves as defenders of simple instinctual humanity against the repressive power of an authoritarian state that sought to train them for military and exploitative rule. In a variety of poetic ways they tried to find liberation from society's controls. A popular antiwar song of those days began with the words "where have all the flowers gone?"

It has always seemed to me that the countercultural groups I saw on campus during the Sixties had very little political focus.[28] They were romantics—a natural evolutionary development of the beat generation explorations into liberated consciousness conducted by a small coterie of artists, poets, and writers in New York and San Francisco during the 1950s. The principal thrust of the counterculture was its pastoral romanticism. It fled from organization and discipline into a world of fantasy, a liberated lifestyle in which everyone did his or her "own thing" without concern for approval or success measured in conventional terms.

Countercultural advocates favored communal life, Oriental mysticism, easy sex, natural foods, and a search for transcendental experiences often enhanced by drugs.

It could not have been accidental that a movement like this first emerged in sizable numbers among California students. California offers the world's nearest approximation to a middle-class consumer's paradise. The power of money and commercial sex is visible everywhere amid the spoils of uncontrolled real estate development. After World War II, when its natural attractions and gentle climate became known to millions of American servicemen passing through to the Pacific, California experienced a continuing flood of immigration from the rest of the U.S., and more recently from Western Europe as well. But its new residents in the postwar era were not the simple, rough-hewn pioneers of earlier times. In the main they were dissatisfied, escaping from earlier failures and searching for a new life in a golden land. These patterns of its recent history have given the state a quality of social restiveness and rootlessness found nowhere else in the world.

In this West Coast celebration of consumer appetites amid natural beauty, countercultural students set themselves up as deliberate strangers in paradise, a self-declared proletariat. They were a living, breathing embodiment of Marcuse's earlier description of a revolutionary force in the Western democracies, but they were not primarily a political movement. Theirs was a personal choice of symbols, utopian values, and lifestyles that turned out, at least for a while, to have immense political impact.

The counterculture spread like wildfire across American college campuses during the 1960s. We observed the symbols of rejection everywhere: rough clothes, disheveled hair, communal living, and the sweetish smell of marijuana. Somehow these young people were trying to define themselves as poor and oppressed, in contradiction to their relative affluence and middle-class origins. Most of them did not try to analyze why they did it. The choice of the countercultural lifestyle brought a new outlook and intense experiences with new friends, and they liked it.

The press and many politicians thoroughly confused the SDS and the counterculture. One was Marxist, highly political, and well organized; the other was romantic and substantially undisciplined. One sought leadership; the other was content to follow and to dream. One advocated violence as an instrument of social change; the other nearly always recoiled from bloodshed.

University administrators in the late 1960s believed the situation to be one in which a small but tightly disciplined Marxist leadership was attempting to build a mass movement out of the romantic rejection espoused by much larger numbers, literally millions, of American countercultural students.[29] Eventually the Marxist leadership effort failed, and the movement began to peter out in the early 1970s with the end of the war in Vietnam and the advent of a harsher economic climate in the U.S.

Intellectuals almost without exception criticize present-day American society as narcissistic. Tom Wolfe has called it the "me generation." But these excesses seem pale in comparison with the self-indulgence of the student counterculture in the late 1960s. Those young people were almost totally self-absorbed in their pursuit of liberation. It is an irony that society's fear of losing them made it possible to accomplish major political reforms. Today the dominance of the white male in the work place is disappearing, family structure is looser, sexual mores have become greatly liberalized—and all these changes derive in some respect from the ideals of the countercultural students of the Sixties. But political reform was not something they sought. It was insufficiently radical. They wanted nothing less than to change the world through a collective visionary experience so that we might abandon war and racism, and discover love.

The student counterculture was a remarkable and, in some ways, a very dangerous force; far more formidable, in my opinion, than the revolutionaries who sought to inspire and manipulate it. Although colorful leaders like Tom Hayden, David Dellinger, and Angela Davis were widely admired by their countercultural followers, the movement itself seemed to defy the ordinary rules of organization and discipline by which political change is accomplished.[30] Hence the attempt to forge a coordinated political effort out of countercultural rejection was probably doomed from the outset. It must have been a disillusioning experience for the leaders of the New Left.

Moreover, in the late Sixties, black students began to organize on campus, using the techniques of group pressure and consciousness-raising pioneered earlier by black leaders of the civil rights movement. Students began to take pride in their blackness and their African heritage. They adopted racial symbols in their clothing and in their hairdos. To strengthen group identity, blacks sought to live apart, eat apart, and think apart from the rest of the campus. When black student organizations pressured administrators, there was, as I have noted earlier, an extraordinary mixture of physical threat and moral anguish in their arguments. Many white administrators began to fear black students during this period, a fear that was welcomed and carefully nurtured by the blacks.

I learned how to overcome this fear. It was evident that we were dealing with tautly disciplined and well-organized people whose object was to negotiate toughly for improved conditions, and not to burn us down as they so often threatened to do. But I never managed to break down the moral barrier—the deep wound in the minds of bright young blacks inflicted by their experience of white racism. With my white skin and white hair, I never succeeded in getting them to trust either me or my good intentions. The curse of racism is that it is double edged.

In the 1960s the leadership of the New Left saw themselves as champions of black revolution in the U.S. They sought to organize black student groups, to teach them socialist ideology, and, if possible, to lead them. But black students were far too experienced and too disciplined to substitute what they viewed as one form of white oppression for another. Few of them were interested in revolution; they wanted to enter American society as equals and gain access to their rightful share of society's benefits denied for centuries to their forebears.

Black student organizations generally rejected New Left leadership. They joined in demonstrations only when it suited their purposes, and they typically refused all blandishments offered to encourage their participation with whites in revolutionary activities. The expectation of the New Left leadership that militant blacks on campus and in the cities would become the shock troops of the revolutionary struggle in the 1960s were rudely dashed. Refusal by black students to participate must have been baffling to those who followed Marcuse's analysis of postindustrial society and who therefore thought they understood the historical role blacks and other Third World people would play in creating utopian socialism.[31]

The frustrations experienced by the leadership of the New Left in failing to organize the counterculture and in being rejected by tightly knit black students, may well have torpedoed the student Left by the early 1970s.[32] Perhaps it was this frustration that accounted for the bizarre acts of terrorism undertaken at about that time.[33] Media-oriented bombings in universities, banks, and in the nation's capital can hardly be construed as thoughtful acts aimed at serious political objectives. They seemed to me to have been cries of frustration, accomplishing little more than to drive the terrorists underground into total ineffectuality. I sometimes wonder whether things came to that ignominious end because the New Left saw the counterculture evolving away from a humanistic crusade with mass appeal for students into an elitist fad attractive to middle-aged artists, writers, and entertainers, which is what the counterculture became in the early Seventies.[34]

In any event, by the mid-Seventies the symbols and drop-out philosophy of the counterculture had virtually disappeared from urban college campuses. They could still be seen in the rural Northeast, along the beach areas of Southern California, and at avant-garde cocktail parties in San Francisco and New York, but the student counterculture had ceased to be a political force.

The special danger posed by the movement in the mid-Sixties lay in its rejection of the fragile ties binding each generation to the next.[35] The generations cannot be easily held together without a foundation of shared values and common purposes that ultimately define a common tradition. Those ties seemed to be virtually on the edge of dissolution among countercultural young people in the United States in the late Sixties. Student alienation was so widespread and so profound that colleges found themselves in a state of constant nervous anxiety. At the time it seemed that a true crisis of values was occurring, in which countercultural youth, inspired and buoyed by the philosophy of the New Left, were rejecting all traditional ideas about study, work, and personal advancement, and trying to find their own way without reference to the past.

These concerns were rooted deep into my psyche by the difficult experiences I went through in 1968 and during the years immediately after. I was astonished when evidence began to accumulate that the counterculture was disappearing from the Columbia campus in 1973. It was being supplanted by determined conformists struggling, not in opposition to a repressive social order, but toward acceptance in law, medical, and business schools. Apparently what we had taken to be an elemental and powerful social movement was only a preoccupation of affluent, middle-class youth. When that affluence began to fade, the counterculture was almost immediately undermined.

But it had to have been more than just that! A prolonged and stressful period of adolescence is now the rule in postindustrial society because of demands for extended preparatory training. These demands produce heavy pressure for advanced study, made more stressful because of the ever-present possibility of ultimate failure. As this enforced extension of adolescence proceeds, young people must either conform or be discarded. Eventually a point is reached at which a significant number may begin to reject the entire regimen. We saw one such point in the counterculture of the Sixties, and I imagine we shall see others again before very long.[36]

It is remarkable that a social phenomenon as powerful as the student counterculture has failed to receive the attention it deserves among analysts of student unrest.[37] My experience in those days was revealing of the elemental power of the movement. Many faculty, junior faculty in particular, were attracted into the counterculture and adopted both its symbols and its philosophical outlook. A few openly opposed the movement because of its anti-intellectual tendencies. Very few social scientists on either side of the issue have been willing to devote serious attention to clinical study of the role played by the movement during the unrest of the Sixties. The major attempt was Theodore Roszak's 1969 book, *The Making of a Counterculture*, but this otherwise fine piece of work is flawed by the author's view of the movement as an emerging humanistic leadership.[38]

That certainly was never true. The narcissistic tendencies of the counterculture would not have permitted its members to endure prolonged struggle or to steel themselves against overwhelming anxieties. Such strength requires a discipline foreign to the movement. The risk was that the student counterculture might have been taken over by more dedicated and disciplined Marxists, who were certainly in there trying.

Marcuse's writings were able to explain and to provide clear logical underpinnings for the inchoate stirrings felt by millions of countercultural students. They saw an ugly world and they tried to withdraw from it into another world of their own making. The initial chapters of Marcuse's *One Dimensional Man* describe a utopian alternative. Although the book is characterized by an aura of radical pessimism, it also provides a withering critique of existing society and its monotone mass culture. These ideas captivated countercultural students. The book became a bible and elevated Marcuse to the role of guru and spiritual father, at least for those whose intellectual capacities were up to the struggle that Marcuse's dialectical reasoning required.

I joined the UCSD faculty as a professor of psychology in July 1965, shortly after Marcuse arrived from Brandeis. A year or so later, a faculty colleague, who had been in Paris during the spring of 1966, mentioned over coffee in the Revelle College Cafeteria that he had seen *One Dimensional Man* prominently displayed on the bookstalls along the banks of the Seine opposite Notre Dame, a place frequented by intellectuals from all over the world. My friend guessed that Marcuse must now be the most famous member of our faculty.

At that time, the relatively tiny UCSD faculty included three Nobel Prize winners and twenty-one members of the National Academy of Science. I really had not read much about Herbert Marcuse, except for a short biographical sketch in *Commonweal* mentioning his emerging status as a hero of the New Left.39 As with many other scientists, my reading did not extend very far into twentieth century social philosophy. I knew far less about Marcuse than about Jean Paul Sartre, which was very little indeed. Could it be that a member of our own faculty had suddenly emerged as an international figure without my knowing anything at all about his work?

After that conversation in the Revelle Cafeteria, I walked over to the campus bookstore, bought a copy of *One Dimensional Man*, and struggled with it for the rest of the summer. It was a complex book cast in difficult prose, but the ideas were new and provocative. Although his English was excellent, Marcuse wrote in the ponderous style of a German philosophical treatise. I thought it surprising that a book as difficult and serious as this one had achieved such popularity.40 It is a tribute to the power of his thought that Marcuse's ideas somehow survived his English writing style.

I was finally introduced to him in 1967. Herbert Marcuse was then 69 years old, tanned and vigorous, chewing on the stump of an extinct cigar, and conveying great personal charm. He was friendly and yet formal. He called me "Professor McGill." With his mane of white hair and wrinkled forehead locked in a perpetually quizzical expression, he seemed to be a perfect model for the classical Herr Professor Doktor of the German universities. I found it impossible to think of him as a dangerous man or as a hero, for that matter.

Marcuse and I did not meet again until shortly after I was appointed UCSD chancellor in June 1968. I never had an opportunity to argue with him about his philosophical position. It was a shame. Although he was obviously a powerful thinker, I found his belief in the power of dialectical logic and his view of tolerance as a form of repression too dogmatic for my taste. It is difficult for a non-Marxist to feel comfortable with the strictures of dialectical thought, and it would have been enlightening to hear Marcuse defend himself against the argument that he had provided no adequate analysis of the circumstances in which his utopian society might actually be realized.[41]

In any case, I simply forgot about social philosophy and buried myself in my own research on auditory sensation, which was coming along very nicely just then.

In the spring of 1968, Marcuse's role as father of the New Left on American campuses and mentor of revolutionary students in Berlin, Paris, and Rome began attracting serious attention from the newspapers in California. At one point it was reported that Rudi Dutschke, a fiery young revolutionary who led student rebels in a number of violent episodes against the government of West Germany, had been invited by Marcuse to visit UCSD.[42] The report created a furor in San Diego, despite Marcuse's repeated denials. In fact, Dutschke never came. He was shot in the head in Berlin by an assassin on April 21, 1968, and was neurologically impaired thereafter. He suffered from severe epileptic attacks and died in Denmark in 1979 at the age of 39, a tragic victim of the violent political passions he had aroused.

The story of the planned Dutschke visit added to other inflammatory accounts of Marcuse's involvement with student radicals on both sides of the Atlantic, eventually producing a major outcry from local citizens and state legislators in California.[43] *The San Diego Union* attacked Marcuse in a series of editorials beginning on May 28, 1968, noting that this "dangerous man" was employed by the University of California and paid by the taxpayers so that he could foment revolution against the country that had given him asylum from the Nazis.[44] The newspaper demanded an investigation by the Regents and Governor Ronald Reagan.

It was useless to explain that we believed Marcuse to be a utopian theorist, not a political revolutionary. People could not or would not grasp the distinction. They were utterly horrified by what they read in the press about communist agitation and bacchanalian revels on American college campuses. If Marcuse was inspiring or even condoning any of this, then the San Diego community wanted him out of UCSD.

On July 1, 1968, Marcuse showed friends a tersely written note he had received in the mail:[45]

Marcuse,
   You are a very dirty Communist dog. We give you seventy-two hours to live [*sic*] United States. Seventy-two hours more, Marcuse, and we kill you.

Ku Klux Klan

A day or so later he learned that an order had been given to Pacific Telephone in his name instructing the phone company to cut off his service. Perhaps it was only petty harassment, but it might also be part of a plot to kill him. Marcuse became alarmed. A few days later, he and his wife, Inge, fled their home in La Jolla and went into seclusion with friends in the Carmel Valley. Later in the month he travelled abroad, as he did nearly every summer. This time, however, Marcuse departed for Europe without returning home to La Jolla.

Just before he went into hiding, Marcuse was interviewed by a local reporter. He insisted that he would return to UCSD because of a sense of obligation to his students. "Quite a few students came to this place because of me, and as far as I can I will not let them down."[46]

On August 13 in Italy he was asked by a reporter representing the *International Herald Tribune* whether he might not be intimidated by threats against his life. Marcuse replied, "The attack on me is only a part of a concerted attack on the university as such. You know this is one of the most reactionary communities in the United States, and they don't want a free university. They don't want a university that tolerates radical opinion."[47]

It was certainly unwise of Marcuse to talk to reporters after receiving what he believed to be a death threat. His remarks were immediately published all over the U.S. and became instant headlines in *The San Diego Union*.[48] People who had never heard of him were now vaguely aware that Herbert Marcuse, described in the newspapers as a communist professor, was teaching at UCSD, paid with taxpayers' funds, and resisting patriotic attempts to remove him. The last thing Marcuse needed was publicity of this sort. It portrayed him to the people of California as a defiant radical entrenched at UCSD. None of it was true, but on the McLuhan plane of existence, shadow is always more important than substance.

Marcuse was far too worldly to seek immortality by setting himself up as an easy target for the Ku Klux Klan. He went into hiding, and when he returned to UCSD in September 1968, there were no more death threats. What might have become high tragedy turned into low comedy as the American Legion entered the picture,[49] prepared to do battle for traditional American values against the evil genius of the New Left.

CHAPTER 4

The American Legion Launches an Attack

On June 21, 1968, the Regents of the University of California selected a new chancellor of the San Diego campus.

There are nine chancellors. Each is the chief administrative officer of a local campus and functions under the general supervision of the president of the university. The appointment in San Diego was planned to coincide with the departure of the retiring chancellor on August first. Accordingly, the new individual would not be expected to take office for six weeks.

Governor Ronald W. Reagan attended the all-day Regents meeting in San Francisco, but he abstained from voting during the brief executive session in which the name of William J. McGill was proposed and approved.

The Regents would have been hard put to find someone with a weaker administrative background. Their new chancellor had once served as a department chairman but had never even been a dean.[1] The problems in 1968, however, were not of the kind that benefit from prior experience with traditional academic administration. Campuses across the country were seething with countercultural rejection and revolutionary rhetoric. Hundreds of college administrators had been driven out of office by unprecedented governance problems. Trustees, sensing the danger, were seeking people with specialized psychological and negotiating skills. The idea of using brute force against students was profoundly objectionable to most of them. Faculty, too, were looking for leaders who would approach confrontation more subtly. Hence, the circumstances that projected me into the chancellorship at San Diego in 1968 were as unique as they were challenging.

Ronald Reagan had been elected governor of California in November 1966 in a smashing victory with a popular mandate to clean the radicals out of the university. Three months after that, Clark Kerr was dismissed as president of the University of California. Although at the time many people believed Governor Reagan responsible for Kerr's firing, one of the Regents told me several years later that the basic cause was a series of unresolved tensions between Kerr and the Regents following the Berkeley student riots in 1964–65. Kerr contends that Reagan and a group of Regents planned and executed his dismissal. I asked Governor Reagan about this in 1978. He denied it, saying that he was not in the room when the Regents made their decision.[2]

Kerr accepted his fate with professional grace and good humor. He told people that he was leaving the presidency of the University of California as he had come to it—"Fired with enthusiasm!" But the tough actions of the Regents and the close proximity of Kerr's dismissal to Reagan's election left the university stunned and resentful.

Governor Reagan's hesitancy about my appointment as chancellor at San Diego was probably not intended to get me off to an excellent start, but he could not have done better. The steely-eyed cynics on the faculty and in the student body were immediately won over and disposed to be friendly. These people believed as an article of faith that no administrator could be acceptable to the Regents unless he had sold out, but after Governor Reagan's abstention they knew I could not be all bad. Sadly, our honeymoon was not destined to last long.

Soon after the name of the new San Diego chancellor became public, reporters began descending on La Jolla, asking what I intended to do about Professor Marcuse.[3] This was prior to the outburst of hysterical publicity over the letter to Marcuse signed by the Ku Klux Klan, but even so he was being depicted daily as a hero of student rebels in the U.S. and Europe. Marcuse was hot copy, and reporters were on the trail of a big story.

I tried to parry their insistent questions by explaining that I was unfamiliar with the terms of Professor Marcuse's postretirement appointment at UCSD. It was not an ordinary faculty appointment, and I would have to study the entire problem before I could tell them anything.

In fact, I understood the conditions of Marcuse's appointment down to the last comma. Less than a year earlier, in the autumn of 1967, while I was chairman of UCSD's academic senate, the faculty had dispatched me on a confidential mission to see Harry Wellman, acting president of the University of California, at his offices in Berkeley.

Harry Wellman was a benign, silver-haired gentleman who looked a bit like Harry Truman. Wellman had been a long-time vice president of the university, and was universally liked. Clark Kerr called him out of retirement to be his senior aide, and in January 1967 the Regents named Wellman acting president when they dismissed Kerr. Their understanding with Dr. Wellman was that he would hold things together until a permanent replacement could be designated. While he was serving in that role I came to see him about a worrisome problem involving Professor Linus Pauling.

Linus C. Pauling, one of the greatest chemists of our age and a two-time winner of the Nobel Prize, was, like Marcuse, the holder of a postretirement appointment at UCSD. Pauling had become prominent in the newspapers during the 1960s as an activist in the antiwar movement. World disarmament and the search for a permanent peace were passions in his life almost as consuming as his devotion to science. In fact, Pauling's second Nobel Prize was the peace prize given in 1962. But he was also an uninhibited individual with a flair for colorful publicity. There was, for example, a classic photograph of Professor Pauling marching in a tuxedo among young demonstrators outside the White House just before joining the President and other guests for dinner.

Since Pauling was appointed at UCSD from year to year by the Regents, the faculty became alarmed over his fate because of the turn to the right in California politics with the election of Governor Reagan. They saw the possibility that the Regents might have little enthusiasm for someone so deeply involved in antiwar protests. My task as a faculty representative was to see to it that Pauling's appointment was not killed on what we construed to be political grounds.[4]

Dr. Wellman was sympathetic but suggested that I be patient and take the matter up with his permanent successor, who would soon be named. It was just the kind of complex diplomatic problem I loved. Waiting also meant that I would have an opportunity to meet the new president of the university, and so I waited.

Not long after President Charles J. Hitch took office on January 1, 1968, I called on him to describe our concerns about Pauling's appointment. He understood at once the pickle we would be in if the Regents should ever deny continuance to one of the most distinguished scientific figures in the world—a veritable giant. It would be charged that Pauling's appointment had been terminated because he was outspokenly opposed to the Vietnam war. Moreover, this charge would be widely believed no matter what other grounds the Regents might advance to justify their action.[5] I asked our people to stay cool while we tried to work out a solution.

A few weeks later Hitch, Wellman, and I devised a scheme in which a resolution would be prepared for submission to the Regents, delegating their authority on postretirement appointments to the president, with the understanding that he would in turn redelegate it to the chancellors. Since the chancellors already had such authority for regular faculty appointments, it was a perfectly reasonable step to take. Pauling's name was never mentioned.

At their May meeting in 1968 the Regents approved the president's recommended change in their standing orders, delegating postretirement appointments to the president and the chancellors of the local campuses. As the Regents' unanimous vote was announced by the secretary of the board, Charlie Hitch looked around and searched for my face in the row of senate representatives near the Regents' table. When he found me, he winked and I smiled back happily. There would now be no fracas over Linus Pauling's appointment because the San Diego chancellor would make it quietly and no one would pay the least attention.

Had I understood then that less than a month later the president of the university would ask me to serve as San Diego chancellor and that the next controversy over a postretirement appointment would involve Herbert Marcuse and would erupt immediately after my selection, I would have fainted dead away. It is a blessing that we never really know what is in store for us.

Despite what I told reporters in June, I knew exactly what Marcuse's appointment entailed, and who in the end would have to make the decision. I would. And if anyone thought that Herbert Marcuse could be quietly reappointed by the San Diego chancellor without an uproar that would spread not only over the whole state of California but eventually to the entire academic world, he was quietly kidding himself.

Then came the Klan's letter to Marcuse in early July. The local newspapers renewed their attacks on him, and UCSD began to vibrate with tension over these repeated threats to Marcuse's safety and continuance. It was understandable. Here was a freshman chancellor not yet even officially in office, and here also was a developing struggle with powerful people in San Diego. The city's largest newspaper was evidently trying to oust Marcuse. His friends felt it necessary to stiffen the new chancellor's resolve by telling him that Marcuse must, repeat *must*, be reappointed immediately. As for the San Diego community, they should be told to go to hell.[6]

I did not think that was such a smart thing to do, but I was also rather fearful of saying it to an aroused faculty. So I holed up in my faculty office on the fourth floor of Urey Hall, trying to keep out of sight until my appointment as chancellor became official on the first of August. It proved impossible.

In mid-July the volatile and, for me at least, frightening situation surrounding Marcuse's status on our faculty was stirred up by, of all people, the American Legion. San Diego Post 6 sent me a letter on July 19, complaining that Marcuse was an admitted Marxist and urging that his 1968–69 teaching contract not be renewed. In fact, in the Legion's view, every effort should be made to revoke Marcuse's current contract. They offered to raise money to "buy up" his contract if no other method could be found.[7]

As it happened, I read about this letter and the Legion's offer in *The San Diego Union* before anything was delivered to me in the mail. It is an age-old tactic in pressure campaigns, but I was new to such things and felt offended. Without consulting anyone I sat down immediately and wrote a formal reply to the Legion. The essential message was:

> The university is bound by a commitment to Professor Marcuse . . . which governs his services to the university during the 1968–69 academic year. I intend to see that this commitment is kept.

The more I thought about it, the more the offer to buy up Marcuse's contract struck me as ludicrous. It was just the kind of approach to the academic life the American Legion might concoct, and I was sorry that my answer had been so stuffy. I should have needled them. When a reporter from *The San Diego Union* mentioned the Legion's offer a few days later, I laughed and said, "They must think Marcuse is a football player."

That seemed to me to be just about the right tone, but when Marcuse's department heard about it, they blew up and sent their chairman, Jason Saunders, around to see me. Saunders explained that his colleagues were concerned because I seemed to be taking the attacks on Marcuse too lightly. The department was deadly serious. In their opinion I should immediately issue a statement denouncing the American Legion for its interference in the affairs of the university. I should also announce that Marcuse would be retained in 1969–70, i.e., next year.

"But, Jason, this whole thing is ridiculous. It is only July. His current appointment has just begun. I am not going to act on any of next year's appointments until spring. Besides, I can't believe that anyone would take the Legion's offer seriously. If they really intend to try to drive Marcuse out, it seems to me that the best approach is to make them look silly. I am trying to diminish this conflict, but the philosophy department seems to want to declare war."

Saunders looked pained. He corrected me gently.

"Bill, it is *The San Diego Union* and the American Legion who have declared war."

After an hour's talk I would not budge on issuing the statement demanded by the philosophy department. Saunders ended our discussion by saying that he would report my position to his department. As he walked out of the office, I could see that he was shaking his head sadly.

The newspapers gave a great deal of play to UCSD's refusal to consider the American Legion's offer.[8] Officials of Post 6 were quoted as saying that the chancellor's decision was evidently final. He had refused to revoke Marcuse's contract. Accordingly, they would now organize a petition from Legion posts in Southern California, and take their displeasure with Dr. Marcuse, as well as their insistence on his removal, directly to the Regents. In the event that the Regents failed to act, the Legion would go over their heads to the state legislature.

Several days after our meeting, Jason Saunders called to report that the philosophy department had met to consider the public attacks on Professor Marcuse as well as the position I expressed on the subject. It was his "melancholy duty" to inform me that the department had lost all confidence in me. The time was late July. I still had not yet officially embarked on my duties as chancellor.

It is difficult now to recall that episode with anything but wry amusement over the irony of a honeymoon that ended more than a week before the official beginning of my term in office, but at the time it was not funny. Both the philosophy department and the American Legion were spoiling for a fight. How could I resolve this problem if the philosophy department refused to give me any elbow room? Later that day I found myself staring at the blackboard in my office musing on the department's expression of no confidence. It brought a sharp twinge of anxiety I had never experienced before. If things were this bad even before I began, what would the chancellor's job be like?

Walter Munk, the newly elected chairman of the academic senate, called the next morning. He wished to speak with me privately about the Marcuse situation and I invited him up at once. In less than an hour Walter was seated amidst the clutter of books and research journals in my faculty office, sipping coffee and exuding warmth. During the more than 15 years I have known him, I have never heard Walter speak a sharp, angry word. He is polite almost to a fault, and he is usually indirect. I sat, coffee cup in hand, waiting for him to come to the point.

It was very simple. Walter had learned about the meeting in the philosophy department. The vote of no confidence was "a lot of silly nonsense that will not help us at all." He wanted me to know how he felt about it. I must have breathed a sigh of relief because Walter cocked his head as he had a way of doing when something he said pleased him. He smiled benignly and then turned to his main business.

Munk was concerned about the alarm in the faculty over these continued political attacks on Marcuse. The American Legion's attempt to buy up Marcuse's contract was the last straw. Something would have to be done to calm things down. Would I be agreeable to a special meeting of the academic senate as soon as he could arrange it? Senate rules required a minimum of five days notice, but Walter did not believe he could get ready in less than two weeks. He had spoken to Walter Kohn, a physicist, and chairman of the senate's Committee on Academic Freedom. Kohn was one of the pillars of the campus. He was perfectly willing to draft a statement supporting Marcuse and expressing confidence in the new chancellor's handling of the matter. It would take only a few days to convene the academic freedom committee, secure their approval, and then pass the statement up to the chairman of the senate with a recommendation for a special meeting. The two Walters would be glad to show me the statement as soon as it was ready.

Munk wanted to know whether this way of handling the sensitivities of our hot problem with Herbert Marcuse would be satisfactory. Would it cause any difficulty between the Regents and me?

I could not imagine any problem with the Regents. There was certainly nothing inflammatory in a statement of support for a colleague under political attack by a newspaper and the American Legion. Moreover, a sensible statement would probably do a lot to help us keep this matter out of the hands of faculty radicals. They were almost hysterical over the thought that the American Legion might want to screen the UCSD faculty for patriotism. As a matter of fact they were not altogether wrong about this. Later discussions with an official of San Diego's American Legion showed that such screening was just what the Legion had in mind.[9] At the time I believed innocently that pressures on universities to conform to the Legion's standards of orthodoxy had gone out of style with the end of the McCarthy era. I was seriously mistaken.

I urged Munk to go ahead with his proposed meeting. A day or two afterwards, he showed me the draft statement of the Committee on Academic Freedom. It was beautiful.

> We wish to assure [Professor Marcuse] and our chancellor of our complete support against the current attempts to silence him, whether they be by well-intentioned citizens, by persons capitalizing on false rumors to agitate public sentiment, or by individuals making threats against his person. . . . We are confident that the great majority of the public supports us in our determination to develop here in San Diego an outstanding university free of violence or threats of violence, and dedicated to the principles of freedom of expression and scholarship without which a democratic society cannot long survive.

Paradoxically the first signs of violence would come during the winter quarter as campus radicals tried to provoke the Governor and the San Diego military into repressive moves against the university. Despite their beautiful statement on Marcuse, the faculty proved less willing to denounce force when UCSD students prevented a Marine Corps recruiter from conducting interviews with other students on campus.

But that part of my story comes later.

As soon as I gave Walter Munk assurance that the statement on Marcuse was satisfactory, a special meeting of the UCSD academic senate was scheduled for August 9 at 3:30 in the afternoon. The philosophy department was predictably dissatisfied with the draft submitted by the Committee on Academic Freedom. It failed to include a denunciation of the American Legion. It spoke of citizens as "well-intentioned." It did not mention Marcuse's appointment. There was in fact nothing of the militant stance sought by the department.

Accordingly, Jason Saunders and another member of the philosophy department drafted a substitute statement condemning interference in the university's affairs by the American Legion and our local newspapers.[10]

When the senate convened on the afternoon of August 9, Walter Kohn was recognized for the purpose of moving the draft statement of the Committee on Academic Freedom. Immediately friends of the philosophy department moved to substitute the tougher Saunders-Jameson version and a debate ensued on the relative merits of the two statements in the context of the motion to substitute. Under the senate's rules this became the first question to be settled.

Walter Kohn was at his unmoving best, refusing all attempts at compromise that might have amended his draft with harsher language. It was soon evident that the senate preferred the more temperate version. Faced with certain defeat, Saunders rose to withdraw his substitute. The stage was set for adoption of Kohn's draft when Seymour Harris, an elderly and famous economist recently arrived from Harvard, asked for the floor.

Harris stated his great dissatisfaction with Marcuse's position on "repressive tolerance" and Marcuse's unwillingness to accord freedom of speech to "erroneous" or "militarist" views. He quoted Arthur Schlesinger's biting sarcasm in a 1968 commencement address critical of Marcuse.[11]

Harris's remarks threw the senate into pandemonium. The Left was clamoring for the floor to answer this unexpected attack from a man whose liberal credentials should have marked him as a friend, not an enemy. It was Seymour Harris, after all, who had been denounced, inaccurately but with great effect, by thousands of conservative Harvard alumni on the grounds that his introduction of Keynesian economics at Harvard had brought socialist ideology to Cambridge. What was he trying to do to Marcuse?

As I glanced around the room from a seat in the first row, I could see dozens of angry faces and waving arms, and I began to fear for the fate of Kohn's meticulously drafted statement. Walter Munk, the chairman, was looking at me hopefully. I raised my right hand and was immediately recognized while the senate slowly quieted down to hear from their new chancellor.

"I am one of Professor Harris's most sincere admirers, yet I find myself in one of those rare situations in which I am at odds with my distinguished colleague. Like him, I do not agree with Professor Marcuse's philosophical views, but that is not the point at issue here. A colleague is under attack by people outside the university. They are trying to preempt our judgment of his scholarly work and our decision about his continuance. We are unable to halt such criticisms, but we must never yield to outside pressures on academic matters.

"I find the statement of the Committee on Academic Freedom reasonable, and indeed a rather beautiful formulation of our scholarly ideals. The statement gives me no problem at all. I welcome the faculty's support of my absolute determination to keep political pressures from influencing academic judgments at UCSD in any circumstances and at any time."

It was a simple little maiden speech, but it evoked a round of applause, an emotional demonstration rarely heard in the staid UCSD senate. Walter Munk was right; they were very worried, but something in their freshman chancellor's appearance or in the tone of his voice convinced them that he would not be pushed around by the American Legion. There was nothing more to be decided.

Walter Kohn's motion on adoption of the statement of the Committee on Academic Freedom passed 109 to 3. Such overwhelming sentiment showed that whatever anxiety I may have felt earlier about serious problems with my old faculty friends over Marcuse's appointment could be put to rest at least for the present. They were disposed to be trusting and leave the matter in my hands. It was a nice outcome.

As soon as the meeting adjourned, I sought out the two Walters to thank them. Walter Munk was characteristically benign.

"You calmed them down, Bill, just as I thought you would. Did you ever suppose you would see half the faculty turning out for a senate meeting in the month of August?"

He was saying that the Marcuse problem was extremely sensitive and we should all be extremely careful. I knew. I knew.

My delight over the senate's rebuff of the hard-liners in the philosophy department ended abruptly the next morning when I read *The San Diego Union's* account of the meeting. The headline was "Academic Senate Supports Marcuse," and the article below simply reproduced the text of the statement approved at the meeting, noting in a final sentence that the senate voted 109 to 3 "to support Marcuse." That wasn't what happened at all. I knew immediately I would be buried in angry mail from citizens and state legislators who could not possibly appreciate our deft handling of faculty militants. These people would conclude only that we were defying their patriotic attempts to drive communists out of UCSD.

The mail did pour in and it was even more hostile than my worst fears led me to anticipate.[12] This was turning into a classic no-win situation: the kind that develops when people on both sides of a dispute have deep feelings and little disposition to understand each other's point of view.

Left alone we were capable of outmaneuvering UCSD's faculty radicals. But when we did it in our oblique academic style, the newspapers would fail to understand what we had done. Success would be interpreted as surrender. The only way to prevent that would be to stay out of the newspapers entirely, but I had no idea how to do it.

The whole country was alarmed over student radicalism. Reporters were on campus continually, covering academic meetings and campus political rallies. The problem was that reporters and editors possessed no experience enabling them to interpret what they saw. They did not trust our explanations. Routinely they would check our views against the views of spokesmen for radical groups. What was printed was a mass of competing claims, making us seem much more troubled and divided than we actually were.

My anxieties about the philosophy department's no-confidence vote were now gone, but they were replaced by even deeper anxieties as I saw an avalanche of public disapproval aimed at Marcuse and the UCSD campus.

Two days after the senate meeting, 32 American Legion posts in San Diego County unanimously approved a resolution reiterating the Post 6 demand that Marcuse's contract be terminated. The text of the resolution included some choice language reminiscent of the heyday of the House Un-American Activities Committee:[13]

> Students are quoted as saying that if hostile elements in San Diego try to get Marcuse out, they are going to have problems with the students.
> We ask the Regents what did they mean? We ask if the above ideas and actions of students who reportedly have been in Marcuse's classes, are the proper foundation for good Americanism, and are the taxpayers of this state paying the bill for this type of education?

So now the Legion was addressing itself directly to the Regents. Regent Dewitt Higgs, a prominent San Diego attorney and chairman of the board, called me to advise that Regent John E. Canaday of Los Angeles, a retired Lockheed executive, had put the status of Herbert Marcuse on the Regents' agenda for the September meeting. Little by little the genie was slipping out of the bottle despite our best efforts to contain it.

Shortly after the special senate meeting, a San Diego legislator arranged a private session for me with Harry L. Foster, judge advocate of the Legion's Twenty-second District (San Diego County). Foster, I was told, was the guiding hand behind the Legion's anti-Marcuse campaign. Mr. Foster came to my home early on a Friday morning, in mid-August. We sat talking in my living room for most of the morning. He was a smallish, grim-faced, bespectacled man in his late sixties. He seemed to be saying that the Legion had no particular complaint against me. If I could assure them that I would decide against Marcuse's reappointment, they were prepared to end their attacks on UCSD and me.

When would I make the decision?

Probably in mid-winter.

Well, then, with suitable assurances as to the outcome, Foster was prepared to guarantee that the Legion would not attempt to embarrass me in front of the Regents or the legislature.

I could give no such assurance. I would eventually have to determine Professor Marcuse's fitness to continue on our faculty. The question was a technical one and could not be decided in advance of the evidence. In any case I would never permit the American Legion to make the decision for me.

Didn't that forecast what the decision would be?

No, it did not. "Frankly, Mr. Foster, I am reasonably confident you are working hand-in-hand with *The San Diego Union* to drive Professor Marcuse out of the university. It is very destructive. If it continues, our attempt to build a first-rate campus in San Diego will be doomed. No one with real talent would want to teach on a campus whose faculty had been chosen by the American Legion."

He denied any involvement with the newspaper or any intent to choose our faculty. Why was I being so damned difficult? Didn't that indicate that I had already made up my mind? After all, the Legion had encountered this sort of problem with faculty communists earlier in San Diego, and had always been able to work out a satisfactory arrangement with the school administration.[14]

"This will not be easy to resolve on a congenial basis. We resent your attempt to screen our faculty. If San Diego State has allowed you to do such screening, it is their affair. We are going to fight it. The Legion ought to wait until I make my decision. If they believe I have made it improperly, they can ask for my resignation."

Foster said the Legion did not intend to wait. They would bring as much pressure on me as possible in order to influence the decision. He hoped I would not be so foolish as to misunderstand how the people of San Diego felt about student radicals, and communist teachers paid with tax dollars.

I got the message. Evidently I was destined for a brief but colorful administrative career.

San Diego has come a long way since the summer of 1968, when that veiled threat was delivered. Although surpassingly beautiful and one of the fastest developing population centers in the Sunbelt, the city has always been regarded as something of a backwater by business executives elsewhere in the nation. Ten years ago they would tell you that San Diego was dominated by aging, right-wing, arch-conservative businessmen, and by retired military. It was seen as a great place to retire, but not overly attractive as a place to do business.

During the decade of the 1970s the city gradually began to shake off this reputation. As I look at it today, San Diego displays a cosmopolitan worldliness that was missing a decade ago. The changes were inspired to some extent by the growth of the university and by the continuing population shift toward the Sunbelt. But the greatest impact occurred when officials in Washington decided to liberalize Navy regulations and to proceed with the full integration of the U.S. Navy. These changes brought San Diego, a big Navy town, face to face with the modern realities of civil disorder, failing discipline, and the double-edged racism that the rest of the country had been grappling with since the early 1960s. It has always seemed to me that America discovered the attractions of its pluralistic character only when it began to face up to the ugly social and racial problems that divided us. Facing such problems, instead of denying them, was the beginning of the curative process. In San Diego, the changes were later in coming than elsewhere.

The political scandals of the early Seventies also had an unusual effect on the city. A number of San Diegans and nearby Southern Californians became caught in the net cast by a new breed of investigative reporters and crusading prosecutors. Under the gun at the beginning of President Nixon's second term were a number of people either in or close to the Nixon administration who were operating with loose ethics at a time when society was no longer prepared to excuse hard-ball politics as a form of patriotic endeavor. One of the principal effects of the Watergate investigations, which figuratively froze the actions of thousands of people, was to convince a rapidly changing San Diego leadership that a scandal over the loss of the Republican Convention in 1972, the collapse of the U.S. National Bank, and the indictment of the mayor for taking bribes from the taxi industry were not isolated events.

Universities flourish in the sympathetic climate created by a liberal community, with its instinctive love of humanistic and scholarly pursuits. Despite my characterization of San Diego in 1968 as dominated by a small-minded, arch-conservative establishment, it would be wrong to conclude that the city lacked enclaves of tolerance. Congressman Lionel Van Deerlin in Washington, Clair Burgener and Pete Wilson in the state legislature in Sacramento, all did their best to protect UCSD from a storm of criticism because of the Marcuse affair. City Attorney Ed Butler, now a Superior Court judge, worked closely with us in dealing with our racial and antiwar tensions. He was under heavy pressure to proceed against UCSD for numerous breaches of order. It required considerable political courage for an elected public official to resist these pressures, but Butler did it.

A number of businessmen and community leaders refused to join *The San Diego Union* and the American Legion in their vendetta. I was buoyed repeatedly by sympathetic contacts with people who evidently understood our ways. There were friendly overtures even among working reporters on the local newspapers, as well as occasional disparaging references to the hard line taken by their editors.

I only wish there had been more such people. When I had my argument with Harry Foster in 1968, San Diego was largely a reflection of a few powerful figures pursuing parochial interests. Prominent in this group was James S. Copley,[15] the owner-publisher of *The San Diego Union* and *Evening Tribune*. Copley newspapers in San Diego were among the most conservative in the nation. Retired Naval and Marine Corps officers were brought in as editorial policy directors and columnists, despite the painful mismatch between the discipline of their military backgrounds and the less orderly events on which they commented. Unfortunately, too, few of them knew how to write.

Another San Diego leader at that time was C. Arnholt Smith.[16] He was the principal figure in the Westgate California Corporation based in San Diego, a conglomerate whose holdings ranged over hotels, the tuna fleet, the San Diego Padres National League baseball team, and most of California's Yellow Cab companies.

Still another was retired Admiral Leslie Gehres,[17] a wartime hero and skipper of the *Ben Franklin*. The *Franklin* was a World War II aircraft carrier that made history when it stood off a concerted kamikaze attack during the battle for Okinawa in 1945, and then limped safely home to the U.S., a near total wreck but under its own power. In 1968 Admiral Gehres worked for Arnholt Smith as a trouble-shooter and mediator in Westgate's labor disputes. He was also Republican state committeeman for San Diego.

If you crossed this powerful San Diego elite, you soon found yourself up to your neck in serious trouble. I believed that Harry Foster was mounting a patriotic effort that was evidently cleared in advance with them.[18] In all probability someone among them had encouraged Foster to undertake the campaign against Marcuse. And now Foster was telling me to watch my step. No chancellor could expect to succeed against the concentrated disapproval of this group of San Diego leaders.

Much of that way of doing things is changed now. Copley and Gehres are dead. Arnholt Smith was ruined in the early Seventies with the failure of his United States National Bank and the bankruptcy of the Westgate

California Corporation. These men and their associates have been replaced by a younger, more broadly experienced leadership group.

Following this thoroughly distasteful discussion with Harry Foster, I put in a call to my cousin, Bill McDermott, in New York City. Bill is a decorated World War II veteran, a double amputee, and an official of the American Legion in New York State. I reviewed the problem I had with the judge advocate of the Legion's Twenty-second District.

Did he know Harry Foster?

"No, Bill, but let me get on the phone. I'm sure I can pull those people off your back."

A few days later he called. "Well, Cousin Bill, you really have a problem out there. They wouldn't listen to me."

There was no hope for assistance from that quarter.

The September meeting of the Board of Regents was held on the UCLA campus. It proved to be a tense affair because of the growing controversy surrounding Eldridge Cleaver and the student-sponsored course, Social Analysis 139X. On Wednesday, September 18th, just prior to the Regents meeting, the state assembly in California formally censured the president and the Regents for their failure to bar Cleaver from lecturing under official auspices in the University of California. No doubt the action of the assembly was timed for its impact on the Regents meeting, because the very next day a similar censure came forth from the state senate.

On the same day, Thursday, September 19th, the Regents Committee on Educational Policy attempted to conduct a review of Social Analysis 139X in a raucous public meeting punctuated by outbursts of shouting and hissing from large numbers of UCLA students in the audience.

The meeting was unusual in several other respects. In the first place, nearly all the Regents were present for what would ordinarily have been a small and poorly attended committee meeting. The presence of so many Regents reflected the board's concern over the bewildering problems posed by Cleaver's course. Second, there was embarrassingly full coverage by newspapers and the Los Angeles TV channels. This kind of treatment was usually reserved for meetings of the full board on Fridays, when Governor Reagan was expected. In keeping with his custom, Reagan did not come a day early even for this highly publicized meeting of the Committee on Educational Policy.

I was relieved that the Governor had not made it. The undisciplined audience made it difficult to transact business, and the presence of Reagan, a polarizing figure, would have made things much worse. It was an excruciating embarrassment for the University of California. All this was before we had any real understanding of the New Left's technique of attacking authority by converting public events into a theater of the absurd.

I was also worried by my own problem with the Regents. There was no connection whatever between Cleaver and Marcuse, but the Regents tended to become angry when their meetings were disrupted. The whole Cleaver episode was a nightmare, and although I wanted a warm, friendly mood when the agenda came to Professor Marcuse, the Regents were uptight and hostile.

The Committee on Educational Policy finally concluded its review of Social Analysis 139X. In deference to the intense feelings it generated, the Regents agreed to put off any decision on the course to the public session of the full board on Friday afternoon. They then went into executive session to consider the Marcuse agenda item. It was their standard way of handling all personnel matters, but the announcement of an executive session produced a near-violent scene as guards attempted to usher people out of the meeting room. Everyone seemed to believe that the Regents were preparing to finish off Cleaver in executive session. With the crowd outside shouting and banging on the closed doors of the meeting room, the Regents finally turned their attention to Herbert Marcuse's status on the UCSD faculty.

Regent John Canaday was a wiry, excitable man with thinning white hair, a florid face, and a quick temper. He began by citing the resolution adopted in mid-August by 32 American Legion posts in San Diego county demanding an investigation of Marcuse by the Regents. All this was bringing the university very bad publicity at a time when we could ill-afford any further decline in public esteem.[19] Would the president explain why the Regents should consider appointing a notorious Marxist whose presence on the faculty was causing us so much grief?

Charlie Hitch puffed rapidly on his cigar, as he tended to do when he became nervous. He motioned me to the table. I acknowledged the unhappy problem arising from the excitement in San Diego over Professor Marcuse. The Regents' telephones must be ringing off the hook. But they should also understand that Marcuse was a perfectly respectable social philosopher with a distinguished reputation in the academic community. He had recently come under attack by the San Diego newspapers and the American Legion because he was considered a hero by the student radicals of the New Left.

We could not allow even a suspicion to arise that the university was permitting its faculty to be scrutinized for patriotism by the American Legion. The Regents must understand that any such impression would hold us up to national ridicule. The faculty were prepared to tolerate doctrinaire Marxists if they were seriously committed to scholarship and were willing to explain their biases to students. Marcuse, however, was no doctrinaire Marxist. He had come under intense criticism in the Soviet Union. I had met him only once, but I had read some of his work and I knew him by reputation. Marcuse was also no revolutionary. He was, as best I could make it out, a utopian theorist.

My advice to the Regents was to stay out of it. Faculty would believe the Regents were judging Marcuse politically rather than academically. Most faculty would be drawn to Marcuse's defense even though they had no use for his philosophical position. They would be understandably fearful that some day they, too, might be judged politically.

We had a perfectly adequate academic mechanism for considering Marcuse's fitness to continue as a member of the UCSD faculty.[20] The Regents should let us use it and weigh our recommendations after judging the quality of our analysis. At all costs, the Regents should not get involved in such a sensitive case as this one before a serious academic review had been carried out. People everywhere, and especially all those angry idealists in the student body, would be scrutinizing the Regents' actions, trying to establish improper political motives.

Besides, fairness to the man himself required that we not act against Marcuse without proper cause. Leave the problem in my hands.

This last was spoken not as a demand, but as an urgent plea. To my complete surprise, Regent Canaday was convinced.

"We simply can't have the American Legion telling the University of California whom to hire and whom to fire. The state constitution makes the Regents independent just so we can resist such pressures. Very well, Mr. Chairman, I move that we leave the decision on Professor Marcuse's status to Chancellor McGill and proceed with the rest of our business. But be careful, Mr. Chancellor."

The show of hands that followed found only Regent W. Glenn Campbell, director of the Hoover Institution at Stanford and a recent Reagan appointee to the board, in opposition. Campbell was almost fanatic in his hostility to Marxists on the University of California faculty. He had a considerable knowledge of and an evident dislike for Marcuse's philosophical position. Accordingly, his vote was predictable. I would never succeed in winning him over.

The Regents had now placed the decision on Herbert Marcuse's future firmly in my hands. During the past six weeks both the UCSD faculty and the Regents had considered the issue, debated it, and decided to back away. I certainly did not know how to solve the problem. Week by week the difficulties it caused were multiplying, but now I had the elbow room I sought. I also had the rudiments of a plan.

After what the American Legion and *The San Diego Union* had done, it was virtually impossible not to reappoint Marcuse. Any other outcome would have made us appear to be knuckling under to the outrageous pressures they had created. It was irrelevant what our real sympathies or reservations about Marcuse might be. The Legion was attempting to enforce its patented anti-intellectualism on our campus and we simply could not yield.

But Marcuse was now 70 years old. While his worshipful admirers believed UCSD fortunate to have him at any age, we were more realistic. Marcuse was certainly a media celebrity, a hero of student radicals throughout the Western world, but celebrities are not as revered by a university faculty as they are in other walks of life. Irreverence is one of the endearing qualities of a scholarly community. By now many of us had read Marcuse and we knew his writing style to be opaque. Whatever Marcuse's power as a philosopher, many of us saw his effectiveness limited by what critics described as his addiction to dialectical pedantry.[21]

These minuses might someday begin to outweigh the plusses of his current popularity. We would then want to retire him gracefully. No other profession is more sensitive to the effects of aging and senescence than is the academic life. The duty of elderly scholars is to teach undergraduates, make no trouble for their departments, and step aside quietly when the time comes. With the Legion and *The Union* continuing their ham-fisted tactics, Marcuse might be made virtually untouchable until the day he died. For his part, he was showing not the slightest sign of willingness to retire voluntarily. Campus jokesters were saying that *The San Diego Union* must be under contract to Marcuse to attack him. It gave him total employment security.

When I took office in the summer of 1968, I thought that, if we could find a way to dampen the public furor over Marcuse, perhaps a solution might be found. Many faculty were displaying skepticism over our concentration on "instant greatness." This label was used to refer to our policy of building departments by opportunistic recruitment of big names without regard for current effectiveness or departmental balance. We had already imported a larger number of professors of advanced age, people with big reputations and big salaries, than any other campus in the University of California. Marcuse, Linus Pauling, Seymour Harris, and a host of other less controversial postretirement faculty members were making UCSD look more and more like an academic retirement community. We were lacking the vitality created by a large, irreverent junior faculty.

These were, as objectively as I can state them, the convoluted opinions held by many senior members of the UCSD faculty as the pressures of the Marcuse appointment crisis began to build. The leadership of the San Diego community, understanding neither the outlook nor the internal tensions of a university, was making a rather simple matter in faculty housekeeping into an academic-freedom crisis of international proportions.

It was becoming impossible for the chancellor to steer a neutral course between San Diego's arch-conservative establishment and the militant liberalism of a substantial part of UCSD's faculty and students. In ordinary times the chancellor's problem was a relatively simple one. He would represent each side gracefully to the other, and also do his best to keep each side from knowing too much about the real sentiments of the other. Since both sides were largely preoccupied with their own affairs, the two worlds seldom intersected, and the system worked remarkably well.

But now, with the power of the New Left growing on campus, and with the public alarmed about student radicalism and the faculty's liberal attitudes, each side was scrutinizing the other as a potential source of danger. The chancellor could not keep them apart. Month by month tension was building toward a collision over Herbert Marcuse.

There was no way to avoid the collision. If we reappointed Marcuse there would be an explosion in the community. If we failed to reappoint him, there would be an explosion on campus. The barely veiled threats emerging from my mid-August discussion with Harry Foster of the American Legion were persuasive evidence that no easy way existed to bridge the differences in outlook between campus and community. All the chancellor might now do was to make his decision at a time and in circumstances designed to minimize the damage.

Gradually, during July and August, faculty leaders and I came to the conclusion that an investigation of Marcuse, his current academic competence and his intellectual honesty, by a blue-ribbon faculty committee, was the most sensible preliminary to our decision on his continuance. I would ask the committee to conduct its inquiry with the utmost care in recognition of the gravity of the charges that had been leveled against Marcuse. If the committee's findings and recommendations turned out to be in favor of reappointment, as seemed highly probable, the integrity of our decision process might conceivably blunt the political attacks that would almost surely follow. If the committee's investigation turned up something completely unforeseen: that Marcuse indoctrinated his students or planned building-takeovers with them, for example, the discovery would create an entirely new basis for a decision. Early in September, I asked Walter Munk to drop by the chancellor's office, and we went over the idea together.

"Bill, when do you want to make this decision on Marcuse?"

I wasn't sure. We first had to get by the September Regents meeting. Governor Reagan was now demanding that the Regents take back most of the authority they had delegated to the president and the faculty over the years. He seemed intent upon suppressing radical activity by attempting to rule the university with an iron hand. Perhaps the Regents might even refuse to let me make the decision.

Munk stared at me in disbelief.

"Do you really suppose they would be so stupid as to violate their own rules? It would turn us into a disaster area in no time at all."

"Walter, the current atmosphere makes anything possible. If I get past the September meeting with my decision authority intact, I suppose we ought to make the Marcuse decision in January. We certainly want to wait until after the election in November."[22]

Munk nodded agreement. A major bond issue providing new construction funds for the University of California and the state colleges would be submitted to voters on the November ballot. But with Regents meetings now continually disrupted by demonstrating students and with political storms brewing over both Eldridge Cleaver and Herbert Marcuse, public confidence in the university was ebbing day by day. The political atmosphere could not be worse. Our prospects for persuading anyone to support a University of California bond issue were already dismal. Neither Munk nor I wanted to do something that would make things worse, and Marcuse was just such a "something."

"Well, Bill, we have a little time. Why don't you worry about getting through the Regents meeting, and I will worry about getting the senate to propose the review committee."

Munk did his work well. Just before the September Regents meeting, he advised me that a five-member committee selected from our best people would be acceptable to the senate. I need not worry about attempts to plant radical faculty or friends of Marcuse on the proposed committee. The people to whom Walter had talked were well aware of my apprehensions over political reprisals against UCSD in the event that Marcuse were to be reappointed. They were determined to set up our internal review faultlessly in order to convince any reasonable critic of the integrity of UCSD's academic evaluations. It should provide an edifying contrast with the unenlightened public harassment of Marcuse carried on by the American Legion. If the Legion was intent on destroying people's reputations in the newspapers, we would try to do things differently.

"Walter, will you sit with the committee and give me your personal assurance that its deliberations are absolutely straight?"

"It's interesting that you should ask, Bill. I had already decided to do that. I will be glad—even honored—to do it."

Accordingly, I went off to the September Regents meeting with a good idea of how we would analyze the pros and cons of Marcuse's reappointment while trying to insulate ourselves from the enormous pressures generated by interested parties. When I urged Regent Canaday to leave the matter in my hands, saying that we had an excellent academic mechanism for determining Marcuse's fitness to continue on the UCSD faculty, I had already made up my mind on the formation of a select faculty committee.

Munk told me later that some of Marcuse's friends in the senate were unhappy about our proposed inquiry. As they saw it, we ought to reappoint Marcuse immediately for 1969–70 and get it over with. A blue-ribbon committee would be a charade. Marcuse was a giant. How could we presume to investigate him?

These people did not concern themselves about political consequences in the same practical way the rest of us did. Some of them were closet radicals who lived with the apocalyptic vision that an ill-advised authoritarian act by the Governor or the Regents might trigger an upheaval in which they would emerge as part of a new ruling elite on campus. After all, Marcuse, like all of us, was an instrument of history. He should be accorded his rightful place in the university, but if Reagan and the Regents tried to prevent it by force, then so much the better. Marcuse's friends would be the principal beneficiaries of the inevitable explosion.

Marcuse's friends were nevertheless prevailed upon to go along with the idea of a select committee. None of them wanted to be on record as opposing a faculty investigation undertaken in the best interests of the campus. Puzzling as that may seem, it is one of the characteristic attitudes of the faculty Left. Nearly all of them are idealists concerned with achieving improved living conditions for the poor and the weak through socialism. If some faculty in American universities describe themselves as revolutionaries, it should be understood as an abstract description. Solidarity with their colleagues is important to them, especially when the contrast between the life of the faculty and the illiberal style of the surrounding community is as sharp as it was in San Diego during 1968.

Curiously, the zeal of leftist elements at UCSD was matched by an equivalent rightist zeal on the part of high state officials. At about this time, Governor Reagan and State Superintendent of Public Instruction Max Rafferty were expressing a simple diagnosis and a simple remedy: we are in revolution; we must crush it with force.[23]

Admittedly, California college campuses were pretty hot in 1968, but there was nothing remotely close to a revolutionary situation. The approach adopted by state officials tended to strengthen otherwise small New Left groups who could point to the Governor's words and actions and cry "fascism" to thousands of sympathetic listeners. In executive sessions of the Board of Regents, the Governor, Dr. Rafferty, and Glenn Campbell told the chancellors that cleaning up the University of California meant getting rid of weaklings and biased liberals who had permitted this revolutionary evil to develop and were now unable to control it.

Associates of Governor Reagan repeatedly urged me to stay calm despite these threatening words. They said that the Governor's bark was much worse than his bite. He was an astute, pragmatic politician who would not, when push came to shove, make stupid mistakes in dealing with the radicals. He simply wanted to make hay at their expense, and he knew that the general public was delighted with his militancy.

Perhaps. Reagan often threatened much more than he really intended to do. But there was little disposition on the part of the Governor or other public officials to penetrate the angry rhetoric of student radicals and try to comprehend the underlying romanticism and nonviolence of the student counterculture. These officials rejected as spineless nearly every carefully thought-out scheme we devised to frustrate Marxist groups attempting to gain control of black students or of the large countercultural segment of the student body sympathetic to New Left causes.

The rigidity of state officials and their inclination to respond to all forms of disruption with counterthreats of force were a source of constant anxiety to the chancellors and would lead to a massive blow-up over "People's Park" later that year. The atmosphere of official threat was obviously very popular with the general public, but it conferred extraordinary power on tiny militant factions as they played the radicalization game by engaging in constant provocations, hoping to bait campus administrations into mistakes that would draw in the police. Whenever that happened during a period of prolonged tension, and it did happen several times, the middle group of politically inactive but sympathetic students would typically "come over," and radicalization of the campus would become a simple matter.

Each chancellor found himself holding a middle ground between the demands of small but ingeniously provocative groups of demonstrators, and angry phone calls from Sacramento threatening intervention if campus peace were not restored immediately. It was a searing experience, one that made us extremely concerned for the safety of thousands of naive, credulous undergraduates in our charge. These young people had no revolutionary ambitions but were easy marks for New Left radicalization in 1968. If the police or the National Guard were to come in, these young people would be hurt. The leaders and organizers would have long since slipped away. Somehow we had to protect excitable students from the worst consequences of their faith in antiheroes. The times cried out for subtle minds and compassionate hearts, but not many of either could be found in California politics during 1968.

In Governor Reagan's case, these inflexible attitudes, coupled with an evident lack of compassion for the romanticism of college students, were surprising. Like many successful politicians, he was a strong and naturally combative man, but during his unguarded moments he also seemed quite affable and outgoing. In private, I found him, as his advisers had said, far more intelligent and pragmatic than his extremist politics led me to expect. Doctrinaire conservatism had made him remarkably successful with California's middle-class voters, but he was hardly naive about conservative ideology in the way that Max Rafferty was. Reagan proved to be a far more complicated person, determined to administer the state in a forceful but not ideologically committed way.

Despite our best efforts, the president and the chancellors were never able to convince the Governor or even to reach him with our analysis of the complexities of student unrest. Reagan dismissed our explanations impatiently, as though they were beside the point. Revolutionaries, he told us, understand only force, and he was prepared to use force whenever necessary. It was puzzling. Eventually I came to the conclusion that the contradictory and sometimes confusing facets of Governor Reagan's personality reflected not only his own background of struggles with communists in the Screen Actors Guild, but also the diverse advice and the wide-ranging briefings he received daily from members of his staff. It was our misfortune that the Governor's education advisers were hardliners lacking either subtlety or successful experience in dealing with radical activity and the tactics of group protest.[24]

The blue-ribbon faculty committee on Herbert Marcuse was established without fanfare in early October. It set to work on the difficult task of evaluating the pros and cons of the philosophy department's recommendation that Herbert Marcuse's postretirement appointment be extended an additional year to 1969–70, and that his salary be increased appropriately. Walter Munk sat with the committee and reported periodically on its progress. In accord with academic traditions of complete secrecy in these matters, no word of the committee's deliberations was allowed to leak out. When Munk briefed me on the committee's progress, he was careful not to offer even as much as a hint on how they might be leaning. Curious as I may have been, I really did not want to know.

It became evident in a short time that the public controversy over Marcuse was at last beginning to come under a semblance of control. *The San Diego Union* and the American Legion realized that I would not act on Marcuse's reappointment until after the committee completed its work, and their report would probably not come in before the first of the year. The stridency of the newspaper's attacks on Marcuse abated sharply in October and November, although "Letters to the Editor" still bloomed regularly with irate complaints aimed at me. Radical students stopped trying to pressure me into reappointing Marcuse immediately. They understood the purpose of the committee's investigation and did not want to do anything that might damage Marcuse's prospects.

There was great excitement in the chancellor's office one day in early November when Herbert Marcuse called for an appointment. Through all the agitation of the summer and autumn of 1968 we had said not a word to one another. When Marcuse came in to see me, it was the first time we had spoken since we were introduced in 1967.

Marcuse was worried about possible delays in our decision. He asked me when I thought it would be made.

"It is not for myself that I raise this. Inge, my wife, keeps asking me where I will be working next year, and I do not know what to tell her."

I advised him that the preliminaries should be completed shortly after the beginning of the new year and that I would make my decision then. As soon as it was done, I would write to him. There would be no delay.

He thanked me and apologized for all the trouble he was causing.

We shook hands. The entire conversation lasted less than ten minutes.

As Marcuse turned to leave the chancellor's office, I stood behind my desk thinking, "So that is the destroyer of Western culture and the seducer of its youth—a professor concerned about his wife's anxiety."

In October and November, I began to spend a great deal of time speaking to Rotary clubs and other civic organizations in San Diego, trying to teach them the rudiments of academic freedom and due process. These talks were regularly reported in the newspapers without hostile editorial comment. As we came to the first of December, I wondered whether we might not at long last have this thing under control.

The Marcuse Decision

CHAPTER

5

Life at UCSD in October and November 1968 was anything but peaceful. All hell was breaking loose over Eldridge Cleaver and Social Analysis 139X. Cleaver came down from San Francisco to give his now famous speech in the UCSD gymnasium on the night of October 4. This was the occasion on which he led an enthusiastic student audience in an obscene anti-Reagan chant. The obscenity was neatly dashed out in *The San Diego Union's* report of the speech, but with sufficient precision as to leave no doubt about what Cleaver actually said.

The mail poured in once more.[1] Many correspondents believed that we should have barred Cleaver from the campus. They denounced us for permitting him to speak. These people could hardly have failed to grasp the significance of barring a militant black man from the exercise of constitutionally protected free speech on a university campus, but they did not think the matter through. Feelings were running so high that few people were thinking at all.

Then, during the November 22 Regents meeting on the San Diego campus, the Regents summarily removed credit for Social Analysis 139X, ostensibly because of their new guest-lecturer rule, but actually because of Cleaver's involvement.

The unprecedented assertion of the Regents' charter authority set off a minor cataclysm in the university. At UCSD there were immediate demands for a student strike and for shutting down the San Diego campus in a gesture of defiance. Three days after the Regents meeting these demands led to the tension-packed November 25th collision between SDS-led demonstrators and the chancellor over Cleaver's course.[2]

Marcuse had been standing in the front ranks of the grimly silent crowd that greeted Governor Reagan as he arrived at the UCSD gymnasium for the Regents meeting on November 22. My staff in the chancellor's office feared that Marcuse might make a public fuss, but he did not. Later that day, however, following the Regents' action denying credit to Social Analysis 139X, he addressed a heated rally of angry students in Revelle Plaza. He announced that he would immediately sever connections with all the administrative committees on which he served because of what the Regents had done.

It was a silly thing to say. Virtually everyone at UCSD knew that Marcuse gave no time whatever to administrative committees, and most of us were content to keep it that way. Marcuse's speech to the rally seemed to be no more than a bit of posturing before the students. If that is what it was, it worked; they cheered him.

Thank God, none of this ever found its way into the newspapers. We were having trouble enough over Marcuse's appointment without being forced to defend his saying that he did not intend to carry out his campus duties.

My November 25 struggle with radical students in Revelle Plaza seemed to leave me greatly strengthened, but it was too good to last. Suddenly, without prior warning, *The San Diego Union* burst forth in a renewed fusillade at Marcuse.

Marcuse, it seems, had gone to New York City after the Regents meeting to speak to a nighttime rally at Fillmore East in Greenwich Village on December 5. The affair was a fund-raiser for the *Guardian*, an underground newspaper. In his remarks Marcuse was quoted as saying that leftist groups ought to develop what he called "political guerrilla forces." These guerrilla forces should become involved in student disorders, racial unrest, and other civil disturbances to advance the cause of libertarian socialism.

The term "political guerrilla forces" was a bit tasteless from someone hoping to persuade the Regents to extend his appointment for an additional year, but it was characteristic of Marcuse's occasional use of flamboyant rhetoric to excite a crowd. Sometimes, as I have noted, he was moved to say things for audience effect. Later in the year, during the upheaval over People's Park in May 1969, Marcuse announced to the cheers of a large audience of UCSD student strikers that he himself was on strike. In fact, a day or two earlier Marcuse had applied for a paid leave of absence until the end of the term to travel in Europe.

Those familiar with Marcuse's philosophical position would have been more alarmed by his reference to advancing the cause of "libertarian socialism." This meant the Marcusian utopia in which freedom of speech, and indeed liberty itself, might be denied to people whose views Marcuse determined to be erroneous or dangerous.3

The speech received national attention, especially the reference to "political guerrilla forces." Here was the father-figure of the New Left calling for underground assaults on the established order in America. Members of the national press, having transformed Marcuse from an academic social philosopher into a kind of Marxist Fu Manchu, were now busily frightening themselves and their readers with the idea that an elderly professor might actually be capable of raising a quasi-military guerrilla force. Those on campus who knew Marcuse well knew that he was not a revolutionary activist. But the tensions of the times were so acute that many intelligent and reflective people were no longer capable of sustained critical thought.

The San Diego Union displayed this self-inflicted anxiety perfectly. There were three days of increasingly excited accounts of Marcuse's December 5 speech, followed by an editorial entitled, "Doctrine of Rebellion Must Go."4

Predictably, another letter arrived from the Twenty-Second District of the American Legion:

> The latest outbreak of Professor Herbert Marcuse in a speech made in New York, December 5th, indicates clearly that he does not intend to refrain from advocating and urging the destruction of our form of democracy. What he is now saying comes close to preaching anarchy.
> . . . We believe you now have sufficient grounds for not only removal, but most certainly you cannot in clear conscience renew his contract. This is not a question of Academic Freedom. A professor's activities off campus . . . must be taken into account when considering the desirability of keeping Marcuse on the campus.

The letter was signed by Harry L. Foster, Judge Advocate.

It was almost unbelievable. Suppose for a moment that Marcuse were trying to bait *The Union* and the Legion into renewed demands for his removal just as the select faculty committee was preparing its report. The Legion's letter and its subsequent release to *The San Diego Union* practically ensured Marcuse's continuance. No one could accuse them of excessive cleverness.

I wrote back in mid-December that the Legion could feel free to hold me responsible for any decision on Marcuse, but that in the meantime they ought to "stop pressuring me."

> It is wholly inappropriate that an issue as subtle and as sensitive as this one, involving as it does a senior academic appointment, should be the subject of undue pressure on the chancellor from local newspapers and from the American Legion.

It had been a long road from mid-July to mid-December. I had tried every soothing device I knew to avoid an open struggle with the American Legion, trying to settle this thing quietly without an academic-freedom fight. Now I had been driven to the point the philosophers urged upon me in July, telling the Legion in simple language to butt out of our affairs. To my astonishment, they seemed to get the message. Back from Harry Foster came a letter saying that the Legion would "leave the Marcuse matter in your hands." Once more a truce had been effected, appropriately just at Christmas time in 1968.

Actually it was not as simple as that. With the intervention of a friendly intermediary, I arranged a meeting with "Captain" E. Robert Anderson, an unusual man who had somehow managed to weave a long career as a naval officer with an even longer career as an editor in the Copley newspapers. At that time he was close to retirement as editorial and news policy director of *The San Diego Union* and *Evening Tribune,*5 having left the Navy in 1955. Joining us was Lieutenant General (Retired) Victor H. Krulak,6 United States Marine Corps, slated to succeed Anderson at the newspaper. Our meeting was set for lunch on January 2 in a private room at the old U.S. Grant Hotel in downtown San Diego.

I had never met Anderson, but I knew General Krulak quite well. In those contacts I had developed a healthy respect for the general's intelligence. He was small in stature, strikingly so for a Marine Corps officer, and he bore an absurd nickname, "Brute." But his body was taut with self-discipline. He stood ramrod straight, and his movements had the quick grace of someone who had spent a great deal of his life in the field. There was also nothing small about his brain.

Krulak had been a gifted military strategist during his career. These qualities of mind came through in our conversations about national politics and world affairs earlier in the fall. Why a Marine Corps general with General Krulak's gifts would want to take on the headaches of running a newspaper, a job for which his background did not suit him at all, puzzled me. He could have done very well as an executive of one of the big airframe manufacturers or in the defense industries burgeoning over Southern California during the Vietnam war. Instead he chose to oversee the editorial policy of *The San Diego Union* and to endure the cynical whispers of the reporters who worked for him. I never understood why. It is always difficult for outsiders to grasp the full context of motives that lead people to undertake hazardous and unrewarding jobs. Krulak may have felt the same puzzlement about me.

In any event, on January 2, after drinks were ordered, Brute Krulak began drawing me out on the New Left and Marcuse's relation to it, student radicalism at UCSD, the role of the faculty in the appointment process, our ideas of academic freedom, and many of my own political views.

Anderson was a white-haired, scholarly looking gentleman, 73 years old and nearing the end of his career. He sat quietly listening to our conversation. The discussion must have matched many others going on at that time in editorial rooms and political offices all over the country, as people grappled with the perplexities of university campuses seething with student unrest. Krulak thought it was a Soviet-inspired conspiracy; I did not. My idea was that our problems were caused by extended adolescence in postindustrial society. It turned out to be a very interesting disagreement.

Neither of them tried to force me into an advance commitment on Marcuse's appointment. In turn, I did not offer my opinion on the American Legion's campaign against Marcuse. In an unspoken agreement, we managed to stay away from what was most on our minds.

Midway through the meal, Captain Anderson turned to me and said, "Call me Andy." I sensed that the account I had given was genuinely instructive to him. As we broke up, Andy asked me to come downtown again soon to speak to his staff. I agreed.

The transformation in *The San Diego Union* began the next morning. All indications that Marcuse existed and was teaching at UCSD virtually disappeared from the newspaper. The daily letters bitterly critical of the chancellor suddenly dropped out of sight. For the next month and a half there was almost nothing about the Marcuse case.

In a few days the volume of mail coming into the chancellor's office dropped off to a trickle, and for a while at least, public criticism practically ceased. It was as though a faucet had been turned off. Circumstances had arranged themselves so that I was seeing the power of the press as an actuality rather than an abstraction. The shutting off of criticism on the Marcuse case was something I sought eagerly at the time, but it has come to disturb me more and more as the years go by and as I continue to think about its implications.

I did go downtown later, on January 31, to the *Union-Tribune* building to speak with Andy's editorial staff in their conference room. It turned out to be quite a grilling. Most of the hard questions on Marcuse were asked on that occasion, but I refused to discuss them. Next day one of *The Union* reporters called to say, only half-kidding, that I was the first fuzzy-minded liberal in history ever to make it into that conference room. When the session ended, Captain Anderson presented me with a memento, a tiny penknife labeled "Copley Press." I wondered what it might signify.

All this diplomatic talk aimed at the editorial staff of *The San Diego Union-Tribune* was my undisguised attempt to get us out of the newspapers for a while and to produce a less hysterical atmosphere in which the select committee might bring in its report. The effort proved to be reasonably successful, despite merry hell breaking out elsewhere in the University of California.

In January the Berkeley campus found itself mired in a student strike engineered by the Third World Liberation Front. The "front" was a coalition of minority students, community people, and radical sympathizers pressing for an autonomous college of black studies with substantial student control over courses and staffing. The Berkeley faculty and administration refused to go along, and the strike followed.[7]

During the January Regents meeting thousands of demonstrators milled around outside the meeting site at University Hall on Oxford Street in Berkeley. Windows were smashed, the police pushed and shoved, and the Regents had to be conducted in and out of the building under guard. When Governor Reagan's limousine pulled slowly out of the University Hall parking area at the end of the meeting, protestors pelted it with eggs. Demonstrators chased the vehicle down Oxford Street as it gathered speed and fled into the darkness. Berkeley was a bad scene in late January, but in La Jolla all seemed serene and peaceful—a calm before the storm.

The month of February 1969 got underway with persistent rumors that the work of the select committee was finished and its report being written. My staff began bringing me daily messages about the dire things in store for us if Marcuse was not reappointed. Something was evidently about to happen. After two months of relative calm, the pressure suddenly began to escalate.

The rumor mill also managed to reach the president's office in Berkeley. My phone was ringing constantly, with Charlie Hitch, the president, or Jack Oswald, his executive vice president, or sometimes both of them together, on the line talking about how to get this thing past the Regents. I told them frankly that I did not see any prospect of an easy time. The select committee would almost certainly recommend reappointment. Oswald reported with equal frankness that any attempt to reappoint Marcuse would evoke serious objections from Governor Reagan and his supporters on the board.[8] Jack had been busy counting noses. We did not have the votes. It seemed to me he was trying to push me, ever so delicately, into declaring against reappointment. Charlie Hitch kept his peace. He said that, whatever happened, we would be in it together.

On Monday, February 3rd, the select committee reported. Walter Munk came into my office with a copy of the document just after it was delivered to the budget committee of the academic senate. Walter told me that he had sat with the select committee all through its deliberations, and that the committee had produced the most honest and thorough analysis of an appointment he had ever seen.

The gist of their report was that among professional philosophers Marcuse was not held in especially high regard. Among sociologists and political theorists, however, estimates of Marcuse's standing tended to run substantially higher. In the judgment of the committee, Marcuse's primary value to UCSD was as an unusually gifted and popular teacher. The committee recommended reappointment, but did not favor promotion to the next higher step in the ranks of full professors.

They had done a thorough job. They had contacted eminent scholars at nearly all the major universities in the United States and Europe. Written opinions of Marcuse's standing in his field were received from no fewer than twenty-four different academic experts. The committee's conclusions were exceptionally well-documented in a field in which ideological disputes and professional rivalries can sometimes produce distorted judgments. There was little room for doubt.

The recommendation of the senate budget committee arrived on February 7. In effect, the budget committee favored both reappointment and promotion. That was to be expected. The chairman was a close friend of Marcuse and one of his strongest ideological allies.

And so there I was, nicely caught in the web I had constructed for myself. But during the long months of faculty deliberations, I had begun to formulate a plan that I shared with no one. If there was any way to bring this thing off without getting chewed up, my plan seemed to offer the best hope, though I could not be sure that any scheme would succeed. Pressures were growing intense, and people on all sides were digging in, waiting for my announcement.

It was clear that I had to reappoint Marcuse on the basis of the select committee's report. It was equally clear that I had to make it a terminal year if I wanted to save us from disaster with the Regents. The select committee's report and Marcuse's age (he was 70 years old) seemed to furnish a basis for making such a two-sided decision and sticking to it in the blasts that were certain to follow from protagonists on both sides.

Accordingly, on February 14, St. Valentine's Day, I wrote Marcuse a brief note stating that I would approve his reappointment for 1969–70, but I would be asking him to retire in June 1970.

I had consulted no one. The letter curtly requesting Marcuse's retirement came as an unpleasant shock to nearly everyone who learned about it. My handling of this sensitive matter had been amateurish in the extreme. The uproar on campus was almost instantaneous. A large group of faculty, thirty or more people, including most of the senior faculty I counted as close friends, demanded to see me immediately. The meeting was quickly arranged for the next morning, Saturday.

They told me that Marcuse would reject my offer out of hand because it seemed to invent a new retirement rule that he interpreted as applying solely to him. The group berated me for taking so critical a step without consulting them. I replied that they had not been notably helpful as I tried to steer the campus through this difficult crisis, and that any other decision would produce damaging reprisals from the Regents. We sat on the edge of our chairs, speaking sharply and staring coldly at one another despite friendships that in some instances extended back over more than a decade.

In the end they pressured me into agreeing to write a second letter to Marcuse, saying that he would be reappointed, indicating that a new retirement policy was being established, one that would apply to everyone, and thanking him for his services.

This second letter was intended to replace my original letter of February 14.9 Missing from it was the key provision that next year would be Marcuse's last on our faculty, as I had counted on in my plan. Instead, the faculty group and I agreed to develop a uniform retirement policy to be enforced at a specified age. It was also agreed we were talking about age 70, and consequently there was little likelihood that Marcuse would be appointed beyond next year.

But it was not completely buttoned up. For the first time I had experienced the mailed fist of an irate faculty, and I was pressured into backing away from what I considered to be a minimally safe course with the Regents.

Looking back on that very rough meeting, I feel I stood my ground fairly well, despite a serious mismanagement of the retirement issue, which provoked the toughest kind of faculty opposition. Those who called the meeting wanted to force me to drop Marcuse's retirement altogether, but I would not do it, and somehow we managed to work out a saving compromise. What a long distance we had come from those civilized days when most of us approached faculty meetings with the idea that nothing could be done if anyone raised an objection!

I came away very depressed from that Saturday morning confrontation with senior UCSD faculty. I had never anticipated being forced to take on old friends like that, but they did not seem to understand that there would be a Regents meeting in less than a week's time. Everything we decided might well be overturned. I was fearful that too much had been given away, increasing the risk of a Regents' veto. The process that led toward an ultimate break with the faculty was now beginning. Neither of us wanted it, but, from that moment, we were increasingly skeptical of each other's judgment.

The familiar, crawling anxiety and a severe headache were primitive warnings of potential danger as I marched out of step for the first time with many of my oldest friends, but there was nothing to be done about it. I could not allow them to push me into a self-sacrificing act, especially when I thought they were wrong. All these pressures were visible to Ann McGill when I returned home on Saturday at two in the afternoon.

"Migod," she said, "what on earth happened to you?"

A press conference on Marcuse was set for Sunday afternoon, February 16. Charlie Hitch had asked me to make the announcement as quickly as possible after the decision to permit the Regents "second thoughts" before their scheduled meeting on February 20–21. It sounded ominous. All the gears were now in motion and I could no longer stop them. In less than two days the decision would be in the newspapers, and I would be running for my life.

At the press conference I announced our intention to reappoint Dr. Herbert Marcuse as professor of philosophy for the academic year 1969–70. A brief statement described the analysis carried out by the select committee of UCSD faculty.

Their report, I said, "delineates and documents Professor Marcuse's eminence as a scholar. He is clearly one of the leading philosophers in the world today and a teacher of remarkable ability."

So much for that. Next came the tough part of the decision:

"As of June 1970 the university will terminate all existing commitments to overage professors, [replacing these agreements] with a policy of expected retirement at a specified age.

"The campus feels that many of its difficulties in the Marcuse case arose from the lack of a clear policy on postretirement appointments.

"We are now in grave difficulties due to the systematic curtailment of resources over a period of years. On the other hand UCSD has made a substantial number of postretirement appointments. [They] are represented more heavily on this campus than on any other campus of the university."

There it was, but none of the reporters turned out to be the least bit interested in our new retirement policy. Nor, as things developed, were there any more serious repercussions at UCSD. The procedures worked out with the faculty a day earlier were eventually approved and implemented without further dispute.

All the questions at the press conference were about Marcuse. Whose advice had I relied on? Had I been afraid of a student revolt if I failed to reappoint him? Had the committee looked into the possibility that Marcuse's teachings might be subversive?

One questioner asked whether I had signed Marcuse's new appointment. The answer was no. I had written to Marcuse that he would be reappointed, but as a courtesy to the Regents I had not yet signed the papers and would not do so until there was an opportunity to discuss the decision with them on Thursday and Friday.

This was to be the final step in my plan. Rather than go before the board with a defiant *fait accompli,* I decided to go up to Berkeley on Wednesday, February 19, and lay out the full logic of our action on Marcuse. I would tell the Regents that I was ethically bound to make the appointment as a consequence of the analysis we had carried out. If they sought to restrain me, I would have no other course than to resign.

It seemed to me that the Regents would understand the friendly intent of my refusal to sign the appointment papers until after I had spoken to them. Even more important, or so I thought, they would find it difficult to face losing a chancellor by attempting to bar him from what he felt morally bound to do. It was an extremely risky business, but the scheme offered at least a possibility of securing assent to Marcuse's reappointment without also inviting severe reprisals from a hostile board.

As events developed, the scheme worked beautifully but not at all in the way I had planned. It created an atmosphere of confusion among the Regents that stymied the opposition to Marcuse's reappointment. Instead of admiring the chancellor's ethical sensitivity, the Governor and several of his Regents became convinced they had been tricked.

Of course, I could not reveal this plan to the reporters on Sunday afternoon or to anyone else, for that matter. The announcement would be interpreted as political maneuvering. Hence there was only my statement that I had not yet signed Marcuse's appointment, and would not do so until I had had a chance to speak with the Regents.

Reaction in San Diego to our action on Marcuse was instantaneous. State Assemblyman John Stull fired off a telegram to the Regents, demanding my immediate dismissal:

". . . UCSD Chancellor William McGill has openly placed himself on the side of those elements which seek to destroy our society and turn the University of California into a battleground."

Another assemblyman announced that he would introduce legislation subtracting Marcuse's salary from the state budget allocation to the university. This action was suggested by Harry Foster of the American Legion, who also said:

> The Chancellor has evidently disregarded the feeling of not only the vast majority of the people in this community but of the State. . . . The decision to renew Marcuse's contract will come back to haunt McGill.

On Tuesday, February 18, the lead editorial in *The San Diego Union* attacked the new retirement policy:

> The mistake was compounded when Dr. McGill also connected the simple decision concerning Marcuse with a new retirement policy which could genuinely harm the university. It could, for example, force the retirement of eminent scholars and genuine scientists.
> Regents of the university must veto Dr. McGill's decision to retain Marcuse another year. They also should seriously reconsider the delegation of broad powers of hiring they have extended to chancellors in view of Dr. McGill's inability to face up to the problem.
> Dr. McGill asked for the privilege of making his own decision. He has made it and now he must live with it.

The brief truce I had engineered with Andy Anderson, editor-in-chief of *The Union*, was now evidently at an end; that was to be expected. What I did not know was that another, totally unforeseen storm was brewing on campus.

On Tuesday afternoon I drove downtown to talk for several hours with DeWitt Higgs, chairman of the Board of Regents. "Dutch" Higgs is the senior partner of one of San Diego's largest law firms. He is a tough, hard-bitten attorney, a tall, slender, sharp-featured man. In 1969 he was 62 years old, but looked much younger. As a Regent, Higgs proved to be a wonderfully warm, decent human being, and a rock of dependability in the midst of the seemingly endless crises afflicting the University of California during the late 1960s. The plight in which the university found itself evoked Higgs's protective tendencies rather than his lawyer's instinct for the kill.

He understood the problems posed for us by the intemperate attacks on Marcuse emanating from the American Legion and the city's two largest newspapers. He did not want the San Diego campus to be torn apart by bitter internal dissension. That Tuesday afternoon, Dutch Higgs carefully reviewed our problems with the board. At the end he volunteered to help me get through the ordeal. It was a great relief for me to have the chairman in my corner, especially because I knew he had hoped I would decide the other way.

At five o'clock an emergency call came into Higgs's office from UCSD. It was George Murphy, the dean of students, telling me that a group of about 150 students and faculty, trailed by several reporters, were camped outside my office door.

"What do they want?"

"They want you to sign Marcuse's appointment. I think you should stay put for a while down there, boss, at least until the reporters leave. I'll keep an eye on things here."

A great many changes had taken place within me since Murphy guided me so shrewdly through my first experience with confrontation in late November. I was more intuitive now about crowds, and more confident of my ability to deal with them.

"No, George. They will only show up at my home tonight if I try to avoid them. I'm coming back. Please tell the people I will talk to them and set up a place where we can meet."

Murphy sounded relieved.

"You're the boss. When can you get here?"

"I can make it by 5:30. Will you call Ann and tell her I will be late for dinner?"

"Sure, boss."

When I pulled into the chancellor's parking space in the darkened UCSD administrative complex, it was 25 minutes later. The floor-to-ceiling windows of the large conference room immediately in front of me were blazing with light. The room seemed to be jammed wall-to-wall with people. George Murphy had posted himself outside. He was carrying his familiar clipboard on which he scribbled notes to himself.

The reporters were gone; thank God for that! Murphy squinted in the deep shadows outside the conference room as he read the demand given by the crowd. It was that I sign Marcuse's reappointment—right now!

Was that all?

"Yes, that's it."

Murphy held open the heavy glass door, and I picked my way with difficulty over tangles of legs, books, and smashed paper bags smelling of junk food, toward the front of the room. Murphy remained posted by the door. As I threaded my way, I could see the shadowy forms of campus policemen standing in the parking lot just outside the plate glass windows that spanned one entire wall of the room.

"Dean Murphy says that you have asked to see me. Here I am. What is the problem?"

The spokesman was Erica Sherover, one of Marcuse's graduate students.[10] She was a prim-looking young woman, with loosely gathered, long brown hair and large glasses. Her lips were drawn into a thin, hard line that bespoke the tension she was under. I remembered she had also been present at the press conference on Sunday.

"The people here do not understand why you have refused to sign Professor Marcuse's appointment. When you speak of 'courtesy to the Regents,' it seems to us that you are reneging on your authority as chancellor. Professor Marcuse must be reappointed immediately, and we are not leaving here until you sign the papers." (Loud applause.)

It was incredible. I could see several faculty members standing in the crowd. They joined in the applause. Were they all so paranoid as to be incapable of seeing that their way of handling the Regents would lead to disaster—not just for Marcuse, but the campus as well? I folded my arms and tried to speak to them reasonably.

"You may stay here all night if you wish; I am not going to sign the papers until I am ready. I do not believe any of you understand what is happening. I have written to Professor Marcuse telling him that he will be reappointed next year. That letter is a commitment binding on the university. (Applause.) I will be going up to Berkeley tomorrow afternoon to explain our actions to the Regents. My job will then be on the line. If the Regents overturn me, I will resign. (Sustained applause.) But you have to understand that this is my responsibility, and I intend to handle it in my own way. Your approach will not succeed in getting the Regents to accept my decision."

And so it went for the next hour and a half. The group seemed intent on getting me to admit that I had, in fact, succumbed to right-wing pressures. As they saw it, the chancellor was trying to save his job by ceding his authority to the Regents and inviting them to overturn his decision. The only way I could disprove the crowd's suspicions would be to sign the appointment then and there. This I refused to do, and we went round and round with each other, each of us repeating the same arguments and getting nowhere.

Most of the confrontational arguments I have had with students or community people have been like that. There is almost no opportunity for genuine communication. The leaders of such groups are trying to exert pressure—to bend the president or the chancellor into acceding to the group's demands. The followers, the faces in the crowd, are emotionally aroused. They see the person they are confronting as evil. His resistance to their pressures is all the evidence necessary to establish his malign intent. No arguments will convince the group. No further proof is really necessary. A tape recorder is always brought along. The microphone is thrust in front of the administrative officer, so that his duplicity may be recorded, scrutinized, and later exposed.

Rarely did these disputes conclude on a moment of such high drama as the one that had occurred in the Cleaver argument in November. Mostly they just petered out into exhaustion. People went home to get some sleep, listen to the tapes, and plot their next moves. During the late 1960s arguments like this managed to get us through countless days of crisis. A long jawboning session can be an effective damper on the emotions of an angry crowd; and there is always the possibility that someone may actually penetrate the thick wall of mutual suspicion and enable people to understand one another a little better.[11]

In this case the argument simply ran down into exhaustion. By seven o'clock nearly everyone in the crowd had drifted away, and the leaders gave up the effort. George Murphy came forward from his post at the door to extract me. As he guided my steps firmly past the piles of trash and the remaining militants, Murphy guessed that this was the end of it, unless my tactics with the Regents should backfire. In that event we would all be in most serious trouble, but it was something he preferred not to think about.

We walked the short distance back to my car, and Murphy opened the door, urging me to go home, eat dinner, and get some rest. Tomorrow

I would be leaving for Berkeley. He wanted me sharp when I faced the Regents.

That Tuesday night the phone at home rang three times with calls from old friends on the faculty urging me to sign the Marcuse appointment before the campus blew up. They meant well and, of course, they did not know what I had been doing earlier in the evening. I was beyond being annoyed with them, saying only they would have to trust me.

This crazy predicament I had fashioned for myself had San Diego's conservative establishment clamoring for my scalp because I had reappointed Marcuse, and nearly everyone on campus believing that by some trick I had not done it. Before going to bed I asked the good Lord not to do anything further to mess up my plan.

The next morning, Wednesday, it poured rain. Late in the afternoon there were some breaks in the clouds and I managed to get on a delayed flight for San Francisco. Just before boarding, I purchased a copy of the *Evening Tribune*, the Copley Press afternoon newspaper in San Diego. As our plane rose out of the murk hanging over San Diego and headed north for the Bay Area, my eye caught a headline on page one:

Reagan Sees New Issue on Marcuse

The Governor was quoted as saying on Tuesday that a new charge had been leveled against Marcuse challenging his qualifications to be a professor. Reagan did not offer details except to add that the challenge came from "citizens outside the campus." He said that he intended to air the matter in executive session at the Regents meeting on Friday and hinted that he would probably oppose extension of Marcuse's appointment.[12]

Now that was odd! At an earlier news conference in mid-January the Governor said he would not intervene in the dispute over Marcuse. The decision, he said, should be left to the campus administration. This sudden shift was just what Jack Oswald had predicted on the basis of his nose count of the Regents. It seemed to augur a political move of some kind. There was no substance to the Governor's report of a new issue on Marcuse's qualifications. The only "citizens" talking this way were the American Legion and their friends. They had been in full cry for nearly a year.

Could it be that Reagan, like UCSD's radical students, had misread my refusal to sign the papers as an invitation to kill the appointment? Didn't he realize my letters to Marcuse were legally binding on the Regents? Good God, what if I had failed to think this thing through correctly and Reagan actually succeeded in restraining me from signing the appointment! The more I thought about it, the more worried I became.

The weather was just beginning to clear in the Bay Area when we arrived. I found myself still fretting over the Governor's news conference. Before I left the terminal, I picked up the *San Francisco Chronicle* and scanned it for news of the Regents meeting. Herb Caen's column said the word was out in Sacramento that Professor Marcuse was a gone goose.

Driving was very soothing in the midst of the nagging anxieties I had brought up from San Diego. My car lights were turned on to illuminate the freeway ahead as twilight fell quickly in the late afternoon. They picked up the signs pointing to the Bay Bridge and Berkeley. Less than an hour away would be dinner and a friendly evening with the president and chancellors.

The talk at those Wednesday evening dinners prior to Regents meetings in the late 1960s nearly always centered on the board's agenda. Because of the powerful political pressures on the Regents, there were sensitive items that the president wanted to discuss and about which he sought advice. During the summer and fall of 1968, and now in the winter of 1969, protests were breaking out on every campus of the university. The agenda was a veritable minefield of problems. Often it seemed that the principal work of the administration—ensuring the continued excellence of the university and planning our future growth—was being shunted aside in the persistent clamor over radical activity.

And so it was on the evening of February 19, 1969. The largest headache of all, at least from my vantage point, was the question before the Committee on Educational Policy reviewing Chancellor McGill's action in reappointing Professor Herbert Marcuse and establishing a new retirement policy for faculty at San Diego.

Charlie Hitch took note of the Marcuse case during our discussion at dinner, but he quickly passed on to Berkeley's big difficulty with Third World student strikers. The Berkeley campus was in a state of emergency. Further trouble was expected at the Regents meeting. The president expressed concern about the impact all this would have on the Governor and his Regents, who were demanding tougher discipline. Everything that could be done in the Marcuse case had been done. The president was sure that Bill McGill would make a strong presentation to the Regents. Berkeley's chancellor, Roger Heyns, wanted to explain the details of new regulations on student conduct that the president would probably announce to the Regents on Friday. The president preferred to make only an announcement that rule changes were coming rather than go into details with the board. The new rules had not yet been reviewed with the faculty, but the Regents might force his hand. Demands from the board for tougher discipline were growing more intense. There was also the problem of crowds of demonstrators expected outside University Hall on Thursday and Friday. Charlie Hitch sat thoughtfully, smoking his cigar and considering his options.

Charles Johnston Hitch was commencing his second year as president of the University of California. He was an economist, a former Rhodes Scholar who had earned a brilliant reputation as a budget and fiscal analyst with the Rand Corporation. Subsequently Hitch moved to the Pentagon, where he performed with distinction as comptroller and deputy to Secretary of Defense Robert McNamara, working among McNamara's bright but sometimes erratic "whiz kids."

Clark Kerr recruited Hitch into the University of California in 1965 to serve as financial vice president. Kerr's keen administrative eye was quick to recognize Hitch's unique talent as a budget and program planner. Hitch would bring exceptional fiscal competence to the operation of a large state university with nine separate campuses and an annual budget not far from a billion dollars. It was something of an irony that the Regents chose Hitch to succeed the man who recruited him when they dismissed Kerr as president in 1967.

Charles J. Hitch was 59 years old in 1969. He was not an overpowering man. In fact, except for his rich, cultivated voice, there was little of the panache that trustees of state universities tend to look for in choosing presidents whose principal job is to impress governors and legislators. Hitch's solemn face and low-key demeanor, together with his first-class mind, marked him as a scholar, and it is certainly true that he was an unusual university president in the sense that he was accepted as an equal by most academics.

Beyond his remarkable talent for fiscal planning, Charles Hitch had one other outstanding quality that matched him to the heavy burdens he was forced to carry in holding the University of California together during the dangerous era (1968–1975) in which he served. He was the most honorable person in the midst of conflict I have ever known. It was simply inconceivable that Charlie would ever lie or attempt to be devious in dealing with the Regents, especially when profound disagreements divided them. You knew without reflection that his presentations of issues would be objective and honest. A direct question always yielded a straight answer. He simply compelled the trust of those around him.

This quality, and his warmth and loyalty to those with whom he worked, made Charlie Hitch an object of great admiration among the chancellors. During Hitch's first year in office our annoyance rose as we observed that Governor Reagan showed the president of the university very little of the consideration we thought he merited. The treatment was formally correct, but openly disdainful. This was not just the Governor's instinctual combative response to perceived adversaries, but something deeper.

Reagan seemed to have the same scornful reaction as the general public did to the vile language and public lewdness that New Left radicals used as shock tactics to proclaim their rejection of conventional morality. He was appalled by it and could not understand why university authorities tolerated it.[13] Hitch, in his own quiet way, sought to protect free expression on campus from the Governor's more ruthless approach to dissent. I think Reagan felt put down by Charlie's understated but unyielding public disagreement with the Governor's analysis of unrest and ways to control it. Governor Reagan, at least at that time, had no interest whatever in protecting the University of California. He sought to remake it, whereas the protection of the university was the first priority of every waking moment of Charlie Hitch's life.

When I once expressed wonderment at the Governor's combative attitude toward the university, a legislative leader explained to me that Reagan had few close friends among politicians in Sacramento. He was a Hollywood celebrity, a deliberate outsider disdainful of the people who, in his judgment, had brought the state of California to the brink of chaos. This attitude certainly did him no political harm. Whenever Governor Reagan attacked the University of California, his popularity zoomed. During his first term, at least, Reagan evinced little concern about the effects of such polarization on a great national institution or on a generation of students disposed to venerate antiheroes.

Whatever the reasons for it, the Governor's hostility affected the attitudes of the chancellors toward him and toward the president. We felt that Charlie Hitch would have difficulty surviving. It evoked our solicitude not only because we admired him, but also because our own survival was dependent on his. Dan Aldrich, the chancellor at Irvine, once put it simply in a toast he offered at an alumni gathering:

"A Hitch in time, saved nine!"

That evening at dinner, my brother chancellors looked solicitously at me, conveying their sympathy for my problem with Professor Marcuse, but they showed themselves to be even more solicitous of the president because of his difficulties with the Governor.

As we plunged into the serious work of planning how to handle the Third World Liberation Front demonstrators, we were determined that nothing should be permitted to embarrass Charlie Hitch before the Regents. Roger Heyns mentioned that police would be used to unblock the entrances to University Hall so as to ensure that the Regents could move in and out without harassment. If demonstrators got out of hand, he was prepared to clear the streets around the building. Evidently, it was Chancellor Heyns who was in the hot seat, and so I relaxed over a glass of wine.

Whether it was the good wine or the good fellowship, or perhaps just the cumulative effects of lack of sleep during the previous week, I found myself so relaxed late in the evening that I fell asleep in the car as Chuck Young, the UCLA chancellor, drove us back to our hotel. I tumbled into bed at eleven o'clock, slept soundly, and wakened thoroughly refreshed at seven on Thursday morning.

Walter Munk and I were scheduled to go before the Committee on Educational Policy in executive session at II AM in the Regents Room on the first floor of University Hall. Seventeen of the twenty-four Regents were there around the table. None of the political figures attended, but that was expected. They would appear tomorrow, Friday, at the meeting of the full board.

I was astonished to see that Glenn Campbell, director of the Hoover Institution, was among the absentees. If any Regent harbored antagonism toward Marcuse, Campbell did. He had told me earlier that he would come to the meeting prepared to read a long list of quotations from Marcuse's writings, which he viewed as establishing Marcuse's unfitness to hold any academic appointment. But Campbell was not there: a hopeful omen.

At the invitation of the committee chairman, Regent Philip Boyd, I began our presentation of the case. When I came to the point describing the formation of the select faculty committee, I turned to Walter Munk and asked him to explain how the committee's investigations were carried out. Munk made an earnest presentation in his best seminar manner. He was almost impassioned in reviewing the care and objectivity with which the committee had addressed its charge. Walter's presentation struck me as extremely effective. At one point he put out his jaw and denounced Assemblyman John Stull for his persistent political interference in our faculty evaluation processes.[14] It was a courageous thing to do, because Stull had entered the room only a few minutes earlier.

At II:45 Regent Boyd called on Mr. Stull, who had requested permission to appear. Stull came to the table, sat down, and read a prepared statement attacking Marcuse's Marxist views. He called on the Regents to veto Marcuse's appointment and dismiss the chancellor for having made it. Regent John Canaday interjected that he agreed with most of Mr.

Stull's criticisms of Marcuse, but not with his conclusion. I wondered hopefully whether my refusal to sign the appointment papers was having the desired effect.

Phil Boyd then looked questioningly toward me. I expressed puzzlement over the content of Mr. Stull's remarks. The "distinguished assemblyman" had been expected to put before the committee some of Professor Marcuse's more objectionable public activities, but the substance of Mr. Stull's complaint seemed to be a political criticism of Marcuse's ideas. This criticism was offered as grounds to deny Professor Marcuse a place on the faculty. I said that in my judgment silencing professors was not an effective way to deal with dangerous ideas. Bad ideas could be overcome only by better ideas. Certainly the history of civilization had demonstrated that ideas could not be suppressed by silencing thinkers.

The morning session concluded on that exchange. Phil Boyd adjourned the committee for an hour's luncheon break. Several of the Regents approached us with compliments on the thoroughness of our presentation. Regent William Forbes asked the secretary to send him a transcript of my reply to Assemblyman Stull. Of course, these Regents were mostly the old-timers who had devoted many years to the guidance of the University of California. They knew the academic life intimately. They were bound to be understanding of the way in which we sought to resolve the Marcuse appointment crisis. The question was whether we had made a similar impact on the thinking of the newer Regents appointed by Governor Reagan. I looked over at Regent William French Smith, the Governor's personal attorney and close confidant, but his face gave no clue to his thoughts. Mr. Smith was too polished a lawyer to allow anyone to see his inner feelings until he was ready to reveal them.

The chancellors gathered around us and offered their professional opinions. The presentation had been effective: cool, matter-of-fact, persuasive. Charlie Hitch smiled and made a thumbs-up gesture of encouragement.

After lunch the committee resumed its deliberations and again I took up our case. I read the text of the report of the select committee. Then came the unique problem of postretirement appointments at UCSD. Several chancellors had tried unsuccessfully to bring them under control. The current dispute over reappointing a 70-year-old professor made control necessary. I explained the complex decision in the Marcuse case, including the termination of all existing commitments as of June 1970 and their replacement by a policy of expected retirement at a specified age.

At this point the Regents began to inquire about the letters of intent.

Both were read aloud. They asked me whether I had signed the appointment papers. I replied that I had not, although I had come to Berkeley completely convinced that the appointment must be made. I was morally obliged to do it.

There was always the possibility that I might hear something at this committee meeting putting an entirely new light on the case. I did not want to confront the Regents with a power conflict similar to those they had encountered in the dispute over Eldridge Cleaver's role in Social Analysis 139X. They had to understand that the appointment must be made. Any other choice would leave me in an ethical situation I could not tolerate.

The Regents turned to their general counsel, Thomas Cunningham, questioning him on the nature of the legal commitment involved in the letters of intent to Marcuse. Judge Cunningham flushed, obviously uncomfortable at having to respond with Chancellor McGill in the room. Phil Boyd saw his embarrassment and suggested a Regents-only session. All of us, other than the president, were excused.

The last two lines of questioning worried me. The Regents were evidently exploring their options by asking whether they could legally block Marcuse's appointment. Had I made a fatal error in refusing to sign the appointment papers?

The Regents-only session of the committee lasted for more than two hours, with no word whatever on what was going on. As the minutes dragged into hours, I became more and more depressed. Why was it taking so long? What could they be doing in there? The situation began to look grim.

The Regents-only session broke at about 4:30 in the afternoon, and they emerged laughing and joking. John Canaday took me aside to tell me that the entire Marcuse issue had now been disposed of. There was no question of dismissing me. Several of the Regents had expressed unhappiness that I had unnecessarily involved them in a matter in which they had no authority. Despite this, they felt that the decision was the only one possible in the circumstances. As things developed, the Regents spent most of their time working on a statement expressing distaste for Professor Marcuse's Marxist philosophy, and trying to include a few words of approval of the job Chancellor McGill was doing. The latter were intended to counter the avalanche of public disapproval that had followed the announcement of Marcuse's reappointment.

We seemed to have got through the Committee on Educational Policy in fine style. If seventeen Regents were agreed on the Marcuse case, there would be no serious difficulties tomorrow with the full board. This impression was confirmed when Regent James Brett, president of the Mechanic's Institute in San Francisco, told me at dinner on Thursday evening that I was mighty persuasive but Marcuse was a bitter pill to swallow.

The dinner was a social affair in Berkeley's beautiful, old Claremont Hotel. It was tendered by the Regents to honor the university administration, and both Governor Reagan and Lieutenant Governor Ed Reinecke were there. In these relaxed circumstances, the struggles and disagreements that divided us were temporarily put aside. We toasted each other as though we were bosom friends and the world was filled with sunshine.

During my presentation to the Committee on Educational Policy on Thursday afternoon, there had been a violent scene across the street on the Berkeley campus. Radical students and Berkeley street-people managed to get into a pitched battle with city police and officers of the California Highway Patrol. The police were on campus to prevent damage to buildings by the Third World Liberation Front.

This struggle between the TWLF and Berkeley campus authorities had been going on for more than a month, and was becoming increasingly ugly. Earlier the Governor had declared a state of emergency, sending in the Highway Patrol over the objections of the Berkeley administration.

The presence of police on campus had the predictable effect of radicalizing large numbers of normally inactive but angry students sympathetic to New Left causes. The issue had now become police on campus, and the original demands of TWLF for an autonomous program of black studies were all but forgotten.

On Friday morning, when we arrived for the executive session of the full board, there was an ominous air of violence on the Berkeley campus. During the night, the Governor had called up the National Guard. Two olive-drab helicopters were perched on the flat roof of a low garage across Addison Street from University Hall. The San Francisco Police Department's Tactical Force was called in overnight under terms of a mutual-aid agreement between the city of Berkeley and other Bay Area police forces. These tough-looking men in blue uniforms were lined up in front of University Hall, keeping the peace as we showed identification cards and entered.

The Regents altered their executive session agenda to insert a special item on the state of emergency at the Berkeley campus. The sheriff of Alameda County and a number of other law enforcement officials appeared at the meeting to attack the Berkeley administration for what they described as lack of cooperation in clamping down on student radicals.

Roger Heyns, the Berkeley chancellor, attempted to explain the subtleties of the patterns of unrest with which we were dealing and the methods we used to handle them, but his arguments were quickly brushed aside by Governor Reagan, who was in blazing form. He said that the problems at Berkeley were part of an organized revolutionary effort in California and that he was determined to crush it.[15] He demanded cooperation from the university.

During the morning's discussion it became clear that the campus police had been removed from the jurisdiction of the Berkeley campus and were reporting directly to the Alameda County sheriff for the duration of the emergency. This was possible because campus police serving the University of California are a branch of the state police. Although the sheriff's office may have felt that such a step facilitated coordination, removing the campus police from the chancellor's authority is always unwise. In this instance it made the Berkeley administration prisoner to policies devised by law enforcement officials who, at least at that time, knew next to nothing about the New Left or about how to counter the subtle provocations engineered by SDS and its offshoot committees.[16]

Law enforcement people kept telling us of an international conspiracy in which SDS was operating through agitators under the discipline of the American Communist Party. These conceptions were evidently drawn from FBI circulars to local police forces, but they bore no relation to anything we were seeing. We thought they were at least 15 years out of date.

The riot-control tactics used by the Alameda sheriff were making things even worse. It was galling and a little frightening to see deadly force used on New Left sympathizers. The police would never get their hands on the radical leaders. They were far too clever to be caught fighting with the cops. It was the credulous and the naive who would be clubbed into submission. These young people needed to be protected from their inclination toward flamboyant gestures as demonstrations of the depth of their commitment. But little likelihood of such protection existed in the present circumstances. It was a classic prescription for tragedy.[17]

The law enforcement presentation to the Regents continued in executive session until lunch time. The board never got around to its executive session agenda; hence the Marcuse case remained in limbo. The unheard agenda items were postponed to a later executive session of the board to be convened immediately after the afternoon meeting. The latter would be held as it always is, in public session following the luncheon break.

The Regents spent much of their public session discussing the emergency at Berkeley. Under pressure, the president agreed to submit toughened rules of student conduct for use in this and similar emergencies. All through the afternoon a huge rally was going on directly across the street from us on the Berkeley campus, but there was no repetition of Thursday's fighting. The sight of the San Francisco tactical force surrounding University Hall was enough to cool the fighting ardor of zealots in the crowd for at least the rest of the day.

Finally, at 3:45 in the afternoon, the public meeting concluded, and the Regents returned to executive session to hear the Marcuse case. Regent Philip Boyd presented the report of the Committee on Educational Policy recommending that no further action be taken and that the Regents limit themselves to a statement. The proposed text devised by the Committee on Educational Policy was circulated by Mr. Boyd.

Glenn Campbell protested that he would not accept this course of action. He had much to say on the Marcuse case, but had not attended Thursday's committee meeting. Now he was being denied an opportunity to present his views. The chairman of the board, DeWitt Higgs, observed that seventeen Regents had attended the committee meeting. They were prepared to support the recommendation of the Committee on Educational Policy.

Campbell, his face contorted with anger, submitted a motion declaring the Regents' strong disapproval of Chancellor McGill's action and their intention to disavow it. Campbell's action was seconded but, just as Governor Reagan began to speak to it, Phil Boyd moved to table the motion.

An angry flush flooded the Governor's face. Seeing it, Boyd apologized. He said that he had not intended to interrupt.

Reagan spoke bitingly and forcefully. He was, he said, angered by the decision and the way it was made. He felt deceived. The Governor had learned only at noon that the Regents were legally unable to overturn the chancellor's action. Reagan reminded the Regents that he was working actively for what he termed "political balance" on the UC faculty. The most effective step toward such balance, in view of what had happened here today, would be to remove these powers of appointment from the chancellors and return them to the Regents.

At this juncture Mr. Boyd reintroduced his motion to table Regent Campbell's censure of the San Diego chancellor. The tabling motion passed in a voice vote.

William French Smith then moved to amend the statement on Marcuse by adding a paragraph which incorporated the language of Campbell's censure and stated that a majority of the board opposed the chancellor's action.

The effect of Smith's unexpected amendment was instantaneous and dramatic. Vernon Cheadle, the Santa Barbara chancellor, had been under brutal pressure for several weeks, caught between campus radicals and irate critics among his alumni. Seated beside me in the row of chancellors adjacent to the Regents table, Vernon suddenly exploded. He leaped to his feet, ran up to the table and slammed his fist down on it, shouting, "Have you any idea what you are doing to this man?"

From across the table, the president, who had never before been heard to raise his voice, yelled at Smith, "Do you care?"

They were concerned that this kind of statement from the Regents, added to the widespread public disapproval of my action in reappointing Marcuse, might undercut me so completely as to force me out of office. It was a lovely gesture of support, but my own anxieties on that score were long past. I rose to my feet in the midst of the angry clamor, feeling strangely drained, and strode to the table. Silence fell immediately when the Regents saw me standing before them:

"I recognize the difficulty that our handling of Professor Marcuse's reappointment has caused for the board. You have your responsibilities; I have mine; and they are different. We analyzed this case to the best of our ability. We brought the Regents a responsible decision based on facts. In the long session of the Committee on Educational Policy yesterday, no contrary facts came to light. It is plain to me that the Regents' objections to Professor Marcuse are political, and, believe me, I understand the objections. I am certainly no admirer of Marcuse's attempts to justify violence and confrontation. But in the discharge of my responsibilities as chancellor, I cannot be guided by political considerations. My obligation is to deal fairly with the faculty and to keep political criteria out of all academic evaluations. This is what I have tried to do."

The superheated atmosphere cooled down rapidly as I addressed the board. A group of moderate Regents, led by Boyd and Higgs, began searching for an agreement to remove the sharp censure of the chancellor implicit in Smith's motion.

Higgs, the shrewd lawyer, thought he saw his moment. He introduced a telegram signed by thirty-seven San Diego business and civic leaders praising Chancellor McGill for his handling of the difficult problems of the Marcuse case.[18] Somehow, during the week, Dutch Higgs must have persuaded these individuals to take a stand against the blanket disapproval demanded by the American Legion, *The San Diego Union*, and the conservative establishment in the city. It was a totally unexpected expression of support, showing that there were many independent liberal spirits in town. As Higgs read the signatories name by name, I looked at the Governor for his reaction. Unlike the cool mask displayed by his lawyer, Bill Smith, Reagan's face was alive with vexation. He had clamped his jaws tightly shut and was slowly shaking his head. He winced several times during the citation. Near the end he yawned.

After considerable haggling among the Regents, a toned-down version of the Smith amendment was agreed upon.[19] The secretary was sent off to have the statement typed. Meanwhile the board turned to a recommendation from the Berkeley campus extending the appointment of a visiting professor of mathematics for one additional quarter. The visitor was found to be objectionable by several Regents because of his close association with a Berkeley faculty member viewed by them as a radical. Another wrangle developed. After considerable debate on whether the Regents should really engage in this kind of political screening, the president's motion to extend the visiting appointment for an additional quarter was approved in a hairline decision, 12 to 11. It had been quite a day!

By now the new version of the statement on Marcuse was typed and circulated to the Regents around the table. Several called over asking whether I found it acceptable. Regent Elinor Heller urged her colleagues to add a sentence of specific approval of the San Diego chancellor. I told them it was unnecessary. Whatever the Regents felt about the San Diego chancellor could be expressed to him privately. The statement was intended to serve other purposes. It was not what I would have written, but I could live with it. This last produced a roar of laughter around the table. Even the Governor was smiling.

The meeting ended on that note. Nearly all the Reagan Regents, Bill Smith included, came over to shake my hand and apologize for the rough treatment they had given me. Smith complimented me on the way I had cooled down the bitter debate. Kathryn Hearst embraced me in tears. These were the private expressions I had suggested, and they said clearly that there were no problems between the board and me. After a long and rancorous struggle, I had emerged from the Marcuse appointment crisis alive and well.

Later on, when I had a chance to relax and think about what had happened, it was evident that my refusal to sign the appointment papers was a near-fatal error of judgment. It did not accomplish my objective of softening the Regents' attitude toward the campus and preventing reprisals. Instead, it implicated the Regents in a decision most of them wanted nothing to do with. When I announced that I wanted to discuss the appointment with the Regents before signing it, I apparently led the Governor and at least one of his supporters on the board to conclude that I was ceding the decision to them. Governor Reagan made it quite clear in the executive session that he felt deceived. Of course, it is difficult to conjecture what the Governor himself was up to. His news conference earlier in the week suggested he was up to something, but when he learned about the letters of intent, he evidently abandoned it.

The next morning, stunned readers of *The San Diego Union* were told that the Regents had backed Chancellor McGill's decision on Marcuse, which was certainly not the case. The Governor was forced to explain to reporters that he had not joined in approving the chancellor's action. He had learned too late that the Regents' hands were tied by Chancellor McGill's letters to Marcuse. A strong implication was left that the chancellor was a pretty devious fellow. Had the papers been signed in advance, as they might have been, none of this commotion would have developed.

On the other hand, the Regents' confusion over whether I had or had not made the appointment certainly did me no harm with UCSD faculty and students. Doubters on campus admitted that the chancellor had been right all along in the way he proposed to handle the Regents. Several people confessed that their unwillingness to trust me had damn near wrecked the strategy. They asked forgiveness for the harsh, last-minute pressures to sign. Forgiveness was easy. I hoped they would not change their minds when they learned what really happened at the board meeting.

Before my departure for Berkeley, I had arranged for a second meeting with the faculty group that had pressured me into withdrawing and rewriting the letter of intent to Marcuse. The purpose of the second meeting was to review the Marcuse decision and hear my report on the Regents meeting. I met with the faculty on Saturday morning in the chancellor's conference room at UCSD.

When I walked in just after 10 AM, to my amazement everyone rose and applauded. For that one brief moment, and on the shakiest of grounds, I was permitted to taste the pleasure that comes with being a hero on campus. George Murphy was standing beside my empty chair joining in the applause as the group waited for me to take my seat. He leaned over smiling and whispered in my ear:

"When this is over, boss, I have to see you."

Later, in the chancellor's office, he explained that on the previous day, Friday, during the late morning, a group of fifteen UCSD students, joined by one faculty member, had physically prevented a Marine Corps recruiter from entering the campus placement office, where he was scheduled to conduct interviews with other UCSD students. The standoff continued for several hours before Murphy wrote the attempt off and asked the recruiter, a Marine captain, to reschedule his appointments for another day.

The officer proved to be very cool. Murphy managed the door-blocking episode so that we could prove it had been a violation of campus rules. It was photographed in detail, and nearly all participants were identified. The incident was the crudest kind of provocation, and it had happened at virtually the same hour I was securing Marcuse's right to teach despite his advocacy of violent confrontations.

It was a remarkable irony, but not the final one. Recently, Walter Munk and I were reminiscing about those wild times at UCSD. He confided that when he returned from Berkeley on that Friday evening, his first thought was to tell Marcuse the good news. Munk drove over to Marcuse's home in La Jolla and rang the doorbell. Marcuse was not in, but Inge Marcuse took the message at the front door. She kept Walter on the doorstep for fifteen minutes, lecturing him about our failure to defend Marcuse or to protect him from the right-wingers who were attempting to drive him out of the university.

Herbert Marcuse in Revelle Plaza, UCSD.
(Courtesy of Rev. John Huber)

Marcuse declaring himself "on strike" at
first People's Park convocation, April 1969.
Immediately behind him and partly hidden is
Linus Pauling. On the extreme left is Walter
Munk. I was seated in the balcony at the
upper right. (Courtesy of Rev.
John Huber)

Angela Davis addressing a rally in Revelle Plaza, October 1970. (Courtesy of Rev. John Huber)

*Large crowd at UCSD awaiting the arrival
of Governor Reagan, November 22, 1968.
The Regents were meeting in the gym at left.
This was the meeting at which the Regents
denied credit for Cleaver's course.* (Courtesy
of Rev. John Huber)

Dean Ernest Mort reading the Chancellor's message to Second People's Park convocation. I was urged by my staff not to appear because SDS would use my presence as an excuse to seize the microphone. (Courtesy of Rev. John Huber)

An argument with students in Revelle Plaza. Barry Shapiro, a graduate student, is on my right. The time is probably May 1969 after the collapse of the student strike over People's Park. (Courtesy of Rev. John Huber)

George Murphy (left) with 1969 UCSD student body president, Jeff Benjamin (glasses), in Revelle Plaza following the collapse of the student strike over People's Park, May 1969. (Courtesy of Rev. John Huber)

The black smudge marks the spot in Revelle Plaza where a UCSD junior set himself afire in an antiwar protest, May 1970. He did not survive. (Courtesy of Rev. John Huber)

CHAPTER 6

Lumumba–Zapata College

A mile east of the La Jolla cliffs towering over Black's Beach, UCSD's northwest quadrant forms a tree-filled right angle pointing to the spectacular fairways and cliff-edge greens of Torrey Pines golf course. The Pacific Ocean sparkles in the distance. Here the land rises gently toward the north before plunging down rugged coastal ravines to meet the sea at the edge of Del Mar. Atop a prominent knoll crowning this far corner of the campus, the new buildings of Third College lie amid ancient eucalyptus and newly planted pine trees.

At first glance the sharp angles and long linear contours of the college seem vaguely suggestive of ranch structures in Mexico or the Southwest. Closer examination reveals that this was what the architect intended. The walls are cream-colored stucco decorated in dark-stained wood. At a distance they could be mistaken for adobe.

The effect is striking. It makes the viewer smile when he discovers an outsized parking lot and a pair of ultra-modern, green-screened tennis courts at the far north end of the college. All of it is pure California illusion, deceiving even the knowledgeable eye into believing for a moment that the contemporary academic buildings and residence halls of

Third College might be part of an old-world hacienda somewhere south of the border.

The architect's mandate was to produce designs in "Mexican and African style, with landscaping of the same nature." This directive was only one of many pronouncements, deeply symbolic and impossible of fulfillment, decreed by the political marriage of blacks and Chicanos responsible for the blueprint of "Lumumba-Zapata College" in March 1969. Political marriages are notoriously shaky, and this one seemed almost beyond consummation. Yet somehow it has managed to survive through the years, still shaky but much less volatile and far more confident than when it started out.

The architect, by enhancing the Mexican flavor of his designs while keeping the buildings low and natural-looking in their western setting, has managed to improve on the preformed concrete of Third College's neighbor to the south, John Muir College, with its odd collection of box-like structures. Third College today conveys a sense of order that seems remarkably permanent. The aura of tranquility is astonishing when I think back on the tumultuous demonstrations, community upheaval, and hostile criticism accompanying the birth of the college in the spring of 1969.

Evans and Novak are syndicated Washington columnists who serve as occasional spokesmen for the conservative right in the nation's capital. These distant critics viewed the early development of Third College with undisguised horror. Their column of September 28, 1970, sounded the alarm:

> By giving black and brown students veto power over faculty appointments in their new Third College at San Diego, McGill not only subverted academic standards but beckoned radical students nationwide to what until recently had been a quiet campus.

The charges were untrue, but the state of alarm was evident. When I read the column, I wondered whether Evans and Novak had ever heard of Herbert Marcuse or Angela Davis.

Although sentiment at UCSD was vastly more sympathetic to Third College than Evans and Novak suggested, and was in fact heavily weighted in favor of the "Lumumba-Zapata" concept, a small group of conservative faculty did its utmost to block final approval of the college by the Regents. A professor of sociology wrote to me on August 21, 1970:

There have been cases in which the college has insisted absolutely . . . that tenured faculty members . . . be either black or brown. I fear this may constitute violations of the 1964 Civil Rights Acts.

Such apprehensions were widespread in the academic world prior to our discovery of the realities of federally mandated and court-ordered affirmative action on behalf of minorities and women. Ironically, the San Diego campus benefited greatly from the racial sensitivities that occasioned this early anxiety. Third College soon became well known as an experiment in minority education. It was carefully scrutinized for application elsewhere, and widely applauded. The college evoked grudging approval of UCSD from tough-minded federal regulators who were attacking colleges and universities for their failure to act vigorously in removing discrimination.

But in the beginning of 1969 fear was widespread in California. We heard persistent, wild charges of reverse discrimination and greatly lowered standards.[1] In point of fact, compared with the shattered standards and ineffectual remediation countenanced by the City University of New York as it attempted to educate large numbers of minority students, UCSD's Third College proved to be a landmark success. Under great political pressure, CUNY simply opened its doors with little advance planning. The intense struggle over Lumumba-Zapata College, on the other hand, led to careful study that attempted to integrate its unconventional, minority-oriented program with the rest of the campus. In any event, when Third College moved into its permanent buildings in 1976, Washington rejoiced while suspicion continued unabated in California.

This initial furor was understandable. Third College had originally been planned with scholarly precision by an eminent provisional faculty, joined in 1967 by an academically gifted and energetic provost. It was to be a traditional undergraduate college centering on historical study. The curriculum of the college would be leavened by work on contemporary social issues and would shun all forms of indoctrination. Virtually overnight this careful academic plan was nearly abandoned. The embryo college became the focus of increasingly bitter controversy as angry black and brown students at UCSD demanded that the college "be devoted to relevant education for minority youth and to the study of contemporary social problems of all people. . . . This college must radically depart from the usual role as the ideological backbone of the social system, and must instead subject every part of the system to ruthless criticism."[2]

On March 14, 1969, when that rude bombshell was hurled at us by militant minority students and their campus sympathizers, both Berkeley and San Francisco State were being ripped apart by violent clashes between police and minority student radicals who called themselves the "Third World Liberation Front." Conflict began in March 1968 at San Francisco State and expanded in January 1969 to Berkeley.3 The TWLF had little difficulty recruiting a few white radicals to its cause. New Left ideologues were only too willing to lend assistance to what they viewed as the beginning of a black revolution in the U.S.

Fighting between the TWLF and the police eventually aroused the sympathies of much larger numbers of incurably romantic countercultural students at San Francisco State and Berkeley. These students were crusading for peace and love, and were content to let the radicals spell out the means by which their elusive goals might be achieved. But radical prescriptions were anything but peaceful and loving; the New Left had its sights on far more grandiose achievements.

What better formula for advancing the day when revolution might sweep across America than a series of revolutionary colleges honoring and teaching the neo-Marxist doctrines of such Third World luminaries as Frantz Fanon, Ché Guevara, and Chairman Mao? And what better way to achieve such a "college" than by confronting Regents and university administrators with the implacable demands of the people themselves?

During the first two weeks of March 1969, UCSD continued to buzz with the climactic moments of the struggle over reappointing Herbert Marcuse, and also with the unexpected blockade of a Marine Corps officer, Captain David Stout, on the steps of UCSD's placement office. There was a special irony in the case of the Marine recruiter because the placement office happened to be in the Camp Matthews area of the campus. Originally Camp Mathews was a Marine rifle-training center that the federal government turned over to the Regents of the University of California in 1964. The thought of a Marine Corps officer forcibly refused access to a former barracks building in Camp Matthews by a group of bearded radical students overtly sympathetic to the North Vietnamese was enough to bring much of San Diego to the brink of apoplexy.4

Charges of campus rule violations were speedily filed against eight of the miscreants. They had been photographed by George Murphy's staff in the act of refusing Murphy's instructions to move away from the placement office steps. I myself wrote to the faculty member involved asking for an explanation of his conduct. At the request of the accused students, a hearing was scheduled before the Committee on Student Conduct. The latter was a joint faculty-student committee whose duty was to review charges of student misconduct, listen to evidence, and present findings to the chancellor.

These wheels of campus justice were turning quite efficiently by our standards. A reluctant faculty can sometimes immobilize administrative discipline, especially in cases that the faculty Left considers unjust. It is done by insisting that the disciplinary procedures conform to unreal standards of perfection. In this case many faculty members were unhappy when we insisted on going ahead with discipline, but they did not attempt to interfere. Later on, when I needed faculty support in denouncing the use of force by campus zealots who claimed to be motivated by high moral principle, the faculty backed me. I certainly could not complain justifiably about the positions the faculty had taken; it was just that they had to be pushed, and I was becoming more volatile and unyielding than ever before. My earlier fears of confrontation had given way to undisguised outrage.

All of these nuances made no impact at all on the people of San Diego. As prompt and effective as we considered our disciplinary procedures to be, they were far too slow to suit patriotic and political groups in the community around us. They were demanding instant expulsion of the student blockaders and immediate dismissal of the faculty member.[5] Although he was a tenured professor, the community considered that constraint relatively unimportant in relation to the sacrilege they were sure he had committed. I was told that professors must never, never do such things; when they do, they automatically disqualify themselves as teachers. It was an understandable moral judgment, though not likely to impress faculty representatives.

There followed two long months of intense criticism and unremitting pressure as we sought to steer a sensible course between angry outside critics and a visibly reluctant faculty.[6] The faculty was hopeful that the entire incident might blow over. Most of them were concerned about the deep revulsion students were displaying over the war in Vietnam. They did not want to anger students by seeming to side with the military. Moreover, now that the Marcuse case was successfully resolved, it was possible to start all over again in a new ambience of mutual respect. Faculty members simply did not consider the Marine recruiter incident important enough to pursue if it would wreck prospects for better relations between students and the administration.

I disagreed. A provocation like that could not be brushed aside so easily. I was at least as close to UCSD undergraduates as the faculty was, and although student hostility to the war was real enough, it did not appear to me to extend to individuals who happened to wear military uniforms. Most students felt no animus at all toward Captain Stout or the Marine Corps.

This protest had not come out of the heart of the student body. It was the work of virtually the same cast of characters that had tried to shut down the campus in November over Eldridge Cleaver and Social Analysis 139X. They were a small clique of SDS students and UCSD faculty searching for opportunities to radicalize the campus. I found it infuriating that they chose to create this incident on the day, and very nearly at the same hour, that I was receiving bitter criticism from Governor Reagan and his supporters on the Board of Regents for defending Marcuse's right to teach in an atmosphere free of political harassment.

One might have expected more understanding from these young radicals if indeed they were the idealists they portrayed themselves to be. It would have required only a temporary concession on one particular day; but no concessions were made at all, and in the final analysis that was why the incident could not be smoothed over.

These people were not idealists. They were zealots. If they felt any emotion beyond commitment to their cause, it was probably contempt for administrators who gave them nothing to fear. I had shaken them in November by besting some of them in public debate, but they saw a unique opportunity in the appearance of a Marine Corps officer on campus and moved without hesitation. They were not fearful of the consequences at all; and they were certainly not sufficiently impressed by my defense of Marcuse to consider holding off.

The realization that this UCSD radical group was at war with me was disturbing. After eight months, the conclusion was inescapable. It was festering inside, poisoning my outlook.[7] I felt a growing irritation with old friends on the faculty because they seemed unable to cope with radical activity. They were unwilling to discipline even a small group of extremists who went out of their way to provoke trouble and who then justified their actions with moral arguments that reeked of hypocrisy. It was obviously phony. Everyone on campus understood what this group was up to. They were trying to force an administrative error that would radicalize us. The faculty knew it, the students knew it, and I knew it. But the faculty would not or could not bring themselves to stop it.

Henry Kissinger, in his book *White House Years*, relates an incident that happened in the spring of 1970. Some of his former colleagues on the Harvard faculty, many of them old friends, came down to the White House not to consult with him or even to argue with him, but to confront him over the administration's decision to invade Cambodia.[8] It was apparently a dismal session, and Kissinger was quite turned off by what he took as sanctimonious arguments advanced by his former faculty colleagues. He tells us that, at the conclusion of the meeting, he realized his transition from the academic world "to the world of affairs" was complete.

Something like that was happening to me, although not so sharply as Kissinger depicts it. Slowly, my faculty roots were being torn up. There were too many points on which my old friends and I disagreed. The people I had to deal with were a real problem. Moreover, I no longer had the same tolerant, gentle manner. I was growing more combative, less willing to accommodate to the passions of politically motivated radicals. An invisible barrier was arising between my former colleagues and me.

Murphy warned that the very intensity of these feelings, even though shared only with him and one or two others, might eventually damage my effectiveness as an administrator. He understood how I felt, he told me. In many ways he was experiencing the same frustrations. "But, boss, you can't let it show. You must be as cold as ice when you go up against SDS and their supporters on the faculty. Nothing will suit them better than to portray you as an oppressor and those blockaders as martyrs. They will succeed in making the argument convincing because you are pushing too hard to make an example of the accused students."

He was perfectly right. Not long after Murphy's warning, SDS flooded the campus with a leaflet entitled, "The Administration versus the People." The key paragraph declaimed:

Dean Murphy and the rest of the administration are not and cannot be neutral arbiters in this environment. They serve basically the same function on this campus as the U.S. military serves around the world—protecting the interests of the U.S. decision-making class, and using very real punitive measures when these interests are threatened. To say that they are enforcing the presence of military recruiters on campus because of "free speech," or "academic freedom," or "rationality" is bullshit! UCSD and its administrators, like the Marine Corps, embody the political biases of American society; we oppose them. Where do you stand?

I quieted down. We went ahead with the disciplinary hearings calmly and carefully. Most of the campus proved hostile to the methods used by the blockaders. Late in March, when I appeared before the faculty senate with a reasoned defense of our policy of open recruiting and called on them to denounce "coercive force in attempts to frustrate the honest effort of this administration to maintain open use of our placement office," the faculty backed me. Later in the spring UCSD students voted overwhelmingly in support of continued access to the placement office for any legitimate potential employer, including the military.

The SDS effort to make martyrs of the blockaders failed because we did not overplay our hand, and our restraint was due chiefly to George Murphy's shrewd guidance.

The eight were disciplined quietly in late May. None was expelled. A note was added to their transcripts stating that they had been placed on disciplinary probation for a year.[9] A letter of censure signed by me was placed in the personnel file of the faculty member. To some critics these actions were little more than a slap on the wrist, but they were calculated to deter protestors from using coercive force in the future. No one would want to risk failure to graduate because of a disciplinary problem.[10]

By mid-May the Marine recruiter incident was closed except for Captain Stout's ceremonial return to campus to complete his interviews. When that day arrived on May 23, it found UCSD in the midst of a major student strike over shootings and injuries that had occurred a week earlier in the street fighting at People's Park in Berkeley. Far greater danger was posed by Captain Stout's return than had ever developed in the original blocking incident on February 21. Faculty reminded me that they had sought to avoid all this by trying to smooth over the incident. I was unyielding.

As the year moved swiftly toward its unexpectedly dramatic climax in late May, everything seemed to unravel at once. Protests and demonstrations directed at the Marine recruiter, military research on campus, Lumumba-Zapata College, and the fighting at People's Park came one after another in waves that threatened several times to engulf us. Faculty and students managed to work themselves into an emotional state bordering on hysteria over the savage street fighting triggered by the Berkeley administration's ill-fated attempt to erect a chain-link fence around People's Park. The National Guard was called out, and shortly afterward a helicopter sprayed clouds of tear gas over much of the Berkeley campus, injuring both innocent and guilty alike in what must surely rank as a classic example of misconceived riot control.

Every campus of the University of California erupted following these incredible events in mid-May. The struggles that ensued drew upon all the strength we possessed as we sought to prevent the same kind of debacle at La Jolla. A thousand angry students marched back and forth across campus for three days, smashing windows, breaking up classes, and trying to break into my office. Niceties were cast aside. This was not the civilized academy to which we had devoted our lives. Nor was it something controlled by debating with angry students. It was a scene out of a nightmare and we had to contain it.

The people and the problems I was forced to confront at UCSD, in the community, and in the state administration were beginning to annoy me, and it showed. Friends noticed the change. They commented that I ought not to take things so personally. How could any of them understand? They did not sit where I sat. In the spring of 1969 the academic landscape was littered with the battered reputations of college presidents unable to contend with their enemies in the New Left or forced to call the police in fruitless attempts to restore order. Claims that none of it was intended personally, or that violent acts against the campus were part of a high-principled attack on society, seemed to me to be dishonest. It did not diminish the hurt meted out to those decent administrators or the harm done to their universities.

Faculty called it the "radicalization game." They were sympathetic with the aims of the protestors, especially with young people protesting the Vietnam war, but they recoiled from any thought of coercion or physical violence. So the faculty moved out of the line of fire and became spectators as the chancellor attempted to bluff, threaten, and cajole angry students into nonviolent expressions of discontent. Most faculty preferred to remain uninvolved until imminent disaster forced them to act.[11]

When the chancellor did well, they cheered him. When he made grave errors, they upbraided him. If things became really bad, the faculty would decide that they had been mistaken in their earlier high opinion of the chancellor's leadership, and, however reluctantly, would attempt to have him removed. I vowed that nothing like that was ever going to happen to me.

Under pressures such as these hardening was unavoidable. But it did not become a problem until May 1969. Before that there were still traces of naive innocence. I suppose it explains why I failed to react with suspicion when a group of black students called on me late one afternoon shortly after the February Regents meeting, inviting me to attend a meeting between minority students and the provost of Third College. The meeting was to deal with the students' views on the academic program and the quality of student life at UCSD's Third College.

In the spring of 1969 Third College did not exist; it was still a blueprint. The faculty expected to submit its academic plan to the Regents some time in the autumn or winter of 1970. The provost, Armin Rappaport, a distinguished historian brought down from Berkeley, had been guiding the preliminary planning of the college since his appointment in 1967.

He formed an advisory committee of minority students to make recommendations on the problems that black and Chicano students would encounter in the courses and residence halls of Third College when it came into operation.

Academics bring a spirit of basic decency to questions of prejudice. Rappaport wanted to create a warm atmosphere attractive to young people of all races and backgrounds. He was deeply concerned about urban social problems. He hoped that the new college would get its hands dirty with these problems and not seek refuge in total concentration on academic coursework remote from the central dilemmas of our time. So Rappaport asked minority students already enrolled at UCSD what he might do to create a more attractive and satisfying environment for them.

He was thinking particularly of dormitory and social life, and the growing tendency among minority students to demand isolation from whites. How could such racial exclusion be tolerated, even in an academic community acutely sensitive to the racial consciousness of minorities, without risking permanent divisions among students and mutually hostile racial groups? If black or Chicano students felt themselves culturally alienated or inadequately prepared for the University of California, and sought isolation to avoid embarrassment, what kind of remediation should the college undertake without stigmatizing those receiving help? These were the questions on which Provost Rappaport was seeking advice as he designed Third College.

The minority students promised to bring in their recommendations by mid-March. The provost, Dean of Students George Murphy, and Professor Dan L. Lindsley would be there to listen. Now I was invited, too.

Dan Lindsley was an eminent UCSD biologist and provisional member of Third College's faculty. Shortly after Martin Luther King's murder on April 4, 1968, Lindsley proposed that the college be named for Dr. King and that it be dedicated to the promotion of equal educational opportunity and improvement of communication between blacks and whites. The proposal was approved "in principle" by the provisional faculty of Third College, but not much was done subsequently. Like most good ideas offered in the aftermath of sudden tragedy it became bogged down in leisurely implementation. By March 1969 no concrete progress toward Lindsley's idealistic objectives had been made. The name "Martin Luther King College" was never officially approved by the campus or submitted to the Regents.

The appointed day for the students' presentation arrived on March 14. They had scheduled it for five in the afternoon, but my last appointment of the day did not conclude until a few minutes after five. Concerned that I was running late, I locked up the office and hurried over to the glass-walled chancellor's conference room a few doors away. Although I was nearly ten minutes behind schedule, none of the students had arrived. The room was virtually empty.

The chancellor's conference room is small in comparison with a theater or a large lecture hall, but in 1969 it was one of the largest rooms on campus, holding two hundred or more when filled to capacity. It echoed with the hushed small talk of the half dozen or so faculty and administrators waiting for the students.

Several members of the faculty were lounging in chairs at the back of the room. Rappaport had seated himself at the head of the polished conference table and was carrying on an animated discussion with Lindsley. Murphy was off to one side staring quizzically out the floor-to-ceiling windows on the north side of the room. He nodded and smiled wanly as I entered. Evidently he would have preferred to be sipping a good dry martini at 5:10 in the afternoon. I sat down next to the provost, listening idly to his ebullient conversation and wondering where on earth the students might be. Fifteen minutes passed with no sign.

All at once they appeared, sixty of them, blacks and Chicanos filing silently and grim-faced into the room. As I swept my eyes from face to face, looking for signs of meaning in this dramatic entrance, Angela Davis took a seat opposite me at the far end of the table. Her hands were folded on a sheaf of typewritten pages, and she stared calmly down the length of the table returning my curious gaze. Whatever else this might be, it was certainly not going to be a discussion of the quality of student life.

All conversation at the head of the table ceased abruptly as the large group of ominously silent students began filing in. They arranged themselves around the long table and in the empty chairs lining the walls of the room. As the bustle of movement died down, it was succeeded by a long, theatrical silence. No sound came from the students. They sat stiffly erect and stony-faced, staring coldly at the tiny administrative group at the head of the table.

The long pause had its effect. I began to feel twinges of anxiety. Miss Davis extracted a pair of tiny gold-rimmed reading glasses from a case on the table in front of her, and without further preliminaries commenced reading from the typed document. Her voice, which I had not heard before, had an unpleasant reedy quality, and dripped with hatred.

"Contradictions," she said, "which sustained America in the past are now threatening to annihilate the entire social edifice. Black slave labor laid the basis of the American economy. Mexican-Americans in the Southwest and black people in the industrial cities and the agrarian South continue to perform the dirty but necessary tasks of building a society of abundance, while systematically being denied the benefits of that society. Therefore, we must reject the entire oppressive structure of America. Racism runs rampant in the educational system while America, in a pseudo-humanitarian stance proudly proclaims that it is the key to equal opportunity for all. This is the hypocrisy our generation must now destroy."[12]

It was the first paragraph of what later became known in the University of California as the "Lumumba-Zapata" demands. Angela Davis read on calmly, and I found myself fascinated by the contrast between the quiet, dignified demeanor of the students and the violence of the rhetoric in the document they were presenting. It was truly a radical proposal, and not just in the political meaning of the term. The entire Third College plan that the provost and provisional faculty had been laboring over during the past two years was to be jettisoned. The curriculum based on historical study would be replaced by courses heavy with Marxist doctrine and steeped in the ideology of Third World revolutionaries. The governance of the college would be in the hands of a board of directors controlled by students.

The college would be named "Lumumba-Zapata" in honor of two Third World heroes: Patrice Lumumba, an African nationalist murdered by agents of Congolese President Kasavubu in Katanga Province in 1961; and Emiliano Zapata, a Mexican revolutionary who died in 1919, shot by an emissary of a government professing to talk peace.

The architecture and landscaping of Lumumba-Zapata college would be in "Mexican and African style," whatever in the world that might mean.

"In order to compensate for past and present injustice," Miss Davis went on, "and to serve those most affected by white racism and economic exploitation, Lumumba-Zapata College must have an enrollment of 35% Blacks and 35% Mexican Americans. Students must be selected on the basis of their potential by an admissions committee controlled by minority students. The University of California admissions requirements must not be used as an instrument for excluding minority students from or limiting their numbers in Lumumba-Zapata College."

As if these demands regarding organization and the admissions policies of Lumumba-Zapata College were not controversial enough, the proposed curriculum was designed to turn my hair several shades whiter when I thought of the reaction we could expect from Governor Reagan and his conservative Regents.

There was to be a course sequence in revolutions.

"Minorities have been excluded from government decision-making and must now develop an original system of self-government. . . . Reading material in this area will include authors such as Lenin, Nkrumah, Marx, Malcom X, Fanon, Padmore, Ché Guevara, and Mariano Azuela."

The students of Lumumba-Zapata College would study economics in order to understand "the economic exploitation of minority peoples in the United States. . . . [as well as] . . . the historical development of capitalism in the western world, including the crucial roles played by colonialism, imperialism, slavery, and genocide."

Other proposed course areas were only a bit less ideological: urban and rural development, health sciences and public health, science and technology, communication, languages, cultural heritage. Some of the flavor of Lumumba-Zapata may be conveyed in the colorful language used to dismiss traditional science teaching. Courses in science at Lumumba-Zapata College would "obviously exclude the theoretical inanities taught at Revelle College as well as the military research conducted at the Scripps Institute."

Finally there was to be a sequence in "White Studies" emphasizing the "negative as well as positive elements of the history of Western civilization."

Angela Davis completed her presentation of the Lumumba-Zapata demands with the description of the course sequence in white studies. The room again fell silent, and only the sounds of stirring feet and squeaking chairs disturbed the eerie quiet.

I looked around at Armin Rappaport, the provost, searching for guidance on how we ought to respond to this thunderclap. For all I knew it might have been the way all planning sessions of Third College were conducted. Rappaport's face was ravaged. He was doing his best to hold back tears brimming around his eyes. Dan Lindsley stared glumly at the floor, while Murphy seemed intent on counting the holes in the acoustical tiles on the ceiling above my head.

Someone had to say something. "What do you wish to do?" I asked. "This paper comes as a complete surprise to me. Do you want me to respond to it?"

"No. We do not want to discuss anything with you now. We will meet with you again on March 26, and we expect you to come prepared to accept these demands."

It was one of the students speaking halfway down the long table. The remark was not exactly impolite, but it was delivered with a snarling contempt that bordered on malevolence.

"Do you have a copy of the paper? I will need to study it."

"A copy will be delivered to your office tomorrow morning."

"Is that all, then?"

"That's all!"

They rose to leave, and as they did, Armin Rappaport cried out, "I have been betrayed!" The students paused, looked at him icily without a trace of compassion, and departed in a body.

As soon as they had gone, I leaned over the provost, who was slumped in his chair. "Armin, did you have any idea this was coming?"

"None. None. I trusted them. They could not have done this alone. They must have had help."

"Well, there is not much we can do about it this evening. Let's pack up and go home."

The next morning, Murphy was in my office full of apologies. He felt bad because he had given me no advance warning, no time to prepare. The problem was that his staff had not warned him, either. Minority students had managed to formulate the Lumumba-Zapata demands and to work out their future strategy without creating so much as a ripple on the surface of the campus. The brusque announcement of a second meeting on March 26 was clear evidence that there was a strategy. But no word of these complex preparations had leaked out. The students and whoever else was involved were certainly well disciplined.

A copy of the Lumumba-Zapata demands was delivered to my office early in the morning. As Murphy leafed through it, I asked him whether Angela Davis might have written the document. The Marxist rhetoric was authentic, and none of the rest of the students seemed to have either the background or the intellectual power to produce a paper of such high quality.

"She may have written it, boss. I just don't know. Armin believes it was done by the faculty advisers to BSC (Black Students Council) and MAYA (Mexican-American Youth Association).[13] The question of authorship is less important than what we do about it."

"For God's sake, George, can you imagine what would happen to us if we were bamboozled into accepting a student-run college with no admissions requirements, and teaching, if that is the word, capitalism as the equivalent of slavery and genocide? I am going to fight it; that's what I am going to do. The planning of Third College is too far advanced to toss it all aside for this damned thing."

Murphy grinned as he saw the show of temper he was paid to keep under control. He urged me to calm myself while he discussed the demands with Armin Rappaport and the faculty of Third College. Perhaps a way might be found to incorporate some of the key ideas into the college program. I told him he was welcome to try. It would take a genius to accomplish any rapprochement between Third College's embryo academic plan and the Lumumba-Zapata demands, but then Murphy was no amateur.

I asked Murphy where he thought this problem might go if we were forced to fight it out with Angela Davis and the minority students along the lines I indicated. He reminded me of the bitter clashes between the police and minority-student strikers at San Francisco State and Berkeley. A minority-student strike at UCSD was a distinct possibility. If that happened, the students would almost certainly reach out for assistance from SDS sympathizers on campus and from militant factions in Los Angeles and downtown San Diego. Both the Black Panthers and the Brown Berets were active downtown.[14]

The prospect of tough street people from Los Angeles and San Diego appearing at UCSD to beef up the demands of our minority students was real enough and frightening. That was the direction the struggles with radical minorities had taken at San Francisco State, Berkeley, and in a number of other places. I made a mental note to call Walter Hahn, San Diego's city manager, to brief him on our new problem. It might soon be his problem, too!

Murphy went off to review the Lumumba-Zapata demands with the provost and members of the faculty of Third College while I set to work drafting our reply. The word was now all over campus about the dignified but resolute confrontation that had taken place on the previous evening in the chancellor's conference room. More indications of a Lumumba-Zapata strategy appeared when booklets containing the full text of the demands began circulating on campus. The student newspapers and various militant groups immediately fell into line behind Lumumba-Zapata, just as Murphy had predicted. It was remarkable that such an elaborate and well-oiled machine could have been kept out of sight until the Lumumba-Zapata group was ready to use it against us.

My administrative staff was apprehensive about all this activity. They asked for a meeting to review our strategy before anything else happened that might further limit our options. We held several long meetings during the next ten days. It developed that what was worrying the staff, and members of the faculty committees as well, was precisely what had concerned Murphy: the spectre of racial conflict on the campus in La Jolla.

We went over the draft of my reply to the demands. The staff thought it was too militant in places, but I insisted on the text because I knew that one day all this would get into the newspapers. The concessionary language we typically used with sensitive minority students would look dreadful in response to the rhetoric of Lumumba-Zapata. Besides, if we were bargaining with them, we might just as well begin from a position as far removed from Lumumba-Zapata as we could reasonably expect to hold.

Accordingly, my reply was put together with considerable advice from the central administration, the college provosts, and the faculty committees. There was, however, one significant omission. I did not consult Armin Rappaport in preparing the draft.

It isn't that he would have disagreed with it. Perhaps the tone was harsher in some places than he might have wished, but Armin would have understood why hard words were necessary. The problem was that he was stunned and virtually desolate because of the unexpected confrontation. Armin believed he had been tricked by the students and their faculty advisers, and he was not wrong about that. He was an honorable man who expected people with grievances to bring them to him, so that he might have a chance to correct things without the embarrassment of a public dispute. Instead, the students had only pretended to be acting on his requests for advice about curriculum and quality-of-life issues. All the while they were preparing a political attack on Third College.

Their document was filled with offensive rhetoric and ideological hokum. The demand for student control of administration and faculty appointments was, and was intended to be, an emasculation of the provost. It must have been demoralizing for Armin to have to sit there and listen to it.

Today, as we look back on the problems of the Sixties, it is usually with the assumption that the inaction of remote, unresponsive university bureaucrats drove students to outbursts of fury and pent-up frustration. As attractive as this explanation may be to contemporary writers, it is far less applicable than its appeal to liberal minds would suggest. After all, most people in the academic life are unguarded idealists. They search openly for a better world than the one they see in corporate life and the halls of government. Armin Rappaport was such an idealist. He was anything but unresponsive. He just could not believe that students would deal with him underhandedly.

In the case of the Lumumba-Zapata demands, the grievances of UCSD's minority students, although directed primarily against society, were vented on a man who, during a time of severe upheaval, was too decent and too sensitive for his own good. The confrontation over Third College was not forced on students by an insensitive, rough-tough administration; it was initiated by students in such a way as to maximize their political opportunities, and Provost Rappaport just happened to be in the way.

Rappaport was 53 years old in 1969. He was a typical professor from an earlier, more golden era: bright, articulate, a conservative, thoughtful man with a taste for good living. There was nothing about him suggesting either hardness or cynicism. On the contrary, he was possessed of an almost boundless faith that seems a bit naive by today's standards. But he was not naive, only sincere and therefore vulnerable.

A day or two after I set about drafting my reply to the students, I tried to call Rappaport. I was told that he had taken the meeting of March 14 very hard and had gone off to Berkeley for a few days to calm down. I should have made a determined effort to locate him and to bring him back as the focal point of our responses to the students. Instead, I stepped into the crisis myself and, in so doing, inadvertently made the chancellor the key respondent to the Lumumba-Zapata demands.

It was amateurish, the first of several major errors I was to make in handling this crisis. Perhaps it would not have made much difference in the outcome, but conducting our negotiations on the future directions of Third College via its provost would have been much sounder administration.

Years later it dawned on me that militant tactics aimed at involving the chancellor were designed to undercut the authority of second-echelon administrators. I then began demanding strict adherence to administrative channels in airing student or community grievances at Columbia. All sorts of people, including faculty and local politicians, warned me that any restriction on access to the president was overly bureaucratic and potentially confrontational. Didn't I understand, they pointed out, that such rigid attitudes were responsible for creating student unrest in the 1960s? These criticisms were not completely wrong, but they were not exactly right, either. There has to be some acceptable middle ground between inaccessibility and administrative chaos. The maintenance of well-understood channels of communication into the president's office offers one of the best ways in which the integrity of an administrative organization can be preserved against erosion from militant action. When the credibility of a dean is undercut, however well-intentioned the action may be, by a president or a chancellor desiring to be personally responsive to student grievances, no militant group will ever respect that dean's authority again. It is an iron law of militant behavior.

But in March 1969 I did not know much about such things. Problems involving militant confrontation were fairly new to universities then. No textbooks were available telling us what to do in a crisis.

There was always abundant advice from other administrators, and from faculty and politicians, but most of it was self-cancelling. Each source of advice tended to neutralize some other source. In the end I had to find my way empirically, following my intuition and learning not only from the mistakes of others but from my own mistakes as well.

In any event, when I stepped into the Lumumba-Zapata dispute and undermined the authority of the provost of Third College, I did it with confident self-assurance that I was taking precisely the right steps to rescue the planning of Third College from the mess in which I had found it after the confrontation with minority students.

On March 26 I delivered my reply to the Lumumba-Zapata demands to a group of approximately 30 minority students gathered in the chancellor's conference room. "I have now had an opportunity to study your proposals and accompanying demands relating to Third College at UCSD. You have told me that the demands are nonnegotiable, but I do not accept the view that your document is aimed at confrontation with the campus faculty and administration. I treat your demands as serious proposals expressing your concerns about Third College and UCSD, and I shall examine them in that way."

The reply turned to issues relating to name, architecture, admissions, financing, and governance. Most of the Lumumba-Zapata demands were rejected, although gently. For example:

"Your demands setting up admission quotas by race or ethnic background seem to be in violation of the provisions of the state constitution and the 1964 Civil Rights Act. Other possibilities should be studied."

"Your proposal for a board of directors and an elected provost is in violation of UCSD's academic plan as approved by the faculty and the Regents. It does, however, have some interesting possibilities and should be discussed."

". . . We cannot simply accede to demands that would put us in violation of the law. Nor can I overturn the complicated academic plans of the entire campus on my own initiative. I can and will support any step within reason and within the law to recruit qualified minority students and faculty in substantial numbers for Third College. . . ."

My analysis of the Lumumba-Zapata curriculum demands began with a blast at the proposed course sequence on revolutions.

"The faculty of UCSD and its chancellor do not propose to engage in the teaching of revolution or in proselytizing for an ideology that links capitalism with slavery and genocide. We are committed to approach all problems in a spirit which precludes indoctrination."

But a number of course proposals in the health sciences, problems of the inner city, fine arts, languages, and cultural heritage were found to be attractive. I suggested that we begin at once to devise independent majors in Afro-American Studies and Mexican-American Studies. These would be available to students in Revelle and Muir Colleges as well as Third College.

The centerpiece of my reply was a bold proposal for cooperation with the local community college districts. A joint program would be established that would offer easy access to UCSD for students at local community colleges where there were heavy minority enrollments.

"What I have in mind is that a junior college student could take courses at UCSD without prejudice to his status as a junior college student, and yet manage to accumulate credit at UCSD and transfer here when ready for our more rigorous program. We might even seek to build a junior college on this campus in order to make a demonstration program of national importance."

This idea for an "experimental college" became the fulcrum of the administration's position on the Lumumba-Zapata demands. It was our major counterproposal and was designed to protect the original academic plan of Third College.

I sought to develop the idea in more detail and in better language for my inauguration speech to the campus on April 11, but the proposal never got off the ground. It was insufficiently radical for some and much too radical for others. The minority students immediately dubbed the experimental college "Back of the Bus College," whereas *The San Diego Union* in an editorial on April 17 dismissed the idea as a "questionable plan" and asked, with unnecessary waspishness I thought, whether any one chancellor had the authority to undermine California's Master Plan for Higher Education.

The penultimate paragraph of my reply displays a brashly confident and somewhat amateurish chancellor.

> Our discussions with BSC and MAYA students concerning special programs for Third College have not been going well. I want to inject myself into these discussions to see that they do go well from this point on. I want to begin by discussing your proposal line by line, and by offering several of my own proposals.

It was, as I have already observed, just the wrong thing to do in replying to the Lumumba-Zapata demands. At our next meeting, the trap I set for myself in the "line by line" peroration was sprung by the minority students with considerable force and great embarrassment for me.

The reply concludes on a peculiarly militant note evidently aimed at the faculty and the general public.

> I want to place before you a demand of my own. It is that we talk and that we do so in the vocabulary and style appropriate to rational discourse and to a university.

Oddly enough, all this was rather well received by the thirty or so minority students who attended our second meeting. They seemed interested in the proposals. They would not, of course, agree to our rejection of their demands for a student-controlled college, but the dialogue made it clear, as Murphy suggested later, that the students seemed far more interested in the issue of student control than in the radical curriculum. That was progress.

Beyond signs of progress on the issues, there seemed to be great progress in tone. The exchanges in this second meeting were carried on in an atmosphere of friendliness and mutual respect that appeared to underline the students' acceptance of the rhetorical demand I laid down in my reply. The tense drama and threat evident in our first meeting was missing entirely. Everyone was quite relaxed. It was almost a pleasant session.

I left convinced that we had done the right thing. The students were turned around; the Lumumba-Zapata demands were effectively derailed, and Third College planning was back on track. Murphy was not so sure.

In my office late that afternoon, he expressed misgivings over Armin Rappaport's evident distance from these discussions. He had tried several times to talk to Rappaport, but Armin was not proving easy to find. Murphy urged me to come to an understanding with the provost of Third College very soon. I should try to aim at building future negotiations with the minority students around Rappaport.

Had we made real progress?

Time would tell, Murphy said. A third meeting with the students was set for April 2.

The third meeting was a disaster from beginning to end. Some thirty-five students, the core group of Lumumba-Zapata protestors, attended. Most of the provisional faculty of Third College came as well.

They wanted to see for themselves the signs of progress we reported from the second meeting.

Even before I sat down, the students were all over me. Someone said: "McGill, we are goddam tired of all this bullshitting around. We are tired of the word games you been playing with us. We are not going to put up with that no more. What we want is answers, and you don't give us no answers. You fuck around with community colleges. You talk about Afro-American Studies and Mexican-American Studies. That's not what we are talking about. We are talking about Lumumba-Zapata College, and you haven't said one goddam word about committing yourself to it!"

It was shattering. The second meeting might just as well never have happened. They wanted no part of it. We were back to square one: Lumumba-Zapata or nothing.

"How can I commit myself to something I don't understand?"

"What do you mean, you don't understand? It's perfectly clear. It's all in writing. You can read, can't you?"

"Let me explain. I am not going to commit myself to a student-run college or to courses in revolution, but I do not think that is what you really want. I am trying to find out what you really want."

"Man, you are playing with us. We are not going to put up with it."

This last was delivered in the middle of angry shouts from the rest of the group. Evidently I had said the wrong thing. Somewhere across the table another student started in on me.

"Look, McGill, we are going to read our demands one by one. You are going to say yes or no whether you agree with them."

"I can't give you a flat yes or no on most of the demands. The answer to most of them is maybe or it depends."

"You are really screwing around with us, man, and it's got to stop. We are going to start reading and, goddammit, we want answers."

With the experience I have now, probably that would have been the ideal place to get up out of my chair, say that I was fed up with the abuse, and walk out. My staff would then say to them that they should not treat the chancellor in that way if they expected to negotiate with him. There would be a long, angry argument. If they were really negotiating, the group would be back in a few days when tempers had cooled, and the atmosphere would be much improved.

I did not get up and leave. I was fearful—all of us were fearful—of a fatal rupture with these paranoid and increasingly militant students. The last thing we wanted was a minority-student strike. All of us sought to reach out to the blacks and Chicanos in our student body. We did not want to fight with them. Added to our ongoing problem with SDS and the military, a minority-student strike would be a catastrophe. No one had yet threatened such a strike, but we were not dense, and we had already thought through what seemed to be developing. The ugly news from Berkeley and San Francisco told us every day to be on guard.

So I sat there as the demands were read "line by line." In each instance a student militant would put the heat to me in the form of a snarling question:

"McGill, what is your answer?"

He might just as well have been asking "McGill, how do you plead: guilty or not guilty?" They were compiling a bill of particulars in order to go back to the campus and complain of the chancellor's unyielding racist attitudes. Soon I would stand indicted as the principal barrier to realization of Lumumba-Zapata College.

With a sinking feeling, I began to comprehend the Lumumba-Zapata strategy. It was to isolate the administration as racists while convincing the faculty and student body of the idealism inherent in Lumumba-Zapata. I had nicely obliged our student strategists by stepping, unbidden, right into the trap they had set. Now they were systematically isolating me.

Oh well, I thought, everyone makes mistakes.

My face set itself in an angry mask, and in response to each new demand I snapped out my answers in barely intelligible monosyllables: "No," "Uh-uh," or occasionally, "Maybe. I don't know what you mean."

Murphy became alarmed when he saw his chancellor being boxed in. He had begun to learn some interesting things about the internal dynamics of the Lumumba-Zapata group. Apparently a significant fraction were not really supporters of the radical curriculum proposed by Angela Davis and her people. The moderate faction wanted a UCSD college oriented toward the needs and interests of minority students. For them the curriculum demands were merely a device to expand the size of the group and hence the pressure they could bring to bear.

Miss Davis and her radical supporters sought to invent a curriculum worthy of a revolutionary college. This was their only interest in Lumumba-Zapata. They had formulated their demands as the first political step toward creating a new radical consciousness within the university. Students and faculty who could be attracted to Lumumba-Zapata College would ultimately change the power balance at UCSD and radicalize the campus in a completely new way. But even at the beginning in March 1969, no clear evidence existed that Angela Davis and her fellow radicals were in charge. Instead there appeared to be a coalition of diverse interest groups cemented together in order to confront the administration. The moderate students were putting on a show of militancy because to stay in contention they had to appear just as macho as Angela Davis and the radicals.

Murphy believed he saw a way in which the coalition could be fractured. To do it we would have to respond positively to the people whose main concerns were a minority-oriented program rather than the furtherance of Third World revolution.

With the chancellor boxed into a completely hostile position, dangerous trends were developing. There was likely to be either a strike led by minority students, or a serious break between the chancellor and the faculty over Lumumba-Zapata. Listening to these angry exchanges between the minority students and me, Murphy decided he could delay no longer. He intruded into the cross-examination, saying that the Lumumba-Zapata document puzzled him. It contained many attractive goals but they seemed to be phrased in ways that forced the administration to concentrate on rhetoric rather than substance.

Would the students or the chancellor object if he, Murphy, were to try to rewrite the document in more positive language that stressed principles to which we might commit ourselves rather than criticisms of existing social conditions?

This proposal set off a brief argument among the students. Several thought Murphy's rewrite would be helpful, but they were immediately silenced by the rest of the group and told not to break ranks. It was Lumumba-Zapata: all or nothing, take it or leave it.

Murphy announced that even without advance approval he would attempt the rewrite and submit his new version both to the chancellor and to the students. They then insisted on a written response to the original demands, and I agreed to furnish it. The clique around Angela Davis evidently had invested a great deal in their bill of particulars.

The third meeting concluded with a bitter exchange. A spokesman for the group announced after whispered consultations that they had no further interest in meeting with me. I stood up flushed with anger and rasped that after the personal abuse and cross-examination I had endured at their hands, I could see no purpose in further meetings with them.

Had I been more experienced, I would have said something like that when they started after me, not after sitting through all their abuse. As it was, my rejoinder was delivered to people who had already accomplished what they set out to do. It was in studying such mistakes and reacting to them that I began tearing out my faculty roots in the spring of 1969. My prescriptions for improvement nearly always involved tough stances and even occasional uses of force. These were things that the faculty as a whole categorically rejected.

Originally, I had entered the chancellor's office with a faculty member's typical preconceptions about university administration. Most faculty secretly believe they can administer a university successfully by devoting an hour or two of their spare time to the task each morning. Administrative problems seem difficult only because most administrators are not very bright! At least that is the faculty view. Few recognize that organizational and financial questions are sometimes quite subtle and far removed from their professional competence.

This observation does not apply to the faculty of business schools, where work centers on organization, management, and finance. At Columbia the business faculty was remarkably helpful in guiding our efforts to build administrative systems and data bases. These faculty also considered university administration a source of fascinating, off-the-beaten-track course material. The relationship proved highly profitable for both of us. Nevertheless, a typical faculty member in the arts and sciences at a major university cannot tell a capital budget from an operating budget, or a balance sheet from an operating statement, much less how to build an organization that will amplify the capabilities of its chief officer. Even worse, during the 1960s, many believed that this kind of knowledge was really not important for running a university. All you need to know, they would say, is where top faculty are, how to recruit them, and how to keep them happy.

Such attitudes probably derive from the fact that before the 1960s there was no class of specially trained professional administrators at colleges and universities. The lower levels of administration were staffed largely by people who had failed to make it into the tenured faculty. During the 1960s, with the growth of organizational theory, crisis management, highspeed data processing, and federal demands for data, a new class of university administrators was born. Today faculty regard them as precious and recruit them almost as carefully as star faculty. But in the late Sixties most faculty still believed that a university could be run out of the president's desk drawer.

It is certainly true that I was unaware of the subtle difficulties posed by the problem of being genuinely and personally responsive to student grievances without undercutting the authority of key subordinates. If I had known, I would have acted more cautiously regarding Armin Rappaport and Third College.

In 1968 most administrators did not know how to respond to confrontation. With the techniques developed in Revelle Plaza during the Cleaver crisis in November, and with George Murphy's skilled tactical guidance, I became good at it quickly. This soon led to a wholly unjustified conviction, after only eight months on the job, that I knew all there was to know about being a successful chancellor in an era of radical confrontation.

The combination of this false sense of security, together with the stresses imposed by the hostile climate in which we were operating, was potentially deadly. It produced self-assured, volatile, and increasingly unwise reactions to each new crisis. The toughening process I was going through helped me to rebound easily from public criticism, but it did not protect me from errors of judgment. In fact, it seemed to stimulate them. When you become less sensitive, more self-assured, and more volatile in an adversarial environment, it is difficult to avoid errors. Slowly I began to see myself surrounded by people trying to do me in. By God, they were not going to get away with it!

Commentators often discuss the "siege mentality" that has obsessed modern American Presidents. The siege mentality is portrayed as though it were some kind of enduring character defect. Really able leaders, it is argued, should be able to rise above pettiness and pursue visions larger than the pleasure of vanquishing enemies. We hear these criticisms inevitably about Richard Nixon, but frequently also in discussions of the leadership difficulties experienced by Lyndon Johnson, Gerald Ford, and Jimmy Carter. President Johnson is generally credited with a modern version of the golden rule: "Do unto others before they do unto you."

It is easier, I think, to recognize the siege mentality in others than to understand it in ourselves. None of us are the godlike creations that the press and the public demand in positions of leadership. We bring to these responsibilities a combination of limited experience and undisclosed weaknesses that may be greatly amplified in the stresses of adversarial struggle. It is true that we also bring strengths, but these are generally slower to emerge, so that the first few months in a difficult administrative job are usually spent establishing control and shoring up weaknesses.

Someone who is overwhelmed by the job typically gets out. The siege mentality tends to develop in those who are not overwhelmed and yet find themselves under continuing stress from the realization that, like it or not, they are at war with determined adversaries. That shattering realization eventually comes to almost all administrators managing large enterprises in which a great deal is at stake. Lincoln felt it; so did MacArthur—to mention just two whose godlike reputations begin to attain human dimensions under closer scrutiny.

The siege mentality is not a character flaw in itself, but a natural, early-stage response to the stress of leadership under adversarial conditions. I experienced it just as virtually everyone else in my position did during the stressful Sixties. With maturity the phenomenon recedes and is replaced by a tolerant understanding, a kind of fondness, for those misguided souls who are trying to cut you up. If an administrator can survive long enough to achieve a modest degree of security in his job, his siege mentality slowly disappears.

The Lumumba-Zapata crisis deepened. Soon after our disastrous third meeting, I wrote out responses to each individual demand and then, taking a cue from Murphy, spoke to the principles that I thought lay behind the demands. The two types of answers proved to be quite different. Murphy went over these responses and agreed to base his rewrite of the Lumumba-Zapata document on the same principles. He would then talk to the minority students, arguing that if they really preferred progress to confrontation, they might try to secure our commitment to these principles in the design of Third College.

Although the approach was the most sensible one under the circumstances, it had a number of serious defects. First of all, it seemed to forecast abandonment of the experimental college idea even before I announced it at my April 11th inaugural. Murphy urged that we try to keep the proposal alive. He would take the position in arguing with the Lumumba-Zapata group that we were genuinely committed to the experimental college but would not force it on our students if they rejected the idea entirely. The chancellor might be willing to consider a minority-oriented Third College, but the radical curriculum and a student-controlled administration were absolutely unacceptable.

Second, if we attempted to break the coalition of moderates and radicals in the Lumumba-Zapata group in the way we were now considering, we would have to make immediate and large-scale alterations in the original plan of Third College. I was now obliged to talk all this out with Armin Rappaport.

This time I made a determined effort to find him, and we were together for several hours. He said he understood the difficult problem he had given me; he would do whatever he could to make it more manageable. Did I need his resignation?

No. I needed solutions, not resignations. We had to find a way out of the crisis without agreeing to a curriculum devoted to Marxist dogma and without accepting the principle of student control. I was getting nowhere in these discussions with the Lumumba-Zapata group. The best way in which he might help me would be to sit down with the protestors and try to work out an acceptable solution—acceptable to him and acceptable to them.

Armin asked me whether it was true that I might be considering replacing his academic plan for a traditional undergraduate college that offered special programs to minority students, with a plan for an entirely minority-oriented program. If this were true, Third College would benefit from sympathetic minority leadership rather than a provost committed to the original ideas.

Perhaps, but I did not know yet what could be done. My preference was for an experimental program on the UCSD campus offered in conjunction with the San Diego community colleges. The Lumumba-Zapata group seemed completely hostile to the proposal. Could we work out some compromise between their interests and the existing Third College plan? I did not know. I outlined Murphy's analysis of the divisions among the Lumumba-Zapata protestors and his belief that a commitment to a minority-oriented Third College might undercut the leadership of Angela Davis and the other radicals. I would accept whatever Rappaport could negotiate with the students just as long as it did not lead to a radical curriculum or to student control.

It was an impossible assignment. Rappaport could see that I was asking him to preserve the experimental college idea and the original Third College plan, while Murphy was being instructed to test the feasibility of a totally new minority-oriented curriculum. Besides, there was now no way in which the Lumumba-Zapata group would take Rappaport's authority seriously. I had inadvertently caused that when I began to negotiate with them personally, and again when I authorized Murphy to rewrite the Lumumba-Zapata demands stressing the goals that the students were seeking. Whatever they were seeking, it was not Armin Rappaport's plan for Third College.

Our strategy was in considerable disarray. We were virtually paralyzed by anxiety over the possibility of racial conflict at UCSD. I was forcing myself to face the possibility and plan for it in view of our disastrous third meeting with the Lumumba-Zapata protestors; but I was also thrashing around, putting out multiple feelers, giving subordinates contradictory assignments, and hoping against hope that something would head off the impending collision.

Armin Rappaport agreed to take over our discussions with the Lumumba-Zapata group. He agreed despite the fact that he now realized, as he told me later, his effectiveness as provost of Third College was virtually at an end.

The inaugural came and went peacefully on April 11. It was one of

La Jolla's best sunny days tempered by cool ocean breezes. Despite the lovely weather, the ceremony was held indoors in the campus gymnasium, because we had received advance warning that at least two groups intended to demonstrate. The gym was more secure against attempts at disruption than an outdoor setting. Typical of those times, the inaugural ceremony was less a splashy display of academic pomp than a simple act of dedication supervised by the president of the university and a delegation of Regents. Even more typical, it came long after the chancellor had lost his virginity. Lumumba-Zapata (about which we were saying as little as possible in public—the Marxist rhetoric would have rocketed San Diego into orbit) was the fourth major UCSD crisis in less than eight months.

Most typical of all the problems of those times was the disparate character of the groups threatening to picket. One, of course, was Lumumba-Zapata. The day before the inaugural, a group of black students asked to see me. They warned that they would set up a picket line unless I stated my commitment to Lumumba-Zapata College immediately. One of the young blacks remarked that they were well connected to the Panthers downtown and could probably bring in plenty of support.

Thoughts of Black Panthers in berets, leather jackets, and dark glasses, perhaps even armed, began flitting through my head as I envisioned them colliding with an ultra-conservative group that was also threatening to picket. The audience and dignitaries might have trouble getting through the militant groups outside the gym. But the threat was overdone. I didn't really believe that our black students would call in the Panthers. I told them they were welcome to picket, provided it was done peacefully. It would add a touch of color to the ceremony in view of the other group proposing to be out there with them.

Next morning I reported this conversation to Regent John Canaday as we robed for the inaugural ceremony. It seemed almost a perfect illustration of the times we lived in. Suddenly tears were in his eyes and he cried out, "Migod, don't they have a shred of decency!"

Nothing came of the threat. There were no black or Chicano pickets —no Black Panthers, no Brown Berets, no students, and no ultra-conservatives either. Three days after the inaugural, Lumumba-Zapata protestors appeared in force outside my office. Their picket signs displayed their opinion of "McGill's Sandbox College," but that was no surprise. Perhaps they did have a shred of decency after all. The threat to picket the inaugural was just one more bit of evidence that they were hard bargainers.

The other protesting group took out a full-page advertisement in *The*

San Diego Union two days prior to the ceremony. Calling themselves Citizens to End Campus Anarchy, they urged the Regents to delay the formal inauguration pending an investigation of my fitness to hold office. Their principal complaints seemed to be my role in Marcuse's reappointment and the Marine recruiter incident. Vice Admiral Albert E. Jarrell was listed as chairman. Membership was both sizable and drawn from all over Southern California. None of the names, including the chairman, were familiar to me. I could not imagine who they were, except perhaps angry taxpayers fed up with what they had been reading in the newspapers, but not very thoughtful about subjecting the university to political pressures.

Somehow, these threats from two angry groups with views that could only be described as polar opposites managed to add to the dignity of the occasion. A reverence for scholarship that few of us had ever admitted before seemed appropriate for marking the continuance of this fragile new university. Although far removed from medieval Bologna and Paris, where universities as we know them in the Western world began, we could feel, on that April morning in 1969, a renewed sense of contact with them. The contact was enhanced by the realization that student unrest has always been a part of the history of universities. We got through it before; we would survive it now.

Toward the end of April, George Murphy brought word that the discussions between Provost Rappaport and the Lumumba-Zapata protestors were not going well at all from our point of view. The minority students were pushing Rappaport, threatening him. He was on the brink of conceding that Third College should be restructured as a minority-oriented college with a greatly enlarged and perhaps even dominant student role in governance and admissions. That in itself was not a major problem, although we could not tolerate student control of the college. There is a great deal of daylight between large-scale student involvement and student control. If the role of students in the governance of the college was the only point in dispute, we could probably work it out.

The difficulty was that the position of the student negotiators remained on dead center. It was Lumumba-Zapata College, all or nothing. Rappaport was preparing to write off all his personal contributions and all his commitment to Third College if it would produce an accord. The students were yielding nothing, nor was there any sign of the hoped-for break between moderates and radicals in the Lumumba-Zapata group.

Looking back at Rappaport's position today with the accumulated experience of more than a decade of hard bargaining with tough student groups, I see that the outcome was predictable. I had given Armin no firm place to stand, nothing really to defend, and no way to assert his authority. The students sensed that. Without strong backing from the chancellor, he was doing what he felt he had to do to keep peace, but what was emerging was not his plan for Third College; it was not even a compromise.

Again Rappaport asked to be replaced by a black or brown administrator. Someone new might be able to lead and inspire the students, whereas Armin could only fight a dismal retreat from the investments of time and energy he had made in Third College. I urged him to hang on a while longer. Our situation was still too precarious.

On April 17 minority groups held a second demonstration outside the chancellor's office. It was considerably larger and more threatening than the picketing that preceded it three days earlier. I happened to be out of town attending the April meeting of the Board of Regents. People who witnessed the demonstration described it as an angry crowd of 80 to 100 people, many of them high school students from somewhere downtown. Over and over they chanted, "Lumumba-Zapata College now!" At the end of the demonstration they delivered an ultimatum demanding implementation of the student demands within two weeks or they would be back to burn us down. Despite the presence of outsiders, the crowd was orderly. No damage was reported.

It seemed to me at this point that nothing was going well. A few days earlier Murphy had delivered his version of the Lumumba-Zapata demands, rewritten in positive language and stripped of offensive rhetoric. The provisional faculty of Third College approved nearly all of Murphy's document, but the students seemed unmoved by it.

The time appeared to be at hand to inform the academic senate of what we were up against. Of course, nearly every faculty member at UCSD had heard about Lumumba-Zapata College by this time. The chancellor's report to the senate would come as no surprise, but I hoped to create a forum for realistic discussion of the demands. I did not want to allow Angela Davis and her supporters to be sweet-talking the faculty while continuing to hard-line the administration. If we were lucky, some variation on the original academic plan of Third College might be worked out. What the faculty had been hearing up to this point was largely the propaganda of the Lumumba-Zapata group. Now it was time they learned the facts.

Late in April Armin Rappaport and I went before the senate to report on the origins and development of the Lumumba-Zapata dispute.

During the 1970s at Columbia I came to realize that in times of prolonged stress the principal responsibility of the campus administration is to focus tension on itself and keep it away from the faculty. The faculty should be able to go about its academic work unburdened by disputes with protesting groups. In this way classes continue uninterrupted, Ph.D. examinations go forward on schedule, and the standards of the institution are maintained. A skillful administration can generally manage to resolve most issues before they ever become significant areas of dispute. The faculty knows about them only through reports in the student newspaper. Often the reports are slanted, but they are written in the past tense, and that has a marvelously soothing effect on faculty nerves.

In most American universities the faculty will endorse such a condition of divorcement if the administration seems to be handling conflict well. When a dispute becomes serious or violence threatens, the faculty will, on its own initiative, attempt to step in as mediator. A campus administration rarely takes a dispute to the faculty and says in effect, "Here it is. We have tried to resolve it, but we are now at our wits end. Please see what you can do with it." This is essentially what I was doing in bringing the Lumumba-Zapata dispute to the senate.

Although editorial writers and lawyers familiar with conflict resolution tend to applaud such administrative tactics, the faculty generally does not. Faculty members believe that the administration is transferring the dangerous consequences of its own ineptitude onto their shoulders. They resent having to deal with urgent pressures that intrude on their scholarly work.

Our move to put the Lumumba-Zapata dispute before the senate was premature and probably a mistake. The potential for acts of violence by UCSD's minority students was a serious matter, serious enough so that the senate might well have been forced to intervene in any event. But the People's Park explosion, which would create major unrest in the form of student strikes on nearly every campus of the University of California, was just about to occur in Berkeley.[15] UCSD immediately became totally preoccupied with People's Park and the resulting student strike. For ten days Lumumba-Zapata College was virtually forgotten. Minority students might then have been willing to retreat from their all-or-nothing stance and work out a compromise with us behind the scenes.

Sometimes it happens. Everything depends on the administration's ability to master the largest conflict it faces. If the administration seems to be winning, other protesting groups scramble to get the best settlement they can negotiate before a vastly strengthened administration turns its guns on them. On the other hand, if the large conflict appears to be going badly, every dissident group on campus will try to join the large protest, hoping to advance its own agenda of grievances. Trouble multiplies rapidly for an administration visibly weakened by conflict. It is another iron law of militancy.

What might have happened in this instance is something we shall never know. I chose to go to the senate with the Lumumba-Zapata dispute on April 23, and after that the senate carried the main burden of searching for a solution until People's Park blew up.

Four meetings of the academic senate were scheduled in quick succession late in April and during the first week in May. Normally the senate convenes once a month, but a growing sense of urgency drove it to try to resolve the tension created by the Lumumba-Zapata demands. Faculty grumbled at this disruption of their academic routine, but they agreed to meet nevertheless. They were even more worried about racial conflict than I was.

Led by Angela Davis, the Lumumba-Zapata protestors were present at these meetings to press their demands. During two climactic meetings on May 6 and 7, hundreds of student supporters, aided by various street people and high school recruits from downtown San Diego, ringed the building in which the senate was convening. They listened with growing restiveness to the parliamentary maneuvers and the frequent invocations of Robert's Rules as the senate debate slipped toward the complexity that only a contentious academic meeting can generate. Loudspeakers had been set up outside the building to broadcast the proceedings.

After first hearing the issues in dispute, the senate tried to persuade the Lumumba-Zapata group to continue negotiating with Provost Rappaport and the provisional faculty of Third College. The students refused on the ground that the provost and his faculty had been shown to have no power.

In the meeting of May 6, Armin Rappaport moved that Third College be governed by a board of directors consisting of three students, two faculty, and the college provost. This proposal was presented as the outcome of an agreement between Rappaport and the Lumumba-Zapata group. It did not reflect his own views. The proposal set off an intense debate that soon broke the senate wide open. Faculty conservatives used every procedural device available to ingenious academic minds to try to block the resolution by having it declared out of order, or, failing that, amending it into less threatening form. The atmosphere grew more and more strained as the parliamentary web grew more complicated. Inside the room, muffled sounds of angry shouts from the people outside could be heard. It seemed only a question of time before the crowd would try to break in.

I asked for a ten-minute recess to allow tempers to cool and to persuade the senate informally that the issue could not be ducked on technicalities. When we resumed, the parliamentary maneuvering was as spirited as ever. A black student rose and denounced "all the silly games you people with Ph.D.'s play." He threatened a student walkout unless immediate action was taken. "BSC-MAYA won't sit and listen to any more parliamentary bullshit."

Finally, late in the afternoon, Rappaport's resolution, stripped of all amendments, came to a vote. It passed 87–34 and the senate recessed for 24 hours. Just before the vote to recess, I urged the members to establish a new Third College planning committee drawn from senate members sympathetic to the directions that now seemed to be emerging.

I found myself strangely depressed by the senate's decision. Right up to the last moment I hoped they might reject Armin's resolution on Third College governance because it was a capitulation to the students. They did not reject it, nor did I rise up to demand that the senate adhere to our traditional form of college governance under a provost. Realizing all the tensions abroad in the senate and on the campus, I hinted and suggested rather than insisted. That is not an adequate prescription for leadership.

Next day I decided to pass up the continuation of the recessed senate meeting in favor of a scheduled session of the council of chancellors in Berkeley. It seemed clear that a minority-oriented college with strong student governance was now inevitable and that the basic decisions had been made on the previous day. Besides, I was weary of all the struggling over Third College. A meeting with the other chancellors in Berkeley offered a pleasant respite. It was nothing of the sort. Trouble broke out at UCSD late in the afternoon of May 7. When it was put down I vowed never to take the easy way out again.

During a break in the council meeting, Roger Heyns told me for the first time about his developing crisis over People's Park, a three-acre, empty lot just off Telegraph Avenue near the Berkeley campus. The university purchased the property in 1967 and cleared it as a site for married student housing, but protracted delays were encountered in finding construction funds. An interim plan was developed to convert the property into a soccer field, but the lot was still vacant in mid-April 1969. Then a group of countercultural street people aided by Berkeley students began fixing it up and planting flowers. They transformed what had been an eyesore into a pleasant, if uninhibited, mini-park with trees, brick walks, benches, flowers, and swings for children. What was frightening about this was that a leadership group of veteran radicals was describing the mini-park as having been seized from the university and given back to the people. It was a symbolic revolutionary act in which students and

Berkeley street people were urged to ignore conventional property rights, take what was theirs, and in so doing add a touch of beauty to their lives.

Heyns was very worried. The university's attorneys were telling him that the Berkeley campus must reestablish control over the property or risk its position of legal ownership.[16] Heyns knew that forcible seizure of the property would become an explosive issue that might again radicalize the campus. He wanted time to work out an agreement in which public use might be permitted until the university needed to clear the site again for housing construction.

Heyns was getting strong objections from University Hall to this kind of pragmatic solution. Berkeley radicals had announced to the newspapers that People's Park was a revolutionary seizure of university property. Regents were already asking hard questions about when and how the university intended to assert its property rights. There seemed to be no way to buy time, no way to avoid a collision.

I returned home to La Jolla at about 7 PM. No sooner had I opened the front door than a radio news bulletin began to describe a break-in at the registrar's office at UCSD. Apparently a large group of students had got into the locked office and were holding it. When I finally managed to get George Murphy on the phone ten minutes later, he told me to relax. It was all over. The registrar's office was now clear, and except for a broken glass door there was no damage.

"Was it the Lumumba-Zapata group?"

"Yes."

"Was Angela Davis there?"

"You better believe it; and quite a few others, including Inge Marcuse."

"How did you get them out?"

"I'll come by the house at about nine o'clock to give you my report, boss. Meanwhile, why don't you have dinner and I'll try to do the same."

Anxiety-ridden meals are among the least delightful of common human experiences. I barely touched dinner while visions of Angela Davis dressed as Joan of Arc surrounded by legions of Black Panthers and Brown Berets flickered through my consciousness. My wife remarked later that I seemed quite calm. Evidently the mask of discipline was taking effect; inside it my brain was seething.

Later in the evening as we relaxed over drinks in my living room, Murphy told me that the senate had reconvened at three in the afternoon. Numerous attempts were made to revive the dispute over Third College governance. A number of faculty senators questioned the legality of the

Rappaport resolution passed on the previous day. Quickly the senate drifted into another parliamentary muddle, with several resolutions on the floor simultaneously and people raising points of order.

One of the resolutions was introduced by Silvio Varon, a member of the faculty of medicine and a well-known biologist. It called for reconstitution of the faculty of Third College so that it would include people committed to the educational needs of minority students. He proposed establishing a new planning committee for Third College consisting of eight faculty members and eight students. The planning committee would be charged with developing a detailed master plan conforming to the governance resolution agreed to by the senate on the previous day. They would have two weeks for consultation with students and faculty before the plan was submitted for endorsement by the senate.

It was almost an impossible task. Varon was recommending that the planning committee devise a successful compromise for Lumumba-Zapata, something that none of us had come close to during the past three weeks. Moreover, this compromise was to be acceptable to the protesting minority students, who still had not budged from "Lumumba-Zapata College now!" And all of it was to be accomplished within two weeks! Varon was sympathetic to the Lumumba-Zapata protestors. Perhaps he knew something about their state of mind that led him to believe his timetable was feasible.

The resolution was not a simple matter for the senate. It consisted of eight numbered paragraphs, each of which would have been sufficient to raise serious questions in the best of circumstances. But in the midst of an emotion-packed debate, and with conflicting resolutions, multiple amendments, and continual points of order, the discussion on the senate floor rapidly became impenetrable. The Lumumba-Zapata group grew hostile.

Several blacks in the angry crowd outside burst into the room and shouted at the faculty senators, "You fuckers are just jiving around. Why don't you get down to business?" When the intruders were escorted out, several senators tried to break the deadlock on the floor. There was a call for a recess. It failed. Someone moved to table all pending business so that the senate could start afresh. It failed, and at that point the Lumumba-Zapata group walked out, angrily trailed by dozens of student supporters.

Murphy asked for recognition. He pleaded with the senate not to adjourn, but to continue searching for a solution. He would go outside and try to persuade the Lumumba-Zapata group to return.

Murphy departed, and a stricken senate turned again to the Varon resolution which, in substance, asked for the abandonment of the original

Third College plan, and put the campus on a hazardous course toward a minority-oriented college with no idea where it would lead. All eyes turned toward Armin Rappaport.

Rappaport rose and told the senate he supported the Varon resolution, despite the fact that its adoption would spell abandonment of everything he had worked for. He conceded that a college of the type demanded by the Lumumba-Zapata protestors was needed "at this point in history," and that in all likelihood he might not be equipped to be provost of such a college. It was a beautiful, selfless gesture at a critical time, and it unblocked the Senate.[17]

Murphy returned. He announced to a hushed room that a sizable group of students had marched over to the chancellor's area and broken into the registrar's office. He called on the senate to act. Murphy did not particularly care what the senate decided, but he needed some decisive action to take to the students. Varon's resolution was then put to a vote and carried 94 to 5.

When Murphy described this scene to me later in the evening I asked him whether it was wise to have injected the sit-in issue just as the senate was about to vote. Opponents would say later that he had stampeded them unfairly. Murphy acknowledged a possible error saying, "At that point I was not necessarily thinking very clearly. I wanted to get over to the registrar's office and get to work." Later Walter Munk, the senate chairman, told me that Murphy's remark was a mistake, but that it made no difference. Varon's resolution would have passed in any case following Armin Rappaport's *beau geste*. Perhaps there might have been more votes in opposition, but the outcome was certain.

With the adoption of a fundamentally new direction for Third College, the senate's work was done and it speedily adjourned. Murphy gathered a group of faculty together. They set out for the registrar's office with a copy of the text of the resolution on Third College.

Meanwhile, several ugly incidents were occurring at the scene of the sit-in. A large sympathetic crowd gathered around the building. Newspaper and television reporters arrived quickly and began mixing with the crowd, looking for information on the protest, and for live-action news. Several reporters were roughed up. Cameras were seized and films exposed.

Inside the building a dean leaving a nearby office stopped to observe the group in the registrar's office and saw a rifle in the hands of one of the people standing in the room.

Murphy and his faculty group arrived outside the registrar's office at about 6:15 PM. A copy of the Varon resolution was handed through a furniture barricade behind the smashed glass door, and two sympathetic faculty members crawled inside to discuss its implications. Murphy was asked to remain outside.

A furious debate arose inside the room over what to do next. Some of the protestors began urging that they leave. The senate had now virtually approved a minority-oriented college. The moderates in the room hoped to go ahead on the basis of the assurances already given. The radicals insisted on further concessions over curriculum. Why give up now when, with a little more pressure, they could get all of Lumumba-Zapata College, curriculum and everything else as well?

After three-quarters of an hour's heated discussion, the protestors put the issue, leave or stay, to a vote among themselves. The decision was very close, but the vote, recounted several times, favored leaving on the basis of the assurances thus far given: 29 votes in favor of leaving and 23 votes for staying.

The problem now was to persuade the outvoted radicals to leave too. Murphy was asked whether he would seek disciplinary action against any students involved in the sit-in. He replied that as of that moment there had been no infraction of campus rules. If they all left immediately, there would be no charges. Murphy's reply clinched it. The group filed out of the office raising their fists in a sign of victory and were embraced by the crowd outside.

"George, you did a fine job, but what about the glass door?"

"Boss, I forgot about the door. I was so damned glad to get them out. I simply forgot about it."

"Someone will have to pay for it."

Murphy thought he might persuade the Lumumba-Zapata group to pay for the door. On May 9 an administrative memo was forwarded to me by the campus business office. It summarized repair costs in the registrar's office "as a result of student activities." The breakdown was:

Door repair	$68.00
Window screen replacement	7.00
Extra custodial clean-up	2.50
TOTAL	$77.50

I turned it over to George Murphy. A day or two later he reported to me, somewhat mysteriously, that the bill had been paid. I never asked him how he did it.

As I listened to Murphy's report of the registrar's office incident in my living room, I could not decide whether we had greater or less trouble as a consequence of Murphy's handling. He had obviously been extremely gentle, and that would give us some public difficulty. Would it settle things down on campus or would our handling be perceived as weakness by Angela Davis and the Lumumba-Zapata radicals, encouraging them to further excesses?

Murphy seemed quite certain that the vote to leave the registrar's office was a decisive event. The hoped-for fracturing of the Lumumba-Zapata group that had guided our actions for several weeks had now happened. The radicals were no longer in charge.

I was skeptical. Rappaport had capitulated. The senate had capitulated, and now Murphy was trying to put a good face on it all, but I was sure he was deceiving himself or trying to push me into a position that he had chosen in advance. Murphy was a very complex man. He was subservient in trivial matters. For example, he liked to call me "boss." But on serious questions he was as tough and unyielding as anyone I have ever known.

Murphy was not deceiving himself. Something remarkable had happened. Silvio Varon's "impossible" resolution somehow finally convinced the moderate minority students that the senate would support their college. The vote to leave the registrar's office was decisive. Angela Davis and her radical supporters had lost their bid for a revolutionary college preaching slavery and genocide as the goals of white society. Soon afterward she lost interest in the Lumumba-Zapata protest and moved on to interests in greener pastures.[17a]

The new Third College planning committee set to work immediately, led by Professor William R. Frazer, a scholarly physicist deeply sympathetic with the idea of a minority-oriented college. During the next ten days faculty and student members of the planning committee held a number of intense discussions and agreed on the outline of a plan.

On May 14 Bill Frazer came in to tell me that he and his committee had finished their task. He showed me the text of a brief document—the revised version of the Lumumba-Zapata demands. Frazer stood next to me as I leafed through it searching for booby-traps. I read:

> The goal of the program is, then, to offer the possibility for minority students to apply the critical and analytical tools of modern learning to the problems they face in their environment and to provide for white students an understanding of the problems involved in present-day society as they prepare to use the same tools. It is hoped that students graduating from the college will be prepared to continue exploring critically throughout their lives what the role of culture and the individual might be in the particular community from which the individual came to

the college, in full awareness that a community is the reality through which all men can be reached in their equality and differences.

The plan was a little gem, a masterpiece. All the strident rhetoric, the Marxist ideology, the indoctrination, were excised. They were replaced by a sensitive and idealistic approach to the needs and interests of minority students, retaining nearly all that was unique in the original Lumumba-Zapata document.

I turned in wonderment to Bill Frazer after studying his paper. He is a serious, scholarly, almost solemn man—at that time a rather young man, 35 years old. The only show of emotion detectable to my gaze was an upward flickering of the muscles at the corners of his mouth as though he were desperately trying to keep from breaking out in a triumphant smile. I said:

"Bill, you and your committee have done an incalculable service to this campus. You have solved the problem. If this is the plan for Third College, I commit myself to it here and now without any qualification. Tell your student members that if they are willing to stick with it and bear all the criticism we are sure to receive, I will get them their college."

The idealism of the UCSD faculty—embodied in Silvio Varon's senate resolution, Armin Rappaport's selfless renunciation of his original Third College plan, and Bill Frazer's transformation of the Lumumba-Zapata demands—had saved the day and set an example that I found irresistible. Instead of arrogant demands and political scheming, what had been produced in the last extremity was beautiful. We began our confrontation in deep anger and now, after a long, bitter struggle, we were preparing to put it aside in mutual compassion.

The struggling was by no means over. Following Armin Rappaport's *pro forma* resignation at the end of the school year in June 1969, the minority students, making full use of their new powers of governance, were determined to select their own provost. I was equally determined not to allow it. I used all my capacity for obfuscation and delay until both parties could agree on a candidate. He had been there all along waiting for us and I wanted him. I had to wait out the minority students until they began to see things that way, too. It required a year, but eventually they came around. Bill Frazer filled in as acting provost until we got it settled.

Our permanent provost was a young black chemist at UCSD, Joseph Watson. He was committed to the students' cause, but he was also extremely determined and unflappable in the most bitter arguments. Joe Watson became provost of Third College in July 1970. When I returned from Columbia in 1980, more than a decade later, Watson was still provost.[18] He had been through a brutal struggle with faculty radicals in 1972 that led to another threatened strike. The issue was whether Third College would become a radical college ruled by majority vote or a minority-oriented college administered by its provost. Watson won. He gave Third College critically needed stability during its fragile early years. Without Watson, the student-centered governance of Third College might have created endless, unnecessary crises in its relations with the rest of the campus. With him, it survived.

The name remains Third College. In turbulent meetings filled with threats during the summer and autumn of 1969, we managed to persuade minority students that the Regents would never agree to "Lumumba-Zapata College." Both parties decided it was best to stay with the name "Third College," at least in the beginning. During the Seventies, repeated efforts were made to give the college a new permanent name, but nothing proved more appealing to its diverse constituencies. The naming dilemma is most easily conveyed in a remark once made to me by a Chicano student expressing irritation with the outlook of black students:

"This college would be better off with a little less Lumumba and a lot more Zapata!"

So "Third College" it has remained, and over the years the name has achieved a certain historic sanctification. Almost no one would want to change it now. Third College at UCSD rings with symbolism and signals a special excellence to the rest of the academic world. It stands for something.[19]

The bitterness accompanying our two-month struggle over the Lumumba-Zapata demands in the spring of 1969 seems far removed now. It is difficult to stroll in Third College today, amid the cream-colored low buildings and the lovely tree-lined walks and remember the turmoil that surrounded the birth of the college. Yet it happened only a dozen years ago.

The struggle was formative in my own development too. I learned a great deal by analyzing the administrative mistakes I made in the early stages of the crisis. That learning proved essential for my later survival in the extraordinarily difficult environment at Columbia University during the 1970s.

My identification as a faculty member eroded significantly during the Lumumba-Zapata crisis. I became more of an adversary, less tolerant of personal abuse from campus radicals than the faculty wished me to be; yet it was also the UCSD faculty that pulled my chestnuts out of the fire when violence threatened over the impasse that developed between the students and me.

Most of all, the struggle taught me not to fear militant black or brown students. Month after month they threatened to burn us down or to harm me, but soon enough I saw that it was artifice. They sensed that white academics were fearful of threats, and they tried to bluff us by playing on our fears. Sometimes, of course, the anger was genuine. Minority students resorted to threats whenever they encountered the endless delays and impenetrable bureaucracy we had constructed to resist the quick changes they demanded. Everyone close to universities knows that by our nature we are extremely liberal about other people's politics and extremely conservative about our own. At first, minority students reacted to this truth by erupting in violent anger. Then they decided in a calculated way that threats of arson, violence, or bombing were the only way to move us. And so they pressured us. After a little experience, I saw through the rhetoric. Any urban administrator will report the same experience in dealing with pressure groups. Apparently the tactics were widely shared in the black community.

Despite their rhetoric, our minority students eventually rejected Angela Davis and her revolutionary leadership. They would not admit it publicly, because they would never denigrate someone who stood up against the white establishment as stoutly as Miss Davis had; but her way was not their way. She sought an agency that would promote revolution, whereas the majority of our black and brown students wanted no more than an institution to serve their needs as they set about claiming what had been denied to their forebears.

When I saw all this, it stirred my own idealism and summoned up my compassion. I wanted to help them get where they wished to go.

It is wonderfully ironic that today when people outside California search for examples of my successes as an administrator in the hazardous era of student unrest a decade ago, they immediately turn to Third College, and to the courage and tenacity necessary for bringing it to birth in such an unfavorable environment. If only they knew that I fought Lumumba-Zapata because I viewed it as Third World propaganda unworthy of a university. My commitment to Third College, while genuine enough, came late in the game. The real achievers were the moderate minority students who knew what they wanted, and the fine, idealistic faculty at UCSD who transformed the strident ugliness of Lumumba-Zapata College into the fragile beauty of Third College, with all its hopes for a better world.

CHAPTER 7

People's Park

Before dawn on Thursday, May 15, 1969, a crew of workmen began erecting an eight-foot high, chain-link fence around a grassy plot formed by Bowditch, Dwight, and Haste Streets near the Berkeley campus. Dawn was an unusual time for fence-building, but this was no ordinary construction project. The foreman hoped to have the job completed before local residents discovered what was going on. Most of them were night people, habitually late risers.

University authorities suggested that sunrise would be a good time to start. They were very apprehensive about community resistance to the fence construction. Nearly everyone anticipated trouble, perhaps even serious trouble, but nothing like the cataclysm that resulted. During the night, as the construction manager assembled his crew and trucked in fence materials, a mutual-aid agreement was invoked by Berkeley's chief of police. At sunrise, contingents from nearby Bay Area police forces as well as state highway patrolmen and Alameda County sheriff's deputies, numbering in all about 150 men, were gathered in the area to protect the workers.[1]

The three-acre grassy plot had become known all over Berkeley as

"People's Park." It was laid out beginning April 20 on a vacant lot owned by the University of California in a run-down section of the city a few blocks south of the campus. The transformation of this familiar eyesore into a laid-back community park was accomplished through an amazing, spontaneous outpouring of volunteer effort by a rag-tag alliance of Berkeley students and Telegraph Avenue street people. At all hours of the day and night uninhibited volunteers, laboring in a carnival atmosphere, enlivened by sweet clouds of marijuana, bottles of cheap red wine, and periodic sexual divertissements, planted grass and flowers, put down brick walks, and installed playground equipment donated by friendly shopkeepers.

The spectacle was incredible, suggesting something of the bazaar in Tehran or a religious festival on the banks of the Ganges. Whatever else it might have been, this was not your traditional America, at least not the old-fashioned, straight-laced America seen from a suburban living room picture window. To gaze at the scene in the park was to be transported into an alien environment filled with strange languages and quaint customs. The hundreds of young people frequenting the place were uninhibited countercultural spirits. They were nearly always loud, often lewd. Occasionally they displayed surges of revolutionary fervor that offended passersby as well as residents of homes adjacent to the park.

And so the neighbors began to complain to the mayor about the weird goings-on in the park and the sounds of bongo drums echoing in the night. The city in turn complained to the university, because the Board of Regents of the University of California was the park's legal owner.

The free-spirited developers of People's Park had never bothered to ask the university's permission to improve the property or even to use it. In fact, a group of battle-scarred Berkeley radicals announced the creation of People's Park as if it were a revolutionary seizure of university land.[2] They said, in the classical rhetoric of the New Left, that the people had transformed an ugly vacant lot into a thing of beauty. Now it belonged to the people. The radicals publicly defied the university to try to take it back.

To anyone even cursorily familiar with the tensions abroad on university campuses in 1969, this situation had "extreme danger" written all over it. While Berkeley's revolutionaries preached the harmony of nature to the park's countercultural developers, they proclaimed a revolutionary seizure to the university and the press. It was one of those diamond-studded revolutionary issues that comes along once in a generation.

As if that were not enough, there were persistent stories about drug and sex activities in the midst of a children's playground. These seemed to be natural modes of self-expression for Telegraph Avenue's street people, but public sex and drug-taking were offensive in the extreme to straight citizens of the city of Berkeley. Tensions between these groups, which ran high in the best of circumstances, threatened to engulf the campus when reports of the lurid goings-on in People's Park focused public concern on the university's ownership role. Why did the Berkeley campus, one of the world's great centers of learning, allow this immorality and law-breaking to go on unchecked? Why didn't the university do something to stop it?

The University of California could not pretend to be an innocent bystander. The little plot of land was purchased in 1967 as a site for married student housing long needed by the Berkeley campus. But the property had been permitted to fall into disrepair after the lot was cleared. Unforeseen funding problems delayed the housing construction, and nothing was done to make effective use of the land on an interim basis. The Berkeley campus devised a plan for temporary conversion into a soccer field, but again there was no money. The lot stood vacant, littered with refuse and abandoned cars, an unofficial free parking space for students and a hangout for drifters until the developers of People's Park moved in.

The neglect was unforgivable in light of the traumatic events of May 15, 1969, and the ensuing two weeks, but it was understandable to anyone familiar with the inner workings of the University of California in 1969. Campus administrators were totally occupied with the unremitting daily pressures of student unrest. Student power and racial injustice were powerful issues on university campuses in 1968–69. At Berkeley these pressures underwent considerable amplification because of the counter-cultural community along Telegraph Avenue. The street people, many of them drifters and runaways attracted to the area because of Berkeley's national reputation as a scene of radical political action, were guaranteed to provide bizarre dimensions to anything happening on campus.[3]

Besides these problems, formidable as they might be for any administration, Berkeley had to cope with the remarkable ingenuity of veteran, in some cases aging, political radicals who had attached themselves to the campus. Such revolutionary types tend to flourish in the nooks and crannies of any large urban university, but the Berkeley radicals of the late 1960s were unusually bright and almost uniquely gifted at devising provocations intended to dramatize New Left issues. Some of these revolutionaries were graduate students, some were junior faculty, but most were simply residents who chose to live in Berkeley to participate in the cultural and political life of the campus.4

The cumulative weight of these sources of tension was exhausting. All the attention and energies of the Berkeley administration were engaged with day-to-day crisis management, as deans and vice chancellors maneuvered to prevent the veterans of the Free Speech Movement from transforming each day's mini-crises into new political causes broadly attractive to students and street people.

Any one of dozens of issues might have torn the campus apart. During the racial conflict of the Third World Liberation Front (TWLF) strike in January and February, a high premium was put on simply trying to get through each day with as little physical damage as possible. In the midst of such stress there was no time for careful attention to detail about a vacant lot or for planning the future. As long as the property posed no immediate problem, it was allowed to recede into the background.5

This administrative weakness reflects traditions of civility that, until the 1960s, had been taken for granted in the academic life for centuries.6 Universities prided themselves on a standard of behavior much above the common forms of civil interchange. Law-breaking was practically unheard of. Only in our most radical years after the middle 1960s did we hear members of the faculty using harsh or foul language in public. Even then, private conversations with those same faculty were almost completely circumspect. The use of obscenity in public was a deliberate vulgarity intended to radicalize listeners through the vernacular of the ghetto. It did not reflect any coarsening of the faculty who adopted the artifice. During the years of radical upheaval most of them remained gentle people with high levels of esthetic sensibility.

There was really no need for systematic crisis management in American universities before 1960. The schedule on which great decisions were made was comfortably slow. Impasses would emerge only after months of consultation and debate. The worst thing that could be said of an administrator was that he failed to consult the faculty adequately.

In the 1960s, however, student pressure tactics imported from the civil rights movement changed the ground rules. These pressures generated such continuing stress that our traditional mechanisms of collegial decision-making and consultative governance broke down. They simply could not keep up with the pace of events. Administrators met around the clock in crisis situations as they sought to deal with fast-breaking militancy and slow-paced faculty decision-making. Soon these administrators became physically and mentally exhausted. By 1969 a rudimentary crisis management team was in operation at Berkeley, but it was virtually overwhelmed by student unrest during the fall and winter months, and even more by the growing intransigence of the Board of Regents. The board had become so hostile to what was going on that it permitted the campuses little latitude for independent decision-making.

The sheer size of the nine-campus system and the complexity of its governance had always made the University of California ponderous and slow-moving. Under the goading of Governor Reagan, however, the Regents were not only a serious bottleneck but a source of hardline policies that few people in the university liked. As the Marcuse case demonstrated, the board was unwilling to delegate responsibility to local campuses or to allow them to respond imaginatively to local problems.

The original plan of the multicampus system envisioned by Clark Kerr had been founded on decentralized decision-making, but as serious differences emerged between militant students and establishment society in the late 1960s, Governor Reagan and his followers on the board became increasingly reluctant to yield authority to local campus officials. The Governor believed us too prone to compromise with dissident groups against what he perceived to be the interests of the general public. He saw himself as representing the public interest in the operation of the university, and his popularity made it clear that he was not wrong when he told us that the public was greatly disaffected with our handling of student unrest.

But something was wrong. It is political heresy to say it, but the fact is, the general public is not always wise in its instinctual reactions to complex social crises. Unlike senior public officials in other states, Governor Reagan chose to exploit his role as an outsider in politics—voicing opinions that the public wanted to hear rather than softening public opinion to protect the state's educational institutions during a time of crisis. We were confronting difficult challenges devised by bright, radical people with subtle minds. These challenges needed to be dealt with imaginatively, but the Governor was unbending.

His approach was simplicity itself. If campus administrators were too weak to smash the radicals, then the Board of Regents would do it. Like all simplistic solutions to our problems, the Governor's demand for greatly increased central authority had unanticipated consequences. It unnecessarily demoralized a sensitive intellectual community accustomed to governing itself. More important, the Regents soon became bogged down in fruitless attempts to decree standards of behavior for the entire university, a realm in which no policy board can be effective. These frustrations so angered the Governor that he demanded even more authority for the board and threatened punitive actions against the university unless he got it.7

Crucial policy issues were postponed while the Regents discussed endless rounds of disciplinary questions. Planning, which ought to occupy the highest priority in the workings of a policy board, was virtually sidetracked. The net result was that the growing need for married-student housing at Berkeley failed to claim the attention of the Regents until the battle of People's Park made it a disciplinary matter. Perhaps many other trustee boards of public universities were similarly preoccupied with discipline in response to the furor over campus militancy, but it seemed to me that the Regents were unusually bogged down.

Berkeley Chancellor Roger Heyns possessed the negotiating skills and the experience necessary to resolve the dangerous dispute over People's Park. Had he ever been free to act, it would have been fairly simple to work out an agreement with the developers of the park permitting them to use and maintain it until the campus needed the property for its own purposes. Even the antagonisms between the street people and the city of Berkeley presented no major difficulty to someone with Heyns's talent for conflict-resolution.

Heyns was so obviously honest and persuasive that he could have convinced both parties to accept his leadership in settling specific complaints as they arose. It was the kind of thing that he did effortlessly whenever he was at liberty to act. But in the case of People's Park the chancellor did not have the authority to negotiate a solution on his own initiative. Any solution would have to be agreed to by the Regents. All of us understood that a limited-term agreement for a user-developed, user-maintained park was unacceptable to a majority of the board, and especially the Governor's supporters.

The principal objection posed by these Regents was that a user agreement is easy to enter into but difficult to terminate. When the agreement expired and the university sought to evict the users of the park so as to convert the property to its own use, there would be an inevitable confrontation. If a fight was in prospect, we might as well get it over with now rather than display weakness before a determined militant group. It would only deepen the resistance later on.

This was the heart of Governor Reagan's philosophy, expressed over and over during that first year of my service under him. He knew that campus revolutionaries constituted only a tiny fraction of the student body. He believed that they were effective because no one opposed them. If administrators took a strong stand, radical activity would quickly disappear. The argument makes sense in many ways, but it cannot be applied without thorough analysis of the situation and clever implementation. In this particular instance, a strong stand led to disaster.

The decision to build a fence around the park was put into effect by the Berkeley administration just one day prior to the May Regents meeting.[8] It was obviously taken with one eye on the Regents. Chancellor Heyns decided to go ahead with the fence rather than face demands from the Regents that he cease his indecision and begin to assert the university's legitimate property rights. In this one instance it seemed advisable to try to act in advance of the Regents and avoid predictable charges of spinelessness. Perhaps the Berkeley radicals were only bluffing earlier when they defied the university to take the park back. Looking at it now, building the fence was a major error. At the time and in the context of the pressures exerted by the Governor, it seemed the best way out of a complex problem.

None of us understood then, neither the Governor nor any of the rest of us, that there are few windows of opportunity in these tense situations. While a window is open, you are relatively free to act, even to use force, with a high probability of success despite the risks; but only while the window is open.

When a militant group seizes a university facility, takes hostages, or engages in any of the acts now familiar as the opening stages of a protest, there exists a brief time when an administration can react forcibly. Generally speaking, this window of opportunity lasts for about 24 to 36 hours. It is necessary to move before the militants have consolidated their position or achieved any significant support from other groups. Even more important for university administrators, the window remains open only until the faculty can mobilize constraints inhibiting the administration from acting without prior faculty consent.[9]

The window had long since closed by the time the Berkeley administration attempted to construct its fence around People's Park on May 15. This was more than three weeks after students and street people began to transform the vacant lot into a community park. The university's first reaction was to try to reclaim the area as a site for a planned soccer field, but the park developers would not leave, and discussions aimed at some acceptable form of joint use broke down because the developers of the park would not or could not promise to end their construction activities.

By May 15 there were literally thousands of protagonists determined to defend People's Park as an idealistic venture contributing a touch of beauty to a tawdry area. It was much too late to retake the park by force or to attempt to build a fence around it without risking a violent aftermath. The fence could have been built without major incident on April 20, but not on May 15.

Another window of opportunity opens up only after much time has elapsed. More often than not, a radical group seizing a facility proves to be a coalition of divergent factions. These subgroups are prone to disagree if left to their own devices. They unite to build up numbers, hoping to confront a university administration with a serious problem if it attempts to move against them.

In such circumstances, prudence suggests that the coalition should not be welded together by attacking it. It is wiser to effect some form of temporary compromise while waiting for natural antagonisms among the factions to split the group apart.[10]

A building seizure typically begins with a great deal of rhetorical exhortation on the achievement of strength through unity, but as time passes disagreements arise on tactics, disputes break out among the factions, and the seizure essentially collapses through lack of a unifying opposition. An experienced administration can easily spot such cleavages in a militant group and wait for it to come apart without force of any kind. A face-saving compromise permits the group to claim victory while abandoning the seizure.

Analytical statements such as these from an administrator experienced with conflict may sound callous to those whose sympathies lie with the student protestors of the 1960s. Even to me such views seem more worthy of a commanding general than a university leader. But in the world I inhabited for more than a dozen years, it was plain that more than idealism was at stake. Student protests were also bitter contests. The longer any contest continued, the greater the urgency among students that they win it. The first duty of any administration was not to lose.

Most of the people who advised me on the art of survival reacted emotionally rather than analytically, and their opinion was divided down the middle. One view was that I ought to handle all protests by admitting immediately that the protestors were right, yielding to them on every disputed point to avoid conflict, and playing up to their idealism. The other view was that I should crack down hard and break the protestors before they broke me.

As that freshman year in the chancellor's office progressed and I gradually became aware of what had to be done, I saw that extremes of compassion or repression were not effective in conflict-resolution. A mixture of force and understanding was required.

The most important rule was to fight as fiercely and intelligently as I could, realizing that most of the protests I confronted, apart from media events, were engineered by opponents who meant harm. The second rule was to listen to the idealism that moved the mass of the protestors, but to do so only after the struggle appeared to be under control. That second step isolated the radical leadership and gave me an opportunity to establish an independent moral position.

Governor Reagan and his followers on the Board of Regents were nearly all captives of the unvarying hard line. Any delay in attacking a militant seizure was a sign of weakness inviting further trouble. Although this policy was said to be based on a realistic assessment of the radicals, it could not have been rooted in the experience of the men who propounded it. The policy was too rigid to hold up in the world in which I operated.[11]

Obviously there are circumstances in which a soft reaction to a militant seizure will be construed as a sign of weakness. In such cases an immediate forceful reaction, a *coup de main*, is helpful in clearing away misapprehensions. This hard line is usually most effective with militant groups that are small and isolated from the sympathies of the rest of the campus. It works, provided that the administrative reaction is surgical; i.e., sufficiently quick and adroit to avoid generating sympathy for the group.

More often than not the militant groups against which I struggled were large and diversely organized. They were alliances of revolutionary and countercultural people pursuing different objectives, united only in their hostility to the world they lived in and to the university administration as a symbol of that world. Such shaky alliances tended to melt away under clever handling, and this almost certainly would have been the case with the groups developing People's Park. If the Regents had given Chancellor Heyns their unqualified backing, permitting him to analyze the problem, devise a strategy, and work through the sources of conflict, there would have been no battle of People's Park. Unfortunately, things were not destined to work out that way.

The fence around People's Park was erected quickly during the morning hours of May 15. As the workmen put up sections, little clusters of angry street people attempted to tear them down but were easily driven off by the police.

At noon a large rally took place in Sproul Plaza on the Berkeley campus. The size of the crowd is difficult to estimate precisely, but it appeared to number in the neighborhood of two thousand people. Anger had been building up all morning as people on campus and in the surrounding community reacted to the university's sudden move. The climax of the rally came at about one in the afternoon, when a young man, the newly elected president of the Berkeley student body, urged his listeners to march to People's Park and take it back.[12]

Less than half an hour later a large crowd converged on the park and confronted police and sheriff's deputies protecting it. From the surging front lines of the shouting, chanting mob, repeated moves were made against the fence. Someone in the crowd turned on a fire hydrant. When the police attempted to turn it off, a fight started. Police began to lob tear gas canisters. Some of the canisters were thrown back by the crowd along with rocks, bottles, and even iron bars. A police car was set afire.

Several wild scenes occurred at the fence during the early afternoon and a number of people, including several policemen, were injured in the fighting. The police were unable to disperse the crowd. It was too large and too angry.

A call went out for police reinforcements. In one of the melées near the fence an officer was stabbed. Police were then issued shotguns charged with birdshot. They fired directly into the crowd driving it, terrified, away from the park and into nearby side streets. Later in the afternoon as street fighting continued, some police ran out of birdshot and changed ammunition to more lethal buckshot.

One rioter was blinded by a blast of birdshot. As many as fifty others were hit and at least a dozen were seriously wounded. It is difficult to estimate numbers more precisely because the wounded were treated at several different hospitals and some took care of their injuries privately. At least five persons were hit by buckshot, including one young man taken to Herrick Hospital with a shattered leg. It is claimed that some of those struck by gunfire were innocent bystanders who happened to wander into the riot scene wondering what was going on.[13]

The most dreadful outcome of all involved an individual who may well have been a bystander. James Rector, 25 years old, a resident of San Jose near the foot of San Francisco Bay, was said to be visiting a friend in Berkeley on May 15 and was shot by a policeman late in the afternoon near People's Park. In the hospital he told doctors treating his wounds that he had wanted to see what was happening at the park. When he encountered policemen in riot gear carrying shotguns near Telegraph Avenue, Rector fled to a rooftop. He said that someone nearby threw a stone down on two policemen in the street below. One of them looked up and pointed at the rooftop. His partner fired at Rector, who was badly hit in the chest and abdomen. Although Rector was alive when admitted to the hospital, he failed to progress and died on Monday, May 19.

It was not immediately certain that Rector had been shot by police. His story was difficult to verify. Subsequent investigation showed that he had a record of petty crime: burglary, receiving stolen property, possession of marijuana. It also showed that his wounds were caused by buckshot, probably from a police shotgun. Exactly what he was doing on the rooftop, whether he may have thrown an object at the police below, are things that have never been established clearly. The only things known with certainty are that he was killed in the rioting and that he had nothing to do with the Berkeley campus or student body.

Late in the afternoon the street fighting tapered off. Police firing shotguns pursued terrified demonstrators through the side streets and on to the Berkeley campus. Students studying in a library on campus far removed from the scene of the action were thrown into a sudden panic when buckshot was fired through a window by police who were chasing demonstrators and firing into the air.

At nightfall the police declared a curfew and Governor Reagan called out the National Guard. Thousands of guardsmen in military uniforms and armed with rifles soon ringed the Berkeley campus while helicopters cruised overhead to spot potential sources of trouble. The whole city of Berkeley lay stunned and seething.

For the next ten days angry students and street people attempted to march and disrupt the life of Berkeley's business district. Law enforcement authorities responded by banning congregations of more than three people. Nearly 1000 arrests were made by police and guardsmen. The arrests included, of course, many innocents who just happened to be in the wrong place at the wrong time. One of those picked up during these sweeps was a hapless postman delivering the mail.[14]

There seems to be no doubt that excessive force was used by police during the street fighting on May 15, in the sweeps through the business district during the next ten days, and in processing those arrested and taken to the Santa Rita prison facility. All the tensions among the countercultural street people, the campus radicals, and Berkeley's straight citizens were released in a sudden spasm of uncontrolled anger. Police and prison authorities, reacting to taunts from people they despised, seemed to lose their professional discipline and attacked the demonstrators with a vengeance. All semblance of prosecutorial rigor or of civil liberties was lost. The demonstrators were not arrested for later trial; they were beaten and punished on the spot.[15]

I first learned of the battle of People's Park at the moment the Regents heard of it. We were meeting in the Faculty Center at UCLA on Thursday afternoon. During an executive session of the Committee on Educational Policy, Earl F. Cheit, Berkeley's executive vice chancellor, was suddenly called out of the room for an urgent phone call. When he returned, he announced that violent street fighting had occurred near People's Park in Berkeley. It began some time in the early afternoon and continued for more than an hour. Cheit said that a large crowd had assembled in Sproul Plaza and marched to the park. There had been gunfire. There were numerous injuries among police and demonstrators. A policeman had been stabbed.

The Regents were genuinely shocked. They immediately adjourned their committee meeting and began to talk among themselves about the public position they should take. I slipped out of the room to call George Murphy at UCSD. He had already heard the news.

Was anything going on in Revelle College?

Nothing. But there would be trouble over this, make no mistake about it. Murphy would go over to Revelle College immediately and keep an eye on things. If anything developed he would call me.

Next morning, Governor Reagan arrived in the midst of a noisy demonstration outside the Faculty Center. I found myself impressed as I had been before by his personal courage, remembering my own fears when I first stood alone in a hostile crowd. While his security people fretted, the Governor emerged from his limousine in front of the Faculty Center, stood for a moment tight-lipped, staring coldly at the demonstrators pressing in around him, and then shouldered his way through the angry, shouting, spitting faces that tried to confront him as he entered the building.

Later in the day, during the open session of the Regents, the room had to be cleared because Dutch Higgs, the chairman, was unable to restore order amid constant booing, shouting, and catcalls from an unruly student audience.

As thousands of demonstrators surrounded the building and pounded on its floor to ceiling glass walls, the Regents resumed their meeting, now with only press and television people present, and a bitter exchange between the Governor and Regent Fred Dutton took place.

Dutton was a Washington lawyer, a Democrat, and a close associate of the Kennedys. He told the Governor that the Regents were making a grave error in cutting themselves off from student concerns. People's Park would be only the beginning of a bitter period in which the Regents, by erecting unnecessary barriers between themselves and the student body, were actually strengthening revolutionaries on the campuses.

Governor Reagan was grim. At those meetings of the Regents in 1968–69 he was never the warm, cheerful figure his admirers saw in public. The Governor's lips were drawn into a tight, hard line that tended to exaggerate the wrinkles around his mouth. He replied to Dutton in an angry, biting flow of words that most of us had heard before.

There were only two alternatives, he said. Either we crush these outbursts or we surrender. Students will obey the law. If they do not, they'd better get out of his way because he will come in with force and he will break them.[16]

It was chilling. I sat there listening to the Governor saying that we might be on the brink of a student revolution. Force was what revolutionaries understood, and he was going to give it to them. None of it made sense. I was sure that the Governor did not believe there was any immediate danger. His idea was that radicals were dominating the university because they were protected by the faculty and no one opposed them. He intended to be the opposition. Could it be possible that we might bungle our way into a holy war? Were we about to drive all those inexperienced, gullible young people, who wanted only to make a dramatic gesture on behalf of a better world, into the hands of revolutionaries?

The meeting ended, but the Faculty Center was still surrounded by a crowd of several thousand students who ignored Chancellor Young's repeated pleas to disperse. The Regents and the Governor would have to be extracted from the building, but the UCLA campus police seemed unable to do it.

After a delay of half an hour a force of about fifty helmeted Los Angeles police arrived. They were in riot gear and carrying batons. Their commander surveyed the situation and then drew his men up in three tight lines at the main entrance of the Faculty Center. He stepped out in the front with a bullhorn to address the crowd.

"I am Lieutenant Nesbitt of the Los Angeles Police Department. In the name of the people of California I command you to disperse."

(From the crowd) "We are the people. Pigs off campus."

Nesbitt gave a sign to his men. They closed ranks, put out their batons in front of them, held horizontally belt-high with both gloved hands, and in perfect discipline took one step forward, then another, and another. Slowly the crowd yielded before the menacing line of blue uniforms, hard hats, and clubs.

"Pigs off campus. Pigs off campus."

The chant came from the crowd, but they were yielding. Step by step the three advancing blue lines moved them down the roadway away from the Faculty Center. No blows were struck. No one was knocked down.

At a point perhaps fifty yards down the road, after the entrance to the Regents' parking lot had been cleared, the front line of police raised their clubs in unison and charged.

The crowd immediately bolted. The three lines of police then wheeled portions of the fleeing crowd center, left, and right in what was evidently a well-rehearsed maneuver. The demonstration was now completely broken up. Thousands simply ran away, chased in three different directions by fifty disciplined men. There were no arrests. It was an awesome display of control by trained experts. As I walked to my car in the parking lot, now completely cleared of demonstrators, I wished somehow that Lieutenant Nesbitt and his men had formed the police contingent confronting the crowd at People's Park on the previous afternoon. The outcome might have been very different.

I was on the Berkeley campus a few days later on Sunday, May 18, to attend a scheduled meeting that went on despite the quasi-military occupation. Late in the morning I flew up to San Francisco, rented an automobile at the airport, and drove over to Berkeley.

I parked the rented car well down on Dana Street only a short distance from the fenced-in People's Park. In the almost eerie quiet that permeated the scene of the street fighting three days earlier, I paused for a few minutes to look around, and then walked over to the campus. Little groups of guardsmen stood on duty at every corner. All were carrying rifles. One nubile young woman, sexually provocative, was trying to present a flower to a young guardsman who stared at the rooftops in an effort to ignore her.

As I entered the campus through the gate at Dana Street and Bancroft Way, helmeted, armed guardsmen were standing spaced about five feet apart along the sidewalk and visible for as far as the eye could see in both directions. Overhead two olive-drab helicopters slowly swung back and forth over the campus at low altitude.

It was a perfectly lovely day. Strollers moved up and down along the sidewalk and little knots of students sat bathed in sunshine on the grass inside the gate. Except for the soldiers, the scene was one of utter peacefulness. An officer appraised people quizzically as they passed into the campus but there was no challenge, no request to identify ourselves.

Inside the gate nothing in the pastoral scene suggested the terror that had suddenly burst out there only three days earlier. There is a curious tranquility about a campus just after a violent emotional explosion. It is as though people are emotionally spent. They search, almost desperately it seems, for some respite in the beauty of nature. If the sun is still warm and the flowers still bloom, life cannot be as ugly as it appeared to be in those awful moments. And people try to go on.

Over the weekend of May 17–18, student organizations all over the University of California were frantically calling each other, discussing

People's Park, and attempting to work out a coordinated plan for expressing their revulsion over what had happened on Thursday. Later we learned that they were considering a universitywide student strike. Murphy came in to see me on Monday morning. Something was evidently going on, but he did not yet have a clear idea of what it might be. His sources among the students were on the verge of hysteria.

Besides, we were barely out of the woods with Lumumba-Zapata College. The senate planning committee set up under Silvio Varon's "impossible" resolution of May 7 had just drawn up its proposal for Third College. The minority students seemed to have agreed to it. Things were beginning to look brighter, but we would not know for certain until the senate met and reacted to the document. That might be tomorrow, Tuesday.

"We just don't need anything else to worry about right now, boss."

I nodded agreement, turned my palms up, and shrugged.

On Tuesday morning, May 20, the waves of irrationality unleashed by the battle for People's Park finally washed across the San Diego campus. At eleven o'clock the phone rang in the chancellor's office. It was the blond, rugged-looking assistant professor of philosophy with whom I had jousted in Revelle Plaza over Eldridge Cleaver and Social Analysis 139X.

He fairly shouted on the line that a student had just died in Berkeley after having been shot at People's Park. I would simply have to close the campus down or there would be an explosion. He would take no responsibility for what might happen unless I ordered a cessation of classes immediately.

I did not have the foggiest idea of what he was talking about. Upwards of fifty people had been hit by birdshot, but there was no word over the weekend that anyone had died. I told the young professor that I could not close the campus down but would try to learn whether there was any new information. He hung up on me abruptly.

I called Berkeley at once and was told about James Rector. He had died at ten o'clock Monday night. People at Berkeley were puzzled over my questions because Rector was not a student there or at any other branch of the university. Conceivably he might have been one of the Telegraph Avenue street people, but their best guess was that he was simply visiting a friend who lived near People's Park. Apparently Rector was a curious bystander whose luck happened to run out during the riot.

I put down the phone feeling almost sick. There would be no way to avoid the deluge now. We might as well prepare ourselves. I dialed Murphy's number. He too had heard the news. Word was all over campus that a Berkeley student had died after having been shot by police at People's Park. It was big, big trouble.

I asked George to come right over so that we might discuss developments and begin to plan. He begged off. Perhaps a bit later in the afternoon; he had some talking to do with students. He would be better able to guide me when he saw how this dreadful thing was hitting them.

Two o'clock found me in my office talking to UCSD's director of planning. The sounds of muffled voices and heavy footsteps came drifting through the walls. Anita buzzed from the reception area. She reported that a large group of students were in the outer office demanding to see me. Without a word of explanation to the director of planning, I jumped up from the desk, strode quickly over to the door, and stepped out into an angry crowd flooding the chancellor's reception area. There were some sixty students and a half dozen faculty. All were very excited and talking at once. I listened to the babble for a few moments, then held up my hands in what I hoped was a commanding gesture:

"This is no place to talk. Why don't you all come with me? We'll find a spot outside where we can be more comfortable and I can at least hear what you are saying."

With that I led them out of the office into a small sunny patio adjacent to the chancellor's conference room. By this time I had learned that when an angry group comes calling, not to seize your office but to air their grievances, it is unwise to wait for them to burst in. Since they cannot keep themselves away from you, you have the capacity to lead them wherever you wish them to be—preferably to some place out in the open air. In that way secretaries and other administrators working in nearby offices can resume their activities. They may be a bit nervous, but at least the crowd has moved on.

I marched over to the patio near the conference room trailed by the entire group. As I turned and faced them they arranged themselves in a neat half circle around me. At the front row of the semicircle stood three faculty members: the philosopher, the professor of German literature, and an assistant professor of French literature. The first two were old friends, so to speak. I knew them now by their first names. They had been involved in every single conflict that developed on campus during the year, doing their damnedest in each one to radicalize the student body. Ron, the philosopher, was the fellow who had phoned a few hours earlier demanding that the campus be closed down. The assistant professor of French literature, Tony, was a Canadian, a self-styled revolutionary, very intense, very articulate, but rather charming, and, I thought, basically harmless.

We argued for nearly two hours. It was one of those long, rambling, ineffectual discussions in which no opinions change. Disputation is the life's blood of any campus, and once involved, students cannot escape it without risking loss of face and loss of sympathy from the rest of the academic community. Hence once I began challenging their arguments, the students could not break off the discussion. I could hold them until tempers cooled and pent-up emotions ebbed away.

Ron, the philosopher, acting as spokesman for the group, demanded that we cancel all classes for the balance of the week so that the campus might mourn James Rector's death.

I said that there were other ways to show our sympathy. Cancelling classes seemed to defeat the very purpose of the university.

The group asserted that Rector was a student at Berkeley and that he had been shot with a .38 caliber automatic.

I said my best information was that he was not a student. To my knowledge he had been hit by buckshot. At that point no one really knew who had done the shooting. We all ought to calm down until the facts became clear. It would take time but that was a small price to pay for knowledge.

Tony demanded that in the meantime I send telegrams to Chancellor Heyns, President Hitch, the Regents, and the Governor condemning them for the roles they played in the battle of People's Park.

I refused. Anything I had to say to Chancellor Heyns would be said privately. He was my friend. The sketchy reports I had received did not seem to warrant any conclusions yet. Wouldn't it be better to calm down and try to learn the facts? I saw no particular point in my sending telegrams to the Regents expressing students' views. If they wanted to send telegrams, why didn't they do it themselves?

The group replied that a telegram from me would carry more weight. And so it went, around and around, getting nowhere. After about an hour and a half of this kind of exchange, Ron, the assistant professor of philosophy, announced to the group that he had had enough. The chancellor was plainly an immoral man who would not be swayed by any argument or even by the murder of a student.

The crowd began to thin out. I saw George Murphy and several of his "baby deans" now standing on the fringes. They had come over to brief me as promised, but found me already in the middle of the trouble they were anticipating.

Finally the discussion ended, and I was able to go back into my office without attracting a crowd.

The deans and I held a brief postmortem in the office. This was evidently only the beginning. A coalition of student groups had asked to use the Revelle College Cafeteria that night for a mass meeting at eight o'clock. Murphy and his staff would cover it. He doubted that anything would happen before then, but he and his people were watchful. His staff had organized itself that afternoon for around-the-clock coverage of the campus until further notice.

It was nearly four o'clock. An important senate meeting on Third College was scheduled at four in Revelle College.

Murphy and I started across campus together. As we traversed the graceful wooden footbridge leading to Revelle College, I described the origins of the fence around People's Park, and the angry argument between Fred Dutton and Governor Reagan at the Regents meeting. Murphy shook his head sadly.

"Boss, sometimes I think we are living in an insane asylum."

A few moments later we entered the Humanities Library Auditorium, where the senate was about to meet. It was flooded with students. Walter Munk, the chairman, was attempting to clear the room as he was required to do under senate rules. Several faculty members, among them Herbert Marcuse, argued that the situation was too grave to permit us to conduct business in the usual way. The senate ought to forget its rules, invite the students in, and try to pass a resolution demanding that the military occupation of the Berkeley campus be lifted. In that way we might keep the lid on at UCSD.

Munk stood his ground. The room would have to be cleared of all visitors. Only members of the academic senate and authorized observers were eligible to remain. The chairman would not call the senate to order until the visitors departed.

No one moved. From a corner of the room came a motion to adjourn in view of the disruption. It was immediately seconded, and carried overwhelmingly by a voice vote. Thus, in less than fifteen minutes, a critical senate meeting suddenly evaporated. Walter Munk took me aside as we were filing out of the auditorium. Despite the excitement over People's Park, he felt it extremely important to get Third College back on track. Munk would attempt to reschedule this adjourned meeting for the next day, Wednesday, at 3:30 in the afternoon.[17]

Murphy and I retraced our steps to the administrative area after the aborted Senate meeting. We immediately closeted ourselves in his office to formulate a plan.

Murphy was suggesting a campuswide convocation at noon tomorrow. The long argument I had with students and faculty outside my office earlier convinced him that there were all sorts of erroneous ideas abroad about who James Rector was and how he was killed. It would be important to get the facts out before an outraged student body did something grossly foolish on the basis of unsubstantiated rumors. Besides, we had to find a way to reassure one another and express the anguish we all felt.

I was dubious. The mass meeting of students scheduled for the Revelle Cafeteria in three hours worried me. What if they decided to call a strike tonight? A convocation at noon tomorrow might well be taken over by a radical leadership and used to promote the strike. It was risky.

As we were debating the proposal back and forth, two members of the faculty arrived, along with the student body president. They joined our discussion. The faculty members had heard a rumor that we intended to cancel classes tomorrow so that everyone could spend the day talking about People's Park and pleading for nonviolent solutions to disputes. The three visitors believed it would offer an excellent way to defuse the atmosphere of crisis now building up rapidly on campus.

I rejected cancelling classes. It was a nonsolution because no one really knew yet what had happened at People's Park. Besides, many students objected to having their studies interrupted in deference to the concerns of other students. It was too divisive. What did they think about a campuswide convocation at noon on Wednesday?

They leaped at it. The student body president, Tom Shepard, was persuaded to take the leadership. At the mass meeting that night in Revelle College, Tom would call for the convocation on Wednesday and request suspension of classes between the hours of twelve noon and one o'clock. He would ask me to lead off the convocation. These actions would be demanded of us in the certain knowledge that we would agree to them. Shepard also asked that flags on campus be lowered to half staff to symbolize our mourning. I agreed. Shepard asked me if I understood that he would have to invite many others to speak at the convocation and that I might find much of what they said objectionable. I understood.

With that we all shook hands and went off, each to his own constituency to secure backing for this temperate response to the events in Berkeley, and to plan for what would surely be a rough day. We could almost feel the rising temperature of the campus and the likelihood of an explosion if we blundered or if something entirely unforeseen should happen.

At about ten o'clock George Murphy called me at home. He was with the provost of Revelle College. The mass meeting in Revelle Cafeteria had just ended. Shepard managed to announce a noon-hour convocation tomorrow, Wednesday, but everything else had been a disaster.

First of all, George reported, at least 700 students were there in the Revelle Cafeteria. He had never seen anything like it since the heyday of the Berkeley Free Speech Movement in 1964. It would be hard to describe what he witnessed as a meeting. It was a mad scene with constant shrieking chants, waving fists, and billowing clouds of marijuana smoke.

"If I sound a bit stoned, boss, you will understand why!"

Our faculty *agitprops* were all there in prominent leadership roles along with the SDS. In the jumble of the night's events Murphy could not recall exactly who had proposed a student strike, but faculty members backed the idea, and it passed by acclamation. No dissent at all. About the only comfort to us was the fact that to bring the entire group along with them, SDS leaders had to agree that the strike would be nonviolent.

"Boss, you were right. The convocation is a mistake. They will use it to promote the strike."

"George, what do they mean by a student strike if they do not intend to try to shut us down forcibly?"

"They will be picketing tomorrow morning and trying to persuade other students to stay out of classes. But I wouldn't put too much faith in the nonviolence pledge, if I were you. This situation offers a gold-plated opportunity to SDS. If they can't shut us down nonviolently, they will try to strong-arm us."

"How long do you think the strike will go on?"

"Their statement at the meeting tonight was that the university would remain closed until the National Guard is removed from Berkeley. I think it might be advisable for you to make a statement that the campus will remain open in spite of the strike vote."

I sat down in the quiet comfort of my living room and composed a statement on a yellow lined pad. I wrote that the campus would remain open. "I will not force students to attend classes, . . . [but] I insist on the right of professors to teach and will protect the rights of all students who wish to attend classes." Then I picked up the phone and called the statement in to the campus public affairs office. My words greeted me in the morning newspaper along with the report of the mass meeting and the strike vote.

Some faculty were critical afterwards. They felt that I was too harsh with aroused students who meant no harm. But after Murphy's report of the strike meeting and the role played not only by SDS but by the same old cast of characters with whom I had found myself at war since last August, there was no doubt about what had to be done. Murphy had not hesitated; nor had I.

We would have to take them on. Later, when it was established that they could not shut us down, I would make peace with the students.

Meanwhile, SDS was going to see some fancy footwork from us. We would make them march all day and plan all night. By god, we would be the first administration in history to exhaust *them* despite the difference in ages. And there would be no recourse to force. No mistakes like that!

I got back on the phone to public affairs and scheduled a press conference at University House at four o'clock the next afternoon, Wednesday. Undoubtedly SDS would be busy all day issuing statements on the success of the strike. We had to counter them. Moreover, Walter Munk had rescheduled the senate meeting for 3:30 Wednesday afternoon. There was no chance now for a serious discussion of Third College's new academic plan. SDS and its faculty supporters would be there in force to demand senate backing for the strike.

Reporters would have to decide whether to cover the senate meeting in Revelle College or the chancellor's press conference at University House on the opposite side of the campus.

Next morning, Wednesday, May 21, students were in front of all the buildings of Revelle College, carrying hand-lettered signs and passing out leaflets, but there were relatively few pickets. As I walked around the college before going to the office, all seemed peaceful.

Murphy reported to me periodically during the morning. Support was not extensive. Roughly 100 students were parading around buildings and through Revelle Plaza. He felt that the situation was under control. Apparently nothing much was due to happen until the noon-hour convocation set for the campus gymnasium at the north edge of Revelle College.

I went over to the gym at noon. A wooden platform had been set up indoors at the west end of the basketball court. The place was jammed when I arrived. More than 2500 students were standing or sitting on the gym floor looking toward the raised platform where someone was testing microphones and a public address system.

The floor was flooded with strike banners and placards. Even more remarkable, dozens of students were wearing white T-shirts stencilled with a red fist and the word "strike" written below it. I wondered how in the world they had time to do the stencilling job, and why in the world they would want to. It seemed more like a festival than a strike.[18]

The convocation opened with my brief appeal for reason and good sense at UCSD in this moment of Berkeley's grief. When I finished there was a smattering of polite applause, the last applause I was to hear until after commencement.

When I finished speaking, I climbed the stairs into the balcony of the gym to listen to the rest of the program. The newly elected student body president, about to replace Tom Shepard, called for student unity across the nine campuses of the university. "The way to get results," he said, "is to strike."

Then Lowell Bergman,[19] a philosophy graduate student and a splendid orator, called up images of black students shot in the back in Orangeburg, South Carolina, and peaceful demonstrators brutalized by Mayor Daley's cops in Chicago. Each blood-tinged sentence was greeted with howls of anger, clenched fists, and waving placards. Bergman urged the students to strike until the university was restructured as a free institution and Berkeley was liberated.

Walter Munk, the senate chairman, made a graceful little talk on the importance of tolerance and restraint. He urged that we learn from Berkeley to look after our own problems.

MAYA and the Black Students Council linked their proposals for Lumumba-Zapata College to the repression now in evidence in Berkeley. Walter had been trying to redirect the attention of the campus to our own Lumumba-Zapata dispute, but few people listening possessed the subtlety to see what he was driving at.

All things considered, the convocation was not as bad as my worst fears led me to believe. It may, in fact, have served a useful purpose by venting a great deal of anger and deescalating hysteria. The climactic moment came shortly after one o'clock, when Linus Pauling and Herbert Marcuse joined each other on the platform in the din of a standing ovation from the crowd.

Pauling told the audience that strikes were legitimate whenever injustices were committed. He was cheered when he said that students, faculty, and UC employees should be "unified against the sort of immorality that is going on in this university."

When Marcuse spoke, the student audience was so quiet I could actually hear my own breathing against his amplified, heavily accented words. Marcuse declared himself on strike until the police and the National Guard were withdrawn from Berkeley. "I just could not go on teaching, business as usual, while those things are happening in Berkeley."

The students leaped to their feet as one person and cheered and cheered their approval. Pauling and Marcuse embraced each other on the platform and the convocation ended.

SDS members immediately seized the microphone to declare an open forum, but the audience had already seen its glimpse of the infinite in that wonderful scene with Pauling and Marcuse. The students began to drift away, and SDS gave up after half an hour.

I sat up in the gym balcony, unnoticed, shaking my head in disbelief over what I had just witnessed. Quite a pair, those two!

On my desk that morning was Marcuse's application for a paid leave of absence beginning on May 24 and extending until the end of the spring quarter. The application and the supporting documents testified that Marcuse's teaching commitments had been met during the fall and winter quarters and that his graduate students were arranged for during the period of requested leave. Thus he could depart the campus, the application stated, with no outstanding obligations at all. Marcuse's declaration that he was on strike was simple grandstanding. I reflected for a moment about the risks I had taken on his behalf in February and about intellectual honesty, the central value of the scholarly life.[20]

As for Linus Pauling, I wondered what those cheering young innocents might think if they knew that a significant part of Pauling's work at UCSD was devoted to a Defense Department contract. I did not consider that to be "immoral," but I knew damned well the students would have—had they known.

I returned to my office in Camp Matthews at half past one still stewing about morality and human frailty. Murphy had arrived a few minutes earlier to report on the morning's strike activity. The situation still seemed to be under control. At noon, just prior to the convocation, the number of marching pickets swelled briefly to 250 people, but throughout the morning the campus experienced no serious interference with instruction. Most classes appeared to be meeting.

George was very concerned about the possibility of a strike resolution at the rescheduled meeting of the senate later in the day. I looked at him in surprise. It seemed almost a foregone conclusion. Why worry about that in view of all our other headaches? I planned to return from my press conference long before the senate adjourned. It was unlikely that the senate would vote to support the strike, but if they did there would be ample opportunity to speak, and perhaps also to tell them what I thought of them.

"So that's where it is, boss?"

"George, I have had it up to here," gesturing with my hand at eye level, "over all the goddam nonsense we have been putting up with this year. When I listened to Marcuse and Pauling this afternoon, I realized I've been wasting my time protecting them. What we are confronting now is too incendiary to allow us to play senate politics as usual. You and I will do whatever has to be done to prevent this strike from getting out of hand. If the senate approves, that will be just fine. Delightful. If they do not, well, perhaps we can both find jobs as consultants to campuses that want to avoid committing suicide."

It was an intemperate outburst and unfair to the faculty. We had been through a great deal together during that incredible year. They had never really let me down. But my feelings reflected the pressure I was under. The process leading to some kind of break with the senate was obviously in motion, and if I had only realized what was happening, I might have disciplined myself to try to prevent it. But I was so intensely involved with fighting the strike that I could not see the obvious.

Murphy asked whether I remembered that Captain Stout, the Marine Corps recruiter, was scheduled to stage a ceremonial return to the campus at our invitation on Friday, just two days later. Captain Stout would be completing the interviews abandoned during the blocking incident on February 21.

"Migod, George, I had forgotten it completely. We simply can't cancel him now after inviting him back here and committing ourselves completely on it. Have disciplinary warnings been placed in the transcripts of the students who blocked Captain Stout?"

"Yes, boss. Oh, we have to go through with the interviews, but they couldn't come at a worse time."

"Does SDS know he will be here on Friday?"

"They know. My informants say there is a plan to arrange a big reception at the placement office on Friday morning. SDS will try to take Captain Stout hostage as he enters Camp Matthews. I am pretty sure the San Diego police know about it. They have informants in SDS."

"What are you saying?"

"Probably, that Captain Stout will come in with a large contingent of police to protect him. SDS will almost surely try to provoke a battle with the cops."

It was another natural—a diamond-studded, gold-plated opportunity. We could expect to have People's Park again, San Diego style. At a minimum Camp Matthews would be teeming with demonstrators, perhaps a thousand of them, on Friday morning. Who could tell what might happen in a tinderbox like that?

Murphy had a plan. He wanted to move the site of the interviews from the campus itself to the University Hospital area in Hillcrest, ten miles to the south. Murphy had already sent someone down there to scout the possibilities. There was a house on Dickinson Street adjacent to the hospital. It would be ideal for our purposes because it was university property and thus conformed to the terms of our invitation to Captain Stout.

SDS would never be able to unravel the plan in time. Murphy would swear the interviewees to secrecy. They were all straight students and we could depend on them.

Was I willing to approve the plan?

It was brilliant. You're damn right I was!

And so I put in a call to a Colonel Kennedy, Captain Stout's superior, in San Francisco. I told Colonel Kennedy we were transferring the site of Friday's interviews from Camp Matthews to University Hospital. He was understandably upset about it and protested bitterly. I suggested that we did not have a choice if we wanted to avoid a violent scene. Moreover we were entirely within our rights in designating the place at which the interviews would take place. And that was it—take it or leave it.

He took it, but under protest. Next day I heard from nearly everyone in the Corps up to General Lowell English, commander of the Marine Corps Recruit Depot in San Diego. I stood my ground. Lowell, someone with whom I got along, told me I was making a serious mistake. All this maneuvering would simply encourage SDS to greater excesses. I asked him to let us fight our campus wars in our own way.

As soon as the new arrangement for Captain Stout's interviews was firm, I called Ralph Davis, the captain in charge of the northern division of the San Diego Police, and confessed what we had done. There would be no need to protect the Marine Corps recruiter from angry crowds as he entered the campus on Friday morning. Davis seemed relieved. He said it was a smart way to handle a ticklish problem.

I invited Captain Davis to come up and spend the next day or two with us at the campus police office in Camp Matthews. We expected it to be a hot period. Almost certainly the police would be receiving anxious phone calls from people on campus as they watched student demonstrators marching back and forth. It was important for him to see what was actually going on and how we were trying to handle it. We wanted no use of force except as a last resort. Hence there must be no surprises.

Davis accepted the invitation immediately. Then he confessed that he had already been up on campus earlier in the day in mufti. It seemed to him that we knew what we were doing.

With these crucial preparations underway, I went over to the senate. Unlike the previous day, the room was a model of decorum. A few pickets marched around Revelle Plaza, but there was no repetition of Tuesday's vain struggle to clear visitors from the auditorium. They wanted no disruption today.

As I took my seat, several excited faculty members converged on me. The campus was alive with stories that a helicopter had sprayed tear gas all over the Berkeley campus shortly after the noon hour on Tuesday, injuring many innocent people. Could it possibly be true? Did I know anything about it?

No, I had heard nothing. "You guys are so uptight you're beginning to believe anything."

In fact, at 1:50 PM on Tuesday a National Guard helicopter attempted to break up a crowd of 4000 people in Sproul Plaza by making repeated passes at low altitude while dropping CS tear gas over the heads of the demonstrators.[21]

Even among Berkeley veterans, faculty and administrators who had been through countless experiences with the police in the years prior to 1969, no one could recall having seen anything quite like it. Because it managed to injure so many people who were, in effect, doing nothing but minding their own business, the helicopter attack on the Berkeley campus was eventually to become a classic in the annals of law enforcement. Specialists in crowd control and police officials would cite it as an example of what not to do in tense situations.[22]

Both the Berkeley radicals and the Governor had now managed to test their theories of forceful action in emotion-laden disputes, and we had a fairly good picture of the results: one man dead, another blinded, up to fifty shot, and a helicopter spewing noxious gas over a university campus so as to injure the guilty and innocent alike.

For the radicals who had fashioned the issue, the total failure of law enforcement officials to understand the subtleties posed by People's Park offered a promise of radicalization beyond their wildest dreams. If, as the New Left hoped, the young people of the country were ready for revolution in 1969, the spark to set it off might easily have been People's Park. The whole affair in the ten days that followed the struggle over the park on May 15 was so sordid, so brutal, and from the standpoint of effective law enforcement so remarkably stupid, as to create a danger more serious than the original street battle. But no revolutionary aftermath of People's Park ever developed. Student revolutionaries proved to be bookish amateurs in their pursuit of violence. When they saw people actually shot and bleeding, they were sickened and terrified. Harsh repression did not drive them deeper into the flames as it does with serious revolutionaries. Instead, New Left students recoiled into depression and narcissism.

The most important outcome of the battle of People's Park was a blizzard of lawsuits citing violations of civil rights. These lawsuits were certainly justified, but it is difficult to see them as part of a revolutionary social movement. The fact is that, except for a tiny fringe of dangerous terrorists, there was no real stomach for violence in the New Left. Revolution was something you practiced on college presidents, who, under the rules of the game, were not permitted to fight back. When the idea was tried against armed police and tough governors, as at People's Park and later at Kent State, the experience of genuine violence simply cut the heart out of the student movement.

But killing and maiming them was not a suitable way to respond to their provocations. Most were romantics, not revolutionaries. Other, more thoughtful means existed for controlling crowds of angry students with at least the possibility of winning them back to the cause of democratic government instead of confirming their hostility.

As for Governor Reagan and his ideas on how to deal with radical students, the Governor seemed surprised by the ineffectuality of old-fashioned law enforcement techniques at People's Park. He was really trying to take maximum political advantage of the confrontational tactics of New Left revolutionaries. The political advantage was there to be gained, as the Governor's subsequent career demonstrated. But he never intended that people be shot and killed. Although Governor Reagan only hinted at it in public, the helicopter gassing of the Berkeley campus must have had him holding his head in disbelief at the ineptitude of the Alameda County sheriff and other senior law enforcement officials trying to carry out his direction to restore order.

After People's Park, Governor Reagan appeared willing to employ more subtle approaches to student unrest. A year later, when shootings occurred at Kent State in Ohio under circumstances not very different from People's Park, the Governor's response was quite sensitive. He closed the University of California down by executive order for a short period. Up until the moment the Governor acted, the radicals were demanding that we shut down at once to mourn the deaths at Kent State and Jackson State. Immediately after he acted, the radicals at UCSD were demanding that we remain open. The Governor was learning.

As soon as the senate was called to order, a student representative moved to amend the agenda by adding a resolution in support of the strike. The amendment was aimed at having the senate debate the strike before any other matter came up. It meant that Third College's academic plan and all other pending business would have to wait for another day. There was some grumbling about this, but the faculty recognized that they could no longer ignore the week's events at Berkeley. A debate on the strike was unavoidable. The amendment was accepted just as I slipped out of the room to be driven off campus to the press conference scheduled for four o'clock at University House.

Reporters expressed annoyance at having to deal with me so far away from the scene of the action in Revelle College, but all of them came nevertheless.

What were my reactions to the strike?

It did not appear to me to be effective. Most classes were meeting. A student "strike" is merely a linguistic gesture unless, in some way, it becomes effective in modifying the university's basic activity. By that criterion the strike was a failure. Anyone taking the trouble to look could see that we were functioning normally. I would not demand that students attend classes, but I was also not going to fold up and go home merely because some students declared themselves to be on strike. The "strike" seemed to me to be a media event, not a real problem at this time.

One of the reporters observed that student strikes had broken out on nearly every campus of the university. Many of the strike demands seemed to be the same from campus to campus. Did this mean that there was a coordinated strategy?

Probably so. They had certainly been spending a great deal of time on the phone with each other.

Why was I so vehemently opposed to the strike? Other chancellors seemed more sympathetic. One had already announced his support of a student strike. Another chancellor had put up bail money for several of his students arrested while demonstrating in Berkeley.

I was opposed to the strike. I could understand the revulsion students must feel over the quasi-military occupation of the Berkeley campus, but they had to recognize that a man had been killed in a street riot. A policeman had also been stabbed. These things were utterly intolerable in a community dedicated to reason. We must avoid all inflammatory acts leading to similar violent incidents here in La Jolla. The only way to emerge from this horror with integrity was through an absolute commitment to nonviolence.

I was pledging myself here and now to nonviolent opposition to the strike, but we were determined to protect UCSD from the waves of irrationality sweeping over campuses everywhere in the U.S. We were equally determined to resist every effort from any quarter to convert the university into a political instrument.

Besides, despite the protestations of nonviolence from the strike leaders, everyone on campus knew that the same cast of characters, the student and faculty radicals who had engineered virtually every disruption on campus during the past year, was firmly planted in the leadership of this strike. How could students reach out to the community around us and make their cause credible when they chose a means calculated to produce so much skepticism?

In view of my pledge of nonviolent opposition, what would I do if buildings were occupied?

"I never speculate. We hope that it will not happen."

The press conference was over. Reporters and TV cameramen packed up their gear, and in most cases, headed downtown. A few wanted to look in on the senate meeting before it adjourned. I gave them a lift back to the campus.

As I reentered the auditorium in Revelle College and took my seat in the first row, I was concerned about the fate of the strike resolution. A faculty member seated behind me leaned forward and whispered in my ear that the resolution in support of the strike had been tabled. The senate was now debating a substitute. It had been amended several times, and the senate was coming close to a vote. The text of the substitute was being written by Professor Sheldon Schultz on a blackboard at the front of the room.

I studied the language of the resolution and my heart sank. It had two parts. The first asked the faculty to meet their classes on Thursday and Friday (the next two days) but to suspend regular activities and devote time to a discussion of events and issues at Berkeley.

The second part of the resolution established a five-member committee headed by Professor Norman Kroll, a universally respected physicist. The committee was charged to go to Berkeley immediately, try to find out what was happening there, and report back to the senate as soon as possible.

The fact-finding committee seemed to be a splendid idea. UCSD was flooded with rumors and emotion-laden propaganda about what had taken place in Berkeley. At the same time the Governor was giving his own version to the press in Sacramento. No one really knew how the street fighting had started, who James Rector was, who shot him, why the helicopter attacked the crowd in Sproul Plaza, or indeed any of the essential facts enabling reasonable people to evaluate inflammatory versions of the People's Park battle circulating in the university.

But the first part of the resolution! It was the senate's way of soothing the great emotional upheaval that had brought so many straight students to support the strike. Nevertheless it seemed completely illogical to me to discuss events at Berkeley before the Kroll committee returned to campus to tell us what had happened.

The more I thought about the contradiction the madder I got. It was another of those sudden surges of anger that came so frequently now that I found myself almost constantly embattled. I had been brought up in the Columbia faculty to believe that the classroom is a sacred place, where only the truth is pursued. Now the proponents of the resolution were proposing to authorize biased classroom discussions before any of the facts about People's Park were really known.

I felt sure the resolution would be defeated. It passed overwhelmingly in a show of hands, as I watched disbelieving. Only a few hardline conservative faculty joined me in voting against it.

I got up out of my seat and stalked angrily from the meeting, followed by Shelly Schultz, who was urging me to come back and speak to the senate about what was upsetting me so. After all, he observed, I had said not one word beforehand in opposition to the resolution.

He was right. I calmed down momentarily and returned to the meeting with my hand raised asking for the floor. Immediately the chairman recognized me.

"The recommendation just adopted," I said, "is irresponsible in the extreme and I will have nothing to do with it. Classroom discussion of events occurring in Berkeley when none of the facts are known, is not teaching, it is indoctrination. I call on all members of the faculty to meet their professional responsibilities to the education of their students."

My statement completed, I wheeled and walked out of the senate a second time, with the eerie sound of total silence in my ears. Bob Hamburger, the assistant dean of medicine, told me later that my face was contorted with rage as I stood there denouncing the resolution. He could see the veins standing out in my neck and forehead as I shouted, and he feared for me.

Back in my office, I composed a brief statement completing the break with the senate. In its essentials it said:

. . . UCSD is not on strike and will not be as long as there is a professor who will teach and a student who will listen.
This afternoon the Academic Senate moved to recommend to their colleagues that they devote all regular classes on Thursday and Friday to a discussion of events on the Berkeley campus. I repudiate this recommendation. This is not teaching in the traditions of UCSD's great faculty. It is the basest form of indoctrination! No one can downgrade the concern we all feel for Berkeley's week of tragedy and violence. I express that concern via my own commitment to reason and debate—to peaceful change and nonviolence. I will not attempt to indoctrinate my students. . . . I intend to meet my class this week and I plan to teach it with every bit of zeal and commitment I possess. This is the only way I know to express my own conception of duty and responsibility.

Suppressed fury and moral preaching show through nearly every sentence. It was an overreaction to what the senate had done, although even to this day my skepticism remains undiminished about what passed for instruction in many UCSD classrooms during those two days. It was at about this time that a young woman undergraduate asked to see me to complain about Tony, the radical assistant professor of French literature. He had told her after one of these classroom discussions of current events that when the revolution came, she would be among the first to be shot!

But the senate had not recommended indoctrination or biased discussions. At a time of great emotional turmoil, these men and women were asking faculty to reach out to their students and try to help them through what must have been unbearable stress. It was certainly not an irresponsible act, though many faculty agreed with me and refused to follow the recommendation.

The senate had, in fact, rejected the strike resolution and, even when I laid them out, refused to alter an earlier vote expressing confidence in my handling of the strike. Evidently they understood the pressure I was under and were doing their best to avoid an open break with the chancellor. When things cooled down by the end of May, I felt a little sheepish at the way I had behaved toward my former colleagues.

Now, more than a dozen years later, I have come to realize that this trauma was an integral part of my growth as an administrator. Few faculty members were capable of handling a campus during those years of "unrest," as we euphemistically label it today. They were too sensitive and decent. Most of them could not bring themselves to do what had to be done to prevent radical activity from getting out of hand. They left that to the chancellor. I had to learn my new role and accept the faculty's unwillingness to participate in it.

When a strike developed or a building was seized, faculty members assumed I would take a hard line. It was my duty, not theirs. Whatever I did, they wanted it done adroitly, avoiding bloodshed or overt repression. They would even accept a *coup de main* against a building occupation, provided it was carried out with style and no one was hurt. Faculty would tell me privately that I had handled the affair well, but public approval was out of the question.

I began to learn this independent role during the People's Park strike in May 1969. The learning was painfully difficult because, like most faculty members, I had always believed that the best administration is conducted in total consultation and close harmony with the faculty. As my hide thickened and I found it necessary to assert my independence, few faculty objected. Most of them understood that it was inevitable and adapted to it. Immediately after my blow-up with the senate, Paul Saltman, who acted as their spokesman, said:

"We recognize the tremendous pressure on him as an administrator and do not want to subject him to more stress, but he has to understand we have to act as faculty just as he has to act as chancellor."[23]

If that two-part resolution adopted by the UCSD senate more than a dozen years ago were to come up again today, I would repudiate it now just as I did then. It was the only thing for the chancellor to do. But I would speak calmly rather than in anger, and would tell the senate that while I understood and sympathized with what they were trying to do, I would have no part of it. The faces before me would then surely smile and nod their understanding, and we would go on to the next piece of business.

That night, May 21, more than a thousand strike sympathizers met in the Revelle College Cafeteria to hammer out their strategy. The meeting was preceded by a candlelight memorial service for James Rector in Revelle Plaza just outside. The students prayed and sang "We Shall Overcome" and Bob Dylan's protest song, "Blowing in the Wind." Then they listened to speeches from several faculty members sympathetic with the strike.

In the long meeting that followed, students discussed ways to make the strike more effective, and how to break the chancellor's hold on the media. They formulated a list of demands that were debated late into the night. The demands included amnesty for those arrested in Berkeley, removal of the police and National Guard, return of People's Park, a public apology from Chancellor Heyns and President Hitch, and an end to military recruiting at UCSD. Again the student strikers committed themselves to nonviolence.

Thursday, May 22, was the worst day of all, especially during the morning. Some classes did not meet. Many spent class time, as the senate had recommended, discussing the situation in Berkeley and even some of those were disrupted by striking students. Reinhard, the professor of German literature, broke into Paul Saltman's biology class urging students to leave because they were needed for strike duty in Revelle Plaza. As it happened, Saltman was taking class time to discuss People's Park. Fewer than a dozen of his 350 students walked out.

But in Revelle Plaza a large crowd had gathered. On several occasions they snake-danced through nearby buildings shouting, "On strike—shut it down."

I continued to hew to my line that the strike was ineffective, but plainly it was having an effect. The campus was growing increasingly demoralized as the day progressed. In Revelle Plaza, a morning-long struggle took place at the flag pole where, in accord with our instructions, the flag had been set at half staff. Some students were attempting to take it down and run up a banner with a clenched fist and the word "strike" printed below. It was the emblem that had magically appeared on dozens of T-shirts two days earlier.

A fight developed between students who objected to having the American flag hauled down and those who were trying to run up their strike banner. Murphy and several of his staff were in the thick of it, trying to keep the antagonists apart.

Repeatedly one flag or the other would be run down. Then there would be a rush by its protagonists and it would be raised again. This nonsense continued through much of the morning. Murphy reported to me that it was all he could do to adhere to my orders on nonviolence. There were at least a dozen people out there he would love to have busted!

The strike banner eventually won out. During the afternoon I received a wire from Harry Foster of the American Legion calling for my resignation if I could not curb un-American activity such as the flag display. We left the strike banner alone until darkness fell. Then we had it removed quietly and locked it up. Next morning the Stars and Stripes were back in their accustomed place, still at half staff in recognition of Berkeley's tragedy.

I spent Thursday visiting administrative departments and bucking up sagging spirits with pep talks explaining our strategy. I told our people I wanted to be seen outdoors as often as possible because the demonstrators found it difficult to stay away from me. In this way I could lead them all over campus. There were repeated questions as to why I had not called the police. I explained that San Diego police officials were already on campus watching us handle the disturbances. They felt we were doing very well. Which was wiser: to call in the police and break heads, or to lead the strikers all over campus until they marched themselves into exhaustion? The argument generally calmed people down.

When it was reported to the strikers in Revelle Plaza that the chancellor was moving from building to building in Camp Matthews talking to the administrative staff, a large group came marching over, trailed by Murphy's staff. The strikers demonstrated in front of the chancellor's office for a brief time, then gathered around the flag pole in the center of Camp Matthews chanting slogans. Someone produced a red flag which was promptly run up on the pole as the American flag was taken down and trampled underfoot.

By the time the marching group arrived, I had already departed for a meeting with the staff of the Scripps Institution of Oceanography. I got back to the office early in the afternoon just as the demonstrators left. One of the office staff had become greatly upset over the flag incident outside and was preparing to leave for the rest of the day.

I found Murphy hunched over the phone inside my office. He had covered his right ear with his hand to block the sounds of disruption from the outer office. When he saw me, he brightened.

Murphy reported that the commitment to nonviolent strike tactics •
still appeared to be holding. Efforts to disrupt classes were meeting with severe disapproval. The strikers seemed to be wearing down psychologically and were now arguing among themselves over tactics. Moderates did not like the business with the flags at all. It suggested revolutionary ideas they despised.

To Murphy's practiced eye, the strike appeared to be losing momentum. If we could handle tomorrow's interviews with Captain Stout, the Marine Corps recruiter, there was a good chance we might break it.

Late in the afternoon, Murphy and I met with San Diego police officials, closeted in their observation post on campus, to discuss Captain Stout's return. Evidently the leaders of SDS were beginning to suspect that something out of the ordinary was afoot. The moment we stepped outside the chancellor's office we were picked up and shadowed by students. I pointed out one young fellow to Murphy. He was dressed in a navy blue T-shirt and running shorts. His long hair was tied up in a neat pony tail with a rubber band, and he was carrying a walkie-talkie radio. When I spotted him, the student had his right ear pressed tightly against the wall of the campus police office trying to decipher the muffled voices inside.

After briefing the police on our plans, Murphy and I took a long walk across campus and ended up in Revelle Plaza, where a crowd was still gathered. We passed a young couple just outside the plaza area. The boy nudged his girl friend as we walked by. I smiled at both of them but they stared straight ahead, grim-faced. I heard the boy exclaim after we passed:

"That was the pig chancellor!"

In Revelle Plaza, the crowd was discussing tactics for Captain Stout's return to campus tomorrow. We heard nothing at all about the plan to seize the captain as a hostage. Speakers were urging their listeners to be out in front of the placement office in Camp Matthews bright and early in the morning.

Later in the evening I issued a carefully drafted announcement:

... Because of the tension currently existing on campus, a direct

result of the strife at Berkeley, and because of threats to personal
safety which come to us from campus and noncampus sources,
the Placement Office, Building 250 on the Matthews Campus,
will not be the site of the interviews.
I have selected a different location. Interviewees will be conducted to this site in order to maximize the opportunity for
orderly interviews and to minimize the risk of injury.

Our objective in issuing the statement was to calm faculty members
who were calling in by the dozens fearful of a repetition of People's Park,
and also to force SDS to spread their people over campus to try to unravel
the mystery of the new interview site.

For most of Thursday night the campus remained very quiet. Again
we had forced SDS strike leaders to plan late into the night, and they were
growing bone-tired. Deans who looked in on meetings in the dorms told
us the students there were bushed.

Linus Pauling spoke to a gathering of students in Revelle College,
urging them to continue their strike as a first line of defense against
growing oppression in California.

"Governor Reagan and his Regents think they own this university
system, but they don't own it. It belongs to the people of California—to
you, the teachers and faculty who help to make it a great university."[24]

Pauling's remarks were reported to me next morning. I could not
disagree with his words except for his support for the strike. But there
was a major flaw in the argument on popular sovereignty. Pauling's
definition of "the people" was much too narrow. The Governor's aggressive suppression of radical activity at Berkeley and elsewhere had already
made him a popular hero in California. Elitist faculty like Pauling were
incapable of understanding such a simple truth, and hence Pauling's
advice to the students was very unsound. A heavy price for inadequate
analysis had just been paid at People's Park and would be paid again in
a year at Kent State. All of us would have to find ways to persuade
students to use the brains God gave them instead of turning to mindless
and self-destructive confrontation tactics that were no longer effective.

Next morning, Friday, Camp Matthews was literally crammed with
demonstrators. There were a number of countercultural types with walk-
ie-talkies trying to learn where we had stashed Captain Stout. At least a
half dozen fancy motor bikes were parked in the midst of the demonstrators, ready to roar off at the moment of discovery to spread the news.

At 10:30 AM a call came in from University Hospital advising us that
Captain Stout and his team had arrived. George Murphy then loaded two

university automobiles with eight interviewees in full sight of the demonstrators. The cars drove off trailed by the motor bikes.

Our dogged adversary, Ron, the assistant professor of philosophy, managed to collect a hundred or so students outside the placement office and was arguing with Murphy just before the cars carrying the interviewees departed. At that moment word was received from SDS scouts that Captain Stout had been located at University Hospital. One of the SDS, an undergraduate, declared the confrontation a victory because the Marine Corps recruiter had been kept off campus. Ron demanded that the group be permitted to talk to Captain Stout at University Hospital. Murphy refused. He was supported in his refusal by twenty faculty volunteers who stood their ground beside Murphy and publicly approved the administration's action to avoid violence.

The recruiting team conducted its interviews in peace and serenity at 115 Dickenson Street. Four demonstrators were seen outside the building.

Murphy drove downtown to look in on the interviews. He called me from University Hospital at noon to report that the plan was proceeding flawlessly. All interviews would be completed by about two o'clock. Things were so quiet down there that he did not think he needed to stay.[25]

Meanwhile, the large crowd in Camp Matthews began to disintegrate as it became apparent that nothing was going to happen. Strike leaders made strenuous efforts to organize a noontime rally in Revelle Plaza to protest the administration's underhanded, strike-busting tactics, but there was no interest in further protest and the strike collapsed during the noon hour. Throughout Friday afternoon the campus was calm and classes met normally. Demonstrators simply evaporated. When Murphy returned to my office at one o'clock, I took him out to lunch and bought him a huge steak.

The senate was scheduled to meet again, this time in day-long session on Saturday, May 24, to try to catch up on all the business accumulated since mid-February in our three months of continuing crises. I was a little nervous about how I would be received after my angry performance late Wednesday afternoon, but the faculty were simply wonderful. One after the other my old colleagues came up, clapped me on the back, and told me that the handling of Captain Stout's return was a masterpiece. Tempers had cooled and there was really nothing to patch up between us.

The first item of senate business was the report of Norman Kroll's fact-finding committee on People's Park. It was a very sober, honest document exposing the essential facts and pulling no punches about the excesses on both sides. When the report was submitted for approval, I asked for the floor and publicly thanked the committee. It was, I said, the first balanced presentation of events in Berkeley I had heard since the whole affair involving People's Park began. A considerable debate arose over the report. Several members of the Senate felt that it had been too rough on the Berkeley administration. They wanted to excise those sections.

Toward the end of the debate I was asked for my view. I told the senate that I, too, disagreed with a number of assertions in the Kroll committee document, but that on the whole I thought it fair. I preferred not to divide the report in order not to divide the senate.

"It is more important for all of us to look to the future and pledge ourselves to nonviolence. We who live the life of reason cannot excuse violence without putting ourselves in contradiction of everything we stand for."

With these remarks, all opposition to the report vanished. It was adopted unanimously, and the senate then scheduled a campuswide convocation for noon on Monday, May 26, to present the report to the entire campus.

Despite our best efforts that was all the business we could do on Saturday. Still another senate meeting was scheduled for Wednesday afternoon, May 28. We simply had to get to the Third College academic plan and settle it, or we would have the Lumumba-Zapata protestors back in our laps again. The senators steeled themselves, agreed to the Wednesday meeting, and then adjourned.

Over the weekend I began to hear rumblings that SDS felt it had been raped by its agreement to accept nonviolent tactics to build up a broad coalition supporting the strike. Murphy called to say there was a plan to seize the microphone from me on Monday. An attempt would be made to take over the convocation. On Monday morning Paul Saltman advised that his students had heard the same story. Murphy and Saltman urged me not to appear. They asked me to write out a statement instead. They would arrange to have it delivered by one of the campus clergy.

Every combative instinct within me told me to go ahead with the appearance, but Murphy and Saltman were adamant. In later years I learned that it is always unwise to be frightened out of a public appearance by the threat of radical activity. It is a signal of weakness to your adversaries. But in the spring of 1969 I was insufficiently confident of my own views to risk a break with my closest advisers, and so I yielded. At about 11 AM, I drafted the statement they wanted. The key words were:

I shall not speak today. I did want to speak. I wanted to ask us to join in a commitment to reason and a repudiation of force. But the need to break the cycle of escalating provocation and response is of such overriding importance that I can do nothing to damage it. The reconciliation that is so essential to all of us is too important to throw away in useless confrontations.

My statement was read at the very beginning of the convocation, and the entire affair went off without a hitch while I sulked in my office. I heard later that Norman Kroll was masterful.

The success of the convocation sealed off the last hope of the strike organizing committee. On Monday afternoon they announced that they were "suspending strike activities temporarily." I went over to Revelle Plaza to spend the afternoon talking to students. It was time now to reach out to them and to tell them I understood what the strike meant to them even though I had to oppose it. Many students were angry with me. They charged me with selling out to Governor Reagan, discrediting them, and distorting the circumstances of the strike at UCSD.

On Wednesday the campus newspaper attacked my handling of the strike in an editorial that struck me as sad rather than bitter. I continued to spend time with any students who would talk to me, trying to convince them that my intent was to protect them. I hoped when they thought about it, they would realize that gestures made in the heat of emotion often do not make sense. By commencement time I managed to patch things up with a few of them, but it was well into the fall term of 1969 before the majority of students put their resentments aside.

Monday night, May 26, at 10 PM Murphy called to report that SDS had just voted to break into my office on Tuesday morning. Handbills were circulating on campus renouncing their pledge of nonviolence. Murphy said he would be in front of my office door very early in the morning with a group of faculty members. I was to wait for his call before coming in.

Half an hour after Murphy's warning, Herbert Stern, the chairman of biology, called to advise me what was up. He had been told by a graduate student. He urged playfully that I sleep late in the morning. I went to bed wondering how many people at the meeting were straight SDS members and how many were plants. I was to discover next evening that the San Diego police also had an informant at the meeting. In any event, I managed to sleep quite well. It was a far cry from the anxieties experienced late in November. I was becoming hard-bitten.

Tom Hull, one of the deans, called at 8:30 AM Tuesday to report that thirty-five SDS arrived outside my office door at 7:45. Murphy met them with a line of faculty blocking the door. Several unavailing efforts were made to rush the faculty line. The students first pleaded and then pushed, but the line held firm. SDS did not want to use stronger tactics; it would ruin them with the rest of the campus.[26]

The group eventually withdrew in frustration. Murphy then offered to produce the chancellor in the conference room a bit later on. It was the only way they would see him. They were never going to get through that line!

Finally, SDS agreed to the proposal, and Tom Hull was dispatched to call me. He advised me to stage my entrance in about an hour—give them some time to think.

When I showed up in the chancellor's conference room at 9:30 AM, a half dozen members of the faculty and 50 to 60 students were there waiting for me. The faculty arranged themselves protectively on both sides of me at the head of the table, and the argument got underway.

It was another long, undirected, semiobscene discussion. I was contemptuous with some students, warm to others, depending on the degree of their commitment to SDS. When the argument threatened to become overheated, the faculty stepped in to say that they should not speak to the chancellor in that way. If the faculty respected the chancellor while sometimes disagreeing with him, so might the students.[27]

It went on like that, for hours, around and around. By noon everyone was drained. There was not a fighting spirit left in the room as the meeting broke up.

It was nearly over. Major disorders were still breaking out nearly everywhere else in the University of California system. The inaugural of UCLA's new chancellor, Charles Young, was virtually ruined by a huge sit-in and hunger strike. Jack Oswald, the university's executive vice president, reported big trouble over the weekend at Davis, Santa Cruz, and Santa Barbara. But at San Diego the strike was ended, SDS had been routed from the chancellor's office, and peace was beginning to bloom again in our hearts.

On Tuesday night I received successive calls from Murphy, Herb Stern, and the San Diego police warning me that SDS had met again. The plan was to throw a custard pie in my face at the senate meeting on Wednesday afternoon. I marvelled at the diversity of these information sources.

The custard-pie incident never came off. I spent the entire senate meeting shifting uncomfortably in my chair and looking furtively for some sign of the pie. Perhaps I might be able to duck faster than they could throw. As I stood before the senate speaking in favor of the Frazer committee's plan for Third College, which would put an end to the dispute between the Lumumba-Zapata students and the administration, the door in the back of the room suddenly burst open. Oh, oh, I thought, here it comes.

But it didn't. Down the aisle toward me marched thirty dead-serious students holding lighted candles. They were carrying a mock coffin labelled "University of California," chanting "The basest form of indoctrination—the basest form of indoctrination."

Of course it was intended to be a serious criticism, but after all the stresses of the past weeks, and after the story of the custard pie, I could restrain myself no longer. I fell back into my chair doubled up and howling with laughter. Tears of relief came streaming down my cheeks unchecked.

On May 30, Memorial Day, 30,000 people staged a dignified, silent protest march along a five-mile route in Berkeley. They had come from all over the state to make their position clear to the university, the police, and the Governor. The crowd was disciplined and the police were circumspect. There were no incidents.[28]

Two weeks later on June 14, UCSD held its 1969 commencement ceremonies on an utterly peaceful and beautiful afternoon. I stood before the festive and yet somehow restrained gathering, speaking solemnly of what we had learned during the year:

Student activists seem to have concluded that university administrators do not budge except under pressure of confrontation. Students themselves, weary of the bureaucracy, boredom, and rigidities of college curricula, rarely approved of violent confrontations but openly supported the objectives of the activists.

As confrontations developed, the public at large and state officials concluded that university administrators were either weak or cowardly and that only massive displays of police force could put an end to such disruptive tactics.

Thus was set in motion an escalating cycle of student provocation and punitive public response until in Berkeley in mid-May all of us saw starkly revealed the utter bankruptcy of both theories of forceful action.

Confrontation has brought change just as student activists knew it would, but the changes have not been exactly what was anticipated. They have taken the form of brutal reprisals rather than increased sensitivity to student concerns.

Similarly the simplistic view that a show of naked force would make student activists go away has resulted in one man dead, one man blinded, dozens shot, and a violent street battle in which anger and mortal fear supplanted the processes of reason which must now be invoked to achieve a settlement.

When I concluded my remarks, there was no applause from the graduating seniors. We all had managed to get through the strike safely, but it would be a while before things could be easy between us again. The conclusion of the moral contest between the students and their chancellor left both parties resentful of the way in which the other had fought. Time would be required to heal the wounds.

CHAPTER 8

The Mighty Are Fallen

The Regents met in Berkeley on June 19 and 20 to conduct an intensive review of People's Park and decide what to do. The Berkeley academic senate, supported virtually unanimously by the other campuses of the university, was insisting that the fence must come down immediately. Governor Reagan remained adamant that radical pressure groups must not be permitted to flout the law by acts or threats of violence.

This impasse was emblematic of hundreds of polarizations that developed on college campuses following violent police actions in the 1960s. It had been encountered earlier at Berkeley with the mass arrests of FSM protestors in December 1964. The same problem tore Columbia University apart during the spring riots of 1968.

All middle ground for sensible discussion and possible resolution of disputes disappears following a major police action, especially one resulting in injuries or large numbers of arrests. Both sides tend to retreat into self-righteous attitudes and seem to relish delivering sanctimonious lectures to each other. Paranoid hatred flourishes in the midst of these deep divisions. Only the healing processes of time or changes in leadership can bring the sides together again. It was obvious to most of us, although not very well understood by the public and state officials at the time, that the sides somehow had to be brought together and the dispute compromised, or the university would remain crippled for an extended period, perhaps permanently.

Roger Heyns understood the problem clearly. While the National Guard surrounded his campus, and marching groups numbering into the thousands sought to disrupt Berkeley's business district, Heyns and his staff undertook intense discussions with the mayor and the city council as well as with groups representing all factions involved in the People's Park dispute.

Out of these discussions a plan evolved, backed by most of the parties. The city of Berkeley would lease People's Park from the university for a defined period and assume responsibility for returning the land in good condition at the end of the lease term. The city, in turn, would enter into an agreement with the diverse groups sponsoring the park, providing for a user-developed, user-maintained community facility. As soon as these understandings were secure, committed to writing, and signed by all parties, the fence would come down.

Architects and urban planners helped to formulate the proposal. They called it imaginative. To the rest of us the plan seemed to offer an excellent prescription for healing the wounds caused by the battle of People's Park, and also to suggest ways in which urban populations and urban institutions might join together to restore decaying neighborhoods.

Heyns came to the June Regents meeting prepared to do battle for his plan. Bright and uniquely persuasive in addressing the ordinary problems of university administration, Heyns in this instance was psyched up at least two or three notches beyond his normal capabilities. I have never seen Roger in better form than he displayed at these meetings—alternately earnest, moralistic, and ironically amusing as circumstances required. He debated brilliantly and with great personal force.

An illuminating exchange between Chancellor Heyns and Lieutenant Governor Ed Reinecke demonstrated Heyns in top form. It followed Reinecke's attempt to substitute a punitive proposal for Heyns's leasing arrangement with the city of Berkeley. Heyns would not hear of it, and demolished Reinecke's arguments in an incisive analysis of their potential consequences. Reinecke then withdrew his proposal, turned to Heyns a little testily, and protested:

"Roger, you drive a hard bargain."

"Governor, I lead a hard life!"

Heyns was then in his early fifties. He was solidly built, clean-shaven, with gray, slightly wavy hair, and a gentle low-key manner. He fitted the stereotype of the benign, fatherly, pipe-smoking professor. But he had survived the rigors of Berkeley's academic jungle for nearly five years, and sad brown eyes reflected the pressures he had endured. They spoke of things no professor had ever seen.

The debate over People's Park came to a climax before the full board on Friday afternoon, June 20. The Regents Room in University Hall was packed. All the Regents were in attendance for this hottest of issues. Governor Reagan was unyielding and uncompassionate, manifesting the ruthless personal force that is his trademark outside the public eye. Heyns was more effective than I had ever seen him as he presented his case for a long-term lease of People's Park to the city of Berkeley.

Unfortunately, as often happened in such high-voltage sessions, the Regents became mired in a series of parliamentary entanglements. Amendments were tacked on amendments until no one knew what was going on. In the end, Regent Dean Watkins, one of the Governor's men, swept aside the tangle by proposing a substitute motion providing that, until such time as the married students housing was ready for construction, the lot would be used as a playing field and a parking lot.

Watkins's motion was backed strongly by Governor Reagan. The strength of the Governor's majority soon showed itself. Even a number of moderate Regents came over. Plainly they were hesitant about elements of the community-based plan that Heyns had worked out. Watkins's proposal carried easily and Heyns went down to a crushing defeat. I remember thinking how insensitive it was to demolish the eccentric beauty of People's Park, with all the misguided idealism that nurtured it, and to do nothing more than pave the place over.

As a matter of fact it never happened. The Governor had second thoughts about the wisdom of the decision. Eventually the fence was taken down and the university left the area an open space, striking an uneasy truce with it community users. In the spring of 1981, twelve years later, the Berkeley campus police issued a warning to students to avoid the park.[1] Police said it was a magnet for criminals, drug dealers, and people with histories of mental problems.

But in June 1969 none of us knew what the future would bring. We saw only the bitterness of the university's defeat. As the vote was announced, Heyns, who was sitting near me, rose without a word and walked out. I was certain he was on his way upstairs to Charlie Hitch's office to hand in his resignation.

When the meeting ended, I ran over to the chancellor's house to try to talk him out of it. Roger was seated quietly with his wife, Esther, sipping a drink. He seemed depressed, but he had not resigned. That would have been a grandstand play, and his strong streak of Protestant morality would not allow him to do it. He had simply slipped out of the room early to avoid reporters.

We sat there for half an hour sipping scotch and soda and wondering aloud whether there was any hope either for us or the institutions we were struggling to hold together. Heyns asked me to stay awhile. The Carnegie Commission on Higher Education would be coming in for a dinner meeting. He wanted to introduce me to them.

Not long afterwards they began to arrive one by one. First, Nathan Pusey, still in the throes of Harvard's great blow-up and very worried about his upcoming commencement. A short while later he resigned.

Next, James Perkins, president of Cornell and a lovely, decent man. His gentle handling of a building seizure by black militants who emerged holding rifles had completely undermined him. Perkins told us that evening in the library of the chancellor's house that he had decided to resign as of July 1.

Then Clark Kerr, one of the first of us to face the pressures of student confrontation and one of the first to fall. Clark listened sympathetically to our recitation of the Regents meeting. He wanted to hear the names of the Regents who had stuck with the president and the chancellor. We named them. Kerr shook his head ruefully. They were very nearly the same people who had been on his side when the Regents voted to dismiss him in 1967.

Slowly the room began to fill with commission members, and it was nearly time for me to go. I had a plane to catch. But I could not resist pausing to study the gathering as the orange light of the setting sun flashed across their faces. Heyns, Hitch, Kerr, Oswald, Perkins, Pusey: the room was like a little museum displaying the collective travail of American universities in that climactic year, 1968–69.

Heyns took me by the elbow, guiding me over to a quiet spot near the front door.

"Roger, I hope you will not resign. I do not think I could bear it if you go."

"You're very nice to say that, Bill, but you will manage no matter what I decide to do. I'll probably hang on."

Then I stole a last look at the animated faces in the library. They seemed relieved by the prospect of a pleasant evening in civilized company.

"Roger, see those men! My heart breaks for them, yet all I can say to myself is that nothing like that is ever going to happen to me. By Christ, it will not happen to me!"

CHAPTER 9

The End of Innocence

It is over now. The prospect of total collapse, seemingly so close at hand in 1969, never materialized. American universities came through the Sixties basically unharmed by the waves of protest washing over them.[1]

Despite the horrendous calamities of my first year in office, the world did not come to an end. Classes continued to meet more or less on schedule. Examinations created more havoc among students than Governor Reagan's political war against the university. We lost our balance and stumbled badly several times, but suspensions of academic activity were rare. Generally we plodded along day after day in what the radicals derided as "business as usual."

Whatever it may have been, it was not business as usual. My predecessor at Columbia, Andrew Cordier, once told me that his key staff would gather in his office each afternoon at five to report progress and drink a toast to the successful conclusion of another day. It was not very different on the West Coast.

In fact, things became far worse before they got better, and still we hung on. The protests during the spring of 1972 at Columbia were the roughest I ever experienced, but when they were brought under control, that was the end. The antiwar frenzy of April 1972 was unprecedented, a sudden outpouring that seemed like an immense spasm of pain. Then just as suddenly the whole thing collapsed. It was as though all the activists in the peace movement had fallen through a trap door.

At first I found the ensuing calm difficult to accept as genuine. What kind of movement was this if such intense emotional arousal and bold commitment could vanish virtually overnight? Was the crusade for peace and justice only a student fad destined for the junk heap alongside goldfish swallowing and phonebooth stuffing? Did restless young spirits begin to ignore abstract idealism when American affluence began to fade? Were they alarmed about their own prospects for survival in an economy suddenly grown ruthless? Or were students responding to more primitive, perhaps even unconscious, pressures that caused them to withdraw from dramatic mass protests into deeply personal expressions of disaffection with society? Did the protest movement run out of steam as new ideas and issues became harder to identify—a kind of exhaustion of the spirit?

In this final chapter I want to examine these questions. Although they are stated here as alternatives, it seems to me that all of them can be answered affirmatively. We must understand that no simple explanation exists for the widespread protest activity of the Sixties. It was a unique form of social conflict resulting from a combination of political, societal, and psychological factors. Some of the most important influences were not clearly visible at the time; their importance has become evident only with the emergence of perspective. It is vital that we understand the complexity of what happened because similar conflicts are quite likely to arise in the future. Many of the psychological forces underlying protest tend to remain constant from generation to generation. Only the social and political problems change.[2]

Despite a voluminous and still active literature on the period, the multifaceted happenings of my Year of the Monkey remain an enigma. The literature offers mostly political explanations of these conflicts, whereas I am searching for more fundamental psychological and humanistic interpretations of the things I saw.[3] Political problems were real enough, but there was also a uniquely intense emotional climate on campus during the late Sixties. It led many students to portray themselves as special victims of an authoritarian and militaristic society.

Where did this climate of arousal come from? Little insight is offered in the current literature. What we find instead are spellbinding political accounts of the meteoric rise of the New Left, and its final disintegration into mutually antagonistic extremist factions. These are important matters for sociologists and historians; less so for me. I am more deeply concerned about what happened to average students than about the organizational dynamics of the New Left. I want to understand what moved the "believers."4 Nothing seemed more important than the multitudes of angry, distraught young faces in the crowds of demonstrators, or the hundreds of tense, emotionally committed people prepared to put their bodies on the line for a cause.

It was the multitudes of followers that lent special force to the era of student protest. Where did they come from? The potential for mass-scale unrest was always there and still exists today; why did it materialize then and not now?

It is tempting to draw the easy conclusion that protests in the 1960s were motivated in large measure by opposition to the war in Vietnam, and that students discovered a new form of media-oriented activist politics that succeeded in forcing the government out of Southeast Asia.

There is no question that such protest activities took place and that they were politically effective. A President in office was forced to withdraw his candidacy for a second term and his successor was harassed almost continually until he himself fell victim to an unprecedented scandal. Henry Kissinger's account of antiwar protests in the period from 1968 to 1972 is very revealing. Media criticism of the Nixon administration was evoked by well-organized antiwar demonstrators marching week in and week out in Washington.5

But the easy conclusion about the basic cause of student unrest in the Sixties, i.e., it was the war, strikes me as too pat and too limited to explain most of what we saw. There are good reasons to doubt that the intense angry climate on campus in that period arose because of the war. Protests on a mass scale had flared up on a number of college campuses long before the war ever became a crucial issue.6 It was in these earlier upheavals that latent student anger first became identified as a matter of concern to university administrators, and the climate of emotional arousal was first understood as an important psychological precondition of protest activity.7

We have to ask ourselves why this angry climate arose when it did, remembering that when America entered the decade of the Sixties, ideology and protest were believed to be out of date. The years since World War II had witnessed a succession of orderly, sometimes even apathetic, adolescent generations motivated principally by the hope of success in business or the professions. If it was not the war that broke the pattern, what did?

During the 1968 presidential campaign, sophisticated antiwar activists moved in to take control of a protest instrumentality fashioned years earlier by a generation of more radical leaders trained in SDS.[8] These early leaders had opposed the war and organized themselves to fight it, but the issues to which they turned at first did not center on the war. It was there in the background like an aching tooth, but it was not what aroused students at the very beginning.

The buzz-words on campus in the early Sixties were *racism* and *student power*.[9] Protests in these areas were unexpectedly successful. A climate had begun to build up on campus that made undergraduates remarkably easy to arouse. They seemed to view themselves as outcasts in a coldly inhumane society. It led them to seek out and venerate a succession of antiheroes whose status as societal victims or as interpreters of student alienation found a special rapport with their feelings.[10]

Radicals devolved quickly on issues that mobilized these feelings. As things turned out, such issues were not hard to find, especially on big campuses undergoing forced expansion to meet the enrollment surge of the postwar baby boom. The classic example was Berkeley's Free Speech Movement (FSM) in 1964–65 which, of course, had nothing to do with the war. The FSM was directed mainly against the insensitivity accompanying unaccustomed bigness.

Many students were lost in the culs-de-sac of overcrowded universities. They saw themselves as useless, neglected cogs in a huge machine. These sustained feelings of alienation were among the basic causes of the climate of arousal at Berkeley.[11] It soon spread to other campuses. Latent anger proved easy to mobilize on nearly every large campus. In the beginning it took the form of irritation at the university's failure to become more actively engaged in the fight for racial justice. Later on it spread to attacks on the university itself because of the irrationality and insensitivity of university bureaucracies.[12]

Even a casual reader of these pages must have been struck by the fact that in 1968–69 I was struggling with SDS and not with antiwar demonstrators. Only one of the five disputes erupting at UCSD during my Year of the Monkey had anything to do with the war. Later on I encountered serious problems with the peace movement, but they were more broadly based and in many ways more emotionally volatile than most of what I saw during my freshman year as chancellor.

In the late spring of 1968 the UCSD campus was already flooded with a free-floating, angry aura of protest not rooted in any particular issue. Hostility toward the administration was just below the surface and no one could be on campus for more than a few days without picking it up.[13] During 1968–69 the surface was broken at least five times by outbreaks of

angry dissent. This intense emotional climate defines the essential difference between campuses then and campuses now. In 1968 the hostility was
almost palpable. On any given day, out of any one of dozens of idealistic
causes, an angry storm might blow up, capable of producing a violent
outburst that could leave us in ruins.

This superheated climate provided the essential precondition for
protest in which SDS and other radical groups thrived. The climate is
gone now. A new generation of radicals still tries to arouse the campus,
but it encounters only apathy from today's students. If one listens to these
new radicals with an ear tuned to the Sixties, there is a note of despairing
isolation in their contempt for student apathy. Such isolation is totally at
variance with the self-assurance and confident exercise of power displayed by radical organizers during the period of unrest.

It would be incorrect to suggest that the climate of arousal on campus
was purely a psychological phenomenon. It was not. There were important psychological components: feelings of alienation, distrust of and
hostility toward administrative authority, frustration with university
bureaucracies. But there was also political anger directed at what students
deemed an unjust society. Racial injustice, the ascendency of technology
over nature, dehumanization of modern life, were the major issues. After
1968 the war in Vietnam became the symbol of all these irritants. Before
1968 they combined, not to produce demonstrations, but to raise the
"temperature" of the campus and keep us in a state of constant tension
throughout the latter half of the Sixties.

Our emotional temperature has now undergone a major downward
fluctuation, influenced by changing political circumstances and diminishing psychological pressures. When that temperature was high, people
were easily excited, crowds formed readily, rumors flew constantly.
Small incidents were blown out of proportion.[14]

Now only the most outrageous events can cause a crowd to form.
Even then, leaders seldom emerge to move the crowd into sustained
action. We see a few brief outbursts, but they quickly subside.

The unprecedented emotional environment of the late Sixties required at least two or three years to develop. It formed a framework of
elevated excitability out of which flowed everything else that happened.
The point of explosiveness was reached at UCSD and elsewhere during
the years between 1968 and 1970. We had to scrutinize every upcoming
event, every offhand remark, every possible source of conflict, for signs
of potential danger.

I remember a rock-concert in the UCSD gymnasium in 1969. The
concert was intended to provide a few hours of pleasant relaxation for our

students in the midst of our political troubles, but it turned out to be a disaster. Hundreds of young people from communities all over San Diego suddenly appeared outside the building, demanding access to an already jam-packed gym floor. When access was denied they rushed the locked doors, threw rocks and anything else they could find, until we gave up trying to control them and called the police.

The police appeared in riot gear less than an hour later. They first sought to calm the crowd, but failed just as we had. As far as we could determine, none of the people trying to break into the gym were our own students. They were outsiders attracted to the campus by news of the rock concert on local radio stations.

The police commander finally gave an order to his men to drive the rioters away from the building. They did so, but in one of those unpredictable errors that no one ever anticipates, the police drove the crowd right into the middle of Revelle Plaza! Students in the dorms looked out their windows at the unbelievable spectacle of riot-clad police in the very center of the campus chasing what appeared to be other UCSD students.[15]

The hostile climate prevailing in those days generally needed much less than that to bring hundreds of infuriated students pouring out of the dormitories shouting, "Pigs off campus." The fracas gave us the fright of our lives. Murphy spent hours in Revelle Plaza using a bull-horn and urging UCSD students to stay calm and remain indoors. He was trying to explain what was going on.

Later we sat down with the police, thanked them for their help, and then pointed out what a near thing it had been. A new plan was drawn up to deal with future outbreaks at social events. Neither we nor the police ever wanted to make that kind of mistake again. In those days you never knew where trouble might come from. Tension was constant.

In 1968 students were protesting many things besides the war. At UCSD, for example, they were upset by what they construed as racism in the Regents' action barring credit for Cleaver's course (Chapter 2).

They were also deeply angered by the American Legion's attempt to set itself up as arbiter of the qualifications of our faculty. Students became distrustful of me because they thought I had yielded to the Legion's pressures during the Marcuse appointment crisis (Chapters 3, 4, 5).

Lumumba-Zapata college became an issue in the spring of 1969. There was a nearly universal belief among our students that UCSD's education of minorities was inadequate. The inadequacy was not easy to explain. Students suspected that it reflected an intentional injustice (Chapter 6).

The battle of People's Park was complex, but students were moved to protest because it seemed to them that the university was insensitive to an enclave of beauty in a rundown Berkeley slum (Chapters 7, 8).

Before the explosive power of the peace movement was really felt, all these other things were going on. In the beginning no more than about ten percent of the student body were committed activists. But nearly all students were, to some degree, sympathetic with the issues raised in campus demonstrations. Many felt a generalized anger as well as a deep sense of disillusionment with traditional society.

At the heart of each campus issue in the Sixties was an unrealizable idealistic view of the universe. Idealism failed for a variety of reasons: either because it was naively utopian, as in the attempt to appoint a black revolutionary (Eldridge Cleaver) to teach whites the evils of racism; or because idealism clashed with vested rights, as happened in the struggle over People's Park. Students were not disposed to compromise their principles to accommodate the needs of others.

Militant leaders of the 1960s were able to galvanize undergraduates because students were easy to arouse and the leaders were charismatic. But there was also a strong attraction between disillusioned students and radical leaders. Both shared the greatly oversimplified utopian beliefs that students regarded as a moral necessity in those days. While the average student harbored only an abstract and essentially passive conception of a better world in which we would all live together in peace and love, the radicals were moved by more grandiose political ambitions. Their agenda called for direct action and revolutionary change.[16] They were willing to take bold steps and manipulate others to advance their cause. The radicals were political down to the soles of their shoes, whereas the students they led saw themselves principally as victims of a coldly unresponsive system. Understanding this difference in outlook is important for understanding the dynamics of student protest in the Sixties.

The leaders and the followers in the New Left all felt that change, any change, no matter how symbolic it might be, would probably leave us better off. One of the puzzling qualities of the mass of students who accepted New Left leadership was their lack of any coherent political plan. Their view was that tearing down something corrupt would improve things for all of us. This was their principal justification for attacking universities.

I have always believed that such ill-thought-out and primitive anarchism had to be at least partly the product of unconscious drives, reflecting unresolved adolescent conflicts with parental authority.[17]

Robert Liebert, whose psychoanalytic study of student rebels at Columbia displays great insight despite, or perhaps because of, an undisguised political sympathy for the radicals, conjectures that unconscious destructive impulses probably did not, in and of themselves, motivate rebellion.[18]

Instead, in Liebert's view, the university administration became a symbol of authority that interacted with unconscious currents of thought already well established in college students as they began to break away from parental control. I could not help noticing how often in those days students would link me with other hated authoritarian symbols. For instance, a portrait once appeared on the cover page of UCSD's radical student newspaper captioned, "Heads I win, tails you lose." The right side of the photo was Governor Reagan's face, the left side was mine! My all-time favorite was a huge banner made of four bedsheets stitched together, billowing from the side of Kent Hall at Columbia during the antiwar demonstrations of 1972. It announced simply:

FUCK NIXON AND McGILL!

Psychologists point out that hostile reactions to authority can be found in every generation of adolescents. Such reactions are normal responses to the socializing restraints imposed by civilization. Oedipal impulses have spawned generational conflict since the dawn of history. Having brought on explosions of public anger in the Sixties, why do they fail to have the same effect now? Why were militant radicals so effective in organizing masses of students then and not now?[19]

It seems to me that the principal answer to these questions, unlike others I have posed, is simple. During the Sixties a remarkable instrument of student protest was fashioned. It had been pioneered by Gandhi in India, and came to us by way of the civil rights movement. The technique involved using the organized pressure of masses of people, more or less nonviolently, to bring the operations of an institution to a halt.

Key to the effectiveness of this technique was astute handling of press and television to generate sympathy for the protestors' cause and to put pressure on university officials to negotiate.

Until the Sixties the awesome structure of university authority was thought to be unchallengeable. Actually, our rules were predicated on universal acceptance and were very fragile. There were no spelled-out grievance procedures for dealing with large-scale disputes. The entire structure of rules crumbled away when it came up against a civil rights-style protest organized by the FSM at Berkeley in 1964.

The effect was devastating. Unwary administrators never anticipated that such powerful protest methods would be used against them. After all, they were supporters of civil rights, not rural sheriffs. Accordingly they walked into every trap set by the protest planners.[20] Each attempt to assert the university's authority raised the stakes until administrators found themselves confronted with the dilemma of arresting hundreds of demonstrators and precipitating a faculty rebellion, or capitulating and unleashing an avalanche of public disapproval. Student leaders had honed their protest skills in contests with tough local law-enforcement officials in the Deep South. Compared with such people, university administrators were pushovers.

As soon as this protest technique was shown to be effective, it immediately spread to other campuses. Rapid diffusion of any form of protest known to produce results is another curious law of militant behavior. Police refer to it as "copycat" rioting.[21]

The diffusion phenomenon shows how thin our veneer of civilization is and how much we lack an adequate theory of behavior on which to base our principles of justice and law enforcement. It will not do simply to assume, as many do, that people granted the full benefits of freedom will want to live together in peace and harmony. That Rousseauvian ideal underlies much liberal thought and is at the heart of our ideas of governance in a modern university, but experience has taught me that it is wrong.[22]

Of course, in referring to militant protests on university campuses, I am speaking of pressure tactics, not rioting. Demonstrations may turn into riots if they get out of hand or are mishandled, but violence is seldom intended. Instead a militant protest is rather like a giant legalistic chess game played on the front pages of the morning newspaper and the six o'clock TV news programs. Little wonder that the faculty came to speak of it as the "radicalization game."

The reader should be aware that special significance is accorded to the term "group protest" in this treatment.[23] Strictly speaking, there is no such thing as a "group grievance." Members of militant groups come to share common grievances and common beliefs, but, as I have tried to explain, it is my impression that these common beliefs are imposed or suggested by protest leaders as they attempt to organize groups for political action.

In the Sixties angry groups tended to form as a manifestation of the intense emotional climate on campus, with all its diffuse stresses and diverse grievances. Where no disastrous event had occurred to rivet attention on a single issue, several angry groups emerged simultaneously. At first there was no central theme of protest. People were diffusely excited. Protest organizers tried to concentrate all this energy—to say specifically what was wrong and what could be done about it. Almost always their message demanded radical political change.[24]

A serious difficulty arises in most popular treatments of campus unrest. They confuse individual grievances with the phenomena of group protest. There is a metaphorical projection of individual feelings into group consciousness. The group is written about as though it were a super-individual. Group protest does not work that way. It is organized, stereotyped, media oriented, and characterized by a form of moral contest with the institution at which grievances are directed. A group protest must be planned and controlled. It is by no means a collective expression of identically outraged reactions, although determined efforts are made to have it appear that way.[25]

When I talked to campus protestors—the believers and followers, not the leaders—I discovered a curious blend of grievance, idealism, and the exhilaration of group action. They were unbudgeable in their conviction that their actions were morally justified. They explained that infringing on the rights of others was acceptable because bureaucratic institutions did not move unless pushed by some form of "extra-legal" prod. And they were obsessed by the need to win their contest with the administration. After the first clash, protesting groups would debate their tactics endlessly, as though it were a competitive sport and they were trying to determine what the next play should be. In many important ways a protest was a contest. Protestors tried to recruit the campus to their cause by portraying the administration as oppressive. They simply did not see any problem in using ruthless tactics to achieve what they deemed as moral ends. They knew they were right.

What followed was an encounter between administration and protestors that might be described as a morality play as well as a contest. The protestors schemed their tough-minded tactics while speaking to themselves and reporters of the high idealism of their cause. After we learned how to defuse such tactics and avoid the escalation of force, we began to apply pressures of our own while calling publicly for a return to civility. The rest of the campus soon became accustomed to the scenario of the morality contest. They would study the administration critically to see whether we were adroit enough to outwit protest groups without making critical mistakes.

The protestors did not have to reflect a significant body of opinion on campus. They needed no more than a suitably idealistic cause and a prescribed tactical plan. Everyone watched in fascination to see how far they could go with it.

The grievances cited by students in those days seemed to me reflective of the diffuse pressures afflicting them. Many grievances centered on the frustrations of student life, but there was also a generalized note of despair: a society as callous as ours, steeped in racism and committed to an unjust war, was not worth living in. I remember once picking up a document on campus entitled *The Student as Nigger.*[26] It played up to the embittered feelings of students and portrayed young people as unjustly trapped in an authoritarian and corrupt environment. The intensity of this alienation was puzzling. We are, after all, discussing the most gifted and successful young people in America; yet they were steeped in disillusionment. No wonder they were so attracted to antiheroes.[27]

I want to return to this phenomenon later. In some ways it restates the psychological problem, but it leads also to philosophical speculation that may offer new insights.

Protests broke out and began to spread in the Sixties because the necessary political and psychological preconditions were there and because protests worked—at least in the beginning. Unrest faded away a decade later because the psychological climate began to dissipate, and because the activity ceased to be effective. We had learned how to counter the protest techniques. Even more important, by 1972 the news media began to view student protest as yesterday's news. They stopped covering it altogether.

Looking back now at the complex and multifaceted disputes at UCSD, I am touched by how fragile and inexperienced we were in 1968—how little we understood of what was going on. It is a reminder if any were needed of the even greater fragility of the thousands of committed students with whom we struggled: not the tough, power-oriented leadership, but the believers and followers who never understood the pressures on them but felt, as perhaps many still do, that they were embarked on a just cause.

The jangled nerves and frayed sensibilities inherited from those experiences took many years to repair. I doubt that the healing will ever be complete for those most centrally involved. Everyone caught up in the bitter struggles of the Sixties paid a price, and no one who lived through those times is ever likely to be entirely at peace again. But at least today we have some perspective in which to frame our understanding of what happened, and to answer the eternal question, why?

As history goes, ten to fifteen years is hardly more than the wink of an eye, but it is long enough to help us sort out our impressions without getting lost in a maze of details and false leads. As we were trying to cope with the upheavals there was a sense of overwhelming chaos that has been etched away with the passage of time. It has left impressions that are quite different from what we believed earlier.

Somehow the political dimensions of the bitter conflicts raging between students and university administrators in the 1960s do not seem as crucial now as they once did. Today no serious person would characterize all scientific research as "war research" in the way that Brad Cleaveland attempted to do at UCSD in 1968.[28] The war is over. It has left deep scars on our psyche and its turmoil wrecked many lives, but it is over.

Racism persists in America. Yet we are no longer in the throes of the racial fears created by demands for black power and amplified by widespread urban rioting in the Sixties. A black middle class with deep roots in American life has begun to emerge, and black voters, indeed a whole range of racially and ethnically defined voting constituencies, are political realities faced by all aspirants to public office in the Eighties.

Thus as we look back at the Sixties, the political controversies of the time no longer possess the devastating force they carried originally. New psychological insights are emerging.

Psychological influences are rarely visible when they are most determinative in shaping human actions. They tend to remain shadowy, hidden even from the actors themselves. These influences become detectable only as we undertake to analyze the forces that shaped an era. Suddenly we begin to recognize a host of familiar phenomena: rebelliousness in the face of doubtful or illegitimate authority; frustration with the bureaucratic regulation of modern life; group membership as a way of coping with stress; peer pressure; aggression generated by frustration; the conviction that one is a victim of society.

All these forces were there in the midst of the chanting demonstrators. At the time they did not appear to be important in comparison with the political events that triggered the student protests. Now they do. It is a matter of perspective.

I began this final chapter with the observation that universities came through the Sixties relatively undamaged.[29] Tumultuous events rarely inflict permanent damage on institutions, at least those with any vitality. Universities, arguably the most independent and fiercely self-protective of all society's institutions, are especially remarkable for their ability to bounce back in the face of turmoil and to continue their preordained activity whatever else may be going on.

Tales of adherence to administrative ritual in the face of imminent disaster abound in the annals of college campuses during the Sixties. Andrew Cordier once called me from Columbia to say that demonstrators were using a battering ram to break into the presidential suite in Low

Library. He said the noise was disturbing an important meeting with his staff. That redoubtable old bureaucrat would let nothing intrude on a meeting with his staff.

The reader will also recall UCSD's luncheon for the Women's Auxiliary of University Hospital scheduled on November 25, 1968, just as SDS was trying to shut us down over Cleaver's course. The luncheon, of course, went on as scheduled. It was moved to a safer locale without explanation, but it went on. We tried to act as though the distractions in Revelle Plaza were inconsequential. Critical to the proof of their unimportance was that they were not allowed to alter any significant element of our administrative routine.

It may well be that adherence to administrative routine serves to protect us from debilitating anxiety during times of intense stress. Afterwards, the contrast between the minutiae of our administrative tasks and the tumult going on all around us often seems absurd. It is said, for example, that the last message from the German army trapped in Stalingrad in the winter of 1943 was a routine weather report.

Damage attributable to conflict is typically suffered by people, not institutions. The sufferers are those luckless individuals whom fate puts in the wrong place at the wrong time. They get caught up in events for which they are not responsible, and are subject to pressures they seek desperately to avoid. They become victims, not in the metaphysical sense adopted by activist students in the 1960s, but in actuality.

One important kind of damage, not typically noted elsewhere but mentioned often in these pages, is the brutalizing that accompanies the experience of conflict. It is sad to remember how quickly it happened. Toughness was necessary. We either developed it or kissed goodbye to our prospects for survival. Student leaders in the early 1960s had learned the art of civil disobedience in struggles with tough law-enforcement officials. When these experienced activists turned their energies to protest back home, there was little to stand against them. No university administrators and few faculty had been through any comparable ordeal.

But not for long. We became hardened too. There was no gentle way to deal with the volatile combination of Herbert Marcuse and Ronald Reagan. Those two incited each other. During the last weeks of the Marcuse appointment struggle at UCSD, every public utterance by either one produced showers of sparks that could easily have set off a major conflict.

Nor was there any gentle way to extract Columbia from the near-catastrophe into which it had fallen in 1968. The fiscal measures necessary to pull the university back from the brink were brutal, and nearly every pressure group with a stake in Columbia's operation objected to them. It was dangerous to ignore the rhetoric of pressure groups threatening violence, especially when no one was sure that the prescribed remedies would work, but it had to be done.

The harsher I became in dealing with provocations aimed at radicalizing the campus, the less forgiving I grew toward young romantics moved by the idealism of the New Left and determined to show their commitment in self-destructive acts. These students needed friendly, realistic guidance, not rough handling. I soon became too thick-skinned to be capable of doing much of it. The problem became the mission of the campus clergy. God alone knows how many young people they saved.[30]

University administrators quickly learned to manage their campuses through a bewildering array of disputes, angry demonstrations, and challenging media events. The conditions under which we operated would probably be deemed unbearable if they were to recur today. We adapted to harshness and found ways to carry on.

In my own case the fear of crowds vanished entirely after one or two successful outings. I learned to plunge into angry gatherings without apprehension about my personal safety. Crowd fear, so paralyzing in the beginning, simply disappeared. It was replaced by a professional concentration on controlling difficult situations before they got out of hand. We learned to reach angry young people before one of them did something monumentally stupid. I once described this professional attitude as a "compassionate state of combat readiness."

Yet some ineffable residue of earlier apprehensions remained. For the first time in my life I discovered a perceptual mode more complicated than simple, undivided experience. Often when I found myself at the center of an angry crowd, a part of my consciousness would seem to detach itself and drift away. I could study what was happening, as if it were from a distance, apprehensive for the poor fellow in the middle of the mess, and yet also scheming what to do next. When I described this phenomenon to a psychiatrist friend, he told me it was a well-documented reaction to stress.[31]

Eventually college administrators of my generation succeeded in neutralizing the ingenious pressure tactics that activist students brought to the campus from the civil rights movement. We learned how to take on the demonstrators in public argument with the whole campus watching, using our experience as debaters to expose the unrevealed political motives of protest organizers. It was a simple case of learning to confront the confronters.[32]

A priceless maneuver for dealing with seizure tactics was taught me by the New York City police in 1971. Several hundred Hispanic students and community sympathizers had seized the basement floor of Lewisohn Hall at Columbia in a dispute over funding. They refused to leave unless we restored budget cuts to a community program they backed. We refused. The impasse went on through the late afternoon and evening. Nothing I tried was effective in persuading them to leave the building. Finally, towards midnight, I called the police.

They came into Lewisohn Hall through a basement tunnel, perhaps fifty men led by an elegant inspector decked out in gold braid. The inspector sought out the leader of the demonstration. He explained that he wanted no violence. If they would submit to a nonviolent arrest, he and his men would lead the demonstrators out of the building to paddy wagons waiting on Broadway.

The demonstration leader cautiously worked out the terms of the arrest with the police inspector: who would stand where, who would be doing what. Eventually it was all arranged. The radical leader knew that reporters and television cameras were set up just outside the building. He wanted the photographs and news stories of his people being led under arrest from a Columbia building after pleading for restoration of budget cuts in a community program.

And so it was done. The inspector and his men led the protesting group upstairs to the front door in accord with the scenario they had worked out. By this time there were fewer than a hundred willing to submit to arrest. As they stepped outdoors with klieg lights blazing and reporters pressing all around, the inspector suddenly stopped, went back to the front door and padlocked it. He told everyone to go home; the fun was over.

The demonstration leader protested that he and his people were under arrest. The inspector stared at him with an expression of profound boredom: "I am much too busy to arrest you tonight. Now go home!"

The next day the demonstrators cried foul and complained they had been tricked, but the rest of the campus smiled. They appreciated adroitness in a rough game with high stakes.[33] That particular community group was wary about taking us on again.

In my mind the most significant costs of the Sixties were psychological, and it was chiefly the students, activists and onlookers alike, who paid. Some paid very dearly.

The experiences of campus leaders and organizers during civil rights protests in the Deep South cultivated their combative instincts, making it relatively easy for them to face arrest, even jail. For these people the threat of arrest in a campus demonstration was not a deterrent; it was a badge of honor eagerly coveted.

The price they paid was exacted chiefly in the desensitization engendered by such experiences. Student leaders developed an almost sanctimonious rhetoric designed to prove that it was really society, not they, who were at fault. In the end, it seemed to me many of them could not tell right from wrong. The thought that they might be doing a gross injustice to faculty or other students did not occur to them, or if it did, faith in their own righteousness overcame their doubts.

The onlookers and believers were very different. Few of them were toughened at all. They were frightened by the political upheavals in which they found themselves. Many lost sleep in bouts of anxiety and self-doubt over the dangers inherent in their commitment to a better world. It required great effort for such young people to cope with the problem. The peer pressure on them was intense.

For some students, the way to handle the pressure was to try for one blazing gesture at a critical moment in which arrest or discipline would be proof positive of their commitment. One can only guess the stresses on undergraduates as they struggled to find the courage to face such dangers. The whole ugly business trapped them at one of the most delicate and vulnerable periods of their lives. Most were still in or only just out of their teens, completely uncertain about who they were or where they fitted. They were only beginning to make decisions on their own. Suddenly they found themselves in the midst of the volatile climate of the campus, alternately played up to and lectured at by student leaders. Many began to feel anger and disillusionment, to question family and tradition. What they heard from radical leaders touched something sacred in their outlook. It was an appeal to moral righteousness. And many were moved to act in circumstances where ordinarily they would be afraid to act.

Persistent anxiety cost them class time and poor grades. Students under this heavy pressure would tell us that they were having trouble concentrating on their studies. Some dropped out of school and never returned. Others made a show of getting themselves arrested in demonstrations, only to struggle later on to have the record expunged because it might damage their chances for admission to medical school or law school.

Most students could not handle the stress at all. They were unable to bring themselves to flat-out defiance of civil authority. They also could not ignore what was going on around them. For these young people the solution was escape into the counterculture, with excitement and relief sought in bouts with "acid" and "speed."

Some broke down completely. Psychiatric counsellors on campus were overwhelmed in those days by young clients desperate for professional help.

In the late Sixties we began to have a serious problem with suicides and accidental deaths.34 The most dreaded episodes began with a telephone call late at night from campus security telling me that a student had been found.

One that I particularly remember came at about midnight after I had gone to bed. It was early in my term at Columbia. When the security man reported what he had discovered, I threw on some clothes and hurried over to Furnald Hall, an ancient dormitory in the South Campus. It was midwinter and icy cold.

On the fifth floor of Furnald, I found the girl, very young, no more than a sophomore, dressed in a navy blue T-shirt and jeans. She had done it to herself, perhaps accidentally. The medical examiner wasn't sure about the accidental part, but he was certain it was a self-inflicted drug overdose. The door to her room was ajar and the corridor outside filled with frightened students talking excitedly in low monotones. They would edge toward the door to peek at the horror inside and then quickly fall back.

She was seated at her desk, her head thrown back as though her last thought was to scream for help. She had sat there dead for more than 72 hours before friends became alarmed and opened the locked room. The body was now swollen and turning dusky gray. I asked the detectives and the medical examiner whether we could not lay her out on her neatly made bed to give her at least the appearance of peace. They shook their heads. Rigor mortis had set in.

In the corridor outside the room stood a student reporter from the *Columbia Spectator*, the campus newspaper. His face was ashen and he looked as if he was about to throw up. When he asked what the police and the medical examiner had told me, his voice caught and stammered violently. I put my arm over his shoulder and told him what I could as he scribbled notes in a shaky hand. I asked him to go easy on her and he nodded. Without another word he thrust the notebook into his jacket pocket and fled.

I remained for a few minutes speaking to the strained young faces in the corridor, trying to explain what had occurred and urging them to go back to bed. Then I walked across the treacherous icy pavement of Low Plaza to my office. I would have to call the girl's parents on my private line.

There is a special problem for participants in any era of dramatic upheaval when they attempt to distill the significance of what they lived through. Temptation is strong to rewrite history in order to justify our own beliefs and actions.³⁵ Memory can be very deceptive. Unerringly it seeks respectability for things done in ignorance and confusion. We all prefer to think of ourselves as moral agents rather than muddled actors in a theater of the absurd.

Former student radicals have been reflecting on the era in print for several years now. There are many, perhaps even the majority, who can honestly say they emerged undamaged and with clean consciences.

They protected the poor, worked to end discrimination, and fought on behalf of the Vietnamese people. And they were successful. Obviously many veterans of campus wars in the Sixties did live up to their ideals.³⁶ I suppose I am obsessed with the other side of the picture because the nature of my responsibilities forced me to see so much of it. It wasn't nearly as edifying as that pretty portrait of idealism, and few social critics want to hear the whole story. It tends to diminish the value of what was accomplished because it rubs our noses in the price some students had to pay. Critics want to remember the era as a time of achievement.

Perhaps not all critics. Recently young conservatives have begun to challenge the activists' recollections of the Sixties. In conservative eyes the era was one of administrative spinelessness, lack of discipline, and moral decay. Both protagonists, I think, tend to overstate their own moral respectability. The period was characterized by a mixture of idealism, brutality, and weakness, lending itself to almost as many interpretations as there were observers. The emotional intensity of the struggles and the moral dedication of at least a majority of the participants makes this Rashomon-like phenomenon perfectly understandable, but the fact that different people perceived the same events in completely different ways should caution us about the dangers of self-sanctification.

I found the Young Americans for Freedom (YAF), a conservative student organization, almost as ruthless in putting pressure on the chancellor or in soliciting outside political help to assure that no issue, however poignant, would be allowed to disturb the academic routine of the campus, as SDS was in trying to shut us down on silly moralistic pretexts. Each group seemed oriented toward fighting the other rather than toward reason.

YAF tended to be a bit more polite than SDS, but only marginally so. The fact is that both sought to impose their views on the rest of us by resorting to adversary pressures. Each wanted to reconstruct the campus in its own conception of truth and morality. Today we would call them single-issue pressure groups.

The greatest problem of all in those days was the widespread abandonment of tolerance and restraint by a variety of people demanding instant perfection and impatient with orderly change. Among the worst offenders was the New Left. It is understandable that New Left radicals of the Sixties would now be trying to prove that their crusade against racial injustice and the war in Vietnam was well intended and high principled. It was. The problems, and they were legion, arose from the way the New Left radicals went about implementing their high-minded intentions.

Other key offenders, less easy to forgive because they were more mature, were some public figures of the Sixties. I no longer find it blood-curdling to look back on Governor Reagan's insistence on the use of deadly force to uphold the law against campus demonstrators. But it is only because we managed to work our way out of the crisis without the total catastrophe many of us feared.37

Governor Reagan and SDS were very much alike in one major respect. Neither had much use for tolerance or restraint if it meant coming to terms with the other. Both seemed to relish being at war. There is a great irony in the fact that the New Left's predilection for direct action and its passion for instant change, as contrasted with the idea of trying to persuade others, has now led to those most hostile to New Left objectives being in charge of the government. If voters are forced to choose between order and chaos, they will choose, and the results will not be pleasing to advocates of radical change.

Direct action, building seizures, and illegal pressure tactics had an unfortunate but completely predictable outcome. They removed the idealistic pursuit of social change from the domain of democratic process to the realm of force. They invited aggressive reactions, my own among them. The backlash, long feared by political moderates following the zealotry of the New Left, has descended upon us with a vengeance. Surely that outcome was not intended.

It is easy to understand why revolutionary leaders of SDS and the Black Panthers would seek to annul the processes of democracy in pursuing their visions of a "just" society. Democracy did not serve their ends.38 They were ruled by ungovernable ambition and convinced that the kind of justice they sought was unavailable through democratic means. It would come only in a revolutionary cataclysm.

But the mass of "believers" had a substantial investment in the survival of democracy. The thought of armed struggle based upon a Third World revolutionary model repelled most of them. They joined in demonstrations because they believed that protest might be a step toward racial justice or the end of the war. Sometimes in the heat of emotion these students went beyond demonstrations into conduct that put them in legal jeopardy, but their intent was only to try to move us. Their goals were justice, peace, and love. The actualization of these abstract virtues was not visible anywhere in the money-grubbing commercial world around them, and they demanded change.

What led so many average, nonviolent, nonrevolutionary undergraduates in the Sixties to sanction abandonment of the slow processes of democracy in favor of group pressure tactics aimed at producing "instant" change by force or threat rather than persuasion?

The question is puzzling, as puzzling as any that can be raised about an era rich in puzzles. There are many plausible explanations, because the influences at work in the Sixties were so exceedingly complex.

Why should we object when students turn to the same pressure tactics widely used in other sectors of society? The acceptability of such pressures is predicated on the belief, now fairly well documented, that a pluralistic society governs itself best through the adversary clash of conflicting centers of influence or power. Groups are expected to differ sharply on public policy. It is assumed they will advance their own viewpoints as forcefully as necessary, and defend their interests against opposition. Harmony of a sort emerges from agreement on little more than the rules decreeing how we should fight.

Beneath the surface of America's traditional two-party governance is a furious clash of special interests: business and labor groups, consumer interests, environmental interests, religious and ethnic groups, pro- and anti-abortion groups. This abbreviated listing barely scratches the surface of our almost unrivaled capacity for internal conflict. Contending groups bash heads continuously in an incredible, noisy brawl. Public policy emerges somehow as the vector resultant of all these forces. We conduct our business in a never-ending swirl of threats, investigations, lawsuits, strikes, sit-ins, press conferences, media events, and a multitude of other less spectacular pressures.

It is a strange kind of governance, frazzling to the nerves, but in mysterious ways workable. Whatever deficiencies the system possesses, it is refreshingly alive in contrast with the lockstep uniformity and bayonet-enforced harmony of the Soviet bloc.

But student radicals in the Sixties elected to go considerably beyond the rules regulating dissent in a system built to foster dissent. Militant picketing and building blockades, seizures of deans' and presidents' offices, breaking into university files, were acts that tended to put students in violation of the law. The fact that such actions involved large numbers of demonstrators did not protect them from legal attack for very long. We began to apply to the courts for restraining orders.39 The issuance of a court order against an illegal demonstration raised the stakes considerably for people prone to take the law into their own hands. The contest was transformed from students versus the administration to students versus the courts.

In the civil rights movement, demonstrators had engaged in mass-scale civil disobedience to test unjust racial segregation laws. The protestors were not at all gentle. They wanted to confront local authorities with the prospect of filling their jails to overflowing or bargaining toward more equitable arrangements between the races. Local officials wisely chose to bargain. It was wise because they were confronting the full power of the federal government in addition to masses of demonstrators determined to shut them down.

Student radicals rarely had government backing, and it could hardly be argued seriously that trespass laws were unjust.40 There never was any intent to test laws by calculated disobedience. Instead students were seeking to change university policies they believed to be racist or warlike. "Extra-legal" actions were necessary, students maintained, because the university would not alter longstanding practices simply because they protested. Meeting their demands was the minimum price the administration would have to pay for withdrawal of militancy.41 It was curious reasoning, and in the long run no one other than the most committed radicals saw it as an effective vehicle for change. At first a majority of nonactivists approved stepping outside the law as a show of commitment, but it was obvious from the beginning that the majority would not go along with a legally flawed protest mechanism once they understood its dangers. Besides, it did not produce the changes students sought and that the radicals had promised.

The faculty was always ready to reexamine university policies in response to well-founded moral objections.42 Despite radical rhetoric arguing the contrary, seizure tactics and moralistic demands were never really necessary. Forcible protest succeeded in shortcircuiting our collegial governance only as long as it continued to achieve results. When we learned how to frustrate sit-ins and seizures, radical students were no longer able to secure backing from the rest of the campus.43

Why then did nonactivist students stand behind "extra-legal" protests in the beginning?

The most obvious explanation is that we in the administration failed to devise any constructive alternatives. It may well be that we tended to look at protest too narrowly and legalistically. Many of us never really understood the broad humanistic goals that students were trying to express, and we forced them into extreme measures to get our attention.

With all the idealism motivating student protest groups, why was it not possible occasionally for the chancellor to make common cause with students, and sometimes sublimate protests by joining them?

This question has been asked frequently by liberal-minded critics. Unfortunately it does not have a simple answer. Most senior university officals of my generation were sensitive, imaginative people who lacked nothing in idealism. It is true that some of them, typically those inexperienced with conflict, became frightened and caught up in the siege mentality when they first discovered that a significant number of student radicals meant to do them harm. It may have prevented these administrators from reaching out to the larger mass of romantic students. That is essentially what happened to me during my first year in the chancellor's office. But many others were quite capable of meeting students halfway and tried to do it.

I knew two college presidents who attempted to guide protest activity by leading it. Both failed. Radical students pushed them into excesses, and other students failed to intervene by controlling the radicals. Both men came to be seen as easy marks. Eventually they were asked to leave office in the face of the public criticism that their sympathetic effort to work with students had unleashed. Although large numbers of students in the Sixties were easy to manipulate, it was not as simple to seduce them this way as contemporary critics, lacking real experience, now try to suggest.44 During twelve years as a chief campus officer I can recall only two, perhaps three, incidents in which the current of idealism was so strong that I was able to enter into it without being obviously manipulative.

One of these incidents was the long reappointment struggle involving Herbert Marcuse at UCSD. The reader will recall that on the very day Marcuse's appointment was authorized by the Regents, a small group of radical students suddenly barred a Marine Corps recruiter from conducting interviews on campus. The overwhelming majority of campus protests resembled the Marine recruiter incident rather than the Marcuse case.

When a hostile group attempts to break into the chancellor's office, or surrounds and jostles him as he walks across the campus, screams obscenities at him, or pickets and chants vulgar slogans in front of his home, it is difficult to dwell on the larger idealism that moves the protestors. These are well-known pressure tactics calculated to harass and intimidate, and they should be understood as such. We saw them as part of the "radicalization game." Ordinary students joined in it, or at least failed to stop it, because they viewed us as adversaries.

Some have suggested that nonactivists were sympathetic to forcible protest because nearly all students were angry, boiling over in fact, with the public's refusal to take them seriously. This view became very popular with the media during the Sixties.

Instances of angry violence did occur, but they were rare and almost always on a small scale.45 The windows of the president's office at Columbia were made of plexiglass when I arrived in 1970. I soon discovered why. Little bands of students would frequently detach themselves from demonstrations and roam the campus throwing rocks or brickbats. These roving bands were wild with fury, but they were numerically insignificant. Nonactivist students almost never participated in that kind of violence. Large-scale demonstrations were always more calculated unless they were badly led. Anger was there, but it was kept in check, disciplined, and made to serve political ends.

Both these factors—administrative refusal to support protest and latent student anger—probably were the causative agents that led a majority of nonactivist students to support the protestors. So was the impatience with which college students viewed bureaucratic delays, especially when demands for change were backed by strong moral feelings.

All combined to create an impression in students' minds that they were engaged in a moral contest with the administration and that they had to win it. Students felt that they were in the majority and also in the right. The impression needed no skeptical testing; it was overpowering. Any opposition was immediately defined as evil. How many times in those days did I hear the singsong chant:

"We are the people—we are the people—we are the people"?

But, as I have tried to suggest, there was something beyond this unsophisticated moral righteousness in the protest activity of the 1960s. Students also needed to portray themselves as victims of society.

Discussions with protestors in those days were nearly always characterized by what seemed to me to be a diminished quality of thought.46 Adversarial habits of thinking, coupled with assumptions of moral rectitude, led protest groups to assert views that I considered virtually paranoid. Whenever I would say this and ask them to apply higher standards of proof to their own beliefs, they would laugh derisively. Proof was unnecessary.

It is not a new observation, but the impact of such intense emotional commitment, unaccompanied by genuine critical skepticism, was almost chilling.47 It shows once more how thin the veneer of our civilization is.

The diminished and quasi-paranoid quality of thought in student protest groups offers a clue to the psychological origins of such groups. If we put aside the idealistic substance of the protests, and also disregard the extra-legal tactics, we are left with the fascinating prior questions of why protest groups formed in the first instance, and what purpose they served.

It is seldom the case that a large number of people decide spontaneously that they have discovered a moral evil against which all feel impelled to act in precisely the same way. Everything in my experience teaches me that, absent a catastrophic incident riveting everyone's attention on a single problem, student protest groups tended to form in the heat of some kind of sustained emotional arousal. In this initial state, the groups were diffusely excited, filled with a diversity of grievances, and very suggestible. Only when such uncoordinated energy was concentrated by protest leaders would the group members come to share essentially the same grievances.

The development of a group or a class believing itself to be composed of victims is a social process not very remote from Marxist prescriptions for the formation of the proletariat. But in modern life, particularly in technologically advanced societies, the struggle seems not to be between a monolithic proletariat and an equally monolithic ownership class, but between countless protest constituencies and the institutions against which they carry grievances.[48]

Astute organizers can capture these diffuse feelings of oppression and victimization, directing them into political action. The objective is to develop an identity for the group and some way of achieving redress from the institutions identified as victimizers.

For twelve years I witnessed the intense competitive struggles in which students tried to survive at a modern university. There were just too many young people competing for too few preferred places. No campus interaction was either simple or pleasant. Undergraduates in large universities needed to push and shove against virtually impenetrable bureaucratic barriers to get even the most elementary things done. It seems perfectly apparent that a great many students were unable to bear the stresses of such continuous infighting.

These pressures seem to me to form the key psychological precondition for the climate of emotional arousal on campus.[49] Coupled with the political horrors of the Sixties, and the existence of an exciting, and at first effective, group protest mechanism, the psychological pressures pushed students into overt action. It is interesting to observe that the stresses are no longer as intense for today's students as they were in the Sixties, and that the protest mechanism has become dated and ineffectual. Hence the climate of emotional arousal has largely disappeared.

Why did so many students of the Sixties react to the intense pressures they faced by banding together as self-declared outcasts from society? Their attempts to find meaning and identity in a universe of overwhelming complexity that threatened to annihilate them seemed to me to be a translation into the academic life of one of the central problems of existential philosophy.[50] It was at this time that the best students discovered and really understood Kierkegaard, Sartre, Camus, and the other existentialists.

The pressures these students faced were no mere philosophical abstractions in the Sixties. Under the unique stresses of the time undergraduates could drift easily into the role of victim. It was so plausible, and it absolved them of moral responsibility in continuing to struggle against a hostile and unyielding environment. Some ceased struggling altogether, satisfied that they had been crushed by insensitive, authoritarian institutions. They viewed their future prospects as hopeless and unbearable.

Such students began to yield their personal goals, spending instead an appreciable amount of their time explaining to anyone who would listen the injustices that had been heaped upon them. They were ready for protest whenever someone came along to identify an appropriate villain and focalize their diffuse grievances. They became easy marks for demagogues and revolutionaries.

The importance of this observation lies in the fact that much of the adversary conflict and demonstration activity engaged in by a whole range of special interests in the U.S. today, was triggered off by the student uprisings of the Sixties.[51] Many people are fundamentally unhappy, searching as students once did for escape from the affronts of bureaucracy and the pressures of daily existence. There is no easy escape. The construction of a sense of purpose in the existential environment that modern life creates is one of the central problems every society faces.

It has become increasingly evident during the last twelve years that some transcendent form of leadership beyond the mere articulation of existential despair and narrow-constituency grievances is necessary not just for undergraduates but for all of us if we are ever to master life in an advanced society with all its complexities, pressures, and frustrations. We must recognize that victimization is a kind of disease, and that there is a special dignity in the sheer continued willingness to struggle.

At UCSD and Columbia I found that we could live with and adjust to even the most brutal pressures. Humor, camaraderie, and a considerable residue of toughness were generally sufficient to get us through the worst times. The alternative to digging in and bearing stress stoically is not a revolutionary cataclysm, as the radicals of the Sixties once fervently preached. It is more likely to be a massive fragmentation of society into groups of self-declared victims narcissistically absorbed in their own grievances, unable to empathize or think of anything else.[52]

For all that, the students of the 1960s were a wonderfully creative, highly original force in American life. Most of them saw establishment institutions as corrupt and violence-prone. They rejected the war in Vietnam, and fought against efforts to mold them into routine and unrewarding occupations. These were good fights.

Students reacted with hostility to universities because they saw us as purveyors of diplomas, not education. In the fresh eyes of our undergraduates, the diploma mills were grinding out certificates of entry into dead-end work situations removed from all vital human concerns. Students viewed college as a competitive rat-race for grades in dull courses, and they were not wrong about that either.

Where could they hear about the philosophical principles that guide one's search for inner peace and self-discovery? Rarely in the classroom or the lecture hall; it was out in the free speech area where the radicals were preaching.

Students of the Sixties wanted to be free to experiment with life, to experience beauty in its fullness. I remember the slogan

Make Love, Not War

daubed over the walls of Columbia's buildings when I moved into the president's office in September 1970.

Of course it was foolish and naive. You cannot change humankind's nature by slogans. It was important to explain to overwrought 18-year-olds that the world crushes naive idealists. Darwin taught us that any species unable to adapt to things as they are becomes extinct. Idealism must always be tempered with intelligent planning if it is to be truly effective in building a better world. Peace and harmony do not come just because we yearn for them. They require intelligence as well as commitment. Most of all, the realization of peace demands that progress be made in single steps.

Many students in that generation were brutally damaged by their search for simplistic utopias, but there was something undeniably beautiful about their crusade.

Freshmen become irritated with me if I seem to suggest that they are one jot less idealistic or less committed than the students who went before them. Today's students are certainly no admirers of the demanding society in which they live. They know too much about poverty, racism, and political corruption. Yet few of them are willing to protest, nor are they duplicates of their apathetic predecessors in the Fifties.

Undergraduates today possess important new qualities. They saw many of their predecessors damaged by ignorance of political and economic realities, and so they react with cynicism to radicals operating with undisclosed political agendas. They are worldly wise beyond their years.

There is a great current interest in family, religion, and cultural roots, but it is not a turning to traditional American ways after a binge of radicalism. Students seem to be trying to rediscover a time when life was simple, when the burdens of existence did not seem so crushing. It is a turning inward, a search for sources of contentment within their own lives.

In a real sense we are all victims of the Sixties. There is not much left now of the lovely naiveté of our youth in World War II. If I were to speak of America today as the "arsenal of democracy," students would laugh scornfully. They have seen too many "democrats" like Franco, Trujillo, and Somoza to fall for such global nonsense in the 1980s. Today's students were mostly children during the ordeal of the Sixties, but they think about that time a lot, and they are very wise.

The time of struggle is behind me now. Nearly all my combative anger has been safely put away again. I hope it will remain hidden forever, emerging only late at night in my recurrent dreams about the students and the ordeals we lived through together. During waking hours, I find myself reacting with a newfound warmth and nostalgia to memories of angry demands that we somehow become better than we are. Those students made me a much more thoughtful person than I used to be. Few of them would believe it, but it is true.

Notes

CHAPTER 1: A MONKEY IN THE GARDEN

1. William Manchester, *Goodbye, Darkness*, Little, Brown, Boston, 1980.

2. Changes in birthrate and immigration statistics have altered the state's population forecasts since the UCSD academic plan was originally formulated. In 1975, the University of California cut back the planned growth of the university. The San Diego campus was limited to four colleges at maximum size, with an overall undergraduate student population of about 8,000. I believe these targets greatly underestimate the potential of the San Diego campus. The area is growing very rapidly under the pressure of the great migration to the sun belt that emerged in the late 1970s.

CHAPTER 2: THE CLEAVER CRISIS

1. The term "media event" may seem cynical in a discussion of campus protests. There were, of course, many legitimate protests in which anger and spontaneity were genuine. But we live in an age of mass communication. "Protest groups" sometimes did not protest; they sought public attention for their causes.

During the 1960s, reporters and TV newsmen were poised for quick trips to the campus whenever word reached newsrooms that something was happening. The campus thus became a vehicle for projecting media messages aimed at the general public.

Media events are easy to spot. Protestors carry neatly lettered placards so as to be visible on TV. They shout carefully rehearsed slogans on cue. There are spokespersons to deliver the message to TV reporters.

Often they would come to us in advance to work out a scenario that assured no interference by university authorities. We accepted this kind of thing as a legitimate exercise of free speech, but after 1970 most of the campus looked upon it with contempt.

Because media events are now commonplace, conceptions tend to develop in the minds of the general public having little to do with reality. Reporters and editors know this, but a protest has primitive impact that attracts an audience or a readership. Hence the transparent character of media events is tolerated by the press. The writer's view is that the whole system of media-oriented "protests" is a sham—an intrusion of populistic show business into news-gathering. It distorts the democratic process. See Todd Gitlin, *The Whole World Is Watching*, University of California Press, Berkeley, 1980, especially page 30. Gitlin was president of the SDS in 1963–64. His media sophistication may surprise readers who look upon student protestors as simple crusaders.

2. In October 1966, the Regents agreed to hold their monthly meetings at each of the university campuses in turn. The policy was intended to familiarize the board with the special characteristics and problems of each campus. By July 1969, security problems forced the Regents to abandon the practice and limit their meetings to secure locations in Berkeley and San Francisco.

3. The Board of Educational Development (BED) was an outgrowth of the Free Speech Movement. Berkeley's academic senate established BED in 1966 to stimulate academic innovation on campus. BED was authorized to review, approve, and administer new and experimental courses that fell outside the conventional jurisdictions of academic departments. Social Analysis 139X, "Dehumanization and Regeneration in the American Social Order," was first proposed to BED by students representing the Associated Students of the University of California. Faculty representatives were not unaware of possible negative repercussions from Cleaver's role. They put the teaching and administrative responsibilities for the course in the hands of four regular faculty members. Cleaver was to be a guest lecturer, a "live source." He was to receive no pay, and his appointment would not carry permanent UC status. These precautions were felt sufficient to ensure the integrity of the course. Obviously they were not. Cleaver contended publicly that the course was his to teach as he wished. The faculty representatives on BED had not reckoned with Cleaver's reaction any more than they had anticipated the huge public outcry.

4. Eldridge Cleaver was jailed on a marijuana charge in 1954 at age 19, and again for assault to kill and rape in 1958. He served nine years in Soledad prison for this second crime. In prison he became a disciple of Malcom X, and wrote his best known work, *Soul on Ice*. Cleaver was released in December 1966, married, and accepted a position as editor of *Ramparts* magazine. He first appeared actively on the California political scene in May 1967, when, as a representative of *Ramparts*, unarmed, he accompanied a group of gun-carrying Black Panthers as they invaded the California State Assembly chamber in Sacramento. In April 1968, Cleaver was involved in a violent encounter with the Oakland police. Two policemen were wounded, eight Panthers were arrested on charges of assault with intent to kill, one was killed. Although Cleaver claimed that he was not carrying a gun, his arrest in Oakland sent him back to prison as a parole violator. He was again released in June 1968, after a hearing in which the judge accused the state of revoking Cleaver's parole out of distaste for his political views. The details of the Oakland shoot-out remain murky, even to the present day.

In July 1968, the Peace and Freedom Party, a California radical group, endorsed Cleaver as their nominee for President of the United States. With the conviction of Huey Newton on September 9, 1968, Cleaver became head of the Black Panther party. In view of all this, it is hardly surprising that the Regents were upset to learn that Cleaver had been invited to teach an experimental course at Berkeley under the sponsorship of the Board of Educational Development.

On September 27, 1968, the State Court of Appeals in San Francisco ruled that the judge who overruled the revocation of Cleaver's parole in June had "acted beyond his authority." For reasons that are not entirely clear, Cleaver was allowed to remain at liberty. On November 2, 1968, he was indicted on three counts of attempted murder and assault with a deadly weapon in connection with the Oakland affray, and released on $50,000 bail. On November 20, the California Supreme Court refused to hear an appeal on the September parole ruling. Faced with returning to prison as a parole violator and standing trial on the assault charge, Cleaver fled the United States for Cuba on December 10, 1968.

He returned to the U.S. from France on November 18, 1975, after nearly seven years as an expatriate. By this time, he had made a complete political about-face. He had broken with the Panthers, experienced a religious conversion, and represented himself as eager to rejoin the mainstream of American life. Five years later he was a lay evangelist, a supporter of President Reagan, and, it was reported, a self-declared member of the Mormon Church.

5. Technically the California state constitution grants all authority in university matters to the Board of Regents. As a matter of practice, however, authority over the development and supervision of the curriculum was delegated to the academic senate under Chapter IX, Section 2(b) of the Standing Orders of the Regents which reads: "The Academic Senate shall authorize and supervise all courses and curricula. . . ." When the Cleaver controversy developed, the Regents attempted to skirt the issue of faculty autonomy and academic freedom by questioning Cleaver's qualifications to teach the course rather than the content of the course. Angry students and faculty rarely acknowledged this legal nicety. Social Analysis 139X was the principal issue before the Regents at their September 1968 meeting. A senior member of the administration suggested using the "Harvard Rule"—i.e., any lecturer who appears more than twice in the same course, must hold a regular faculty appointment.

After a long and acrimonious debate, the Regents drafted a resolution limiting guest lecturers to one lecture and permitting the president of the university to make exceptions to this rule. It was this resolution that was eventually ratified by the board at its November 22, 1968, meeting at UCSD.

Some idea of Governor Reagan's position in the debate may be conveyed by a resolution he offered at the Santa Cruz meeting in October. It can be summarized as follows: Article IV, Section 9, of the California Constitution gives the Regents full power over the university. The Regents are authorized, but not required, to delegate authority. The Regents can withdraw delegated authority if the faculty abuses it. The Berkeley academic senate has not read the California Constitution carefully. We owe it to the people of California to correct this misconception. Therefore: The academic senate has no autonomous power. Whatever power it has is limited to specific delegations. The Board of Educational

Development has no power to initiate courses. The Regents approve degrees. The Regents, president, and the chancellors appoint the faculty upon the advice of the academic senate and the administration. The right to approve an appointment is different from academic freedom and free speech. University facilities cannot be used for Cleaver's course. Faculty who accredit 139X will be disciplined. Credits earned in the course cannot be applied to a degree.

The toughness of Reagan's position shocked and angered the faculty. In November, Reagan adroitly withdrew his resolution in favor of the "one lecture" rule. He said that he was always willing to compromise.

6. At the meeting at San Diego, the Board of Regents decided that since Social Analysis 139X had not been brought into conformity with the guest-lecturer policy established in September, students enrolled in the course would not receive academic credit. This decision was within their constitutional power but conflicted with the delegated authority of the academic senate to "supervise all courses and curricula."

7. The general public in California was genuinely shocked to discover the Marxist orientation of a number of leaders of the FSM. For example, Bettina Aptheker, daughter of a well-known member of the Communist Party, was a leading member of the FSM steering committee. People jumped to the erroneous conclusion that the thousands of students who associated themselves with FSM were communists. This simplistic view was particularly significant in shaping later public responses to student protest on the national scene, because the Berkeley upheaval played a seminal role in subsequent unrest. In the public mind it was all a communist plot. While the Berkeley crisis yielded beneficial long-term changes in university policy and curriculum, it also polarized the California electorate and seriously damaged public support for the university system. A detailed, though somewhat biased, account of the Berkeley conflict of 1964–65 can be found in Max Heirich, *The Spiral of Conflict: Berkeley, 1964*, Columbia University Press, New York, 1971.

8. We received more than our share of angry letters at UCSD. I have saved the choicest examples, of which the following is typical. Notice that this taxpayer is quite aware of our vulnerability because of the pending university bond issue.

> President of UCSD,
>   How can you possibly along with your collegues [*sic*] be so terrible as to spend the taxpayers money by standing by and letting a criminal with a sick mind such as Cleaver speak in a so-called top notch college as UCSD? I can't believe that a person in your position and your intelligence could do a thing like this. Submitting our young Americans to such vulgarity and ideas to over-throw our Government and things that all Americans fight for in the service. I'll guarantee you I'll not vote "yes" on tax bonds to help schools with things like this and the unrest in students. The unrest is caused by just such people. I absolutely can't believe it. How can you people stand your consciences?
>   Sincerely yours,
>   A San Diego taxpayer.

9. In his 1966 campaign against incumbent Governor Edmund Brown,

Reagan came down hard on the "Berkeley mess." He attacked the cost of the university, the soundness of its education. He blamed President Kerr for his handling of the FSM. In Reagan's view, administrators should be able to control students. Two years later, on October 9, 1968, in a speech before the California Bar Association, Reagan was still making political hay at the expense of the university. He noted the increase in gun sales in California and asserted that the public was arming itself because it had lost faith in government protection. He cited campus crises as one of the major causes of this public apprehension, calling the university problem "the biggest problem facing California. . . . Colleges are not going to become launching pads for anarchy. Those who cannot get their education within the framework of our system can get it elsewhere." See *The San Diego Union,* October 10, 1968, B-1.

On October 17, at a board meeting in Santa Cruz continuously disrupted by demonstrating students, the Regents rejected Reagan's demand (see note 5) that they strip the academic senate of its authority to develop experimental courses. A few days later, angered by this refusal to bar Cleaver's participation in Social Analysis 139X, he said, "The people have not turned this institution over to the faculty to rule by insubordination, or to the administrators to rule through appeasement and capitulation, or to the students to rule by coercion." *The San Diego Evening Tribune,* October 21, 1968, p. 1.

Reagan's tough approach was enthusiastically supported by average voters in California. He argued that if students were unwilling to abide by university rules, they should be thrown out, opening places for others who might appreciate the educational opportunities offered by the state. If administrators were unwilling to stand up to students and faculty, they should be removed. If the faculty could not handle curriculum planning in an "acceptable" manner, authority over curriculum should be returned to the Regents. Not even the Regents themselves were spared. In Reagan's view, if the Regents refused to deal with these problems, it was time to reorganize the board and find people who understood their duty. By the spring of 1969, the Governor gained his majority among the Regents and they began to implement his views.

It is difficult to reconcile this hard-ball approach with the "nice guy" political image Reagan projects.

He is regularly underestimated because people pay attention to his facile public utterances rather than his public actions. When Reagan was first elected in 1966, faculty and students derided him as "our acting Governor." They learned in a hurry!

10. At the September Regents meeting in Los Angeles:

> Speaking in favor of Regent Grant's substitute motion, Governor Reagan stated that, as evidenced by thousands of letters he has received, Mr. Cleaver's participation in the course is unacceptable to the people of California. He called attention to possible actions which might be demanded by the citizens of the State if Regent Grant's substitute motion was defeated—a. investigation of the university administration by the legislative committee which is presently examining the university, b. submission to the voters of initiatives which would change the structure and control of the

university, giving to the Legislature control in many areas which it does not now have.

Minutes, University of California Board of Regents, Sept. 20, 1968, p. 9.

11. The *La Jolla Light* headline for Thursday, October 10, read, "Panther Leader Speaks. Presidential Nominee Cleaver Predicts Revolution." Cleaver attacked everyone. Governor Reagan became "Mickey Mouse Reagan," Max Rafferty was "Donald Duck Rafferty," and America became "Babylon." How does the "new" Cleaver explain these rhetorical excesses? In *Soul On Fire,* he writes, "Governor Reagan and Max Rafferty . . . launched into my classroom appearances with the inspiration of holy war. The effect was marvelous. There was enormous support from young people all over the West, particularly on the large college campuses." Eldridge Cleaver, *Soul On Fire,* Word Books, Waco, Texas, 1978, p. 100. Beyond this admission, he attributes his words to "rocketing paranoia." Cleaver maintains that Panther rhetoric, while adopting much of its vocabulary from the Black Muslim movement, was never founded on hatred of whites. *Ibid.,* pp. 92–100.

12. The meeting of Sunday, November 24, was organized by the Steering Committee of the Faculty Ad Hoc Committee on Academic Freedom. Radical faculty interpreted the Regents' action as an administrative ban on Cleaver's right to speak. In a private letter to the chancellor, one faculty member who attended the meeting characterized it as "highly charged." Another said, "Only in the Sunday evening meeting was there developed the hysteria that was the driving force behind events. In addition to some sensible remarks, a number of suicidal proposals were made." A conservative senior member of the faculty said, "In fifty years of teaching, I have never been so disheartened by faculty behavior as I was by the Sunday night meeting. My only consolation is that the injudicious comments and proposals emanated from a relatively few members of the faculty." In the words of another commentator, "The whole Sunday evening operation was nonsensical. It is nonsensical to try and make official sense of it now. It is nonsensical to try and make sense of the effects without making sense of the immediate cause."

The meeting produced a number of resolutions, ranging from moderate to extreme, that were placed before the academic senate the following Tuesday. Fortunately, by Tuesday the climate on campus had cooled. Resolutions to close down the campus or censure the Regents were abandoned. Instead, the senate resolved that the Regents had "gravely violated academic freedom by retroactively cancelling a course approved by a duly authorized body of the UC Berkeley Academic Senate." This was a strong statement, but not censure or open defiance. The senate further requested that the AAUP investigate the University of California on the grounds that the Regents' actions were a breach of academic freedom. In answer to student demands for a more relevant curriculum, it established a committee to deal with curriculum reform. The last motion of the meeting, passed by a unanimous vote, was a resolution directed to the chancellor: "Bill, put another roll on the player piano and keep playing." I never understood what they meant, but it sounded friendly.

13. Minority-student grievances centered on faculty hiring practices, the relevance of current curriculum, and the availability of educational opportunities.

They echoed demands being made by minority students at other institutions, especially at Berkeley and San Francisco State.

14. The signature heading on the yellow pad read, "I intend to cancel my classes tomorrow, November 25, so that I and my students may participate in the Convocation planned to discuss the current university problems relating to recent Regental action." This was a statement of individual conviction, and certainly did not imply support for a two-day strike. Unfortunately, when the list of faculty signatures was published by strike activists, it was appended to a statement calling on faculty to back the strike.

15. It was Murphy, in fact, who ordered the arrest of a nonstudent during a dispute over the legality of a CORE table in front of Sproul Hall. The man had refused to identify himself. This arrest set off the celebrated "police car entrapment" incident of October 1, 1964. Heirich, pp. 143–144.

16. On Wednesday, November 13, after an extended strike by Third World Liberation Front students and several days of violence on campus, President Robert Smith closed the San Francisco State campus. Governor Reagan and the state college trustees, deeply angered, gave him until November 20 to open the college and keep it open, "at bayonet-point if necessary." On Tuesday, November 26, Smith resigned. He was succeeded by S. I. Hayakawa, who opened the campus with the help of the San Francisco police, fought a media campaign in his tam-o'-shanter against the militants, and went on to become a folk hero in California. Hayakawa displayed great personal courage during this episode, but it seemed to me he was running for political office from the moment he stepped on the barricades. New Left ideologues were so preoccupied with seizing power they could not understand the boost they were giving to Sam Hayakawa's political ambitions.

17. The chemist was Professor James Arnold, who was widely admired by students. He never hesitated to mix it with them when we were in trouble. He was and is a superb human being.

18. Actually there was no written employment contract, only an inscrutable appointment form. But its terms and conditions were well understood by both Regents and faculty.

19. I was referring to the convocation in Revelle Plaza, but the Regents seemed to be putting on a political circus of their own at the time.

20. We used to speak of them as the "Del Mar crowd." These were countercultural people living in communes and rooming houses in Del Mar. Although not UCSD students, they appeared regularly on campus with guitars, guerrilla theater, and packs of barking dogs. It was a truly bizarre scene, long since vanished as skyrocketing real estate values in Southern California drove the counterculture out.

21. The faculty cited here, together with one or two others, will reappear frequently in the text. They constituted a core group of radicals working closely with SDS. These people used their academic freedom quite improperly to try to radicalize the campus. During the Cleaver incident, I suddenly realized they were

uninhibited by the ethical restraints accompanying faculty rank. Several times I asked the senate to discipline them, without success. My hardening attitude toward such faculty militancy eventually led to a blow-up with the senate in May 1969 over People's Park. I have omitted names here because several still hold faculty positions. They have quieted down now, and seem to want to forget the past.

22. At the close of the winter quarter, he returned to Jamaica, as required by U.S. immigration laws, for what he believed was a routine interview pending issuance of his resident visa. In May 1969 the American consular officer in Jamaica informed him that his application for a resident visa had been denied as a result of unspecified activities deemed illegal under the McCarran-Walter Act.

23. Women have, of course, moved light years from the kind of affair I am describing. Today it would be denounced as sexist, but it was commonplace at universities in 1968.

I, too, have changed. Even before the end of that academic year I had seen so much conflict that I was completely preoccupied with survival. I doubt that I would have had the patience to go through with an affair such as this, with all its elements of social ritual, when just across the campus people were attempting to shut us down.

I suppose it is better for those women and for me that such changes have occurred. But thinking about how it is now, and how it was then, saddens me a little. We have gained a great deal in personal dignity, but I fear we have also lost something that was oddly graceful.

24. The speaker was, of course, Brad Cleaveland (see note 26). Cleaveland was a formidable opponent. He was very bright, very convincing, and thoroughly radical in his outlook. In the SLATE "Supplement to the General Catalogue" at Berkeley in 1964, Cleaveland wrote, "The multiversity is not an educational center, but a highly efficient industry: it produces bombs, other war machines, a few token 'peaceful' machines, and enormous numbers of safe, highly skilled and respectable automatons to meet the immediate needs of business and government." Analysts agree that the SLATE Supplement had a major impact on Berkeley students, making them receptive to the arguments of the FSM. Heirich, pp. 99–101.

The issues Cleaveland was raising were the very ones that had closed down San Francisco State during the previous week. UCSD, with its emphasis on big-dollar scientific research, much of it government-funded, was vulnerable to this kind of attack. By the spring of 1970, government-funded "war" research would emerge as a major radical issue at UCSD.

25. He was right. In 1968, by even the most optimistic estimates, only 3.8% of the UCSD student body was made up of minority students. By 1970 this figure had been raised to 11%. In 1980 it was 19%.

26. Brad Cleaveland currently lives in the Bay Area. He supports himself by working as a carpenter and remains actively involved in radical intellectual groups. He no longer remembers our confrontation in Revelle Plaza. For him, I suppose, it was all in a day's work.

Barry Shapiro also lives and works in the Bay Area. He is said to be disillusioned with politics, and interested now in cultural reform. He works for the East Bay Men's Center, an organization offering alternatives to typical male roles in society.

27. After her acquittal in a celebrated trial based on the abduction and killing of a Marin County judge in June 1972, Angela Davis became a veritable saint of the Marxist world. She travels by train behind the Iron Curtain and is greeted by excited crowds of children who present her with bouquets of flowers. Moscow radio and television regularly report on her activities in the U.S. It seems to me that this sanctification does not suit Miss Davis. She is more at home in front of a crowd urging them to action. Fortunately she is not a powerful speaker. Given her other gifts, it is difficult to imagine the mischief Angela Davis might have done had she been able to excite crowds during the Sixties.

CHAPTER 3: AN AGE OF ANTIHEROES

1. Robert Nisbet, *Twilight of Authority*, Oxford University Press, New York, 1975, pp. 102–112.

2. It is true that portions of the electorate have their heroes. President Ronald Reagan is seen as a true champion by American conservatives, and Ralph Nader remains the darling of young radicals who view the country as corrupted by business interests. The point I am making is that the times we live in polarize the electorate and effectively bar public officials from moving substantially beyond their political origins to reign as national heroes. That status is reserved for sports greats and TV celebrities. The present chapter will examine some of the antiheroes chosen by students.

2a. The issue arises because students were attracted to some very unusual heroes in the Sixties.
There is an extensive literature on the concept of the "hero" in contemporary historical and literary criticism. My own thinking has been heavily influenced by Robert Nisbet's view of political heroes as identifiable in relation to a set of values deemed sacred by a societal unit. (See Robert Nisbet, *Twilight of Authority*, pp. 102–112.) Although modern critics offer diverse typologies or classifications of heroes (generally seeming to favor revolutionary heroes, i.e. freedom fighters), it is evident that the terms "hero" and "villain" are relativistic. We devolve upon those who seem to embody values we accept as sacred. Hence my "hero" is certain to be someone else's "villain."
The people elected as heroes by students in the Sixties cannot be easily assigned to the continuum defined by the hero-villain polarity. They stand somewhere off-scale in that they lack many of the qualities that caused classical heroes to transcend human dimensions: i.e. grace, courage, strength, breadth of vision. Students chose as their models people who were either societal outcasts or who gave special voice to the alienation that students felt.
I have called these figures "antiheroes." The usage conforms reasonably well to the dictionary definition although perhaps not to contemporary literary usage.

The important point is that these "antiheroes" taken collectively offer special insights into the values of students in the Sixties.

3. The most articulate generational analysis comes from Lewis Feuer in his book, *The Conflict of Generations: The Character and Significance of Student Movements*, Basic Books, New York, 1969. Feuer argues that generational revolt is historically inevitable because of its relation to the oedipal conflicts characteristic of adolescent youth. This thesis has drawn considerable criticism on theoretical and historical grounds. It is, however, many orders of magnitude superior to generational explanations of student unrest appearing in the popular media during the late 1960s. The generational problem will be taken up again in Chapter 9.

4. Apologia in which the Sixties are interpreted as a moral crusade are bound to increase as numbers of young radicals begin to age at their typewriters. One need only mention Richard Flacks, *Youth and Social Change*, Markham Publishing Co., Chicago, 1971, and, more recently, Todd Gitlin, *The Whole World Is Watching*, University of California Press, Berkeley, 1980. A notable exception to the tone of self-justification among middle-aged veterans of the New Left is a remarkable doctoral dissertation by Harold Jacobs, *The Personal and the Political: A Study of the Decline of the New Left*, Department of Sociology, University of California, Berkeley, 1978. Jacobs offers a thoroughly balanced, and to this reader, compelling analysis of the inner contradictions of the New Left that led to its ultimate disintegration. As far as I know this dissertation has not been published.

The literature on student protest in the Sixties is voluminous. An excellent summary of research and current opinion on the subject can be found in a bibliographical essay by Molly Levin and John Spiegel, "Point and Counterpoint in the Literature of Student Unrest," in Donald Light, Jr., and John Spiegel, *The Dynamics of University Protest*, Nelson-Hall, Chicago, 1977, pp. 23–50. The best bibliographical aids appear to be Albert J. Miller, *Confrontation, Conflict and Dissent: A Bibliography of a Decade of Controversy, 1960–70*, Scarecrow Press, Metuchen, N.J., 1972, and Philip G. Altbach and David H. Kelley, *American Students: A Selected Bibliography on Student Activism and Related Topics*, Lexington Books, Lexington, Mass., 1973.

5. A well-known critic of the New Left argued that the early ideals of "participatory democracy" were soon abandoned in favor of power tactics.

> In the universities, participatory democracy has now been replaced by a new doctrine which decrees that when democratic procedures either do not exist (as indeed they do not in many sectors of many universities) or when a democratic system fails to respond to deeply felt needs (as with the Vietnam war) then it is quite legitimate to engage in disruption and disorder to bring about change. This argument has attracted the support of substantial minorities of students and even of faculties, though it has been less effective among the American people at large.
> The new doctrine, which we see exemplified at Nanterre and Columbia, is a far cry from the ideals of participatory democracy, especially in the early days of the New Left when meetings were open to all, when discussions to gain consensus went on endlessly,

when there was deep soul-searching about the morality of engaging in activity that provoked the violence of political opponents and police. Under the auspices of the new doctrine, the rights of the majority are held in derision, and political opponents are prevented from speaking or being heard. Tactics are worked out to strip authorities of dignity through staged confrontations, to arrange matters so that violence will erupt for the benefit of the press and television, to win over basically unsympathetic students who, owing to their commitment to fairmindedness, will almost always be "radicalized" by exposure to police intervention. In effect, we have moved from the ideal of politicized masses with direct control over their fate—an unlikely form of organization in any case, to the quite cynical manipulation of the masses by those who themselves object to "formal" democracy and to the public order and tolerance that are its foundation.

Nathan Glazer, *Remembering the Answers*, Basic Books, New York, 1970, p. 184.

6. This criticism, I should stress, is limited to key leadership figures. Apart from these leaders there were many other young radicals who used their opposition not to seek power, but to attempt imaginative forms of social engagement: experimental colleges, tutorial groups for minority children, community organization. None of it was conventional scholarly activity, but it was highly creative and hardly subversive.

It is virtually impossible to be a socialist without possessing a central core of compassion for victims of injustice. The curious thing about New Left leaders with whom I dealt was their lack of compassion. Perhaps I drew a poor sample, but I do not think so. I suspect it reflects the rapid growth of revolutionary ambition among the leaders of the New Left during the 1960s and the fact that most of them came from comfortable, upper-middle-class backgrounds. Few had ever experienced hardship in personal terms.

* 7. Mark Rudd, "Columbia: Notes on a Spring Rebellion," in Carl Oglesby, ed., *The New Left Reader*, Grove Press, New York, 1969.

8. Peter Clecak, *Radical Paradoxes*, Harper & Row, New York, 1973.

9. Typical of such exploitation was the college lecture circuit. Radical leaders were in heavy demand for campus speaking engagements during the 1960s. They demanded huge lecture fees paid from student funds. These "revolutionaries" had the best of all possible worlds. They made violent, inflammatory speeches, and yet marketed themselves like any bourgeois entrepreneur. The radical pixies, Abbie Hoffman and Jerry Rubin, played this game with astonishing success. They are now accorded a place in the history of the era, but I think they were really creations of the media who tried to make a fast buck by riding a popular wave of the times. Leading radicals were on the college lecture circuit continuously. Student tastes have changed now. Hoffman and Rubin have been replaced by new antiheroes, exemplified by Charles Colson and G. Gordon Liddy. It was and is a lucrative source of income. Cleaver was paid $750 by students for his appearance at UCSD on October 4, 1968.

10. Dellinger's analysis was delivered in the baccalaureate sermon to the

senior class of Columbia College on May 30, 1971, in Saint Paul's Chapel. He was chosen as baccalaureate speaker by the Class of 1971. I found his address remarkable in several respects. It was delivered extemporaneously with great sincerity and no bombast. Obviously Dellinger believed every word. And yet nearly all his conclusions seemed to me to be ridiculous. The veneration of antiheroes in Columbia College at that time was such that the graduating seniors accepted it all without challenge. They gave Dellinger a standing ovation when he finished.

11. Much of the rhetoric of New Left writers and orators centered on the confrontation between people as thinking beings capable of self-fulfillment, and bureaucratic institutions, generally portrayed as unfeeling and unresponsive. This acute polarization between the individual and the state is one of the existential consequences of modern technology and population growth. Its legacy can be seen in the antinuclear movement, the environmentalist movement and, ironically, in the antigovernment bias of the extreme right-wing in the United States.

Obviously the war in Vietnam provided a moral issue of great appeal to students, but campus orators dwelt on deeper questions. They criticized the competitive nature of American society, the disappearance of family and other human-sized associations, our loss of "love." We began to hear that people were more important than institutions, and that love was more important than patriotism. It was a humanism that asked why things had to be the ugly way they were. It appealed to students because it proposed to recast society in ways that would stress goodness.

Coupled with this was a conviction that hope for the future lay with youth, that the fresh perspective of young people somehow assured their decisions would be morally right. Left intellectuals on campus, frustrated by the war and remote from national decision-making, found a constituency among these young people.

Inevitably the university was caught in the middle. Radicals charged that the university's principal role was to serve the government. They demanded reforms that would make us a vehicle for political expressions hostile to government. As university administrators contemplated their tax-exempt status and their need for public funding, they could not help resist such demands. Students had to learn that in a democratic society, change must be undertaken in incremental steps, not by enunciating moral imperatives. But students were young, idealistic, and impatient.

12. One of the remarkable changes in campus life between 1968 and the present is the disappearance of the New Left as the major force in determining what issues will be discussed in public forums.

13. It can be argued that the FSM uprising at Berkeley in 1964 and the big explosion at Columbia in 1968 were expressions of dissatisfaction with campus life. I do not mean to split hairs here. I am saying that serious demonstrations almost never broke out because of the quality of food in the cafeteria or the lack of heat in the dorms. These things produced real dissatisfactions, but they fueled other political fires burning at the same time.

If you want to understand a student protest, look at the protest demands. Do not zero in on deeper dissatisfactions and assume that if those needs were met there would have been no protest. It is largely true, but not relevant. Proceeding that way permits some scholarly analysts to brush aside the political aspirations of Marxist radicals in positions of leadership, and concentrate on the less crucial determinants of protests to avoid facing the role of the ideological left. On the other hand, after Berkeley and Columbia most of the public viewed student protests as a Marxist plot. Every real problem I faced had both elements and was best dealt with by recognizing each in its appropriate role.

14. There are innumerable examples of this principle: the sudden decision to "capture" the police car at Berkeley in October 1964; the decision to invade the dean's office at Columbia in April 1968 after the failure of the confrontation at the gym site in Morningside Park; the speech by the "straight" student at UCSD during the Cleaver episode in November 1968. In student protests an angry crowd, even when it knows why it is angry, is still diffusely upset. Someone needs to emerge to tell the crowd what is wrong and what to do about it. Out of such opportunities radical leaders are born. See R. Serge Denisoff (ed.), *The Sociology of Dissent*, Harcourt Brace Jovanovich, New York, 1974, especially an article entitled "Social Movements" written by Herbert Blumer, pp. 8–9. The role of leadership in student protests will be discussed in a more detailed way in Chapter 9.

15. Marcuse was born in Berlin in 1898 of middle-class Jewish parents. He studied at the University of Berlin and at Freiburg, where he developed an early interest in Marxist thought and politics. He completed his doctorate at Freiburg in 1922, then began a study of Hegel's ontology and philosophy of history under Heidegger. For an excellent discussion of Marcuse's early philosophical development, see Sidney Lipshires, *Herbert Marcuse: From Marx to Freud amd Beyond,* Schenkman Publishing Co., Inc., Cambridge, Mass., pp. 2–13. Marcuse's major works include:

Negations, Routledge & Kegan Paul Ltd., London, 1968.
Reason and Revolution: Hegel and the Rise of Social Theory, Routledge & Kegan
     Paul Ltd., London, 1954.
Eros and Civilization, Beacon Press, Boston, 1955.
Soviet Marxism, Routledge & Kegan Paul Ltd., London, 1958.
One-Dimensional Man, Beacon Press, Boston, 1964.
A Critique of Pure Tolerance, (with R. P. Wolff and Barrington Moore, Jr.)
     Beacon Press, Boston, 1967.
An Essay on Liberation, Beacon Press, Boston, 1969.

A complete bibliography of Marcuse's works can be found in *The Critical Spirit,* edited by Kurt Wolff and Barrington Moore, Jr. Marcuse died in West Germany in 1979.

16. The Frankfurt Institute of Social Research was founded in 1923 by Hermann and Felix Weil. Through the years the institute's research centered on social issues approached from a Marxist perspective. After 1930, under the leadership of Max Horkheimer, the institute turned to philosophical and psychological speculation, or, as it was called, "critical theory." During the period of exile in the United States, the institute boasted several important intellectuals: Theodore Adorno, Leo Lowenthal, Franz Neumann, Karl Wittfogel, Erich Fromm, Otto Kirckheimer, and Herbert Marcuse. Of these, Marcuse maintained the most serious commitment to critical theory as developed by the school during the 1930s.

Student unrest in the 1960s, the search for new cultural values distinct from those of a technologically oriented society, the emergence of dissent, and the growing recognition that social, cultural, and political issues must be treated in a unified way, led to the popularization, through Marcuse, of ideas developed earlier within the Frankfurt School but little known in the United States before 1960.

An excellent discussion of the work of the Frankfurt School can be found in Martin Jay, *The Dialectical Imagination*, Little, Brown and Co., Boston, 1973. The author extends this study to 1970 in his article "The Frankfurt School in Exile," *Perspectives in American History*, 1972, Vol. 6, pp. 339–385.

17. Butler was active in Republican Party politics during and after World War I. He drafted several party platforms, and ran as a Presidential candidate. For a long time he served as an adviser to the party on foreign affairs. His writings during the 1920s rarely mention the growth of communist and fascist power. Butler's major interest was in achieving lasting peace via the Locarno Treaties guaranteeing the borders of contending states in Europe. It is a far cry from Marcuse's apocalyptic view of historical forces.

18. This point will be discussed in detail in Chapter 5. For now it is sufficient to say that no fixed terminal age for postretirement appointments existed at UCSD. The policy was intended to make the new campus attractive to senior professors with big academic reputations who were forced to retire elsewhere. Marcuse was only one of many such appointments.

19. Interviews with Marcuse appeared in *The Los Angeles Times, The National Observer,* and *The London Daily Express,* to name a few. He was featured in popular news magazines like *Time* and *Newsweek.* He became the subject of a film made for French National Television, and gave interviews to Belgian television and the BBC. In June 1968 he was featured on NBC's "Today" show. On August 20, 1968, *The San Diego Union* commented angrily on photographs of Marcuse meeting the representatives of the North Vietnamese government at the Paris peace talks. Academic recognition accompanied popular interest. In September 1968, Marcuse was elected president of the Pacific Division of the American Philosophical Association.

20. Like many favorite student quotations from Marcuse, this one is taken somewhat out of context. It appears as a paraphrase and extension of Schiller's *Aesthetic Education*, in a passage in which Marcuse develops Schiller's concept of the aesthetic to try to show that the "desublimation" of reason allows the release of sensuous perception. Certainly the idea of radicalizing Schiller ought to give one pause! Seen in its entirety, the passage becomes quite harmless. Herbert Marcuse, *Eros and Civilization: A Philosophical Inquiry into Freud*, Beacon Press, Boston, 1966, p. 191.

21. Herbert Marcuse, *One Dimensional Man*, Beacon Press, Boston, 1964, p. 7.

22. *Ibid.,* p. 245.

23. This idea is most fully developed in Marcuse's essay, "Repressive Toler-

ance," Wolff, Moore, Marcuse, *A Critique of Pure Tolerance,* Beacon Press, Boston, 1967.

24. The text of the Port Huron Statement can be found in Paul Jacobs and Saul Landau, *The New Radicals: A Report with Documents,* Vintage Books, New York, 1966, p. 155.

25. Since its founding, SDS has gained annually in both chapters and individual members. Founded by fewer than 60 students from 11 institutions, by 1964 it had about 2,000 members on some 75 campuses. In 1966, the numbers had grown to almost 20,000 in nearly 200 institutions. Currently (1968), chapters in 275–300 colleges and universities enroll nearly 30,000 individuals. These figures apply only to formal members: many more students can be rallied to participate in the discussions, programs, and demonstrations which SDS catalyzes.
E. Joseph Shoben, Jr., Philip Werdell, and Durward Long, "Radical Student Organizations," in Julian Foster and Durward Long, *Protest! Student Activism in America,* William Morrow & Company, New York, 1970, pp. 208–209.

26. The internal struggles of SDS during the second half of 1968 are vividly described in Kirkpatrick Sale, *SDS,* Random House, New York, 1973.

27. The term "counterculture" is used by social scientists to describe a large-scale phenomenon reflecting major alterations of academic, social, cultural, and artistic values in the U.S. I refer here only to the precursors of this movement that began appearing on U.S. college campuses during the early 1960s. I saw countercultural students for the first time when I visited the Bay Area in 1963. It was apparent that the counterculture was already well-developed there, yet no sign of it existed at Columbia. By the mid-Sixties the movement had spread to Haight-Ashbury, Telegraph Avenue, and the East Village. In 1970 it was preoccupying nearly every established institution in the United States.
For a fascinating discussion of the counterculture in the large meaning of the term, see William L. O'Neill, *Coming Apart: An Informal History of America in the 1960s,* Quadrangle Books, Chicago, 1971.

28. The sympathies of countercultural students lay with the New Left, but the nature of the movement precluded easy political organization. It was a collection of free spirits who sought change in symbolic ways calculated to drive any disciplinarian, left or right, up the wall. Countercultural young people were not disposed to concentrate on a single political issue, or on any issue, for very long. They existed outside the terms of reference of organized groups with dependable lines of authority.

29. There are no solid figures known to the writer on actual numbers of "alienated" or countercultural students. In 1968 I estimated them to be one-third of the student body at major universities. Hence the number may well have been in the millions. It seemed to me at the time to be a serious value crisis. It is a very difficult problem in taxonomy because the alienation ranged from faddish adoption of long hair and ragged clothing to complete philosophical commitment to a new way of life. However one defines the borders of the counterculture, I am trying to convey here and elsewhere in the text my conviction that most protests

were organized, and the issues devised, by a bright, tightly knit and largely Marxist student leadership. The audiences, the faces in the crowd at sit-ins and demonstrations, were mostly countercultural students trying to press for a better world by demanding instant change, though not really accepting all the theoretical analyses set forth by their leaders.

30. The exaggerated independence of countercultural students was justified by such labels as freedom, self-expression, and self-fulfillment, but it also bespoke a total lack of discipline, perseverance, or serious thought. Maintenance of the countercultural lifestyle required an investment of time and energy that deflected its devotees from the more serious ideological preoccupations of their Marxist leaders.

31. The role of black students in the unrest of the 1960s was evidently a complex one. They were an independent third force wooed frantically by both radicals and campus administrators. SDS humiliation at the hands of its Black Panther allies in 1968 was one of the worst moments in the movement. See Sale, p. 566. To the writer's knowledge, the history of black student unions on college campuses during the Sixties remains to be written. It would be a fascinating contribution to America's social history.

32. Historians of the New Left maintain that the end came much earlier, following a collision between the Revolutionary Youth Movement and Progressive Labor for control of SDS in 1968. This internal struggle did indeed seem to tear SDS apart, but as a practical matter the New Left careened on with two, sometimes three, heads through the antiwar demonstrations of the period 1968–72. After 1972 the collapse came quickly. I often wonder whether the fatal struggle between RYM and PLP would have occurred if SDS had been successful earlier at organizing blacks and countercultural students into a popular youth movement. The collision seemed to reflect disputes within the organization over how to rescue an initiative that had suddenly gone wrong.

33. One of the outcomes of internal struggling for control of SDS was the emergence of a terrorist faction, the Weathermen. See Harold Jacobs, ed., *Weatherman*, Ramparts Press, San Francisco, 1970.

34. See O'Neill, p. 267.

35. See Feuer, pp. 385–435.

36. The idea of extended adolescence as a source of unrest fostered by the educational requirements of advanced society appears to be due to Kenneth Kenniston, *Youth and Dissent*, Harcourt Brace Jovanovich, New York, 1971, pp. 6–8; see also F. Musgrove, *Youth and the Social Order*, Indiana University Press, Bloomington, Ind., 1965. My thinking on this topic has been greatly influenced by arguments addressed to American business by the labor economist, Ivar Berg. Berg holds that the demand for educational credentials, i.e., degrees or special certificates as a condition of employment, has had the effect of systematically extending adolescence for the convenience of personnel offices. See Ivar Berg, *Education and Jobs: The Great Training Robbery*, Praeger, New York, 1970, especially pages 185–194.

37. A great deal of research has been devoted to the counterculture, but much of it deals with aspects of the movement unrelated to campus unrest or the curious relation between SDS and the student counterculture. Historians of the SDS occasionally speak of "hippies," a reference to the counterculture that I have studiously avoided. It suggests drug freaks and social misfits, whereas I am referring to altruistically motivated students. In any case, the theory of blacks and countercultural youth as the designated shock troops of SDS's revolutionary plan deserves more attention than it has received thus far from analysts of the New Left.

38. Theodore Roszak, *The Making of a Counterculture*, Anchor Books, New York, 1969.

39. *Commonweal*, December 22, 1967.

40. I hope that I am not alone in this reaction to Marcuse's English prose. I found him as formidable as any abstract mathematician, relieved only on occasion by such catch phrases as "the power of negative thinking." See Marcuse, *One Dimensional Man*, p. 124.

41. The so-called Left Hegelians, including Marx and Marcuse, view history as a guided evolutionary process with discrete epochs defined by successively more advanced economic and political systems. The latter are deemed unstable because the conditions that build each epoch also contain contradictory elements that eventually destroy it. Transition from epoch to epoch is necessarily disruptive (i.e., revolutionary), because it is based upon comparisons by masses of people of their current condition with an ideal they apprehend only dimly. Thus they are led to rebel against forces that restrain them from realizing the ideal. The existence of a guiding ideal is a very important feature of the dialectical process, as it enables analysts to identify its terminal state of perfection.

All dialectical thinkers seem to accept the premise that the evolutionary process gathers strength as it proceeds to transition. It is viewed as moving like an avalanche. For Marx, the class struggle is the force that builds and strengthens the proletariat. For Marcuse, the more psychologically repressive a society is, the greater the explosive force of its disenfranchised elements.

This commitment to the inevitability of an explosion, of a building avalanche deriving from contradictions in a particular epochal stage, appears to the writer to be the dogmatic feature of Marcuse's thought. The evolutionary process might just as well peak at a particular epoch if, instead of a gathering avalanche, the process undergoes destructive subdivision, as happened with SDS. For Marcuse, such disintegration would be evidence only that a social movement was false in the first instance. But the difficulty is an important one among non-Marxists. The test of any model is its ability to predict. How does one know in advance which movements carry the stamp of history? Can such a theory ever be proved wrong?

42. The flap grew out of an article in the *Bonn Advertiser*, a West German newspaper. It said, "Rudi Dutschke, SDS [Socialist German Student Organization] ideologist from Berlin, will probably travel to America in the foreseeable future. As reported by a well-informed source in Bonn, Dutschke made up his mind to accept an offer to become an assistant to Herbert Marcuse, the German

professor of philosophy who teaches at the University of California, San Diego, California." This report was picked up by *The New York Times*, May 15, 1968, and "The Periscope" column in *Newsweek* magazine, June 10, 1968. All three stories were published in *The San Diego Union*, June 6, 1968.

Apparently Dutschke had continuing problems with his head wound. While he was still hospitalized in Germany, Marcuse visited him. Marcuse reported that he urged Dutschke, his wife, and son to visit him in San Diego and enjoy the San Diego Zoo. Soon afterward, Dutschke's wife, Gretchen, an American citizen, applied for immigrant status for him. At that time it was reported he was considering attending San Jose State College in Northern California.

Marcuse always denied that he extended Dutschke an invitation to come to UCSD, either as a student or as a faculty member. He claimed he urged Dutschke not to take such a step because of the "hostile atmosphere" in the United States. It seems unlikely that Dutschke could have entered the university as a student, since he was already completing a doctorate in Germany. In the political climate of that time his appointment to the UCSD faculty would have been well nigh impossible. *The San Diego Union*, on September 4, 1968, p. 1, reported that Dutschke had abandoned plans to visit the United States for reasons of health.

The matter was never raised with me. It was one of those nonissues that somehow can never be put to rest in a paranoid time.

43. Some of this mail is still preserved in the files of the UCSD chancellor's office. It illustrates how far public opinion was from supporting the freedoms of speech and association most Americans take for granted. What stuck in the public craw was the fact that Marcuse was being paid with state funds. People were hostile to his revolutionary views, but the fact that he was formulating them while being paid with their money was just too much. As a matter of fact, the argument raises an interesting question on how dissident faculty can be protected from public disaffection in a tax-supported university.

44. *The San Diego Union* attack culminated with an editorial published on June 11th, entitled, "This Is An Order," demanding that Marcuse be immediately removed from the university. It concluded, "There is now the threat—and it is indeed a threat to the peace and security of our university—that 'Red Rudi' will come here under the auspices of Herbert Marcuse, professor of Left Wing philosophy at the college." The editorial seemed to be aimed at arousing the military community in San Diego. It did little to convince UCSD's cosmopolitan faculty that the city knew how to get along with an intellectual community.

45. This text and the account of Marcuse's sudden flight are taken from Kenneth Lamott, *Anti-California*, Little, Brown and Co., Boston, 1971, pp. 174–187.

46. The *Desert Sun*, Monday, August 5, 1968.

47. *International Herald Tribune*, August 13, 1968.

48. *The San Diego Union*, August 14, 1968. A dispatch datelined Rome carried the headline "Marcuse in Italy Challenges Legion."

49. This letter, addressed to Chancellor William J. McGill, dated July 19,

1968, and signed by the American Legion Post 6, can be found in the UCSD files of the papers of Chancellor McGill, Special Collections, UCSD Central Library.

CHAPTER 4: THE AMERICAN LEGION LAUNCHES AN ATTACK

1. In the winter of 1964, Jacques Barzun at Columbia suggested I consider an appointment as vice dean of the graduate faculties. I refused. Columbia was already beginning to pulsate with radical activity and New York City was verging on chaos. The very idea of being a dean made my blood run cold. Barzun thought I was silly, and as subsequent events proved, he was right.

In any case, after that feeler, or more precisely because of it, I decided to flee to Southern California and a quiet, scholarly career in scientific research and teaching. The decision to leave Columbia enabled me to escape the explosion there in 1968, but it also brought me unaware into a dangerous situation in the University of California.

Life there was anything but benign in 1968. I found myself struggling with Ronald Reagan, Herbert Marcuse, and Angela Davis. In the end I came to realize that there was no escape from the problems of society in 1968. All of us had to take a stand. Mine turned out to be a dogged resistance to the use of the university as a political instrument. It eventually brought me into conflict with virtually everyone: the Governor, the Regents, the legislature, SDS and most other radical students, the extreme right, and much of the faculty left. All of them wanted to reconstitute the university in their own vision of truth, making us much less open and tolerant than our traditions mandated. Mine was, I suppose, a reactionary mission, but I am proud of it. An age-old adage says, "If it ain't broke, don't fix it!"

2. The official version of Kerr's dismissal by the Regents is quite candid, but incomplete on several essential points. It can be found in Verne A. Stadtman, *The University of California 1868–1968*, McGraw-Hill Book Company, New York, 1970, p. 483.

In 1968, Kerr allowed himself to be interviewed regarding the matter. The account is given in Bill Boyarsky, *The Rise of Ronald Reagan*, Random House, New York, 1968, p. 229. In essence, Kerr says that the Governor and a group of Regents conspired to have him dismissed.

3. Reporters from *The San Diego Union* were under instructions from their editors to pump me on Marcuse. On June 23rd *The Union* published a long interview, including hard questions about leftist groups on campus, the Vietnam war and draft protests, and the pending university budget. It was not a gentle way to begin, but it was in fact only a gentle foretaste of what was coming when *The Union* and the American Legion undertook to drive Herbert Marcuse out of the university.

4. In February 1971 at Columbia, I wrote an angry letter to the university senate after two classes were broken into by militant demonstrators. The letter demanded protection of the right to teach, saying "I did not spend the last three years in bitter struggle defending the teaching rights of Linus Pauling, Angela

Davis, and Herbert Marcuse only to watch such rights trampled at Columbia." A friend on the faculty asked me what I was talking about. "I know about Marcuse and Angela Davis, but Linus Pauling?" His question projected puzzlement and disbelief. I smiled beatifically and replied that one day I would explain. To the best of my knowledge this story has never been told previously. Pauling himself never knew. It illustrates the quiet way in which an academic community can handle its most explosive problems. The style is one I have come to love. It was briefly submerged in the paranoid struggles of the Sixties, but I am happy to report that it is back again, alive and well.

5. The Regents, like students during the 1960s, were not immune from self-destructive acts. The president and the chancellors were forced constantly to deflect the board from taking political vengeance on the faculty left during the Reagan era. Such acts did great damage to the university's reputation, as the Regents' later attempt to fire Angela Davis demonstrated.

6. Marcuse's friends on the faculty were deeply offended by statements I made to *The San Diego Union* on June 23. Among other things, I said that a telegram congratulating the Zengakuren in Japan for rioting against U.S. Navy servicemen was "an ugly and tasteless act." Marcuse was a signer, as were many other faculty. I also told reporters that it was not my impression that Marcuse was an "active publicity seeker." People told me I ought to be more careful about embarrassing faculty in the newspapers. However, I could make amends by signing Marcuse's appointment immediately.

7. Letter to WJM dated July 19, 1968, and signed by "San Diego Post 6, George W. Fisher, Commander" (copy to Regents).

8. The story was carried in the *Los Angeles Times* on July 27, 1968, under the headline "Chancellor Rejects Legion Bid to Buy Up Marcuse's Contract." Harry Foster of the Legion was then quoted as saying, "We don't intend to drop the matter. We will direct all of our attention to the Regents."

9. The details of this threat are discussed later in the chapter. It was made during a long and disturbing private conversation with Harry Foster representing the American Legion.

10. There is no record of the Saunders-Jameson draft statement in the files of the UCSD chancellor's office. The reference here derives from a letter written by me to Dr. John S. Galbraith dated August 26, 1968. The letter is in the university files.

11. Seymour Harris's attack on Marcuse is described in WJM to Dr. John S. Galbraith (8/26/68, UCSD files). Schlesinger's address was delivered at City University of New York as Senator Robert Kennedy lay dying in a Los Angeles hospital. It was published in *Harper's Magazine*, August, 1968, pp. 19–24. Some idea of the bite in Schlesinger's sarcasm toward Marcuse's anti-liberal utopia may be gleaned from Arthur M. Schlesinger, Jr., *The Crisis of Confidence*, Houghton Mifflin, Boston, 1969. See especially pp. 36–38.

12. Since June, an angry deluge of mail on Marcuse had been showering not only on me but also on the Board of Regents, the president of the university, and

the Governor's office. The power of the mass media to stimulate angry mail is a phenomenon of great importance in a democracy. The effect is almost Pavlovian. Mail disappears when the problem is no longer cited in the press. The phenomenon is worthy of careful study by schools of journalism. It is a remarkably effective pressure tactic. Consider for a moment this example, which appeared in the *Evening Tribune,* June 22.

> Editor:
> What is Dr. Herbert Marcuse, admitted Marxist and darling of the extreme left, doing teaching philosophy at UCSD and being paid with my money?
> Who are the people at UCSD who brought him here? What [*sic*] at UCSD apologizes for him, saying he is a "good teacher"? How can a man with this commitment to Marxism teach philosophy objectively? Who is attracted to his classes?
> Dr. Marcuse is from Germany. He could have gone to a Marxist country when he left Germany. Instead he chose to come here and enjoy the fruits of our capitalistic society. Why?

I also received the following from a neighbor:

> Sir:
> Enclosed is a picture of a very evil man [Marcuse]. We had hoped your attitudes towards him would be other than indicated in your interview with Mr. [Homer] Clance [a reporter for *The San Diego Union*].
> As far as we are concerned, we desire no further social contacts with you.

13. The full text of the resolution can be found in *The San Diego Union,* August 12, 1968.

It cited statements, attributed to Marcuse, that students who disrupted Columbia University had been influenced by his writings, and concludes with, "We believe we have said enough to lay the foundation for serious provoking [*sic*] thoughts by the Regents and urge you to do everything possible to prevent the issuance of a teaching contract to Marcuse in 1969–1970."

14. Liberal San Diegans were quick to cite parallels between the Marcuse affair and the case of Dr. Harry Steinmetz, professor of psychology at San Diego State University. Steinmetz was attacked during the McCarthy era by Harry Foster and Major General George Fisher of the Legion's Un-American Activities Committee. Eventually San Diego State dismissed Steinmetz in 1954 under the Dilworth Act, which made it a cause for dismissal if a state employee refused to testify before a congressional committee, in this case HUAC. Steinmetz died in 1980 without ever receiving legal redress or even retirement benefits.

Harry Foster once compared the two initiatives: "Under the Supreme Court rulings since 1954, we probably would not be able to get rid of someone like Steinmetz. Professors know they have this protection and abuse it. There are parallels in the Steinmetz and Marcuse cases. Steinmetz made no bones about participating in left-wing organizations; Marcuse admits to being a strong Marxist." Harold Keen, "The Threat to Marcuse," *San Diego Magazine,* August 1968, pp. 33–34.

15. James Copley was a nice man who built a successful but very unusual newspaper empire based in San Diego. For many years the director of editorial and news policy of *The San Diego Union* was a retired naval captain. He was succeeded in 1969 by a Marine Corps general. The newspaper's editorial policy was not directed by professional journalists until shortly after Copley's death, when Helen, his widow, took over the management and moved the paper into the mainstream of professional journalism. Copley was born on August 12, 1916, in St. Johnsville, New York. His parents died in the great influenza epidemic of 1917. In a stroke of good fortune, the orphaned child was adopted in 1920 by Colonel Ira C. Copley, an Illinois utility executive, congressman, and publisher. When Colonel Copley expanded his newspaper chain to include a number of small Southern California newspapers, including *The San Diego Union* and *Evening Tribune*, James Copley, recently graduated from Yale, went to work on the staff of the Culver City (Calif.) *Star News*. Two years later he moved to the Alhambra *Post Advocate*, then the Glendale *Newspress*. In 1941, he came to *The San Diego Union*. At the time of his death in 1973 at age 57, Copley had built the corporation bearing his name into a major publishing enterprise. He was chairman of the Copley Publishing Corporation, chairman of the board of the Copley News Service, publisher of *The San Diego Union* and *Evening Tribune* and editorial page editor of *The Union*. He was active in San Diego civic affairs, and a close friend of governors and presidents. A prominent San Diegan said of him, "I have never met a more dedicated American."

16. C. Arnholt Smith was convicted on May 7, 1979, of income tax evasion and grand theft. His once-powerful San Diego-based Westgate California Corporation was torn apart after 1974, when bank receivers liquidated its assets in an attempt to make good the debts of Smith's U.S. National Bank. The latter was the first part of Smith's financial empire to collapse. Currently, Smith's appeal against an $11 million judgment is pending.

17. I had a serious private talk with Admiral Gehres in October of 1968. He chewed me out continuously about the way in which I was running UCSD, yet I was so awed at meeting the famed hero of the *Ben Franklin* that I could not respond to him in kind. At first I thought I was encountering the moral outrage of a naval officer angry with what he took to be our unwillingness to enforce discipline. I had heard plenty of that from the San Diego military in 1968–69. But as we talked, I began to realize that the admiral was trying to put political pressure on me in the Marcuse case. He kept threatening to go to the Governor and the legislature with punitive actions aimed at UCSD unless Marcuse was dismissed. I came away from that meeting immensely saddened. What do you do when you discover that one of your heroes is an imperfect man?

18. In an interview with *The New York Times*, October 6, 1968, Foster admitted that he had never heard of Marcuse until the anti-Marcuse editorials appeared in *The San Diego Union*. "The Marcuse matter," Foster said, "was brought to my attention by certain officials of the community here whom I'm not privileged to name, who hoped the Legion would move because otherwise there might be considerable trouble on campus here."

The *Times* story goes on to note that Legion Post 6 raised, almost overnight,

$20,000 to give the university to buy up the professor's contract for the coming year.

Who put up the money?

"They were some people here in town—some Legion members and quite a few businessmen—altogether about 15 individuals." *The New York Times*, October 6, 1968.

19. John Canaday was a Los Angeles aerospace executive in his early sixties. Although not a Reagan appointee, he was a strong supporter of the Governor's aggressive approach to campus discipline. Added to the Cleaver problem and in the midst of systemwide campus disruption, the Marcuse issue was just one too many for Canaday. He knew it was an election year, and that our bond issues and budgets were very much in doubt. Canaday was also an old-fashioned Regent who loved the University of California as he remembered it. He felt there was still a chance to save us from public disavowal if we would only crack down on radical activity. He tried to lead us in that direction.

20. Here I was hinting at a select faculty committee established by the UCSD senate to consider the merits of Herbert Marcuse's reappointment in 1969–70. The committee played a crucial moderating role in the dispute over Marcuse. Its files are now locked away from public view. All my references to the committee's work are drawn from contemporaneous monthly letters written to my predecessor, John S. Galbraith, between October 1968 and March 1969.

21. It has always seemed to me that while Marcuse was a notable philosopher, his use of dialectical argument made his prose style a challenge for the uninitiated reader. Here is just one example: "While the reversal of the trend in the educational enterprise at least could conceivably be enforced by the students and teachers themselves, and thus be self-imposed, the systematic withdrawal of tolerance toward regressive and repressive opinions and movements could only be envisaged as results of large-scale pressure which would amount to an upheaval. In other words, it would presuppose that which is still to be accomplished: the reversal of the trend." Wolff, Moore, Marcuse, *A Critique of Pure Tolerance*, Boston, Beacon Press, 1965, p. 101.

22. 1968 was an election year. We found ourselves the focus of many rhetorical exchanges between candidates. Dr. Max Rafferty was challenging Democrat Alan Cranston for the U.S. Senate. In appealing to conservative voters, Rafferty chose decency and the Red menace as his campaign themes. Such things brought him inevitably to devastating commentaries on the moral condition of the University of California. Meanwhile, Jesse Unruh, a Democrat and speaker of the assembly, began campaigning on behalf of Democratic candidates and in anticipation of his own run for the governorship in 1970. Unruh's campaign theme was an updated version of Reagan's when he challenged Governor Edmund (Pat) Brown in 1966: the Governor promised to clean up our great university, and it is still a mess. The struggle over Eldridge Cleaver's course had unified Reagan and Unruh in angry public opposition to the university. We could not let the Marcuse appointment become this kind of issue without risking serious reprisals from outraged voters. The only solution was to stay out of the newspapers. It was proving very difficult to do.

23. Max Rafferty seemed to believe there were simple solutions to every public problem. He was an effective, articulate, and very popular speaker, prone to see the Red menace everywhere endangering our children. The press could always count on him for a quotable quote. His comments made good old-fashioned horse sense unless you knew something about the issue at hand. When that realization dawned on me, I began to see him as a glib but ungifted public official.

24. The Governor's principal education adviser was Professor Alex Sherriffs of the University of California, Berkeley. Alex Carlton Sherriffs was born in San Jose, California, in 1917. He earned a Ph.D. in psychology at Stanford in 1946 and soon became internationally known as a research specialist in developmental psychology. From 1958 until 1966, Sherriffs was vice chancellor for student affairs at Berkeley. It was Sherriffs who ordered the cessation of student political activities on the 26-foot strip of pavement outside the Bancroft Way entrance near Telegraph Avenue at the opening of the fall term in 1964 (see Heirich, 1971). This action triggered a series of increasingly volatile collisions with politically active students that became known as the Berkeley Free Speech Movement. Sherriffs' professional background in guidance and developmental psychology made his hard-line handling of these political protests difficult to understand. Perhaps he acted under pressure from the Regents or state politicians. Whatever the facts, his handling of the FSM protests ultimately led to dismissal from his administrative post in 1966. Sherriffs was certainly hurt professionally by the FSM.

It was with this background that Governor Reagan named Sherriffs in 1968 as his Special Assistant for Education, a post he held until 1973, when he became vice chancellor for academic affairs for the California State University and College system.

Sherriffs was almost certainly the principal figure in an informal group of conservative faculty who met periodically with the Governor to advise him on university and state college affairs. The existence of the group, which in effect bypassed the advisory role of the leaders of both institutions, was never acknowledged. It exemplified Mr. Reagan's delight in political hard-ball as well as the dangers faced by any institution finding itself on his blacklist.

CHAPTER 5: THE MARCUSE DECISION

1. Dear Mr. McGill, How proud you must be of serving corruption so efficiently! What a fine disservice you have done the students of the university and indeed all of us who are concerned with helping our young build the moral and spiritual strength which they will need for the difficult days ahead in our country.
Sometimes, 'we the people' feel helpless, but provoke us enough with affronts to decency such as allowing Cleaver, a paroled convict of the slimiest sort to exhort in the filthiest of language the students to violence, and we shall find a way to put an end to the idiocies and the poisonous thinking which are being allowed to flood our campuses.

Sincerely and determinedly

2. These events, ending in the long debate with SDS leaders on whether

or not UCSD should be shut down following the Regents' action on Social Analysis 139X, were described in Chapter 2.

3. During the Sixties, Marcuse became increasingly committed to his authoritarian stand. Some of his most chilling positions can be found in an essay entitled "Repressive Tolerance" in Wolff, Moore, Marcuse, *A Critique of Pure Tolerance*, Boston, Beacon Press, 1965, p. 109. Following a paragraph in which he deplores the manner in which democratic institutions permitted the growth of fascism, Marcuse goes on to say:

> The whole post-fascist period is one of clear and present danger. Consequently, true pacification requires the withdrawal of tolerance before the deed, at the stage of communication in word, print, and picture. Such extreme suspension of the right of free speech and free assembly is indeed justified only if the whole of society is in extreme danger. I maintain that our society is in such an emergency situation, and that it has become the normal state of affairs. Different opinions and "philosophies" can no longer compete peacefully for adherence and persuasion on rational grounds: the "marketplace of ideas" is organized and delimited by those who determine the national and the individual interest. In this society, for which the ideologists have proclaimed the "end of ideology," the false consciousness has become the general consciousness—from the government down to its last objects. The small and powerless minorities which struggle against the false consciousness and its beneficiaries must be helped: their continued existence is more important than the preservation of abused rights and liberties which grant constitutional powers to those who oppress these minorities. It should be evident by now that the exercise of civil rights by those who don't have them presupposes the withdrawal of civil rights from those who prevent their exercise, and that liberation of the Damned of the Earth presupposes suppression not only of their old but also of their new masters.

4. *The San Diego Union*, December 12, 1968. The text of the editorial is worth reading as an example of the jittery spirit abroad in the country.

DR. MARCUSE HARMS UCSD
DOCTRINE OF REBELLION MUST GO

> With his usual and perhaps deliberate flair for goading the society that protects him, Dr. Herbert Marcuse has again embarrassed and hurt the University of California at San Diego and all of higher education in the United States of America.
>
> Marcuse, a philosophy professor at UCSD, advocated in a speech to the "New Left" in New York that militants develop "political guerrilla forces" to foster "libertarian socialism."
>
> He shared the platform with the ilk of H. Rap Brown, former head of the Students' Non-Violent Coordinating Committee and other seditious and racist speakers of similar disrepute.
>
> But Marcuse said what in essence he always has said. He himself admits that his philosophies, if they can be dignified by this term, inspired the violence at Columbia University, the Sorbonne in Paris, and Berlin.

Anarchists at the University of Rome carried during their rioting placards with "Marx, Marcuse, Mao." French revolutionaries showed signs with "Marx, Mao et Marcuse." And his recent book was advertised with the blurb, the three Ms, "Marx, the God; Marcuse, the prophet; Mao, the sword."

Marcuse advocates "moral, political, intellectual and sexual rebellion of youth." He advocates violence to change the democratic system in the United States. The American Legion properly notes this is "close to anarchy."

Marcuse preaches rule by the "intellectual elite." He favors limitations on the free press. He would suppress what he calls "false ideas." Like Stalin or Hitler? He is a socialist and avowed anti-American. "I believe," Marcuse says, "nobody is free in this society. Nobody."

It is naive and unacceptable to assume that Marcuse advocates any different ideas in his lectures at UCSD. He has never spoken them elsewhere.

Nor can the UCSD administration insist with any degree of intellectual honesty that Marcuse is presenting "new" ideas. Marxism, not a philosophy but a critique of capitalism, is more than a century old. It has been disproven time and again in practice. Is there any more rotten society or repressive one to people than Russia, or Communist China, or Cuba?

Chancellor Wm. McGill has said UCSD could be properly suspect by the community if it had fifty Marcuses and no opposing views. Does it have an opposing view in the philosophy department?

The American Legion is reasonable, moderate and correct in asking that Marcuse's contract not be renewed after June 30 when it expires. If a face-saving reason is needed, Marcuse is three years over the 67 year university mandated retirement age.

The issue is not one of academic freedom. Nobody seeks to deprive higher education of that. Too often in Marcuse's case this cry has been one of false pride and ego, or self serving.

The issue is one of balance in views that encourages true intellectual inquiry and academic freedom. This is what Marcuse is hurting.

5.   E. Robert Anderson was born in 1895 in San Francisco. He served in the U.S. Navy both actively and as a reservist for 35 years, retiring in 1955 with the rank of Captain. Anderson was also a career newspaperman. He left Reno, Nevada, in 1923 to become city editor of the old *San Diego Sun*. He then moved to *The Union* in 1925. When the latter became a Copley newspaper in 1928, Anderson began a long career as a Copley editor and executive, ending in his retirement in June 1969.

6.   General Victor H. Krulak was born in Denver, Colorado, January 7, 1913. He graduated from the U.S. Naval Academy and was later honored by a Doctor of Laws degree from the University of San Diego. Krulak rose from the rank of 2nd Lieutenant in 1934 to Lieutenant General in the Marine Corps prior to his retirement. He was commanding general of the Fleet Marine Force in the Pacific during the war in Vietnam, and served in the Pentagon on the staff of the Joint Chiefs. On June 2, 1968, General Krulak retired from the Marine Corps and

returned to San Diego. On June 10th he joined the Copley newspapers as vice president of the Copley Press, Inc., and president of the Copley News Service.

7. Pressures for "relevant" curriculum caused great tensions and considerable violence at both Berkeley and San Francisco State in early 1969. We were already hearing the same kinds of rumblings in San Diego. They were at the heart of the dispute over Cleaver's course. Soon they would erupt, full blown, in the Lumumba-Zapata controversy. See Chapter 6.

8. Jack Oswald spent a great deal of time on the phone with the Regents lobbying for the administration's positions and testing their sentiments on important agenda items. He was likable and easy to talk to. The Regents could confide in him without fear that their views would be spread around. As a consequence, Oswald's forecasts of votes on crucial issues were generally right on the button. If things were close or if we were sure losers, there was still some time to finesse difficult agenda items before the board voted. Except for the vote on People's Park (described in Chapter 8) which was a surprise, we generally knew of our defeats ahead of time.

9. File copies of both letters are in my UCSD papers. They are also discussed in a contemporaneous letter (March 2, 1969) to John S. Galbraith: Special Collections, UCSD Central Library.

10. Inge Marcuse died at the age of 59 in 1973. He then married Erica Sherover in 1976.

11. Critics with little personal experience in managing or resolving conflict tend to look for carefully crafted solutions as they might be devised by a professional mediator. In its highest form, bargaining between conflicting parties is an orderly enterprise in which each party tries to get what it seeks without giving away something that cannot be yielded. The resulting compromise is a monument of rationality. But conflict follows these rules only in circumstances where a legally mandated conflict-resolution process is imposed. In real conflict you confront the problem of intense anger between the conflicting parties. When anger is aroused, it generates confused paranoia, and the emotional dynamics of crowd situations emerge. See, for example, "Perspectives on Collective Violence," Chapter 1, in *Collective Violence*, J. F. Short, Jr., and M. E. Wolfgang (eds.), Chicago, Aldine-Atherton, 1972, pp. 3–32.

12. As noted in the text, the abrupt change in the Governor's position had all the indications of a political move by an astute politician, but I was never able to determine what lay behind it. In October 1968 I had a talk with Admiral Gehres, who hinted that he intended to go to the Governor and the legislature over Marcuse. Gehres was Republican State Committeeman from San Diego. A group called *Citizens to End Campus Anarchy* emerged in March 1969 to protest delays in disciplining students who had blockaded the Marine recruiter. It is possible that their representatives talked to the Governor earlier about Marcuse, since they were closely linked to Gehres. Pressure groups tend to surface on most controversial topics, and it is difficult to believe that Reagan would have taken this particular one seriously. More likely, he was opposed to Marcuse's appointment from the very beginning and was simply waiting for the right moment to make his move.

13. Many of Mr. Reagan's most important speeches in his first campaign for Governor of California have been collected in a slender volume called *The Creative Society,* published by The Devin-Adair Company, New York, 1968. On May 12, 1966, he spoke at the Cow Palace near San Francisco on "The Morality Gap at Berkeley." The speech was inspired by charges contained in a report from the Senate Subcommittee on Un-American Activities that the Berkeley campus had become "a rallying point for Communists and a center of sexual misconduct." Centerpiece of the report was a description of a dance, attended by minors, at which there were rock-and-roll bands, marijuana, and porno movies.

> How could this happen on the campus of a great university? It happened because those responsible abdicated their responsibilities. . . . These charges must neither be swept under the rug by a timid administration or by public apologists for the university. The public has a right to know from open hearings whether the situation in Berkeley is as the report says.
>
> The citizens who pay the taxes that support the university also have a right to know that, if the situation is as the report says, that those responsible will be fired, that the university will be cleaned up and restored to its position as a major institution of learning and research. . . . Administrators should be told that it is their job to administer the university properly and if they don't we will find someone who will (pp. 126–127).

14. Assemblyman John Stull represented the 80th Assembly district, which included La Jolla, in the state legislature. After twenty years in the Navy, Stull retired with the rank of Commander to become executive director of the 1964 Goldwater campaign in the northern part of San Diego County. In 1966 Stull ran successfully for the assembly. From the moment of his election he became a thorn in the university's side.

He copied Governor Reagan's tactic of campaigning against the University of California, although not with Reagan's imagination. Stull's line, which in view of what was going on at UCSD, proved quite popular with his constituency, was that nearly all UCSD problems were due to incompetent leadership. His prescription was simple: Fire them! In 1967 he demanded the firing of Chancellor Galbraith, in 1968 Professor Marcuse, in 1969 Chancellor McGill, in 1970 Vice Chancellors Murphy and Saltman. Between times he attacked university land purchases and opposed UC bond issues. He sponsored bills that would prohibit display of the Viet Cong flag on any university campus, reduce the university budget by the amount of Marcuse's salary, and force the university to submit to line by line budget review. He advocated the creation of a popularly elected Board of Regents, an end to faculty tenure, removal of independent appointment authority from the chancellors, and elimination of faculty governance. The high point (or perhaps the nadir) came in September of 1970, when, in a political speech, Stull said that if McGill's plans for Third College went through, "he may yet prove the greatest revolutionary of them all."

I should note that after saying goodbye to John Stull, five hours on an airplane brought me to Columbia and Bella Abzug. Ms. Abzug used to lecture me periodically on my unremitting conservatism, which in her view oppressed the daycare advocates and tenants groups among her constituency. Nothing measures the diversity of this country better than the transition from John Stull to Bella Abzug! My great misfortune was that both were very much alike in their determination to bring the university under political control.

15. Minutes of the UC Board of Regents, February 21, 1969, p. 15. The minutes of the meetings of the UC Regents are carefully edited before they become a matter of public record. Nevertheless, even in the minutes, Governor Reagan's anger is evident.

16. It is not surprising that operational law-enforcement people knew little about the complex structure of the New Left in 1969. They depended on inaccurate FBI bulletins for information on SDS and other revolutionary groups.

More surprising is the fact that senior government and intelligence officials were equally in the dark. During the Watergate investigation it was revealed that at about this time (1969), a vice president of the University of California was retained by the CIA to brief the agency on the nature of the New Left and the radicalization techniques employed by SDS. This vice president, since retired, was a bright, engaging man who displayed great interest in my experiences and often talked to me about them. Apparently these discussions were promptly relayed to the agency.

The clincher was President Nixon's 1970 decision to implement the so-called Huston Plan, ignoring constitutional restraints on intelligence-gathering against left-wing student groups. It did not go anywhere, but it illustrates the frustration then prevailing in the government. Few people could believe that SDS was an indigenous radical organization. They kept searching without success for its foreign sources of control.

17. It must be remembered that the decade of the 1960s was an era of transition for law enforcement as well as for our other national institutions. Before that period police had little experience in handling large numbers of people who might be aroused by what they saw as hostile or brutal acts by law enforcement. Police typically did not have effective community relations liaisons with the growing ethnic and minority communities in urban areas before the 1960s. Senior officers believed that crowd tensions should be controlled by a show of force or by force itself.

The urban riots of the 1960s and the crowd situations on or near university campuses presented totally new problems for these old-fashioned, tried-and-true concepts of law enforcement. It was discovered (as we discovered on campus) that ill-timed shows of force often made matters worse. Moreover, the courts took a strong position protecting civil liberties and making it difficult for police to attempt to quell disturbances by mass arrests.

In 1968 the younger, urban-trained law enforcement people understood our ideas about radicalization. The senior people did not. They felt that radical activity was protected by the faculty and was a problem only because, in their view, it was unopposed. They wanted to oppose it with force. All of these conflicting ideas eventually came under test in mid-May during the struggle over People's Park. It was the tragedy many of us feared.

Much of what I subsequently learned at Columbia on the subject of handling crowds came under the tutelage of New York Police Commissioners Patrick

Murphy and Michael Codd, and from Inspector Mike Lonergan. They knew what they were doing.

18. The text of the telegram read as follows:

> The central issue at UCSD is not the hiring or firing of Dr. Herbert Marcuse. The central issue is whether the chancellor of a great university shall have the freedom to govern his institution in accordance with his own best judgment and his conscience, subject to review by the Board of Regents.
>
> The undersigned declare their unqualified confidence in Chancellor William McGill. We believe Dr. McGill is acting in what he sincerely considers to be the best interests of the university.
>
> We commend Dr. McGill for following his own conscience and exercising his own judgment, rather than bowing to pressures from those outside the university who would diminish or usurp his authority.
>
> We deplore any attempt to force Dr. McGill to resign, or to bring about his removal as chancellor.
>
> Furthermore, we do not believe the Marcuse crisis can be resolved by removing Dr. McGill.
>
> We believe the chancellor understands the problem and is entirely capable of resolving it in his own way. And we have full confidence that the Board of Regents will perform their duty.
>
> Accordingly, we reiterate our trust in Dr. McGill and urge the Regents, in reviewing Dr. McGill's decision, to make clear their support of Dr. McGill as chancellor of UCSD.

J. Floyd Andrews	Lewis Silverberg
James W. Archer	Frank Hope Jr.
Jack L. Bowers	Jack Walsh
Malin Burnham	Milton Fredman
Armistead Carter	Alvin R. Cushman
Franklin F. Evenson	Harry Callaway
Ferdinand Fletcher	Walter Zable
Willis H. Fletcher	Dr. Gordon Sproul
Ed Butler	Dr. Jonas Salk
Elliott Cushman	George A. Scott
Arthur Jessop	Joseph Slater
Stephen P. Cushman	Clinton McKinnon
Claude Blakemore	Dr. Jacob Bronowski
A.B. Polinsky	Leonard J. Zanville
Hamilton Marston	Norman B. Foster
Robert Peterson	Carl M. Esenoff
Richard Silberman	Clayton H. Brace
Ned Kimball	William A. Seligman

Dean Haskins

19. The following is the amended statement approved by the Regents:

> After an exhaustive review and within the authority previously vested in him by The Regents, Chancellor McGill has renewed Professor Herbert Marcuse's contract for one year with the University of California, San Diego. Although there has been a commitment made to him the matter was discussed today by The Regents.

A substantial number of them strongly disapproved of this action. Steps are now being taken to reconsider the delegation to the Chancellors of power over faculty appointments and returning such authority to The Regents.

CHAPTER 6: LUMUMBA-ZAPATA COLLEGE

1. Consider Assemblyman John Stull's opinion, voiced in *The San Diego Union* on September 15, 1970, after I had departed UCSD for Columbia:

> UCSD's Third College is a "wild and woolly experiment in racism" that will lead to demands for their own colleges by "every radical and militant in the United States." . . . it will "enforce the most overt racism, discrimination and segregation and, in a perversion of academic standards, it will inevitably and eventually result in eliminating the university itself" . . . "I have received information that McGill gave out tenured faculty appointments in this Third College to unqualified faculty."

2. A copy of the original LZ college demands can be found in Special Collections, UCSD Central Library.

3. The formation of the so-called Third World Liberation Front at San Francisco State is described graphically in William Barlow and Peter Shapiro, *An End to Silence*, Bobbs-Merrill (Pegasus), New York, 1971. The reader is warned that this book is part of the flood of slanted literature written between 1968 and 1973, idolizing the New Left. In their introduction the authors observe, "Lest there be any question about our 'objectivity,' both of us were deeply involved in the strike. . . . While we were writing strike propaganda for the student newspaper . . . we first conceived of the book."

4. Because of this history, the blockade of a Marine Corps officer on the steps of a former barracks building in Camp Matthews had a symbolism that extended far beyond the act itself.

5. A strange situation developed in the aftermath of the blockade. One of Murphy's staff, Dr. John Geddes, director of the placement office, suddenly went public. He began to write politically toned articles and inflammatory public letters about the incident despite Murphy's vigorous objections. Murphy believed that Geddes was attempting to focus political and community disapproval not on the blockaders, but on UCSD. Geddes refused Murphy's directions to stop. We also learned that Geddes was working as an education adviser to Assemblyman John Stull, our most persistent critic. Powerful faculty decided that Geddes should be fired. I was extremely annoyed by Geddes's unintended conversion of the fifteen students and faculty who blocked Captain Stout into martyrs, but I also told the faculty that academic freedom to take unpopular positions could not be limited to the radical left. Geddes would not be fired for what he was saying off campus. I now believe that Geddes had political motives. We could have disciplined him for refusing to follow his superior's directions, but it would have resulted in an uproar. Geddes resolved the problem for us by resigning in June on his own initiative.

6. This was during the period of daily black-bordered "countdown" advertisements in *The San Diego Union* reading:

__ DAYS

Have Gone By Since 11 Militant Students
And 60 To 80 Sympathizers at UCSD
ILLEGALLY BLOCKED

A MARINE CAPTAIN

FROM

Holding Scheduled Recruitment Interviews
No Disciplinary Action Has Been Taken
By UCSD Chancellor William McGill
WHY NOT?

Ad Sponsored By Citizens To End Campus Anarchy
V. Adm. Albert E. Jarrell, USN(RET.) Chairman
P.O. Box 2391—La Jolla, California 92037

The ads appeared daily for more than two months.

7. At this point a question of credibility arises. Writers and critics who venerate SDS will no doubt claim that I simply did not know how to handle pressure. My adversarial reactions were an injustice to students acting out of pure idealism. The language is familiar in apologia for the New Left.

To these doubters I commend the following remarkably frank analysis of SDS objectives, because it is a faithful reproduction of the rhetoric I heard over and over again in those days:

> As well as attacking the university for its participation in war research and exploitation of surrounding working class communities, we must challenge the other main function of the university, which is to turn out corporate morons to take up the task of administering the world. The university is not a place devoted to human development which "makes a few destructive mistakes." The university is a place dedicated to the perpetuation of class exploitation and class oppression. . . . Our strategy therefore must be an attack on the entire institution of the university, a challenge to its purpose and to its right to exist. Wherever possible, we must strive to shut it down—shut it down rather than "reform" it, because as long as the society exists in its present form the university can only function to achieve the aims we have just discussed.

Cathy Wilkerson, Mike Spiegel, Les Coleman, "New Left Notes," October 7, 1968. Reprinted in Chapter 10 of *Student Power, Participation and Revolution*, John and Susan Erlich, eds., Association Press, New York, 1970, p. 70.

8. Henry Kissinger, *White House Years*, Little, Brown, Boston, 1979, pp. 514–515.

9. Students on disciplinary probation are barred from extracurricular activities and are subject to the withholding of degrees if the terms of the probation are violated.

10. The environment in 1969 was not conducive to reason. Much tougher

actions were required with the same people in 1970. We secured a court order enjoining them from specified disruptive activity. A number of them violated the order, were arrested, convicted, and jailed. By that time I had become so incensed with these people, I made a special point of testifying against them.

11. This analysis was first suggested to me in 1968 by Roger Heyns while he was Berkeley chancellor. I often discussed it with other presidents, particularly with Andrew Cordier during our period of overlap at Columbia. The language in the text, however, is my own. It is a bit more ironic in tone than my two teachers would have wished.

12. The similarities between the Lumumba-Zapata demands and the BSC and TWLF demands at San Francisco State are unmistakable. Similar language emerged also from the TWLF at Berkeley in January 1969.

Late in 1968 Third World students at San Francisco State demanded the creation of a school of Third World studies with fifty full-time teaching positions and a black studies department with twenty full-time teaching positions. In addition, they insisted upon autonomous control within these new divisions, immunity from supervision by the California State College trustees, open admissions for all nonwhite students, and complete control over student financial aid.

13. The Black Student Council (BSC) and Mexican-American Youth Association (MAYA) were registered student organizations at UCSD, entitled to use university facilities and supported in part by student fees. The register was kept in the office of George Murphy, dean of students. When students rallied in Revelle Plaza, they used microphones and amplifiers supplied by the university. Such equipment was kept in the dean's office and was available to all registered student groups. We did not attempt to offer or deny facilities to student organizations on the basis of their political views. Learning to accept being told off by a young person using facilities you have provided for his extracurricular enjoyment is an interesting experiment in self-discipline. Grievances should be freely aired in a student community. It then becomes possible to respond, and I do not exclude as a suitable response out-arguing students and taking their audience away from them. A university should be a civilized, but never a soft, place.

14. The local FBI office, apparently under instructions from the very top of the Nixon administration, was gathering information on the Panthers and other New Left militant groups on the ground that these people posed a threat to national security. An agent from the San Diego FBI office called on me at about this time to request our cooperation in supplying campus files on minority students alleged to be operating with militant groups. He was particularly interested in Angela Davis. I refused. The files had been put together with the understanding that they would not be used against the interests of our students. We would give them to the FBI only under subpoena.

In 1968 many responsible officials, including the President and the Governor of California, seemed ready to believe the country was threatened by revolution. None of it made sense to me. We had substantial trouble, but it would be a great exaggeration to speak of it as a national security threat treatable by intelligence-gathering against militant students. The radicals were spreading enough paranoia about tapped telephones and FBI surveillance without giving them actual justification. As things turned out, nothing ever developed out of the FBI overture, and, of course, the revolution that the politicians were afraid of never came. After considering the monumental errors made by law enforcement in the battle over People's Park, errors that might have created a militant revolutionary movement in many countries, I concluded that the New Left was long on rhetoric and short on commitment. The U.S. was simply not in revolutionary condition.

15. The People's Park controversy and the upheaval in the University of California following the street fighting in Berkeley on May 15, 1969, are discussed in Chapter 7.

16. Lawyers tend to be apprehensive whenever an institution fails to exercise its property rights in deference to student or community unrest. Courts have held that such failure in certain instances grants a license to the public which may not be withdrawn by mere reassertion of a previously unexercised right.

The problem is that laws governing property and the ideals of students do not match well. A cardinal philosophical principle of the New Left was that it valued people and devalued property. Whenever the university attempted to assert its property rights against the interests of the poor, or even against established community groups, we had a fight on our hands. We would be told by students that the university is a humane institution with a special role in society. It should not place its property interests above the interests of people. At the same time our lawyers would advise us that if we did not control university property, we would be failing in our duty as fiduciaries. These cross-purposes lay at the very heart of the People's Park controversy. They illustrate the ingenuity of veteran Berkeley radicals in choosing an issue certain to pose a fatal dilemma for the University of California.

17. When Armin Rappaport resigned as provost of Third College, he returned to the UCSD faculty as a full professor in the department of history. He served as department chairman, has authored an impressive list of books and articles in his field, twentieth century U.S. diplomatic history, and remains one of the most popular teachers in the university. While he still laments the fate of the original Third College plan, he seems glad to have returned to the role of an active, productive senior scholar.

17a. Angela Davis's version of these events can be found in her autobiography.

> We had put up a fierce struggle. Large numbers of UCSD students had experienced the radicalization that was occurring on campuses throughout the country. The university hierarchy decided, apparently, that it was best to make concessions we were demanding, rather than risk a prolonged disruption of campus activities. To tell the truth, we had not really expected them to agree so readily to our notion of the third college. And when they did, those of us leading the movement knew that despite our victory—of which all of us were proud—Lumumba-Zapata College would never become the revolutionary institution we had originally projected.

Angela Davis, *An Autobiography*, Random House, Inc., New York, 1974, pp. 197–198.

18. In 1981 Joe Watson was named vice chancellor for undergraduate affairs at UCSD. Simultaneously Bill Frazer became university vice president for academic affairs with offices in Berkeley. He had been professor of physics at UCSD. Both men made their administrative reputations with the success of the Third College experiment.

19. There is no question that Third College is very different today from Lumumba-Zapata college. In 1970 the college had 106 minority students out of a total enrollment of 167 students. In the fall of 1979, the college opened with 1671 students, 624 of whom were minority students. It is clear that in the course of its ten-year development the college has become increasingly attractive to both white and minority students. The curricular interests of the students have also changed. While the original L-Z curriculum demands focused on social issues and radical perspectives, these demands were never adopted. Currently, Third College's curriculum is moving in the direction of the hard sciences. Of all Third College students 49% major in natural sciences, engineering, and mathematics. Many Third College graduates attend medical and other graduate and professional schools. The college has been active in the development of innovative programs offering minority undergraduate students practical research experience in the high-powered laboratories of the UCSD campus. The Third College administration hopes to establish UCSD as a national center for training minority scientists.

CHAPTER 7: PEOPLE'S PARK

1. It is difficult even now to find an unbiased account of the events at People's Park on May 15, 1969. Guided by my memory of what happened, I have selected among several sources. The best is Chancellor Roger Heyns's written report to the May 23, 1969, special meeting of the Berkeley academic senate. As far as I know, this 45-page document has not been printed. I have relied heavily on it. One of the best sources in print is Kenneth Lamott, *Anti-California: Report from Our First Parafascist State*, Little, Brown, Boston, 1971. Despite his title, Lamott proves to be an accurate and careful reporter. His account of People's Park is given on pp. 154–170.

For authentic information on police preparations and police injuries, the best source is Governor Reagan's speech to the Commonwealth Club, San Francisco, on June 13, 1969. Writers sympathetic to the protestors tend to overstate the size of crowds, numbers of police, and the motives of the protestors. See, for example, the chronology in *People's Park*, Alan Copeland, ed., Ballantine Books, New York, 1969. This is a collection of superb photographs with a chronology of the park on pp. 109–118. Both Lamott and this source give the number of police as 250. The figure in the text comes from Governor Reagan's report.

2. Virtually all sources agree that the origin of the park traces to an article in the *Berkeley Barb* on April 18, 1969, calling for a large-scale community effort to begin construction on April 20. The *Barb* article said, "We will police our own park and not allow its occupation by an imperial power." Handbills circulating in the park and picked up by Berkeley campus police spoke of violent retaliation if the university attempted to move against the project.

3. The Berkeley street people in most instances were not political revolutionaries but countercultural dropouts. They enjoyed spoofing what they considered a square and stuffy university. When they appeared for a rally in Sproul Plaza or at a public ceremony on campus, one could never quite tell what might happen. Generally it was harmless, but inevitably it was extravagantly eccentric.

4. Some of these revolutionaries were veterans of the Free Speech Movement. A good account of the ethos of the community surrounding the Berkeley campus during the early 1960s can be found in Chapter 1 of Max Heirich, *The Beginning, Berkeley 1964*, Columbia University Press, New York, 1970. It should be noted that this environment also spawned the Symbionese Liberation Army, a truly bizarre revolutionary sect. As far as I know it had no connection whatever with the university.

5. It should be noted, however, that despite all the competing demands on its energies, the Berkeley administration secured approval from the university's central financing agency for high-priority loan funds to build a playing field at the Haste-Bowditch site. The approval came on April 4, 1969, two weeks prior to the article in the *Berkeley Barb*. Apparently Berkeley officials sensed that something was up.

6. It is true that our early history was somewhat volatile. Students at Bologna, Paris, and Oxford rioted regularly in the Middle Ages. Keeping them in check often required the most forceful measures. Historians now point out, partly in jest but not without good reason, that more blood was spilled in the Oxford High Street than on many battlefields of Europe. Yet all this volatility was long ago.

In 1811 a Columbia College commencement was disrupted at Trinity Church in New York City when Columbia President William Harris took exception to remarks made by a student speaker. The president refused to hand the student his diploma, whereupon the graduating class became enraged and proceeded to attack the faculty. The learned gentlemen had to take to their heels to avoid bodily harm.

But even the 1811 commencement at Columbia was an aberration until the 1960s. Politeness in civil interchange has characterized the academic life in America almost since its founding.

7. The Governor's pressure to centralize authority in the hands of the Board of Regents encompassed a wide variety of disciplinary and administrative areas. The press, however, gave most of its attention to the Governor's attempts to restore direct regental authority over the appointment process on campus. The Marcuse affair had put this issue squarely in the public eye. In the March 22nd issue of *The San Diego Union*, Reagan said that revoking chancellors' rights to confer tenure on faculty members "would put back into the hands of the Regents the right to have some authority." In April 1969, the Regents voted to assume veto authority over the campus chancellors in the matter of hiring and promotion of faculty.

8. The decision to build a fence was in fact announced by Chancellor Heyns in a memorandum to the campus on May 13, 1969, three days prior to the

May Regents meeting in Los Angeles. In the memo no date was indicated for the fence construction.

9. The reader should note that this precept, which virtually every experienced university administrator will endorse, runs directly contrary to suggestions in the literature based upon the Gandhian theory of nonviolent protest.

> If the authorities arrest or haul off demonstrators near the beginning of the demonstration, they may lose community sympathy and appear as intransigent, rigid dictators, just as the protestors described them. At the same time, they will probably make the protestors more entrenched, more cohesive, more determined. If, however, the authorities call in the police after waiting some time for the protest to end and after making several overtures to negotiate as soon as the students stop demonstrating, then the action will seem justified. . . . The community may even come to see it as the authorities' duty to remove a disruptive element from the community.

"Directed Resistance: The Structure of Tactics in Student Protest," Donald W. Light, Jr., *The Dynamics of University Protest*, Nelson-Hall, Chicago, 1977, pp. 69–95.

Light's argument is applicable only when the administrative response to a seizure (let's face it, not a "demonstration") is sufficiently abrupt and maladroit to generate widespread sympathy for the protestors. I have found such sympathy to be automatic only in communities inexperienced with protest. When you have been, as I have, through twelve years of persistent attempts at protest by seizure, you find a majority of the faculty eager to end any seizure quickly if it can be done. They know perfectly well what is implied when, for example, a group seizes the campus computer center, chains the doors, and threatens to wreck it unless their demands are met.

The important point to understand is that seizures and related pressure tactics, by their very nature, force the administration to respond. The response must be chosen after a careful assessment of the problem as well as the reactivity of the large audience of faculty and students who stand aloof, watching the game. The basic criteria for administrative response are that it must (1) diminish the problem and (2) permit continuation of the strategy on successive days.

The reader will now understand why it is sometimes necessary to act before the faculty mobilizes. Many who have read the sociological literature on student protest may think they know better how to deal with pressure tactics than experienced administrators.

10. UCSD's handling of the Lumumba-Zapata protest is an instance of this precept; so is the response to the student strike at UCSD described in this chapter. The classic case was Edward Levi's masterful handling of a major building seizure at the University of Chicago in 1969. He ignored the demands of the protestors, isolated them by refusing to use force against them, and waited for the coalition to come apart. Eventually it did. The protestors departed with nothing to show for their efforts.

11. I hope it is clear from the text that I believed Governor Reagan's approach to student protest to be rooted in his sure instinct for doing the politically

popular thing. He became, as it were, the projection of the voice of the average citizen on the Board of Regents. We, on the other hand, were attempting to handle disruption professionally rather than politically. Our primary concern was to avoid damaging thousands of naive, countercultural students sympathetic to New Left causes, who were prone to make gestures that got them into trouble. At the time politicians used to speak hopefully of the "silent majority," a large force of sympathetic students who would support the administration. To the best of my knowledge this majority never existed. It was an invention of political minds that never understood what was going on on campus.

12. Sympathetic accounts of this rally in Sproul Plaza give the crowd size as nearly 6000. The figure in the text comes from Governor Reagan's Commonwealth Club address (see note 1). Most reliable sources agree that the young president-elect of the Berkeley student body used such words as "Let's go down and take the park." See, for example, Henry F. May, "Living with Crisis, A View from Berkeley," *American Scholar*, 1968–69, 38:588–605. The individual involved later denied he said it. What he said or meant is no longer important except for his conscience.

13. See Frederick Berry, Thomas Brooks, and Eugene Commins, "Terror in a Teapot," *Nation*, 1969, 208:784–788, for a graphic description of the injuries and degree of involvement of some who were shot. The text draws upon page 786 of this article.

14. The reference to the postman is in Professor May's *American Scholar* article, p. 594.

15. The Berry, Brooks, Commins article in the *Nation* displays the powerful anger felt by civil libertarians over tactics used by law enforcement people in clearing the streets, breaking up crowds on campus, and making arrests following the initial street battle on May 15. One needs to have lived in a university community to understand the effect of such excesses on academic civil libertarians.

16. Governor Reagan, in his June 13, 1969, Commonwealth Club speech, said it again with almost as much force.

> Those who administer and teach must make it plain that they will not be coerced by threats of force from that little group that is commanding so much of their attention. They must spell out in advance to that tiny minority the kinds of misconduct they will not tolerate and that there will be no negotiation with anyone who threatens violence. . . . If they will follow this and stand firm—the university can dispose of that kind of revolution within the week.

17. At this point the special committee on Third College chaired by Professor William Frazer had prepared its report in response to the Varon resolution of May 7. The committee was trying to claim the senate's attention so the report could be discussed and, they hoped, appraised. But on May 20, the entire campus was in orbit over People's Park. It was difficult to think of anything else.

18. The sudden appearance of dozens of white T-shirts bearing the strike symbol might be considered an encouraging bourgeois episode in the heyday of the New Left. I presume that students bought them from some sharp operator.

In a deeper sense, this incident displays the superficial nature of the average student's commitments to radical causes and the unconscious oedipal drives moving students. These were not revolutionaries; they were adolescents. Is there any wonder, after the blood spilled at People's Park, that the chancellors felt protective about students and hostile toward both the hard radicals who had created this mess and the law enforcement people who so thoroughly misunderstood what was going on?

19. Lowell Bergman left the university soon after I did and worked as a free-lance reporter in the San Diego area. Currently Bergman is a West Coast producer for a major television network and is the cofounder of CIR, the Center for Investigative Reporting, a public-interest research group.

20. Marcuse did in fact take his leave. He had an academic version of the "captain's paradise." He was on strike and on paid leave at the same time.

21. The crowd had been obstreperous. Following a noon-hour vigil for James Rector, they had tried to march off campus toward Berkeley's business district, but were blocked by guardsmen. They then turned round and moved toward the chancellor's house on the west side of campus. Police followed them and drove them away, using tear gas and clubs. The crowd began to drift back toward Sproul Plaza. Then a public announcement was made, apparently by campus police, that "chemical agents" would be dropped. After that the helicopter came in. Unfortunately, noxious fumes spread all over the campus and into the adjacent side streets.

Students tried to flee the rolling clouds of gas, but many were overcome. Children playing in the Strawberry Canyon recreation area on campus, patients in nearby Cowell Hospital, and young people in several elementary and secondary schools near the campus were affected.

22. The helicopter incident was mentioned to me as a horrible example by several senior police officers in New York City during the 1970s. They wanted to know if I had witnessed it.

23. *San Diego Evening Tribune,* May 22, 1969.

24. *San Diego Evening Tribune,* May 23, 1969.

25. Later in the day I received a phone call from the dean of medicine complaining bitterly about the use of the hospital site for Captain Stout's interviews. The dean pointed out that, historically, hospital facilities are considered off-limits in political and military confrontations. He wanted to stay neutral. I listened to him politely, but after the nature of the complaint became clear in the first two or three sentences, my mind switched off.

26. I cannot say enough in praise of these courageous faculty volunteers. They were a motly group of twenty or so, drawn from nearly every department on campus and diverse in their politics. What brought them together was a common revulsion for violent protest.

An unusual incident occurred during the face-off at the chancellor's office door. One student, Ned Van Valkenburgh, attempted to lead a group of twenty-five others inside "to make an appointment." There was a struggle at the door, and Murphy inadvertently slammed it on Van Valkenburgh's hand. In an inspired use of our grievance procedures, Van Valkenburgh subsequently filed a complaint with the senate committee on academic freedom. The committee heard the complaint in due course and issued a report urging everyone to use better manners. On December 8, 1969, as this report was about to be issued I wrote an irate (and hence revealing) complaint to the committee:

> It is difficult for me to disagree with the Committee's precepts on courtesy in personal interactions. Nevertheless the citation of such precepts as bearing on the incident at hand seems a bit remote from the point. I was not in my office during the blocking effort. I did, however, sit through a long and utterly brutalizing interview in the [chancellor's] conference room with those who had sought to enter my office earlier. I can tell you it was an ugly business from beginning to end.
>
> The Committee must bear in mind that Deans Murphy and Hull were neither discourteous nor provocative in carrying out their duties. They have the responsibility for maintenance of campus peace in a climate of freedom. As I read the account of the event, the first recourse to force was sought by Mr. Van Valkenburgh. It is but one more example of the equally valid precept that forceful steps undertaken with moralistic intent usually set in motion an escalation process that none of us know how to control.
>
> ... A climate of freedom requires due regard for more than Mr. Van Valkenburgh's right to enter my office over the Dean's objection. It requires some sensitivity to the chancellor's freedom, that of his secretarial staff, and the right of the Deans to perform their legitimate duties peacefully.

These are not the words of a pleasant academic diplomat.

27. In the chancellor's files there is a brief, wonderful record of this meeting written by a middle-level administrator:

> Chancellor McGill met this morning at 9:30 to hear demands presented by the Radical Students Union (i.e., SDS) with other concerned students present. The RSU approached the meeting pessimistically and their expectations were fulfilled. McGill meandered and some people in the room shouted insults; there were, however, brief moments of clarity.
>
> Many if not all of the RSU members left in disgust. The discussion went on, at some times heated, but for the most part in a lower key.

28. The Berkeley march is described in Lamott, *Anti-California*, pp. 167–170.

CHAPTER 8: THE MIGHTY ARE FALLEN

1. *Los Angeles Times*, March 13, 1981, p. 21.

CHAPTER 9: THE END OF INNOCENCE

1. The prospect of collapse was not due to a revolutionary threat but to the predicament in which universities found themselves as protesting students and overreactive public officials both turned their wrath on the campus. There was great concern that a number of institutions might be hurt by a combination of public disavowal, alumni disaffection, and reduced student enrollment. In most instances confidence was quickly restored when it became evident that educational standards were being maintained despite the turmoil. Nevertheless universities did change. Relations between students and university administrators were altered sharply as students became more involved in university governance. We saw students brought into academic senates and governing boards. Student places were created on presidential search committees. These and similar changes were greeted with nearly universal approval. They strengthened institutions by making them less autocratic and better able to cope with internal disputes.

2. The constellation of causative factors producing the elevated emotional arousal of the Sixties was unique and is not likely to be repeated identically. But it would be quite incorrect to conclude that protest is no longer a matter of concern. As this chapter proceeds, an argument will be developed stressing the role of sustained emotional arousal as a psychological precondition for student protest. Part of the climate of arousal during the Sixties was engendered by antipathy to racial injustice in America. Part of it was due to the war in Vietnam, but much of it was traceable to new circumstances faced by young people trying to come to terms with modern society: alienation created by large institutions, frustrations accompanying greatly enhanced bureaucratic regulation of contemporary life, enforced extension of adolescence produced by heavy demands for education in a modern state.

3. I do not mean to suggest here that psychological determinants of student protest are more important than political determinants. The political ideals of the protestors have been discussed by many writers, whereas psychological pressures on students remain largely unexamined. There is a rudimentary literature on psychological factors in student protest, but many commentators have a distinct aversion for such inquiry. They believe it centers on irrational determinants, denigrating the rational motives and ideals of the protestors. I try to challenge that argument in this chapter, but it is important to warn readers unfamiliar with this material about its extreme sensitivity. In fact, the claim is encountered occasionally that it is unreasonable even to raise questions about the unconscious motives of students without also probing the motives of faculties and administrators. (See, for example, J. P. Spiegel, "The Group Psychology of Campus Disorders," in Donald W. Light, Jr., and John Spiegel, *The Dynamics of University Protest*, Nelson-Hall, Chicago, 1977, p. 141.) Such judicial appraisal is necessary. There is much to be discovered, but one should not attempt to bar consideration of psychological factors in student protests on grounds of fairness. These influences are too important to be ignored. At some point we must cease bickering over who was moral or who was right, and begin asking ourselves what was going on. They are two different realms of discourse.

4. The term "believers" is used here interchangeably with "followers." Classifying protesting crowds into those who preached and organized, and those who believed and followed, is a crude but useful analytical step. Eric Hoffer developed the "believers" syndrome in a fascinating book, but I think he overstates the case *(The True Believer,* Harper & Brothers, New York, 1951). In any event there seemed to be two distinguishable groups in most political demonstrations I saw during the Sixties. The classification is crude because there was actually a continuum of political involvement among believers, ranging from sophisticated ideological commitment to near-total ignorance of the issues. Moreover, the sophistication of the leadership varied. Some demonstrations were organized by self-elected, ad hoc committees of experienced radicals. Others were put together by elected student leaders who usually displayed little skill, bumbling along until taken over by radicals at a key moment. Still other demonstrations were spontaneous and leaderless.

The majority of the demonstrations I saw were managed by well-organized, ad hoc protest committees. Distinctive handbills would appear on campus advertising a forthcoming rally. The flyers carried a brief message outlining the nature of the protest. Speakers would be listed, often including one or two prominent outsiders. There would be music or guerrilla theater entertainment. The leadership had to design and run off the handbills, book the space, arrange for speakers and the sound equipment, as well as for the entertainment needed to attract a crowd. They also had to design a scenario for the rally if it was preliminary to an intended direct action such as a sit-in or building seizure. This was generally done at a long meeting on the night before, and it was serious work.

Certain views were held in common by leaders and followers, but there were also sharp differences. New Left leaders projected utopian visions of a better world. The followers accepted New Left leadership and longed for the utopias, but they rejected violent means. Believers were far more passive than their leaders wished them to be.

5. Henry Kissinger, *White House Years,* Little, Brown and Co., Boston, 1979, pp. 509–517, 1190–1201.

6. The point is evident throughout the text and seemed evident to administrators who served during the era of unrest. Yet the war in Vietnam was always there in the background, and some scholars maintain that "disaffection from the war [was] a major determinant of student militancy even in protests that [were] manifestly not about the war." See R. B. Smith, "Campus Protests and the Vietnam War," in J. F. Short, Jr., and M. E. Wolfgang, eds., *Collective Violence,* Aldine Atherton, Chicago, 1972, pp. 250–277. I do not know how to cope with arguments claiming hidden causes. Another example is the claim that unrest was attributable to parental permissiveness. Such claims are implausible but impossible to disprove. At the very least they fail to explain the rapid spread of unrest in diverse societies: Germany, France, Italy, China, Japan. After playing a role in the era and studying its complexity, I have an aversion for all simple explanations.

7. I have in mind here a sustained, free-floating, subsurface tension that triggered off innumerable small incidents, any one of which could turn into a major storm. The tension is said to be "free-floating" because it was not rooted

in any specific grievance. Since it failed to dissipate during periods of calm, it is also called "latent anger." The tense emotional atmosphere it created is denoted as a "climate of arousal." I first wrote about this climate in an article that appeared in the *La Jolla Light*, July 24, 1969, later republished in several places:

> Nothing is more obvious than the reality of student anger. The phenomenon extends to many junior faculty members and graduate students. Anger is directed at the war in Vietnam, racism, poverty and exploitation in our cities, and the evils of a faceless society.

8. This new generation of anti-war activists included Allard Lowenstein, Sam Brown, Rev. William S. Coffin, Dr. Spock, and a host of others. They were determined to drive Lyndon Johnson from office and alter the government's war policy.

9. "Student power" was a term chosen by the radicals to signify a range of issues involving personal student concerns. It was intended to summon up contextual meanings evocative of "black power." This militant label is not at all helpful for conveying the frustration felt by students caught in the never-ending ellipses of university bureaucracy, where no one has the power to approve what you want to do and the only way to get a decision is to apply to some other office. But such frustrations are exactly what created a significant part of the climate of arousal. Frustration and alienation, in and of themselves, seldom led to protests, but they created an angry context in which students first began to listen to charismatic radicals painting word pictures of a New Jerusalem. A better term than "student power" might have been "bureaucratic bestiary."

10. These feelings are identified by other commentators as a form of alienation. Like much else in Marx, the term "alienation" is easy to comprehend but virtually impossible to confine in any simple definition. A splendid paper on the New Left written by Martin Oppenheimer did much to clarify my understanding of what students meant when they described themselves as alienated. Oppenheimer labels the feelings of victimization cited in the text as "alienation from the meaning of existence." He quotes Durkheim: "Under these conditions, one would lose the courage to live, that is to act and struggle, since nothing will remain of our exertions." A key argument of this chapter is that such alienation made students especially receptive to the leadership of New Left antiheroes. Martin Oppenheimer, "The Student Movement as a Response to Alienation," *Journal of Human Relations*, XVI, no.1 (1968), pp. 1–16.

11. In 1965, as an aftermath of the Free Speech Movement, the University of California established a committee to study educational problems at Berkeley. The introductory section of the committee report describing the alienation, frustration, and anger of Berkeley students remains one of the best descriptions of the climate of arousal I have ever read. It is difficult to believe that this perceptive analysis was written in 1965. This section of the report makes clear that, while the war in Vietnam was in the background in 1965, it was not yet considered an important factor in student unrest. See *Education at Berkeley, Report of the Select Committee on Education*, University of California, Berkeley, 1966, pp. 11–36.

12. The special attraction of New Left philosophy can be readily under-

stood if we remember that it preached participatory democracy and individual control of decisions central to one's life. These principles involve a categorical rejection of all forms of bureaucratic control. Alienated students responded warmly to the possibility of such nonelitist governance. The problem was that no one knew how to make it work in a mass society.

13. The latent anger was easily recognized by trustees. Many of them spent many hours with us listening to students' diffuse grievances and trying to fathom their alienation. Parents also saw it, but rarely understood it correctly as a climatic phenomenon extending considerably beyond their own children. Most public figures spent no time at all on campus and hence had no idea of what the problem was.

14. The idea of an "emotional temperature" is meaningless, but it suggests rapidly moving particles, many collisions, and rapid transmission of disturbances. This is what I am trying to convey.

15. Of course, it is irrelevant whether the police were chasing UCSD students or outsiders. The distinction would not change the brutality of what was happening. But a riot at a rock concert is itself a very brutal event, and there comes a point in trying to deal with a violent crowd when reason is completely ineffective. The crowd must be broken up before it injures innocent people or destroys valuable property. This type of primitive violence is different both in degree and in kind from the calculated pressure tactics used by demonstrators in political protests. The problem in 1969 was that deadly force was sometimes employed against both types of crowds. In this instance we did not have a chance to explain to our students what was going on. Perhaps they might have been opposed to dispersing rioters at a rock concert, but using such force against political protestors would have brought to the surface all their latent anger immediately.

16. Because many of the radicals were Marxists, it is easy to jump to the erroneous conclusion that they were under some form of external discipline and that student protests were part of a secretly organized subversive plot. Most law enforcement officials subscribed to such views. The major difficulty is that student leaders brought a variety of competing visions to their work, ranging from classical Soviet Marxism-Leninism, to Trotskyite, Maoist, Castroite, and Marcusian versions of neo-Marxism. Although we tended to lump all radicals together, the fact is that they were as much at war with one another as they were with us. Ultimately it was these bitter internal ideological disputes that caused the New Left to collapse. At the time we seldom saw evidence of the rivalries. New Left radicals would try to mask their personal differences in order to confront the administration in a posture of unity.

17. I am aware of the sensitivity of this problem. It is important to avoid any suggestion that the motives of student protestors were irrational while my own motives were both pure and completely sensible. I have tried to be candid about my fears, weaknesses, and errors of judgment. I am not proud of my combative reactions to the protests I faced. The reactions were simply there and must be accepted as phenomena. So should it be with student protestors.

But now that the unrest is over, we ought to try to get an understanding of the latent anger characteristic of the period. The fact is that it was not all high-minded idealism, and not understood by the students themselves. In addressing myself to the psychological phenomena of student protests during the Sixties, I am following Currie and Skolnick's admonition that "invocation of Oedipal conflict to explain some of the characteristics of protest movements would be useful if it were a response to the issues raised by empirical analysis—[i.e.] there were well-observed phenomena that seemed difficult to explain without some such approach." Elliot Currie and Jerome H. Skolnick, "A Critical Note on Conceptions of Collective Behavior," in J. F. Short and M. E. Wolfgang, eds., *Collective Violence*, Aldine-Atherton, Chicago, 1972, p. 70. See also Carl J. Crouch, "Collective Behavior: An Examination of Some Stereotypes," *Social Problems*, XV (1968), pp. 310–322.

18. Robert Liebert, *Radical and Militant Youth*, Praeger, New York, 1971. The discussion on which I draw here can be found on page 106.

19. This question must be posed and answered whenever we attempt to invoke unconscious psychological drives as explanatory concepts in student protest. The drives appear to change very little from one generation to another. If they were key factors in producing the unrest of the Sixties, why doesn't unrest occur now or indeed in every generation? Hostility to symbols of authority probably played a contributory role in heightening the climate of arousal, but was not in and of itself sufficient to account for either the form or the political objectives of the protests that actually occurred.

20. At Berkeley in 1964 the FSM was beginning to run out of steam after three months of continuous organizational effort by a small group of activists who had masterminded the protest. Suddenly, with no prior warning, the administration sent out letters to four protest leaders summoning them before a disciplinary tribunal. Immediately handbills began circulating on campus advertising a rally on December 2:

> Chancellor Strong has summoned Arthur Goldberg, Mario Savio, and Jackie Goldberg before his Faculty Committee on Student Conduct. These three students have been singled out—from among thousands—for their participation in the demonstration of October 1st and 2nd. . . .

The clumsy attempt at selective discipline intensified student feelings. A huge crowd appeared for the rally. Mario Savio made a classic speech, urging them to bring the Berkeley campus to a halt by putting "your bodies upon the gears and upon the wheels, upon the levers, upon all the apparatus . . . to make it stop. And you've got to indicate to the people who run it, to the people who own it, that unless you're free the machine will be prevented from working at all." More than a thousand students marched into Sproul Hall, Berkeley's administrative headquarters, where late that night and next morning, 773 persons were arrested. M. Heirich, *The Spiral of Conflict, Berkeley 1964*, Columbia University Press, New York, 1971, pp. 265–278.

21. See *Report of the President's Commission on Campus Unrest*, U.S. Govern-

ment Printing Office, Washington, D.C., 1970, pp. 20–35. The mass media probably played a significant role in this diffusion process. "Night after night, television film of events on one campus carried the methods and spirit of protest to every other campus in the country." *Ibid.*, p. 28. This source also contains an unusual bibliography on student unrest. It includes several invaluable contemporary treatments of police practices, theorizing by law enforcement agencies, and discussions of legal problems posed by codes of student conduct and injunctions against campus disorders (References 93–139).

22. It can be argued that the problem is not with the Rousseauvian ideal but rather with the widespread anger felt by students because of a variety of grievances relating to poor education and excessive bureaucracy. If that anger and its causes had been faced realistically, protests might not have spread in the way they did. The point is a telling one. Still, I have never been able to understand the intensity of the angry climate in the 1960s. University faculties were far more receptive to grievances and much more willing to change in response to moral criticism than most commentators admit. The case for militant protest was never as strong as has been depicted. Moreover, protests did not break out on a large scale until they became the faddish thing to do.

23. "Group protest" is a form of collective behavior. In crowds, situations arise that reflect the interactions of crowd members. They are not well described by asking individuals, as reporters sometimes do, to recount their own feelings.

24. There is a voluminous literature on "crowd theory" in the sociology of collective behavior. The arguments presented here are based on direct observation of hundreds of student protests over a period of twelve years. The treatment is original in the sense that it was not formulated by poring over the literature. There are, however, many points of contact between this analysis and the literature on collective behavior. A subset of that literature dealing with social movements produces descriptions quite similar to those found here.

For example, Lawrence Stone's essay, "Theories of Revolution" in R. S. Denisoff, *The Sociology of Dissent*, Harcourt Brace Jovanovich, New York, 1974, pp. 385–398, describes four social stages of revolution that will be familiar to readers of these pages. The first stage is characterized by "indiscriminate, uncoordinated mass unrest and dissatisfaction, the result of dim recognition that traditional values no longer satisfy current aspirations" (pp. 397–398). Stone also points to the emergence of two distinct types of leaders (hence the leader-follower relation), "the prophet who sketches the shape of the new utopia upon which men's hopes can focus, and the reformer working methodically toward specific goals."

In the same volume, Herbert Blumer writes on social movements *(ibid.*, pp. 4–20). Consider the following description of the role of agitators as defined by Blumer: "The other situation is one wherein people are already aroused, restless and discontented, but where they are too timid to act or else do not know what to do. In this situation the function of agitation is not so much to implant the seeds of unrest as to intensify and direct tensions which people already have."

These descriptions are so close to what I saw that the theory of student protests in the Sixties would appear to be a special case of the theory of social movements.

Crowd tensions in student protest are also analyzed in the text. I attempt to formulate the dynamics of protest demonstrations (apart from media events), as pressure tactics aimed at forcing the administration into concessions. The literature on crowd pressures extends back to the classic work of LeBon (1897) and Freud (1921). Gustav LeBon, *The Crowd: A Study of the Popular Mind,* Macmillan, New York, 1897. Sigmund Freud, *Group Psychology and the Analysis of the Ego,* W. W. Norton, New York, 1959. Many of LeBon's ideas are now rejected for good ideological and empirical reasons, but his book is full of insights for anyone who has studied and actually faced crowds.

The best modern treatment of generalized beliefs in crowds may be found in Neil Smelser's *Theory of Collective Behavior,* Free Press, New York, 1963. One of the best descriptions of the crowd interplay in a student protest is given by Richard A. Berk, "A Gaming Approach to Crowd Behavior," *American Sociological Review,* XXXIX (1974), pp. 355–373. It is very similar to what I experienced.

25. This view of student demonstrations as harnessing crowd behavior in pursuit of well-defined, rational (although unpopular) objectives, is not far from Skolnick's view of political protest. J. Skolnick, *The Politics of Protest,* Simon and Schuster, New York, 1969. We appear to part company, however, over the extent to which this rational structure is understood by members of the protesting group. In most of the demonstrations I saw the rationale was the creation of an ideological elite. This leadership portrayed the protest as a unanimous, outraged reaction to specified administrative abuses. Protest leaders tried to generate supportive public reactions by depicting the group's objectives in the simplest and most sympathetic ways, ways the public would understand, yet seldom revealing the full ideological agenda of the leaders.

26. Jerry Farber, "The Student as Nigger," *The Student as Nigger: Essays and Stories,* Contact Books, Los Angeles, 1969, pp. 114–128.

27. The intensity of the disillusionment is still puzzling. Barbara Ward once remarked to me that it had robbed an entire generation of American college students of the spontaneous joy that should accompany youth.

28. This was Brad Cleaveland's position in the debate over Cleaver's course described in Chapter 2. One of the special problems of the Sixties was the moral position taken by many undergraduate students that we avoid even symbolic involvements with the war in Vietnam. Hence, students objected to research on burns done by university physicians under sponsorship of the Department of Defense. They felt it corrupted us. Students were trying to define a new code that would insulate the university from corruption by forbidding work deemed morally wrong. Few understood that it had been tried before in the Middle Ages and that our principles of academic freedom were formulated in reaction to the church when it attempted to decree what teachers would be allowed to say or do while remaining true to the gospel.

29. Obviously there was short-range damage, some of it severe. But it proved relatively easy to correct, and the long-term reputations of nearly all of America's major colleges and universities survived unblemished.

30. The history of the campus clergy in the Sixties is still to be written. At

the time the public heard a great deal about religious antiwar protestors. What was written was mostly unfavorable, but I saw much that was spiritually uplifting. Religious counselors arrived as representatives of campus ministries provided by the major denominations. When they discovered the climate of intense emotional arousal, disillusionment, and despair, they were deeply moved. Religious counselors began operating in close ecumenical harmony as academic advisers, psychological guides, draft advisers, all-night friends for students in deep anxiety or on "bad trips." It was a missionary work of incalculable value to distraught young people and to us. The campus clergy were our unsung heroes. There were, of course, a few bad apples. A Jewish trustee once lamented to me that Judaism lacked an equivalent of excommunication. He had in mind a certain religious counselor, but such individuals were rare.

31. R. D. Laing, *The Divided Self,* Penguin Books, New York, 1965, p. 66.

32. For readers whose emotions lie with the protestors, the very act of resisting might appear evil or at least ill-conceived. Advocates must understand that yielding to idealistically motivated protest is not evidence of morality. It did not, in point of fact, generate admiration. The first duty of any administration was to survive, and to do that we had to learn how to frustrate direct-action tactics. Debating the leaders proved to be one of the most effective ways.

33. The trick played on these demonstrators by the police inspector succeeded with an unwary community group that was neither well-organized nor very popular on campus, but tactics such as these can be dangerous. Radical students tend to view the chancellor as a political schemer who has achieved his position by manipulating an establishment they reject. In such cases it is essential to conduct a conflict honorably and with excruciating fairness, as though every point were a matter of principle. The chancellor's word must be *absolutely* dependable and must be given with *absolute* clarity, because it is received in an intensely paranoid atmosphere in which words are subject to distortion and misunderstanding. My negotiations with the Lumumba-Zapata protestors are an excellent example.

Oddly enough, the campus never demanded that I adopt the same rigorous standards with all protesting groups. When a group (generally outsiders) seemed to students and faculty to be particularly vicious or untrustworthy, anything in my repertoire was acceptable, provided only that no one was injured. It shows how we had all been made callous by our repeated experiences with seizure tactics.

34. There are several implications here that must now be made explicit. A basic assertion of this chapter is that tensions created by the bizarre psychological climate on campus during the Sixties produced severe emotional distress among students. They sought relief in a variety of ways. Some turned to radical activity and others to the drug scene in trying to cope with environmentally generated tension. Others simply dropped out. It follows that reportable events, such as accidental drug overdoses (i.e., "bad trips") and suicides, must have been unusually marked during the Sixties. Moreover, there ought to be a provable connection between such phenomena and changes in stress level.

An excellent characterization of student reaction to the superheated campus climate is given by H. Hendin, *The Age of Sensation,* W. W. Norton, New York, 1975. Hendin is a psychiatrist at Columbia University who presents the human dilemmas of the average student with remarkable perception and tenderness. His depiction of these pressures is what I saw.

Data on suicides are unambiguous in showing a rapidly increasing incidence among college students during the time period in question (see A. M. Parker, *Suicide Among Young Adults,* Exposition Press, New York, 1974, pp. 121–122). Similar conclusions can be established for accidental deaths (exclusive of motor vehicle accidents) in the 15- to 24-year age segment of the population. See P. C. Holinger, "Violent Deaths Among the Young: Recent Trends in Suicide, Homicide, and Accidents," *American Journal of Psychiatry,* CXXXVI (1979), pp. 1144–1147, especially table 3. It is not clear that incidence reaches a peak in the early Seventies. It may, in fact, continue to rise. If psychological pressures are now diminishing, we should expect to see a peak similar to that observed in older age groups during the Depression era. It is still too early to tell.

In the case of 15- to 24-year-olds, linking suicides and accidental deaths to the stressful emotional climate of the Sixties is a more difficult problem. There is positive evidence of such linkage (see Parker, *Suicide Among Young Adults,* p. 121). Most commentators identify emotional isolation rather than generalized stress as the principal causative agent in campus suicides. R. H. Seiden, "The Problem of Suicide on College Campuses," *Journal of School Health,* XLI (1971), pp. 243–248, argues that the relation "may be [one] in which drugs, social withdrawal, and suicides [are] all used as different means of escaping unbearable situations." This is precisely what I had in mind.

Good data and in-depth analyses in these areas are hard to come by. Most writers acknowledge the unpleasantness of the subject as making for serious errors of underreporting. It is unfortunately true that campus administrators regularly suppress information on drug use, drug overdoses, and attempted suicides on campus because of the potential damage to the reputations of the young people involved as well as to our institutions. For example, data on suicides and accidental deaths should always be combined in analyzing campus tensions. Reporting physicians try to spare families unnecessary pain by giving young victims the benefit of every doubt. It leads to more or less deliberate misclassification. There are many other such problems. The reader should understand that nothing in this area is simple or easy to prove.

35. I expect to be charged with rewriting history, and so be it; it is the Rashomon phenomenon again.

36. There is a splendid article in the *Chronicle of Higher Education* written by one of these remarkable young people. He resents the belittling of his idealism by politicians who now want to curry favor with conservative voting constituencies. Douglas S. MacKay, "The Crusade to Rewrite the History of the 1960's," *The Chronicle of Higher Education,* May 18, 1981, p. 56.

37. Mr. Reagan, despite many errors in understanding and handling student unrest, served effectively for two terms as Governor of California and retired successfully in 1974 to seek the Presidency. He was not just a presentable and articulate communicator. He was also a very forceful and combative man, a

genuine leader. His combination of traits is unique in recent American politics. At the same time, the Governor was not deeply thoughtful about radical politics. He reacted to provocations by using a sledgehammer on his adversaries. In other words, he played their game. If we had been facing a more broadly gauged and more cleverly led social movement, it might have been catastrophic. At best, it disillusioned a generation of romantic students who wanted no more than to show their commitment.

38. It is somewhat galling to hear these young leaders lauded today for revering "participatory democracy." At the time I was reading reports of all-night meetings in which the scenarios of major demonstrations were worked out in advance. It convinced me that the leadership was power hungry. Participatory democracy had been a superlative idea in the early days of SDS, but by the late Sixties it became a veneer for manipulating the mass of true "believers."

39. The problem was to transform the arena of combat from the campus to the courtroom. The authority of the courts is far more attractive than deadly force in keeping order on campus. I first heard of temporary restraining orders in 1969, when Columbia University went into the New York courts to enjoin the illegal occupation of Columbia buildings. During the spring of 1970, I succeeded in getting a similar restraining order in the California Superior Court over the initial skepticism of the university's attorneys. It worked remarkably well.

40. The value of a court order lay precisely in the fact that student protestors never intended to challenge unjust laws. Nonactivist students were willing to participate in sit-ins up to the point of immediate personal danger if the adversary were the administration, but few of them were prepared to risk contempt of court.

41. This is what is meant when we speak of a "moral contest" between students and administration. In the long run, disputes were settled most effectively by avoiding force or even court orders. An agreement could usually be worked out in which demonstrators were persuaded to abandon their seizure in return for a face-saving concession from the administration. They could then claim they had won, and life would go on as before. If that tactic failed, and if we also failed to bluff the demonstrators out, the next step was to go into court.

42. Many faculties acted to ban classified research on campus and bar their members from clandestine associations with intelligence agencies. The intent was to deal with moral objections to practices that had sprung up during the Cold War era without much thought or prior discussion. Radical students, of course, were not appeased by such changes. Their political views were formulated in moralistic terms and hence created a limitless set of demands, as Neuchterlein has pointed out (p. 620). J. A. Neuchterlein, "Neo-Conservatism and Its Critics," *Virginia Quarterly Review*, LIII (1977), pp. 607–625.

43. Just as a technique of protest spreads rapidly when it is known to be effective, it begins to recede when someone devises effective countermeasures. In the adversarial society we have built this kind of tactical contest goes on all the time.

44. Students in protest demonstrations seemed to be quite suggestible but they accepted leadership only from those they admired. I often remarked on how difficult it was to be persuasive with a crowd amid constant boos and catcalls, while every word spoken by such antiheroes as Angela Davis was received with rapt attention. College presidents who tried to lead demonstrations continued to be viewed as adversaries and outsiders by their students. See Crouch, "Collective Behavior," pp. 312–313.

My technique of debating with protestors before the leaders had managed to set the agenda or had focused the crowd's energy was effective precisely because students were suggestible. But it did not permit me to lead the demonstrators in an agenda I had determined; it enabled me only to frustrate the radical leadership by neutralizing their efforts to organize the crowd.

45. A leaderless, angry crowd is dangerous because it is unpredictable. If it is sufficiently large, it must be broken up lest someone be killed or injured when the crowd turns on him. Most police tactics with crowds are devised for dealing with such leaderless violence. It took some time for the police to realize that attacking a political demonstration only amplified the level of anger, creating a far more serious problem after the attack than before, because the crowd multiplied.

Roaming, rock-throwing groups on campus were nearly always leaderless and generally very small. We let them spend their fury and cleaned up after them. Boarded up, smashed plate-glass windows were a common sight on campus in the late 1960s, almost as common as graffiti.

46. This observation is sure to cause difficulty with sociologists and social psychologists who view protesting crowds as carrying out rational courses of action. See, for example, R. A. Berk, "A Gaming Approach to Crowd Behavior," *American Sociological Review*, XXXIX (1974), pp. 355–373.

47. The observation is not new because it traces back to Freud (1921) and LeBon (1897). It is important, however, to avoid any hint of mysticism with concepts such as "group mind," i.e., regression of crowds to a more primitive state. The fact is simply that it was remarkably difficult to reason with groups of angry student protestors. It is an important observation and I do not want to lose it merely because some may find it politically objectionable.

48. The victimization phenomenon is even more prominent in protest constituencies that develop under the unremitting pressures of urban life.

49. I have not discovered in the literature on social movements a citation of the importance of this intense emotional climate as a precursor of serious protest. The climate of arousal was obviously a central factor in student protests. It caused crowds to form, rumors to fly, and small incidents to be magnified out of proportion to their real significance. I think it quite likely that a similar climate builds up in most revolutionary situations and becomes the emotional engine that drives revolutionary crowds.

50. William Barrett, *Irrational Man*, Doubleday, New York, 1958 (also in paperback Anchor Books edition, 1962). See especially pp. 23–41 in the paperback version.

51. There is an intimate connection, for example, between the growth of the women's movement and the student movements of the Sixties. Jacobs argues that one of the key factors leading to the collapse of SDS was its failure to comprehend the restiveness of its women members. See Harold Jacobs, *The Personal and the Political*, pp. 406–453. Jacobs draws many of his ideas from Sara Evans, *Personal Politics*, Alfred A. Knopf, New York, 1979.

Today's environmental and antinuclear organizations had their roots in countercultural initiatives that were so appealing to students in the mid-Sixties.

52. Signs of this fragmentation are becoming visible in the heavy emphasis on job stress that has emerged in modern labor bargaining. We read of "teacher-burnout" or "air-controller's fatigue" in relation to jobs not ordinarily considered to be unusually stressful. In 1981 the U.S. air controllers went out on strike. A psychologist, C. David Jenkins, who had studied them referred to their behavior as "alienated":

> The controllers are frustrated at [what they perceive as] the bungling, inflexibility and irrationality of management and the unresponsiveness of the whole hierarchy. . . . Most people faced with that kind of stress become depressed or anxious [but the controllers] instead take it out in pugnacious, aggressive behavior, brushes with the law, speeding tickets, fist fights, mental problems.

Los Angeles Times, August 13, 1981, p. 3.

The parallel with the students of the Sixties is arresting. Even more striking is the fact that it was Ronald Reagan, as President of the United States, who promptly fired them when they struck.

Bibliography

Bacciocco, Edward J., Jr.: *The New Left in America: Reform to Revolution 1956 to 1970*, Hoover Institution Press, Stanford, 1974.

Barlow, William, and Peter Shapiro: *An End to Silence: The San Francisco State College Student Movement in the '60s*, Bobbs-Merrill Co. (Pegasus), New York, 1971.

Barrett, William: *Irrational Man*, Doubleday, New York, 1958.

Berg, Ivar: *Education and Jobs: The Great Training Robbery*, Praeger, New York, 1970.

Berk, Richard A.: "A Gaming Approach to Crowd Behavior," *American Sociological Review*, XXXIX (1974), pp. 355–373.

Berry, Frederick, Thomas Brooks, and Eugene Commins: "Terror in a Teapot," *Nation*, 1969, 208:784–788.

Boyarsky, Bill: *The Rise of Ronald Reagan*, Random House, New York, 1968.

Breines, Paul (ed.): *Critical Interruptions: New Left Perspectives on Herbert Marcuse*, Herder and Herder, New York, 1970.

Califano, Joseph A., Jr.: *The Student Revolution: A Global Confrontation*, W.W. Norton & Co., New York, 1970.

Carnegie Commission on Higher Education: *Dissent and Disruption: Proposals for Consideration by the Campus*, McGraw-Hill Book Company, New York, 1971.

Cleaver, Eldridge: *Soul on Ice*, McGraw-Hill Book Company, New York, 1968.

Cleaver, Eldridge: *Soul on Fire*, Word Books, Waco, Tex., 1978.

Clecak, Peter: *Radical Paradoxes: Dilemmas of the American Left: 1945–1970*, Harper & Row, New York, 1973.

Cohen, Mitchell, and Dennis Hale (eds.): *The New Student Left—An Anthology*, Beacon Press, Boston, 1966.

Copeland, Alan, and Nikki Arai (eds.): *People's Park*, Ballantine Books, New York, 1969.

Crouch, Carl J.: "Collective Behavior: An Examination of Some Stereotypes," *Social Problems*, XV (1968), pp. 310–322.

Davis, Angela: *Angela Davis—An Autobiography*, Random House, New York, 1974.

Denisoff, R. Serge, and Robert K. Merton (eds.): *The Sociology of Dissent*, Harcourt Brace Jovanovich, Inc., New York, 1974.

Diggins, John P.: *The American Left in the Twentieth Century*, Harcourt Brace Jovanovich, Inc., New York, 1973.

Education at Berkeley, Report of the Select Committee on Education, University of California, Berkeley, 1966.

Erlich, John, and Susan Erlich (eds.): *Student Power: Participation and Revolution,* Association Press, New York, 1970.

Evans, Sara: *Personal Politics: The Roots of Women's Liberation in the Civil Rights Movement and the New Left,* Alfred A. Knopf, New York, 1979.

Farber, Jerry: "The Student as Nigger," *The Student as Nigger: Essays and Stories,* Contact Books, Los Angeles, 1969, pp. 114–128.

Feuer, Lewis S.: *The Conflict of Generations: The Character and Significance of Student Movements,* Basic Books, New York, 1969.

Flacks, Richard: *Youth and Social Change,* Markham Publishing Company, Chicago, 1971.

Freud, Sigmund: *Group Psychology and the Analysis of the Ego,* translated and edited by James Strachey, W.W. Norton, New York, 1959.

Gitlin, Todd: *The Whole World Is Watching,* University of California Press, Berkeley, 1980.

Glazer, Nathan: *Remembering the Answers: Essays on the American Student Revolt,* Basic Books, Inc., New York, 1970.

Heirich, Max: *The Spiral of Conflict: Berkeley, 1964,* Columbia University Press, New York, 1971.

Hendin, Herbert: *The Age of Sensation,* W.W. Norton, New York, 1975.

Heyns, Roger: *Chancellor's Report to Emergency Meeting of Berkeley Division, University of California Academic Senate,* University of California, May 23, 1969, 45 pp. (unpublished manuscript).

Holinger, P. C.: "Violent Deaths Among the Young: Recent Trends in Suicide, Homicide, and Accidents," *American Journal of Psychiatry,* CXXXVI (1979), pp. 1144–1147.

Jacobs, Harold: *The Personal and the Political: A Study of the Decline of the New Left,* Unpublished doctoral dissertation, Department of Sociology, University of California, Berkeley, 1978.

Jacobs, Harold (ed.): *Weatherman,* Ramparts Press, 1970.

Jay, Martin: *The Dialectical Imagination: A History of the Frankfurt School and the Institute of Social Research 1923–1950,* Little, Brown and Company, Boston, 1973.

Jay, Martin: "The Frankfurt School in Exile," *Perspectives in American History,* 1972, Vol. 6, pp. 339–385.

Kissinger, Henry: *White House Years,* Little, Brown and Co., Boston, 1979.

Laing, R. D.: *The Divided Self,* Penguin Books, New York, 1965.

Lamott, Kenneth: *Anti-California: Report from Our First Parafascist State,* Little, Brown and Co., Boston, 1971.

Lasch, Christopher: *The Culture of Narcissism,* W.W. Norton & Company, Inc., New York, 1979.

LeBon, Gustav: *The Crowd: A Study of the Popular Mind,* Macmillan, New York, 1897.

Liebert, Robert: *Radical and Militant Youth,* Praeger, New York, 1971.

Light, Donald, Jr., and John Spiegel: *The Dynamics of University Protest,* Nelson-Hall Publishers, Chicago, 1977.

Lipshires, Sidney: *Herbert Marcuse: From Marx to Freud and Beyond,* Schenkman Publishing Co., Cambridge, Mass., 1974.

Lockwood, Lee: *Conversation with Eldridge Cleaver, Algiers,* McGraw-Hill Book Company, New York, 1970.

MacIntyre, Alasdair: *Marcuse,* Wm. Collins & Co. Ltd., London, 1970.

Mackay, Douglas.: "The Crusade to Rewrite the History of the 1960's," *The Chronicle of Higher Education,* May 18, 1981, p. 56.

Manchester, William: *Goodbye, Darkness,* Little, Brown and Co., Boston, 1980.

Marcuse, Herbert: *Eros and Civilization,* Beacon Press, Boston, 1955.

Marcuse, Herbert: *An Essay on Liberation,* Beacon Press, Boston, 1969.

Marcuse, Herbert: *Five Lectures: Psychoanalysis, Politics and Utopia,* Beacon Press, Boston, 1970.

Marcuse, Herbert: *Negations: Essays in Critical Theory,* Beacon Press, Boston, 1968.

Marcuse, Herbert: *One Dimensional Man: Studies in the Ideology of Advanced Industrial Society,* Beacon Press, Boston, 1964.

Marcuse, Herbert: *Reason and Revolution: Hegel and the Rise of Social Theory,* The Humanities Press, New York, 1954.

Marcuse, Herbert: *Soviet Marxism: A Critical Analysis,* Columbia University Press, New York, 1958.

Marcuse, Herbert: *Studies in Critical Philosophy,* Beacon Press, Boston, 1972.

Mattick, Paul: *Critique of Marcuse,* Herder and Herder, New York, 1972.

May, Henry F.: "Living with Crisis, A View from Berkeley," *American Scholar,* 1968–69, 38:588–605.

Neuchterlein, J. A.: "Neo-Conservatism and Its Critics," *Virginia Quarterly Review,* LIII (1977), pp. 607–625.

Nisbet, Robert: *Twilight of Authority,* Oxford University Press, New York, 1975.

Oglesby, Carl (ed.): *The New Left Reader,* Grove Press, New York, 1969.

O'Neill, John (ed.): *On Critical Theory,* The Seabury Press, New York, 1976.

O'Neill, William L.: *Coming Apart: An Informal History of America in the 1960's,* Quadrangle Books, Chicago, 1971.

Oppenheimer, Martin: "The Student Movement as a Response to Alienation." *Journal of Human Relations,* XVI, No.1 (1968), pp. 1–16.

Parker, A. M.: *Suicide Among Young Adults,* Exposition Press, New York, 1974.

The People's Park: A Report on a Confrontation at Berkeley, Office of the Governor, Sacramento, Calif., 1969.

The Report of the President's Commission on Campus Unrest, Arno Press, New York, 1970.

Reagan, Ronald: *The Creative Society: Some Comments on Problems Facing America,* The Devin-Adair Company, New York, 1968.

Robinson, Paul A.: *The Freudian Left: Wilhelm Reich, Geza Roheim, Herbert Marcuse,* Harper & Row, New York, 1969.

Roszak, Theodore: *The Making of a Counterculture,* Doubleday, New York, 1969.

Sale, Kirkpatrick: *SDS,* Random House, New York, 1973.

Schlesinger, Arthur M., Jr.: "America 1968: The Politics of Violence," *Harper's Magazine,* August 1968, pp. 19–24.

Schlesinger, Arthur M., Jr.: *The Crisis of Confidence: Ideas, Power and Violence in America,* Houghton Mifflin Company, Boston, 1969.

Seiden, R. H.: "The Problem of Suicide on College Campuses," *Journal of School Health,* XLI (1971), pp. 243–248.

Short, J. F., Jr., and M. E. Wolfgang (eds.): *Collective Violence*, Aldine Atherton, Chicago, 1972.

Skolnick, J.: *The Politics of Protest*, Simon and Schuster, New York, 1969.

Smelser, Neil: *Theory of Collective Behavior*, The Free Press, New York, 1963.

Stadtman, Verne A.: *The University of California 1868–1968*, McGraw-Hill Book Company, New York, 1970.

Vickers, George R.: *The Formation of the New Left: The Early Years*, D.C. Heath and Company, Lexington, Mass., 1975.

Weber, Ronald (ed.): *America in Change: Reflections on the 60's and 70's*, University of Notre Dame Press, Notre Dame, 1972.

Wolff, Kurt H., and Barrington Moore, Jr. (eds.): *The Critical Spirit: Essays in Honor of Herbert Marcuse*, Beacon Press, Boston, 1967.

Wolff, Robert Paul, Barrington Moore, Jr., and Herbert Marcuse: *A Critique of Pure Tolerance*, Beacon Press, Boston, 1965.

Young, Nigel: *An Infantile Disorder? The Crisis and Decline of the New Left*, Routledge & Kegan Paul, London, 1977.

Index

283

About the Author

WILLIAM J. McGILL, formerly President of Columbia University from 1970 to 1980, was Chancellor of the University of California, San Diego during the tumultuous period 1968–70. Prior to his administrative positions, Dr. McGill has taught psychology at Columbia, UCSD, MIT, and Harvard. He and his wife now live in California.